MEXICANS
IN THE
MAKING OF
AMERICA

MEXICANS
IN THE
MAKING OF
AMERICA

NEIL FOLEY

THE BELKNAP PRESS OF
HARVARD UNIVERSITY PRESS
Cambridge, Massachusetts, and London, England
2014

First printing

Library of Congress Cataloging-in-Publication Data

Foley, Neil.
   Mexicans in the making of America / Neil Foley.
      pages cm
   Includes bibliographical references and index.
   ISBN 978-0-674-04848-5
   1. Mexican Americans—History.   2. Mexicans—United States—
History.   3. Immigrants—United States—History.   4. United States—
Relations—Mexico.   5. Mexico—Relations—United States.   6. National
characteristics, American.   7. United States—Ethnic relations.
8. Transnationalism—History.   9. United States—Emigration and
immigration—Social aspects.   10. Mexico—Emigration and
immigration—Social aspects.   I. Title.
   E184.M5F65 2014
   973'.046872—dc23
                                                         2014010425

For Angela, querida madre de nuestras hijas Sabina, Bianca, and Sophia
And for Latin@s—Past, Present, and Future

CONTENTS

PREFACE

Some readers might wonder why a person with a non-Latino name like "Neil Foley" would feel the urge or the need to write about Mexican Americans and Mexican immigrants. It never occurred to me, growing up in the suburbs of Washington, DC, in the 1950s and 1960s, that I was any different from the kids I went to parochial school with. We were all "white"—no African Americans or other Latinos attended my elementary school. Most blacks lived in the capital city, as did the tiny Latino community, mostly Central Americans who settled around 18th and Columbia Road in a neighborhood called Adams Morgan. In those days the words "Latinos" and "Hispanics" were not much in use. That came later, in the 1970s, about the same time that I began to ponder the challenges our immigrant grandparents faced in making the journey to the United States.

My father, Raymond Patrick Foley, was the son of impoverished Irish immigrants from County Kerry, Ireland. He was the youngest of seven children born in Brockton, Massachusetts. His mother, Julia Sheehan Foley, died shortly after he was born. His church gave him a scholarship to attend Boston College, where he studied Spanish and subsequently made a living as a Spanish translator for the FBI and the Department of Justice.

My mother, Maria Lilia Trejo, one of nine children, was the daughter of Mexican immigrants who crossed the border into New Mexico before it was illegal to cross without papers. Today she would be called an "anchor baby." They met during World War II. Like my father, she was a devout Catholic, but practiced the rituals and rhythms of "folk Catholicism" that she was brought up with. Her devotion to the Virgin Mary included our praying the rosary every day after dinner during the month of May while our neighborhood friends played ball in the street. At home I listened to my mother's scratchy records of Mexican *ranchera* music and grew up thinking her enchiladas, tacos, tamales, frijoles, and sopapillas were American food, which of course they are. But not everyone thought so at the time. This was long before Taco Bell spread from California to the East Coast.

We were a family of eight children in a suburb where Anglo families were much smaller. We were different that way. But so far as I knew, I was as American as anyone else. I spoke unaccented English, and nobody ever told me to "go back to Mexico." My Anglo name partially masked my ethnicity, which was hardly necessary since few Anglo Americans in the suburbs of Washington had any contact with or understanding of Latinos.

Today Latinos are in all fifty states, and by midcentury nearly one in every three Americans will be of Hispanic origin. Although many Americans believe that Hispanics are newcomers to the United States, Hispanics have been in North America long before Anglo Americans began their relentless march to the Pacific in the nineteenth century. *Mexicans in the Making of America* chronicles the history of Mexicans in the Southwest and the continual northward migration of Mexicans across the international border, established in 1848, to a region that once belonged to Mexico. In the last half-century, immigration from Mexico and other countries has made America one of the most culturally rich nations in the world, and that, I argue, augurs well for the future of the United States. The children of Latinos today will rescue a graying nation whose non-Hispanic white population continues to decline. They will provide the labor and the tax revenues to support elderly whites, whose numbers are projected to more than double between 2012 and 2060, from 43.1 million to 92.0 million. In countless other ways Latinos will replenish and restore America in this century, if given half a chance.

I began researching and writing *Mexicans in the Making of America* almost a decade ago, about the time Congress passed the Secure Fence Act in 2006, calling for the construction of a 700-mile fence on the border with Mexico to prevent unlawful entry into the United States. *Time* magazine called it the "Great Wall of America," although the fence, built in part by undocumented Mexican immigrants, hardly compares to the Great Wall of China, except in its objective to keep out "invaders." Fortunately for me, my mother's parents crossed the border almost a century ago, before the creation of the Border Patrol—or I wouldn't be here today.

As an "anchor baby" born in the United States to "illegal alien" parents, my mother was supposed to grow up and take advantage of the social welfare system, if you can believe Rush Limbaugh and his ilk, and sponsor relatives from Mexico to come over with "family reunification" visas. She did neither. What my mother did do, along with my father, was raise a family of eight children during the springtime of the 1960s, hammer us daily with the importance of studying and getting good grades, and never let us forget that we owed our good fortune to God, la Virgen María, and more angels and saints than I can remember. She suffered her share of indignities as a brown-skinned "Mexican" when she first moved from New Mexico to Washington, DC, but she rarely told us about them. This book, in part, is her story and that of millions of other Latinas and Latinos whose ancestors are indigenous to North America, and without whose labor the American Southwest could not have been developed.

The United States themselves are essentially the greatest poem. . . . Here is not merely a nation but a teeming nation of nations.

—Walt Whitman, Preface to *Leaves of Grass* (1855)

Settled by the people of all nations, all nations may claim her for their own. You can not spill a drop of American blood without spilling the blood of the whole world. . . . We are not a narrow tribe . . . our blood is as the flood of the Amazon, made up of a thousand noble currents all pouring into one. We are not a nation, so much as a world.

—Herman Melville, *Redburn* (1849)

PROLOGUE

"America's Changing Colors"

America today has long ceased being a nation in "black and white." The color of America has been changing since the end of World War II, slowly at first and very rapidly in the last four decades. Today anyone who has visited urban public schools can see the growing number of children from India, Korea, Japan, Guatemala, Mexico, Dominican Republic, China, Vietnam, Nigeria, and many other countries. Already generations of children have grown up in an increasingly multicultural nation where millions of immigrants from Asia, Latin America, and increasingly Africa have changed the face of America and challenged the notion of America as a nation of "English only" citizens. But no other language is heard more often on the street corners, in urban stores and suburban malls, and in the workplace than the Spanish language—and no immigrant group stands out for its sheer size and sweeping presence like the Mexican immigrant population. Multicultural America, like multilingualism, is the gift—or the price, depending on your point of view—of an economically interdependent world in which peoples globally are on the move, following borderless flows of capital and finance. Mexicans, like other immigrant groups, come to America looking for work and economic opportunities, much like Koreans in Japan, Turks in Germany, Algerians in France, Tunisians in Italy; and Irish, Indians, and Pakistanis in Great Britain. But unlike other immigrant groups, Mexicans, like the Native Americans before them, lived for hundreds of years—thousands, in the case of American Indians—before the first Anglo-American settlers crossed the Mississippi River into the present-day American West and Southwest.[1]

For over two decades the debate on comprehensive immigration reform has been ongoing with little agreement about how to manage, much less control, the historical movement of Mexicans to El Otro Lado (the Other Side). The construction of a 700-mile fence along parts of the border after the passage of the Secure Fence Act in 2006 may have scored points for the politicians who supported the measure, but few Americans believe a fence alone will stop continual migration from Mexico. Certainly Mexicans themselves don't believe it. As comedian George Lopez put it, if the United States were to build a moat along the border and stock it with alligators, in three weeks Mexicans would be "selling belts and wallets" on the U.S. side. Americans will always want Mexican laborers, Lopez quips, because "we do the best work: cheaper, better, faster."[2]

While the pace of Mexican immigration from 1970 to 2000 has been unparalleled in U.S. history, the pattern of Mexicans migrating north from Mexico began centuries ago. For hundreds of years after the conquest of the Aztec empire, Spanish colonists and their Indian converts founded towns and established missions in the present-day states of the Southwest and the Southeast from Florida to California, as well as the northern states of Mexico from Tamaulipas to Baja California. The towns and cities from Los Angeles to San Augustine, Florida—and from San Francisco and Santa Fe to Mexico City—define a zone of settlement and transnational migration that some scholars call Greater Mexico, partly because the region once belonged to Mexico, and partly because the people and culture continue to be heavily influenced by continuous migration from Mexico.[3]

Long before the arrival of Anglo Americans in Texas in the early nineteenth century, Spanish colonists and mestizo settlers had founded Santa Fe (1609), El Paso (1659), San Antonio (1718), and Los Angeles (1769), to name but a few. In Florida the Spanish founded Saint Augustine in 1565—the oldest, continuous European settlement in the continental United States. Spanish colonists from central Mexico crossed the Río Grande at El Paso del Norte (the Northern Pass) almost a decade before the English settled Jamestown in 1607. As one author put it, "If Americans hit the books, they'd find what Al Gore would call an inconvenient truth. The early history of what is now the United States was Spanish, not English, and our denial of this heritage is rooted in age-old stereotypes that still entangle today's immigration debate."[4] Some Anglo Americans with deep roots in the Southwest, many of whose ancestors crossed the Sabine River from Louisiana to Mexican Texas in the 1820s—most of them illegally—have come to recognize this history. "It is a fact," wrote the editor of the *El Paso Herald-Post* in 1950, "that there were [Spanish-speaking] people here seventy-five years before an Englishman landed at Jamestown. Their descendants are still here and, compared to them, the Puritans are recent immigrants."[5] Or as one Latino author aptly put it: "We were here when here was there."[6]

So if Mexicans have been living in the U.S. Southwest long before the United States was the United States and provided much of the labor to develop the region, why do so many Americans today believe that Mexican immigrants represent a grave threat to our nation unlike that of any other immigrant group in our nation's history? Is it because "they take our jobs" or is it something more disturbing, more menacing, like "they are changing our culture instead of us changing them"? Do they fear that Mexican immigrants, unlike most immigrants from Europe, do not assimilate as quickly into the American mainstream, if at all? Or that they come in such large numbers, many of them illegally, that they threaten to overwhelm Anglo culture in many cities where they already outnumber blacks and non-Hispanic whites?

In the past Anglo Americans didn't fear Mexicans so much as need to control how many immigrants to let in to provide the labor force for the rapidly expanding economy. In the states that share a 2,000-mile border with Mexico—California, Arizona, New Mexico and Texas—Mexicans are, and always have been, a palpable, salient reality, and non-Hispanics have grown accustomed for at least a century to hearing Spanish spoken throughout the region. With the creation of the border at the conclusion of the U.S.-Mexican War in 1848, Mexicans crossing the unmarked border came as migrant laborers long before the 1917 Immigration Act required that immigrants pay a head tax and pass a literacy test. Despite the creation of the Border Patrol in 1924 and attempts to limit illegal entry, the northward migration of Mexicans to the United States has been continual, transnational, and virtually unstoppable for over 150 years.

Since 9/11 and the tightening of the border—the so-called Tortilla Curtain—the illegal entry of Mexicans has been reduced but by no means eliminated. The construction of a 700-mile fence has shifted the flow to over 1,000 miles of unfenced border, much of it in the Sonoran desert and along stretches of the Río Grande. Now Mexicans risk dying in the deserts of Arizona and New Mexico, or drowning in the Río Grande, to have a shot at the American Dream. They also risk apprehension by the Border Patrol and Immigration and Customs Enforcement (ICE), deportation, and in recent years, jail terms in detention centers. But they come nonetheless.

Mexicans are not coming here to breathe the air of political freedom or escape religious persecution. They come here to work. Wages in the United States are more than ten times higher than in Mexico, where the official minimum wage in 2013 was $5.10 *per day* in the highest-paid zones, which includes Mexico City and other cities.[7] Over half the urban population survives in the informal economy as unlicensed street vendors selling everything from tamales and tattoos to pirated movies and music, whereas in the United States Mexican men earn upwards of $8.00 per hour cutting grass, washing dishes, cleaning offices, picking fruits and vegetables, and working in construction, while women change the beds in hospitals and hotels across the country, or work as nannies and maids for urban upper-middle-class families.[8] One thing is for certain: Mexicans did not face all the obstacles and hazards of crossing the border illegally, of leaving behind their families and communities, of risking apprehension and imprisonment, to collect welfare or panhandle on street corners in New York or Los Angeles in exchange for a "God bless." They can do that in Mexico, where sadly millions are reduced to begging just to survive, despite the fact that Mexico's economy is the eleventh largest in the world and the second-largest economy, after Brazil, in Latin America.

Mexican immigrants, as has often been said, are doing jobs that few Americans want to do. In the South and Midwest they now work in poultry factories, meat packing plants, tobacco fields, construction, agriculture, and other occupations once filled mainly by African Americans and working-class whites. In seven of the ten largest cities in the United States—New York, Los Angeles, Houston, San Diego, Phoenix, Dallas, and San Antonio, in that order—Latinos now outnumber blacks, and they already outnumber non-Hispanic whites in Los Angeles, San Antonio, and El Paso. Taken together, Latinos and African Americans outnumber non-Hispanic whites in the five largest cities—New York, Los Angeles, Chicago, Houston, and Philadelphia. In 2003 the U.S. Census Bureau reported with excessive fanfare that Hispanics had surpassed the population of African Americans to become the nation's largest minority group—a milestone that has made Latinos a "hot ticket" for businesses eager to capture their growing market share. Today many Americans fear that this "silent invasion" of Latino newcomers will overwhelm American culture and transform the United States into a "third world" country. They are skeptical that Mexicans will assimilate and become productive members of society rather than a drain on its social welfare resources, medical and health services, and public schools. Many African Americans, on the other hand, feel torn between their historical commitment to equal rights and nervous apprehension that Mexicans take jobs from them, and in some cities and towns compete with them for coveted positions on school boards and city councils.

Fear of Mexican immigrants is by no means a new phenomenon in our history. Generally during times of national unrest and anxiety, such as economic recession or war (including the War on Terror), many Americans displace their fears onto illegal aliens and especially the danger to the United States of illegal immigration across the border with Mexico. During World War I the *New York Times* carried the front-page headline "Anarchists Flock Here from Mexico—Dangerous Aliens Smuggled across the Border at the Rate of 100 a Day."[9] During the 1920s politicians and pundits in the Southwest made the eugenic argument that Mexican immigration would "destroy white civilization"—an unsavory, politically incorrect phrase repackaged today as the need to preserve "Anglo-Protestant culture."[10] In the depression of the 1930s, over half a million Mexicans were voluntarily or forcibly deported to Mexico because jobs had become scarce and local relief programs were intended primarily for Anglo Americans.[11] During World War II the United States signed a bilateral agreement with Mexico to import tens of thousands of "braceros" (manual laborers, mainly farm workers), but at the height of the anticommunist hysteria of the Cold War 1950s, the Immigration and Naturalization Service launched "Operation Wetback," a quasi-military operation to round up and deport Mexican immigrants.[12] The recession of the 1970s again raised the specter of Mexicans overrunning the country and ruining the economy, leading to increased border security and public debate on immigration restriction.

Over the last three decades the concern over Mexican immigration has never been far beneath the surface of public and political discourse. Employer sanctions and limited amnesty were enacted in the mid-1980s, and the 1990s witnessed a backlash against Mexican immigrants in California that resulted in the passing of Proposition 187 to deny medical, educational, and social services to undocumented immigrants and their children. And since 9/11 many politicians have targeted the border with Mexico, and the ease with which Mexicans and other immigrants cross it, as the single most dangerous threat to our national security. Thus in 2003, ICE was created within the Department of Homeland Security to enforce immigration laws and "to protect the United States against terrorist attacks." According to its website, "ICE does this by targeting illegal immigrants: the people, money and materials that support terrorism and other criminal activities."[13] Our border with Mexico was never more than a line in the sand from Tijuana to the Río Grande, and crossing the border was never, until recently, a serious challenge to Mexicans desiring to work in the United States. But to think that "targeting illegal immigrants" from Mexico is going to protect the United States from terrorist attack is surely misguided.[14] Arresting, jailing, and deporting Mexicans may increase the price of the food we eat, but probably not the level of protection against terrorist attack.

For many Americans, Mexican immigrants nevertheless represent a threat even more serious than terrorists because unchecked immigration from Mexico, they argue, will fundamentally change what Harvard political scientist Samuel Huntington called America's "core Anglo-Protestant culture," which he said is "central to American identity." "There is no Americano dream," he declared. "There is only the American dream created by an Anglo-Protestant society." Huntington feared that if the flow of Mexicans into the country cannot be stopped, then America won't be "America" anymore; it will be "two peoples, two cultures, and two languages." More ominously, he predicted, "If this trend continues, the cultural division between Hispanics and Anglos could replace the racial division between blacks and whites as the most serious cleavage in U.S. society."[15] Some expressed views even more grim than Huntington's. Tom Tancredo, former Colorado representative and chairman of the House Immigration Reform Caucus, claimed that illegal immigration had a "death grip" on the nation and warned, "We are committing cultural suicide. . . . The barbarians at the gate will only need to give us a slight push, and the emaciated body of Western civilization will collapse in a heap."[16]

Huntington's and Tancredo's fears are not new. Over 200 years ago Founding Father Benjamin Franklin took a dim view of German immigrants: "Why should Pennsylvania, founded by the English, become a colony of aliens who will shortly be so numerous as to Germanize us instead of our Anglifying them?" Franklin believed that only the English were "purely white," and called Spaniards, Italians, French, Russians, Germans, and even Swedes "swarthy" Europeans who would not make good Americans.[17] Today the descendants of "swarthy" Swedes, Italians, Poles, Irish, and Mexicans, as well as of "tawny" Africans and Asians, recognize that their immigrant and slave ancestors helped make this country what it is.

Deep somewhere in the American national psyche resides an almost primal fear that immigrants will continue to come in such numbers that America will be transformed into something radically different, alien, and fundamentally un-American. Many worry that the unparalleled surge of Mexican immigrants will "Mexicanize" us rather than our Americanizing them. They worry that America will become a bicultural, bilingual nation that has lost its core Anglo-Protestant culture—forgetting that preeminent cities like Los Angeles, New Orleans, San Antonio, New York, Chicago, and Miami long ago ceased being Anglo-Protestant cities, if indeed they ever were. Still, many Americans firmly believe that only strict enforcement of our 2,000-mile border with Mexico will prevent the United States from entering a period of rapid decline and loss of their identity as "true" Americans.

These fears are fed by the dramatic demographic changes since the passage of the Immigration Act of 1965, which eliminated national origin, race, or ancestry as a basis for immigration to the United States and replaced it with a race-neutral system of quotas and "preferences," such as for family members of resident foreign nationals and immigrants with occupational skills. Would-be immigrants from Asian and Latin-American countries began packing their bags and heading to the United States in record numbers. They invited other family members to join them, who in turn invited more family members, setting off a process of chain migration that continues to this day.

The increase in the Latino population since the 1965 immigration law has been unprecedented in the history of the United States. In 2010 the census counted 50.5 million Hispanics or Latinos, making up 16.3 percent of the U.S. population, compared to 4.5 percent in 1970. Most of the increase after 2000 has been due to natural increase rather than immigration, as recent birthrates confirm: in 2010 one of every four babies born in the United States was born to a Latina mother. By 2050 the Latino share of the nation's total population is projected to nearly double, from 16 percent to 30 percent, when nearly one in three U.S. residents will be Latino.[18] The United States now has the second-largest Latino population in the world. Only Mexico's (112 million) exceeds the U.S. Latino population. Put another way, there are more Latinos in the United States than there are in Spain.

The overwhelming majority of Latinos in the United States (nearly two-thirds, about 34 million) are of Mexican origin. Puerto Ricans, who are U.S. citizens, constitute the second-largest group at 9.5 percent, followed by Salvadorans (3.8 percent), Cubans (3.6 percent), Dominicans (2.9 percent), Guatemalans (2.3 percent), and smaller numbers from other Central and South American countries. Not surprisingly, then, the overwhelming number of Mexican-origin Latinos in the United States is what drives the media, politicians, pundits, and the public to focus almost exclusively on the problem of immigration from Mexico—and why *Mexicans in the Making of America* focuses mainly on this fastest-growing segment of the U.S. population.[19]

In recent decades Mexican immigrants no longer confine themselves to the border states, but seek job opportunities in the South, the Midwest, and New England (especially nonmetropolitan New York), where they establish new communities of Latinos. In the South, where their numbers have increased dramatically in the last two decades, particularly in North Carolina, Arkansas, Georgia, and Alabama, it is not uncommon to find grits and frijoles, hash browns and huevos rancheros on the same menu—or where, as one scholar put it, "the gumbo of Dixie gives way to the refried beans of

Mexico."[20] Immigrants from the Caribbean and Central America, particularly Dominicans and Salvadorans, continue to immigrate to cities on the East Coast, where they join Puerto Ricans and other long-resident Latinos, U.S. citizens and immigrants alike. As early as 1990, *Time* magazine noted in a cover story on "America's Changing Colors" how some cities had already become twenty-first-century melting pots: "At the Sesame Hut restaurant in Houston, a Korean immigrant owner trains Hispanic immigrant workers to prepare Chinese-style food for a largely black clientele."[21]

But the fear that America will one day be no longer "America" is overblown and fundamentally unwarranted. The fact that we share a 2,000-mile border with Mexico and that Mexicans have been migrating north for over a century helps to explain the sustained and highly visible presence of Spanish-speaking immigrants in the United States, particularly in major cities from Los Angeles to New York. But out of the plurality and diversity of religious beliefs, languages, cultural practices, and national origins, the overwhelming majority of U.S.-born children of immigrants grow up speaking English and buying into American popular culture even as many retain their native languages and customs for generations. Every Latino immigrant group, whether Mexican, Salvadoran, Dominican, or Guatemalan, experiences the slow but steady process of social, cultural, and economic adaptation to life in the United States.

America will surely look different with so many immigrants from Latin America, Africa, and Asia, but the same could be said of the United States in the early twentieth century, when Americans worried that Italians, Jews, Irish, Slavs, and others presumed to be racially inferior could not be assimilated into American life and culture. A few generations later, many Jews attended Harvard and Yale, where they had been subject to admission quotas until the 1930s. In 1934 Franklin D. Roosevelt made Columbus Day a federal holiday, and Italians and non-Italians across the country held Columbus Day parades. The Irish went from being a despised and despicable breed of inassimilable Catholics and racial inferiors to American patriots celebrated each year on Saint Patrick's Day by thousands of green-beer-swilling Americans of non-Irish ancestry. The election of President John F. Kennedy in 1960 broke the glass ceiling for Irish Catholics after a century of hostility from the nation's Protestant majority. After World War II Mexicans were singled out for praise when every statehouse from California to Texas thanked Mexico for its support during the war and passed resolutions to celebrate Cinco de Mayo to "honor our neighbor, Mexico for her courageous fight for freedom." State governments also commemorated September 16, Mexican Independence Day, in recognition of the Mexican people's "love of liberty . . . and the debt of gratitude which all of us . . . feel for the great contribution made in the building of our society by our citizens of Spanish-speaking origins."[22] While participating in American society has been more difficult than building it, generations of Mexican Americans have made slow but steady progress from the margins to the mainstream.

The path to becoming American for Mexican immigrants is historically well trod, even as immigration from Mexico has been continual for more than a century. Like the Irish, Italians, Poles, Jews, and Germans, Mexicans have faced difficult challenges and obstacles, but two or three generations later, their descendants have become, in varying degrees, acculturated to American life—which is not the same as saying that they have become part of mainstream, middle-class America as did many, if not most, descendants of immigrants from the turn of the twentieth century. The vast majority of today's immigrants hail from Asia, Latin America, and Africa—not Europe—and enter a society that has become increasingly intolerant of non-European immigrants. In addition, America's economy today is radically changed and so are the opportunities for recent immigrants to find a secure and permanent niche. Sociologists have observed that there are many ways of acculturating to American society: as peddlers, plumbers, and professors, as well as prison inmates. Some call this "segmented assimilation," meaning that immigrants assimilate into different strata of American economic and social life, from the middle class and less prosperous working class to the marginalized inner-city underclass.[23]

Despite the hardships they face in today's changed economic landscape, their children attend public schools where they learn English, however imperfectly, and gradually—inexorably—become "Americanized." Whether in neighborhoods in Los Angeles, Chicago, or New York—or rural areas in the South and Midwest—they grow up mainly bilingual and bicultural, acquiring an understanding and appreciation of American culture and values in both Spanish and English. According to the 2000 census, less than 10 percent of the Hispanic population lived in households where no English was spoken, and among children the number was just 2 percent.[24] The children of immigrants today drink deeply from the fountain of American popular culture—from hip-hop music to urban dress styles and American fast food—in short, all the things European and Latin-American nations generally regard as uniquely (and deplorably) "American." When they grow up, Mexican Americans often marry Anglo Americans, African Americans, Native Americans, and Asian Americans, while many young non-Hispanic Americans listen to Latin pop and are increasingly learning Spanish and other foreign languages to better compete in the growing global economy.

Assimilation is, of course, a two-way street. America has already changed considerably in this respect since the early twentieth century, and many Americans today have been around long enough to witness the profound changes in our demographic makeup since the 1960s, when it was taken for granted that the vast majority of Americans were "white." When I was growing up in the suburbs of Washington, DC, in the 1960s, one rarely heard references to Mexican immigrants, much less "Hispanics," a word that did not gain popular usage until the 1970s and 1980s.[25] The Southwest, of course, was—and always has been—a very different place from the South, the Midwest, New England, and the Mid-Atlantic States. From New York to Georgia, whites and blacks circled each other suspiciously, but neither group knew much, if anything, about Mexicans. Non-Hispanics had never heard of a taco, much less Taco Bell. Their familiarity with Mexican culture extended to the antics of the Frito Bandito, the ad character on TV who stole corn chips at gunpoint from Anglo Americans; and the popular Looney Tunes character Speedy Gonzalez, who was a mouse like Mickey, only faster, particularly with the señoritas. Almost fifty years later, few Americans have not eaten Mexican food and even fewer can claim never to have met a Latino. Times have changed, and so has America.[26]

Mexico too has changed. Since World War II it has become progressively more Americanized. The impact of Americanization is everywhere felt, from the growing influence of American popular culture—language, food, music, dress—to the ubiquity of franchise chains like Burger King, McDonald's, Starbucks, and Papa John's, including the growing number of Wal-Marts, 7-Elevens, Sam's Clubs, and even Taco Bells that are displacing Mexican outlets. Mexican journalist and cultural critic Carlos Monsiváis observed that Mexicans have adapted U.S. modernity to their own ends and assimilate America "without assimilating." In other words, he argues, "Americanization is Mexicanized." By the same logic, however, the "Latinization" of the United States is also Americanized, especially since so many immigrants arrive already partly Americanized through the global forces of the media, technology, and popular culture. "In Mexico the border with the United States is found everywhere," Monsiváis metaphorically notes, "and as regards our culture and our economy, all Mexicans live on the border."[27]

As early as the 1920s the Mexican intellectual José Vasconcelos observed how Mexicans living in the six border states with the United States had become victims of the barbarous process of Americanization, which he disparagingly called "apochamiento," roughly "gringoization."[28] In northern Mexican cities like Monterrey, for example, Mexicans go "trick-or-treating" on Halloween, the night before celebrating their own holiday, the

Día de los Muertos (Day of the Dead). The commercialization of Christmas in Mexico is everywhere apparent, especially in department stores where young children line up to sit on Santa's lap, weeks before celebrating the more traditional Día de los Reyes (Day of the Kings) on January 6. The dual forces of Americanizing Mexico and Latinizing the United States continue apace, as Mexican immigrants adapt to life in the United States and as non-Hispanic Americans, particularly the younger generation, increasingly learn Spanish, eat enchiladas, tacos, and refried beans, dance to reggaetón, merengue, and Latin pop, and generally do not feel threatened by media portrayals of Mexican immigration as a "silent invasion," a latent terrorist threat, or the advance guard of the "reconquest" of the Southwest—a "Trojan burrito," as the author Richard Rodríguez put it, within the walls of Fortress America.[29]

As Latinos, and Mexican Americans in particular, continue to move, however slowly, into the mainstream of American life, Latinos will become ever more central to American culture and society throughout the twenty-first century. For more than a century Mexican immigrants and their U.S.-born Mexican-American offspring have been making and remaking America, literally building and servicing it, at least in the greater Southwest, as well as doing all the things that other Americans do, like raise families, work hard, pay taxes, buy homes, fight wars, and in other ways contribute to the well-being of the nation, much like other immigrant groups and their descendants throughout American history. Their path to acceptance as bona fide Americans has not been easy, but generations of Latinos in the United States, particularly in the Southwest and West, and cities like Chicago, New York, and Miami, have made their mark on American culture and politics, and will continue to do so in important ways for the rest of the twenty-first century.

In the chapters that follow, *Mexicans in the Making of America* argues that the United States, from the moment it signed the Treaty of Guadalupe Hidalgo ending the war with Mexico in 1848, sealed its destiny—and Mexico's—as two nations, separate and unequal, inextricably linked by geography and bound together by generations of Mexican Americans and Mexican immigrants. The history of Mexicans in the United States must be understood within the context of relations between Mexico and the United States, particularly in the middle and latter-half of the twentieth century, when migration from Mexico was greater than at any time in the history of North America. As the nation's third-largest trading partner, Mexico will continue to be linked to the United States in important ways for the foreseeable future. Even the periodic anti-immigrant hysteria of the post–World War II era—from the backlash against "wetbacks" in the 1950s to Arizona's SB 1070 in

2010 to limit constitutional rights of unauthorized immigrants—has not diminished the growing cultural, lingual, and economic ties that increasingly bind Mexico and the United States.[30] The role of Mexican immigrants and Mexican Americans is therefore central to the story of the making of the United States—at least that part that was Mexican America—since before the United States was the United States.

As with other marginalized groups, particularly African Americans, World War II was a watershed in American history for the struggle of second- and later-generation Mexican Americans for full citizenship rights and equality with Anglo Americans in the schools, on the jobs, and in the history books. Mexican Americans had long insisted that being of Mexican origin did not make one less American, any more than it did Italian or Irish Americans. America's long history of white supremacy became increasingly untenable after World War II, and Cold War Soviet propaganda never tired of pointing out American hypocrisy in supporting democracy around the world while denying equal rights to its nonwhite citizens at home. More than a half-century later, young Americans are increasingly more accustomed to and accepting of the idea that America has become far more racially diverse than at any time in our history.

In a broader historical sense, *Mexicans in the Making of America* illustrates what the United States has been reluctant to acknowledge for most of its history, namely, that it is a thoroughly composite culture of racially blended peoples that defies the notion of some normative or static understanding of what it means to be "American." It is in part the history of the United States coming to terms with having seized the northern half of Mexico in the 1848, as well as the islands of Puerto Rico, the Philippines, and Cuba in 1898, and the fear that it may have bitten off more than it can safely chew. In examining the ways in which the United States has coped with the very thing it often denies—that it is not, nor has it ever been, a purely Anglo-American nation—*Mexicans in the Making of America* reveals how the United States has become more of what it has always been, only this time, in this century, with a rapidly growing population of U.S.-born Mexicans and other Americans of Hispanic descent. It is in this story of regional, national, and transnational struggles of Latinos and other marginalized groups to enjoy full citizenship rights that we witness the making and *remaking* of American culture into something more democratic, more egalitarian, more accepting of difference—in short, more American.

1

THE GENESIS OF
MEXICAN AMERICA

Generations of Americans grow up learning about the voyages of Christopher Columbus in 1492 to the islands of the Caribbean, although no American can recall Columbus ever having set foot anywhere in present-day United States. That's because he never did. We learned in elementary school that the Pilgrims arrived somewhere on the coast of Massachusetts in 1620 (near a commemorative stone called "Plymouth Rock"), and that the first permanent English settlement was established in 1607 in Jamestown. We may recall that the Vikings, or Norsemen, explored and for a brief time settled parts of Canada around the year 1000, but our knowledge of what happened between 1492 and 1607 is often a bit nebulous, although the history of Spanish exploration and settlement in what is now the United States is well documented. So why do we learn about the late-arriving pilgrims and virtually nothing about the earlier explorations of the Spanish, let alone the earlier settlements of mixed-race "mestizos," in North America?[1]

Before Canada, the United States, and Mexico existed as modern states, their first peoples took shape in bands, clans, tribes, towns, and cities. These peoples made kingdoms, nations, and empires. Of course, these social and political entities rested on materials that indigenous peoples had discovered, invented, cultivated, and developed as they migrated across the continent. When the English founded Jamestown, they survived because of Indian corn, a food discovered and cultivated in central Mexico, then dispersed throughout North America, through informal and commercial exchange over hundreds of years. On first contact then, the ancestors of Anglo Americans encountered Mexican food—turkey, squash, beans, tomatoes,

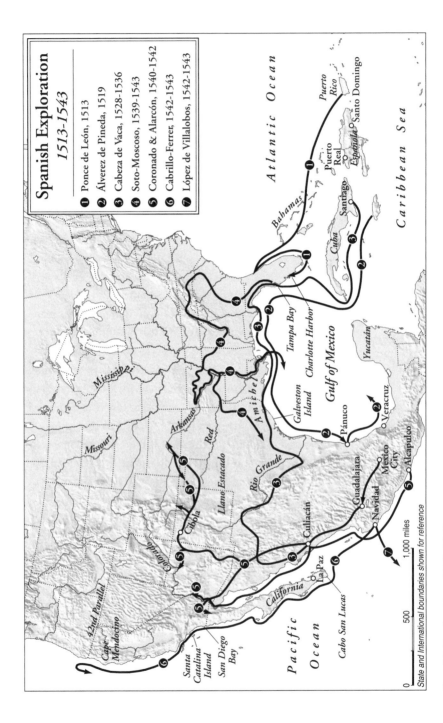

Spanish Exploration, 1513–1543.

chocolate would follow in both the near and distant future. The native ancestors of mestizo Mexicans made these foods, foods their Spanish ancestors encountered even before their entry into the Aztec empire.[2]

The first European to set foot on what was to become the United States was Ponce de León, who landed somewhere on the eastern coast of Florida in 1513—over three hundred years before the United States acquired Florida from Spain—and christened the region "La Florida" for the abundance of colorful and fragrant flowers there. During the next three decades Spanish explorers and conquistadors like Hernando de Soto, Álvar Núñez Cabeza de Baca, and Francisco Vásquez de Coronado were the first Europeans to traverse the Appalachian mountains, the Mississippi River, the Grand Canyon, and in the case of Coronado, the high plains of central Kansas where he thought he might find the fabled city of Quivira and all the gold that the Spaniards expected to find there. In 1565, over fifty years before the Pilgrims made landfall, Spaniards founded St. Augustine, the first permanent settlement in the United States (on the Florida coast) and explored much of the present-day U.S. South and Southwest, as well as the shoreline from Bangor, Maine to Florida, and the Pacific Coast as far north as Oregon. By 1600, the American empire of imperial Spain had become, according to one geographer, "a prodigious creation . . . extending from the Río Grande del Norte to the Río de la Plata at the southern portal to Peru."[3] In other words, as the Mexican novelist and essayist Carlos Fuentes put it, "the Hispanic world did not come to the United States, the United States came to the Hispanic world."[4]

It is not surprising that U.S. history privileges the English colonizers over the Spanish, but it is nevertheless important to recall that much of what we call the American Southwest was permanently settled by Spaniards, mestizos, and their Indian allies centuries before the arrival of westward-moving Anglo Americans in the 1820s. Even before the United States took the northern half of Mexico in the 1848 U.S.-Mexican War, Anglo colonists (some with their slaves) began pouring into the territory from Texas to California where they first encountered Mexican people. From the start Anglo Americans regarded the Mexicans as little better than Indians and utterly incapable of becoming civilized members of the Anglo-American republic. Of course, Mexicans as a whole were principally of indigenous origin, a biological and visible fact that stoked the fears many Anglos had of racial intermixing. Although anti-immigrant rhetoric today has changed over the last 200 years, many of the anti-Mexican sentiments Anglos expressed in Texas in the 1820s continue to inform the fears of Americans today who worry that Mexicans are "reconquering" the Southwest and potentially every major city in the United States.[5] The origins of *Mexicans in the Making of America* begin with "first contact" between Anglos and Mexican citizens in Texas in the 1820s and the annexation of the northern half of Mexico in 1848.

The signing of the Treaty of Guadalupe Hidalgo in 1848 ending the U.S.-Mexican War resulted in the social, political, and economic displacement of Mexicans throughout the Southwest, despite U.S citizenship conferred by the treaty and guarantees to respect their property rights. Conquest meant that American racism against blacks in the South would be extended to Mexicans and other "foreigners," like the Chinese, as well as to the original inhabitants of the land, the numerous Indian tribes of the American West.[6] The consequences of the war were disastrous for Mexico, and its effects are still being felt today as Mexicans continue to immigrate to the United States across a border imposed on their country by war—a border recently militarized with high-tech surveillance technology, including the use of unmanned aerial drones, and the construction of a 700-mile barrier fence, all poignant reminders of conquest.

The long history of Spaniards, Christianized Indians, and Mexicans in the United States begins with a prior conquest—the Spanish conquest of the Aztec empire almost 500 years ago and the northward expansion of colonial New Spain into the present-day Southwest, a conquest that set the stage for the making of Mexican America. Spain's colony in North and Central America, New Spain, endured for three hundred years—from 1521, when Hernán Cortés presided over the defeat of the Aztec empire, until 1821 when Mexico achieved its independence from Spain. While the history of the native peoples of Mexico—among them the Olmecs, Toltecs, Maya, Aztecs, to name a few—stretches back many thousands of years, most historians trace the beginning of modern Mexico to the first encounter between Cortés and the Aztec emperor Moctezuma. Cortés had come to the New World in search of rank, fame, and wealth, particularly gold, as had most Spaniards. A Spanish soldier who fought in the conquest of Mexico explained that he came to the New World "to serve God and his Majesty, to give light to those who were in the darkness and to grow rich as all men desire to do."[7] With candor and clarity, he expressed the dual purpose of Spanish conquest: to convert the Indians to Christianity and to extract from their labor the wealth in the mines and soil of the New World. Through the violence of conquest, a people would evolve who expanded northward as they fashioned the "Spanish" borderlands.

The Aztecs, a warrior band of nomadic tribes from the coastal region of Nayarit in northwestern Mexico, were relative newcomers to the Valley of Mexico, having consolidated their power over the region only a few decades before the arrival of the Spaniards. The Aztecs demanded tribute from the natives they conquered, which included human sacrifices to their god Huitzilopochtli. Because of their very dominance, the Aztecs constructed the foundation of cultural and political unity on which the Mexican nation would later be built. With the help of a captured Indian slave, Malintzin ("La Malinche"), who served as Cortés's interpreter and mistress, the Spaniards were able to form important political and military alliances with Indian tribes, such as the Tlaxcalans, who hated the Aztecs more than they feared the Spaniards. For good or ill, Malintzin would symbolize the intermixture of Spaniard and Indian that would make the Mexican nation.[8] Like some of the coastal tribes near Veracruz, the Tlaxcalans welcomed the Spanish as allies against their Aztec overlords. In the fall of 1519, when Cortés marched on Tenochtitlán, the Aztec capital and future site of Mexico City, he was accompanied by thousands of Indian allies determined to end their vassalage under the Aztecs.[9]

Cortés's march inland to Tenochtitlán revealed a great deal about the violence that begot New Spain and the Mexican people. In Cholula, a large city about sixty miles from the Aztec capital, the Cholulan *caciques* (tribal chiefs) welcomed the Spaniards and their Indian allies, but secretly had plotted, apparently on orders from Moctezuma himself, to trap and destroy the invaders. Malintzin learned of the plot from a Cholulan woman and promptly warned Cortés, who devised a plan to teach the Cholulans—and the Aztecs—a lesson in Spanish retribution. With the aid of his Tlaxcalan and Cempoalan allies, Cortés ordered the wholesale slaughter of over 6,000 Cholulans, among them many of their priests and *caciques*. Upon hearing the news, Moctezuma believed, according to one chronicler, that further resistance was futile and reluctantly admitted Cortés and his men into the capital city of the Aztec empire, a city soon made the capital of colonial New Spain and later Mexico, including the states that would become the "Southwest."[10]

When one of Cortés's soldiers, Bernal Díaz del Castillo, first laid eyes on the Aztec capital as he entered the city from the causeway of Iztapalapa, he was struck by its immense size and grandeur, comparing it to "the enchanted scenes we had read of in Amadis of Gaul, from the great towers and temples and other edifices . . . that seemed to rise out of the water . . . for . . . never yet did man see, hear, or dream of anything equal to the spectacle which appeared to our eyes on that day."[11] With about a quarter million inhabitants, Tenochtitlán was larger than any city in Spain, and only four European cities—Naples, Venice, Milan, and Paris—had populations larger than 100,000 in the early sixteenth century.[12] Moctezuma's offer of friendship and gold to the Spaniards triggered a gold rush that would bring thousands of Europeans to Mexico and the Americas.

After formal exchange of greetings, Cortés and his men moved into the emperor's palace and quietly held him prisoner. Relations between the Spaniards and the Aztecs grew increasingly difficult, particularly among the Aztec nobles who deeply resented the house arrest of their emperor. In the spring of 1520, while Cortés was away from the capital, his first officer, Pedro de Alvarado, suspected that the nobles had plotted against them. He decided upon the same course of action as had Cortés in Cholula: he surrounded thousands of them, unarmed, in the courtyard of the temple during a religious ceremony, and on Alvarado's signal the Spaniards massacred them. Unlike the Cholulans, however, the Aztecs rose up in rebellion, killed a number of Spaniards, and laid siege to the palace where the Spaniards retreated and were essentially trapped. Cortés managed to fight his way back into the palace and, under the cover of darkness, the Spanish force fled the city, losing more than half its men, including many of its Tlaxcalan allies. In many ways, the creation of New Spain owes as much to indigenous peoples as the Spaniards whose Indian allies vastly outnumbered them.[13]

A year later, Cortés returned with reinforcements and retook the city in August 1521 after a spirited defense led by Moctezuma's nephew, Cuauhtémoc. Moctezuma was killed the year before, although whether his death was at the hands of the Spaniards or the Aztecs has never been established. What is clear, however, is that a relatively small band of Spaniards was able to maintain control over the vast Aztec empire in part because of deadly microbes they carried with them from across the ocean—small pox, measles, and other contagious diseases endemic to Europe but unknown in America. With no prior exposure, Indians had not acquired immunities against them. Eight million Indians, about one-third of the native population, perished within a decade of the conquest, prompting many Indians to believe that their gods had abandoned them. Their defeat, in other words, owed as much to infestation as invasion. Without the plagues, the Spanish demographic imprint on modern Mexico would have been minimal—not unlike the impact of the Dutch on South Africans.[14]

News of Cortés's victory over the Aztecs emboldened other Spanish opportunists to undertake expeditions in search of gold and glory. Many medieval legends circulated among the Spaniards about the existence of the Seven Cities of Cíbola and Quivira, mythical places of fabulous wealth that many Spaniards believed lay in the vast uncharted region to the north of Tenochtitlán, including Aztlán, the Edenic place of origin of the Mexica (Aztecs). Cortés himself believed in the existence of a northern province of Amazons, "inhabited by women, without a single man, who have children in the way which the ancient histories ascribe to the Amazons." These fantasies would take the Spaniards and their more numerous mestizo and indigenous allies into what is now the southwestern United States.[15]

The most famous of these expeditions culminated in the failure of Francisco Vásquez de Coronado to find the mythical Quivira in what is now the heartland of America. Coronado organized his expedition based on a report of Fray Marcos de Niza, a friar who claimed to have seen one of the fabled Seven Cities (in present-day Arizona) and reported that it was larger and more magnificent than Mexico City. Coronado set out from Compostela in the northwestern region of New Spain in 1540 with a large force of over a thousand natives and about 335 Spaniards.[16] In New Mexico Coronado's men encountered a native called the Turk, who told them of the fabulous wealth of Quivira where "pitchers, dishes, and bowls were made of gold."[17] The Turk and Pueblo Indians had apparently deceived Coronado about the existence of Quivira in order to lure him into leaving their villages and never returning. Indeed he took the expedition as far as the present-day town of Lyons in central Kansas. As far as the Zuni and Pueblo Indians were concerned, the Spaniards demanded so much food, clothing, and shelter that they were themselves in danger of starvation and exposure to the elements. They understood well that Spaniards would do anything and go anywhere to find cities of gold, and it required no great strategic plan to tell the Spaniards that great wealth lay a little farther away—as far away from the Pueblo settlements as possible. The Pueblo Indians had asked the Turk, as Coronado later learned, to take them "to a place where we and our horses would starve to death." In the middle of Kansas with nothing but "cattle and sky," as one chronicler recorded, they were far from starving, but neither had they come such a great distance to marvel at the herds of buffalo. Discouraged, Coronado had the Turk garroted and his disillusioned force returned to Tierra Nueva, "the new land," as they called New Mexico.[18] After having explored much of present-day Arizona, New Mexico, Texas, Oklahoma, and Kansas, and spent much of his personal wealth underwriting the expedition, Coronado failed to find the legendary cities or treasures of gold and silver. For the following fifty years, the viceroyalty authorized no further expeditions into what is now the United States, choosing instead to consolidate its control over Indian labor in the Valley of Mexico and the newly discovered silver mines in Zacatecas and other locations in the central corridor of Mexico.[19]

As the sixteenth century drew to a close, the Crown decided to establish a permanent presence in the northern borderlands to protect the wealth of its mining corridor and provide a base for Franciscan friars to convert the Pueblo Indians. In 1596 Juan de Oñate led an expedition to the north by way of present-day El Paso, Albuquerque, and finally Santa Fe, where he established the first permanent colony in 1608. In that city his Tlaxcalan Indian allies founded the barrio of Analco, where the Chapel of San Miguel, the oldest church in the continental United States, still stands today. Although humble Pueblo villages were a far cry from the splendor of Tenochtitlán, the Pueblo Indians farmed their own land, providing Spanish and mestizo settlers with a solid agricultural base to establish churches, missions, presidios, municipalities, and other institutions of Spanish colonial society in what we now call the Southwest.[20]

Spaniards maintained control over hostile natives mainly by acts of brutality, torture, and the point of the sword, a pattern established early on by Cortés, Coronado, De Soto and other *adelantados* (entrepreneurs commissioned by the Crown). The natives, in turn, plotted rebellions, ambushes, and other forms of guerilla warfare to resist Spanish rule. In 1680 united Pueblo tribes launched a full-scale revolt against the Spaniards and the Franciscan friars, who often brutally punished the natives for continuing to worship their native gods. In a few short weeks the Pueblos had driven the Spaniards out of New Mexico north of El Paso. They destroyed the missions, killed most of the priests, and over 350 of the province's 2,500 colonists. As one Spanish officer observed, "The heathen have conceived a mortal hatred for our holy faith and enmity for the Spanish nation."[21] Although the Spaniards reconquered northern New Mexico in 1693, some Pueblo Indians continued to resist Spanish exploitation and desecration of their culture. The penalty for disobedience was generally the same: an arraignment followed by execution, torture, or enslavement. Many abandoned their pueblos entirely rather than submit to Spanish rule, while other Christianized Indians fled southward with the Spaniards and reconstructed their pueblos near El Paso, where their descendants remain in present-day Texas.[22]

In distant northern settlements like El Paso and Santa Fe, Spaniards, mestizos, and Indians frequently intermarried, since Indians vastly outnumbered Spaniards and virtually no constraints existed against the intimate mixing of Spaniards, mestizos, and Christianized Indians. Juan de Oñate, the wealthy, aristocratic founder of settlements near present-day Santa Fe, was himself married to Isabel Tolosa Cortés Moctezuma, the great granddaughter of the Aztec emperor and the granddaughter of Hernán Cortés.[23]

MEXICANS IN THE MAKING OF AMERICA

As the distinction between Spaniard and Indian became increasingly blurred, mestizos often took advantage of their vaguely defined status to move within both Pueblo and Hispanic social circles.[24] Shortly after Oñate's *entrada,* the Spaniards were adapting—assimilating, we would say today—to the native culture. In 1601 a Spanish official, Ginés de Herrera Horta, reported that he had met "a Spanish boy, who . . . grew up among the Indian boys. He knew the language of the Picurís or Queres better than the Indians themselves, and they were astonished to hear him talk."[25] Growing up among the Indians was the norm for most Spaniards in the north, where education took place largely in the missions, and Spanish settlers and Hispanicized Indians often worked in close proximity to each other. Spaniards used Tlaxcalans, for example, to colonize and "civilize" the "Chichimecas" of the northern frontier as far north as the Río Bravo. Their mestizo offspring formed a racial category that was encoded in the law and indicated a social status above the Indians but below the Spaniards. The population we would recognize as "Mexican" was thus fashioned both north and south of today's border.

Mexicans were not only the mixed-race offspring of Spaniards and Indians. Spaniards imported as many as 200,000 African slaves during the colonial period to augment the Indian labor force, which had been greatly reduced as a result of small pox and other diseases. While many maintained their culture in places like Veracruz, the port of entry for most Africans, most intermarried with the mestizos, natives, and Spaniards.[26] The Spaniards freely mixed with all groups, but they were also obsessed with maintaining legal and social distinctions among the various mixtures, and to that end created a system of classification, or "castas," for the various types of racial mixtures. The principal categories included mixtures of Spanish with Africans, Indians, and mestizos: a Spaniard and an African produced a "mulato"; a Spaniard and an Indian produced a mestizo; a Spaniard and a mestizo produced a "castizo." When these mixed-race persons married others of different racial mixtures, they produced offspring who were classified with the names of animals, such as "lobo" (wolf) and "coyote," while other subcastes yielded more exotic names, such as "jump backwards, kinky-head, hay-seed, whitey, darkey, sambo, village mulatto, stay-up-in-the-air and I-don't-understand-you, or there-you-are." The more distant one's ancestry from "pure-blooded" Spaniard, the more bizarre the racial category.[27]

In reality, racial identities were highly contingent and fluid, depending on a variety of factors, such as social status, skin color, language, and other factors. A light-skinned castiza might pass as mestiza. A mestizo might pass as "español." The complicated racial nomenclature hardly reflected the reality of shifting racial identities in New Spain, particularly in the northern borderlands, including New Mexico, where it was possible to be born "indio" (Indian) and, through conversion to Catholicism, fluency in Spanish, and perhaps adoption into a Spanish family, grow up to be mestizo. In other words, while some passed as belonging to a higher socioracial status than they actually were, others passed into a new racial identity as a result of social and economic advancement. The profusion of crisscrossed color lines in Spanish colonial society made it impossible to know with any certainty whether or not dark-skinned individuals had earned the privilege, through petitions to the colonial government, to be called "blanco."[28] "When the colour of the skin is too repugnant" for some petitioners to "get themselves *whitened*," wrote the German explorer and geographer Alexander Von Humboldt, the petitioners are often granted the right to "consider themselves as whites *(que se tengan por blancos)*."[29]

Spaniards were of course the most powerful and privileged group. The colonial elite was divided into two classes of Spaniards: "peninsulares," Spaniards born in Spain; and "criollos," Spaniards born in the New World. Criollos were not "creoles" in the sense of being racially mixed; they were Spaniards born in Mexico rather than Spain, and for that reason alone were not entitled to hold the highest positions in the colonial bureaucracy. This distinction was an important factor in the war for Mexican independence, as many criollos sided with insurgent Indians to overthrow Spanish rule. But already by the end of the eighteenth century intermarriage among peninsulares, criollos, mestizos. and afromestizos had become more acceptable and their offspring, through a decree issued in 1805 called Limpieza de Sangre (Blood Purity), could be accorded criollo status.[30] Thus, while race and color mattered in the New Spain's social structure, they differed markedly from the black-white divide that characterized the racial regime of the future United States, and that would put Mexicans on the "colored" side of the color line.

Maintaining power based on one's status as "Spanish" operated one way in central Mexico where the vast majority of the population lived, in contrast to the sparsely settled northern borderlands where fewer people were able to claim "pure" Spanish ancestry. Wealth and resources were concentrated in central Mexico, not in the remote northern borderlands, like New Mexico, Texas, and California, where the elites were mostly mestizos. Of the estimated 13,204 people married in New Mexico between 1693 and 1846, only ten persons listed their parents' birthplace as Spain.[31] These mestizo northerners were the focus of racial ridicule by the Anglo Americans who would pour into the region. In their eyes Mexicans were hardly differ-ent from the Indians with whom they waged constant warfare.

While missionaries had been anxious to convert the Indians from Cali-fornia to Texas, the viceroyalty of New Spain early saw little to be gained, at least economically, from further investment in northern mission enterprises. For one thing, vast distances separated the northern settlements from the more populated and prosperous settlements to the south, making effective government and control in the north both difficult and expensive. In the late seventeenth and early eighteenth centuries, however, the Crown took measures to protect its northern frontier from foreign threats: missions and presidios were established in east Texas in the 1690s as a buffer against the French in Louisiana, and settlement of California was authorized as a *cordon sanitaire* against the encroachment of English and Russian settlers in the Pacific Northwest. Aside from their importance to the defense of New Spain, however, the northern settlements held little interest for Span-ish secular authorities in Mexico City, a perspective that later contributed to the loss of Mexico's northern territory to the United States.[32]

Relations between the United States and Spain preceded those with Mexico. Spain assisted the United States in its war for independence, as Spanish troops, including mestizo cowboys from Texas, pushed across the Mississippi River to recover Florida from the British. Thus, "Mexicans," as New Spain's people were then increasingly called, fought in the revolution that founded the United States. Moreover, at the war's end the United States' entire western and southern borders were with the Spanish empire.[33]

Even before the United States had won its independence from England, Spanish officials had long feared the territorial ambitions of the Anglo-Saxon settlers and the threat they represented to colonial New Spain. The Span-ish ambassador to France, the Count of Aranda, prophesied in 1783 that the newly independent English colonies would one day seize Spain's North American colonies and rule the continent: "This federal republic has been born a pygmy, but the day will come when it will be a giant and an enormous colossus on those regions. . . . Then its first steps will be seizing the Flori-das in order to dominate the Gulf of Mexico and once it has obstructed New Spain's trade, it will aspire to conquer the vast empire, which will not be able to defend itself against such a formidable power established on the same continent and contiguous to it."[34]

The expansion of the United States from pygmy republic to colossus of continental dimensions was not simply the result of the work of "civi-lized men . . . driven onward by the hand of God."[35] War and revolution in Europe contributed handily to the expansionist goals of the early republic.

Shortly after the British recognized the independence of its former colonies in 1783, the French Revolution of 1789 initiated a period of war that preoccupied Europe for the next twenty-five years, providing the fledgling United States with the breathing space it needed to set up its system of government and to develop trade and commerce throughout the states and with other nations. A major break for the United States came in 1803 when France, then on the verge of war with England, abandoned its plans for a French empire in North America and sold the Louisiana Territory. In one stroke the United States had doubled its size and pushed its borders thousands of square miles toward the older Spanish colonial frontier extending from California to Texas (although Thomas Jefferson claimed, incorrectly, that Texas was included in the Louisiana Purchase). In 1819 Spain and the United States signed the Adams-Onis Treaty in which Spain ceded Florida to the United States in return for recognition of Texas as part of New Spain. The United States took full advantage of the conflicts and wars in Europe to wrest Florida away from Spain and Louisiana from France, at a time when those countries could not spare the resources to defend their colonies in North America. Thus, even before Mexico's independence, Hispanic geographic and demographic power was retreating before the Anglo-American advance.[36]

Mexico was not faring so well as the young republic with which it shared the North American continent. Having declared its independence from Spain in 1810, it fought a series of bloody and costly battles for eleven years before actually gaining it, while at the same time its neighbor to the north (and east) was enjoying the fruits of neutrality from European wars (even as it waged war with the British empire in 1812) by occupying itself with commerce, trade, and westward expansion. After independence, Mexico was virtually bankrupt. After years of war, first with Spain and decades of civil strife and conflict between "Centralists" and "Federalists" afterward, the Mexican government stumbled from one financial crisis to another. Many mines, a major source of revenue for Mexico, had ceased to operate for lack of capital and an endemic labor shortage. Many of the *haciendas* (plantations and large livestock ranches) that were the backbone of agricultural production still lay in ruins, in part because of the scorched-earth practices followed by the insurgents and royalists during the decade-long war of independence. Twenty years after independence in 1821, the wife of the Spanish minister to Mexico described catastrophic consequences of the war on Mexico City and the surrounding countryside: "ruins, everywhere—here a viceroy's country palace serving as a tavern, where mules stop to rest . . . there, a whole village crumbling to pieces; roofless houses, broken down walls and arches, an old church—the remnants of a convent."[37] To complicate matters, the Spanish government had built only three highways in all of Mexico during the colonial period, and these were in a state of serious disrepair. If transportation formed the veins through which flowed the blood of commerce, Mexico was suffering, according to one historian, from "a form of pernicious anemia."[38] In the early nineteenth century, the tide of demographic, economic, and military power rolled west with the Anglo-American empire.

No longer a pygmy, the colossus came knocking at the Texas door in the early 1820s, when both Spain and newly independent Mexico were far too weak to resist. Mexico mistrusted the intentions of the Anglo settlers, many of them squatters ("illegal aliens") and slaveholders, but gambled that by giving them generous and cheap land grants, and requiring them to become Mexican citizens (and Catholics), they would become loyal citizens of Mexico and serve as a buffer against further expansion of the United States.[39]

When Anglo settlers first encountered Mexicans in Texas, they had little understanding of the people, history, institutions, and culture of Latin Americans in general. What Anglo Americans did know was that Mexicans were very little like themselves. After hundreds of years of Spanish rule, most Mexicans were Catholics, a religion that Anglo Americans disdained for its "superstitions" and subservience to Rome. Catholics could not be trusted to put the interests of the nation before their obedience to the Pope. "The people of [Spanish] America are the most ignorant, bigoted, the most superstitious of all the Roman Catholics in Christendom," wrote John Adams, Founding Father and second president of the United States. "Was it probable, was it possible, that . . . free government . . . should be introduced and established among such a people . . . ? It appeared to me . . . as absurd as similar plans would be to establish democracies among the birds, beasts, and fishes."[40] Just as God had given man "dominion over the fish of the sea, and over the birds of the heavens, and over the cattle, and over all the earth, and over every creeping thing that creepeth upon the earth," the Anglo dominion over Mexicans and Indians did not include integration into the body politic any more than it did for fish, fowl, or cattle.[41]

Even more disturbing to Anglo Americans was the mixed-race appearance of Mexicans. After centuries of *mestizaje*—the blending of Indian, Spanish, and African peoples—Mexicans represented the racial degradation that supposedly resulted from Europeans mixing with the natives they ruled and sometimes enslaved. Anglo Americans rarely mixed with, much less married, the Indians they defeated, who eventually were "removed" to

Indian Territory (Oklahoma) and reservations throughout the American West. Indians in Mexico, though disfranchised, formed an integral part of the nation and in many regions outnumbered *mestizos* and Spaniards.[42]

Anglo Americans' assessment of Mexican women, however, was not nearly as harsh, even though by New England standards they were morally lax and sexually permissive. These mixed-race women exuded a sensuousness that did not go unnoticed by Anglo men. Anglo women were scarce in San Antonio, where an Anglo settler from Ohio caught his first glimpse of a "Spanish" señorita. He practically became unhinged as he recalled his barely concealed concupiscence upon their first meeting: "Her features were beautiful . . . her complexion was of the loveliest, the snowy brightness of her well turned forehead beautifully contrasting with the carnation tints of her mouth, her pouting cherry lips were irresistible and even when closed seemed to have an utterance . . . but I have no such language as seemed to be spoken by her eyes else might I tell how dangerous it was to meet their luster and feel their quick thrilling scrutiny of the heart as tho' the very fire of their expression was conveyed with their beamings."[43] Certainly being the object of Anglo lust had its advantages. Mexican women who married Anglo men, like Jim Bowie of Alamo fame, were among the first Mexicans to have the racial and cultural identity of "Spanish" conferred upon them by Anglo men anxious to whiten their "half-Indian" Mexican señoritas—and especially their half-Anglo children.

Nonetheless, before Texas rebelled, Anglo Texans had firmly established in their minds that Mexicans were more like Indians and black Americans than Germans or French. One Anglo Texan wrote that Mexicans were "the adulterate and degenerate brood of the once high-spirited Castilian." Sam Houston, in an address to rally support against Mexico, explained that the "vigor of the descendants of the sturdy north will never mix with the phlegm of the indolent Mexicans no matter how long we may live among them," and asked his fellow compatriots if they "would bow under the yoke of these half-Indians." A newcomer Anglo-Texan regarded Mexicans as "degraded and vile," whose "unfortunate race of Spaniard, Indian and African is so blended that the worst qualities of each predominate."[44]

While the economy was in shambles and Mexico paralyzed by political infighting, the United States sent its first ambassador in 1824, Joel Poinsett, with instructions to purchase Texas and push the border with Mexico farther southwest to the Río Grande. The Mexican government refused repeated offers to sell California and New Mexico and finally asked for Poinsett's recall in 1829 because of his frequent interference in Mexican domestic politics, a pattern of diplomatic trespassing that foreshadowed the "big stick" diplomacy—and military intervention—of the early twentieth century. Throughout the next two decades Mexico continued to suffer from military coups, bitter political antagonisms between conservatives and liberals, centralists, and federalists over the form and scope of national governance, including a sizable number of politicos who favored the establishment of a monarchy and closer ties to Spain. Meanwhile efforts continued in the United States to secure congressional approval for the acquisition of Texas.

Instead, as every student of American and Texas history knows, the settlers (including some Mexican *tejanos*) rose up in rebellion against the Mexican government in 1834. The principal Anglo colonizer of Texas, Stephen Austin, believed that it was the manifest destiny of Anglo Americans to "redeem Texas from the wilderness"—to "*Americanize* Texas."[45] The conflict between Texas and Mexico, Austin wrote, was nothing less than "a war of barbarism and of despotic principles, waged by the mongrel Spanish-Indian and Negro race, against civilization and the Anglo-American race."[46] The enterprise of Americanizing Texas was best expressed by William H. Wharton, one of the staunchest supporters of Anglo rule in Texas: "The justice and benevolence of God will forbid that the delightful region of Texas should again become a howling wilderness, trod only by savages, or that it should be permanently benighted by the ignorance and superstition, the anarchy and rapine of Mexican misrule. The Anglo-American race are destined to be forever the proprietors of this land of *promise* and *fulfillment. Their* laws will govern it, *their* learning will enlighten it, their enterprise will improve it."[47] Such sentiments did not bode well for the future of Anglo-Mexican or U.S.-Mexico relations.

Although the Mexican government had banned slavery, Anglo Americans were determined to exercise their constitutional rights (in a foreign country) to own them. Most Texas histories pay scant attention to the contentious issue of slavery in the Texas conflict with Mexico, preferring instead to view the conflict, whether implicitly or explicitly, in terms of liberty-loving defenders of the Alamo versus backward, despotic Mexico. This simple paradox lies at the heart of the Texas creation myth, celebrated by numerous Alamo movies and books. Henry Clay, for example, asked, "By what race should Texas be peopled?" and responded that only liberty-loving Anglo Americans could save Texas from becoming a "place of despotism and slaves."[48] Clay was clearly not opposed to Texas being a place of black American slaves. His concern was that white people would be equivalent to "slaves" under Mexican rule (which denied them their God-given right to own slaves). Shortly after Sam Houston's victory over the Mexican Army in

1836, Texas became the independent Lone Star republic that was the envy of the South, for it made the protection of slavery a central feature of its constitution.[49] Texas became officially "Americanized" nine years later when it was annexed to the United States as a slave state.

In 1845 a Democratic newspaper editor from New York, John L. O'Sullivan, coined the phrase "manifest destiny" to justify the absorption of northern Mexico and Oregon into the United States: "The American claim is by the right of our manifest destiny to overspread and to possess the whole of the continent which Providence has given us for the development of the great experiment of liberty and . . . self-government entrusted to us."[50] The providential basis of O'Sullivan's "American claim" was less a matter of rational policy than religious faith. Expressions of the English settlers as God's Chosen People, however, date back to the founding of the nation.[51] Two years after the signing of the Declaration of Independence, the New England merchant and courier during the Revolutionary War Elkanah Watson rhapsodized over "the decrees of the Almighty, who has evidently raised up this nation to become a lamp to guide degraded and oppressed humanity."[52] In a speech in the House of Representatives a few years before the U.S.-Mexican War in 1846, Caleb Cushing celebrated the "spectacle of the Anglo-American stock extending itself into the heart of the Continent . . . advancing with . . . the preordination of inevitable progress, like the sun moving westerly in the heavens, or the ascending tide on the seashore, or . . . as a deluge of civilized men rising unabatedly and driven onwards by the hand of God."[53] The gleam in the eye of the expansionist encompassed not just the northern territory of Mexico, but extended to the Pacific Northwest as far as the Arctic Ocean.[54]

That Texas would enter the Union as a slave state complicated matters, but in the end the forces of expansion overshadowed the slavery question and Texas was annexed by joint resolution of the U.S. Congress in 1845 at the end of President John Tyler's term in office. His successor, James Knox Polk, set his sights on acquiring California and was willing to risk war with Mexico. Taking advantage of Mexico's endemic political infighting and the sorry state of its economy, Polk sent General Zachary Taylor to march from Corpus Christi on the Nueces River, which was the recognized southwestern border of Texas, to the mouth of the Río Grande near Matamoros, Mexico. There they clashed with the Mexican Army and lives were lost on both sides. President Polk claimed that Mexico "had shed American blood on American soil" and asked Congress to declare war on Mexico. Although many Americans, including Abraham Lincoln and Henry

David Thoreau, believed that the United States had provoked the war in order to acquire California, the voices of territorial expansion drowned out those of peace.[55]

It was hardly an even match. At the time the population of the United States had reached 20 million compared to Mexico's 7 million. Mexico's bankrupt economy stood in sharp contrast to its neighbor's dynamic and expanding one, and while the war dampened political factionalism between the North and the South in the United States, it crippled Mexico's ability to govern, much less defend itself against attack.[56] In two years the war was over. Equipped with modern weaponry, advanced artillery, and abundant resources, U.S. troops attacked along four fronts: Colonel Stephen Kearny marched overland to Santa Fe, New Mexico, where the Mexican governor Manuel Armijo offered no resistance. General Zachary Taylor continued his march south to Monterrey and Saltillo, Mexico. Commodore Robert Stockton took Los Angeles, California, although shortly afterward he faced a revolt by the Californios. Seeking to force Mexico's surrender as quickly as possible, President Polk sent General Winfield Scott with seventy troop-ships to Veracruz. After bombarding the port for a few days, his troops stormed the city and Veracruz surrendered. From Veracruz Scott marched his troops to Mexico City over essentially the same route taken by the conquistador Hérnan Cortés to the Halls of Montezuma over 300 years earlier.

The Mexican Army was no match for Scott's highly trained and equipped army. After a series of defensive battles, the city surrendered, although many civilians and even children—the revered *niños héroes*—joined in defense of the city. To the utter humiliation of the Mexicans, the American flag flew over the National Palace for the ten months that General Scott's army occupied the city. With instructions from President Polk, the U.S. peace commissioner, Nicholas P. Trist, negotiated the Treaty of Guadalupe Hidalgo, which formally concluded the war and ratified the loss of half of Mexico's land, including Texas, whose independence in 1836 Mexico had refused to recognize. Trist undertook his assignment with anguish. When Mexican treaty commissioner Bernardo Couto remarked to him at the treaty's conclusion, "This must be a proud moment for you; no less proud for you than it is humiliating for us," Trist replied: "We are making peace, let that be our only thought." Later Trist told his wife and others present: "Could those Mexicans have seen in my heart at that moment, they would have known my feeling of shame as an American was far stronger than theirs could be as Mexicans. . . . My objective throughout was not to obtain

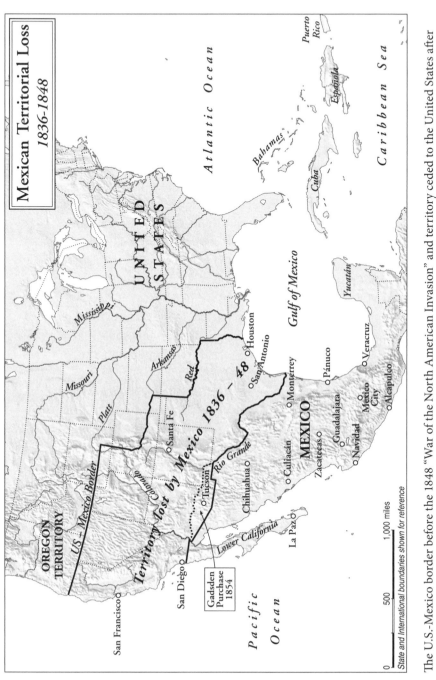

The U.S.-Mexico border before the 1848 "War of the North American Invasion" and territory ceded to the United States after the war.

Mexican Territorial Loss
1836-1848

UNITED STATES

OREGON TERRITORY

Territory lost by Mexico 1836 – 48

Gadsden Purchase 1854

MEXICO

Mississippi

Missouri

Platt

Arkansas

Red

Colorado

Rio Grande

US – Mexico Border

San Francisco

San Diego

Tucson

Santa Fe

Chihuahua

Culiacán

Zacatecas

Guadalajara

Navidad

Mexico City

Acapulco

La Paz

Lower California

Houston

San Antonio

Monterrey

Pánuco

Veracruz

Yucatán

Gulf of Mexico

Atlantic Ocean

Pacific Ocean

Caribbean Sea

Bahamas

Cuba

Española

Puerto Rico

0   500   1,000 miles

State and international boundaries shown for reference

all I could, but on the contrary to make the treaty as little exacting as possible for Mexico . . . . In this I was governed by . . . the iniquity of the war, as an abuse of power on our part."[57]

For many Mexicans the treaty dictated not only the humiliating loss of half the nation's territory, but also, as two historians of Mexico have noted, "an amputation, a painful surgery designed only to conserve what was left."[58] Perhaps this sad moment in the history of Mexico was what reputedly moved the late nineteenth-century dictator Porfirio Díaz to utter, "Poor Mexico, so far from God, so close to the United States."[59] On the other hand, in winning the war the United States could not have imagined that the new 2,000-mile border and the newly acquired territory—from California to Texas—would continue to be the destination of millions of Mexicans through the opening decades of the twenty-first century.

After the war with Mexico, the United States faced the challenge of incorporating the vast territory of northern Mexico, as well as the resident Mexicans, into the U.S. polity. Mexican residents who did not formally declare their intent to remain citizens of Mexico within one year after the signing of the Treaty of Guadalupe Hidalgo automatically became U.S. citizens. No doubt this must have come as a shock to many Mexican *pobladores* (settlers), who had lived in the region for centuries of Spanish and Mexican rule, in some cases going back to the founding of Santa Fe in 1609. But they did not number in the millions as their posterity would in the twentieth century. At the time of the U.S.-Mexican War, the population of Indian and mestizo Mexicans living in the vast territory ceded to the United States numbered between only eighty and one hundred thousand, most of whom lived on subsistence farms and small ranches in California, New Mexico, and Texas. Except for the most elite Californios, who often intermarried with Anglo Americans, the vast majority of Mexicans lived their lives apart from Anglo Americans in their own *colonias,* or Mexican neighborhoods. But that would soon change as Anglos flocked to the new territory in search of cheap land—and later cheap labor.[60]

Throughout the latter half of the nineteenth century huge swaths of land were being parceled out to Anglo-American settlers and later the railroads. Mexican landowners struggled to hold on to their land in areas like South Texas and northern New Mexico where they still outnumbered Anglos. Articles VIII and IX of the Treaty of Guadalupe Hidalgo specifically guaranteed that Mexican property rights under U.S. rule would be "inviolably respected." In reality, Anglos' lust for land could no more be constrained by treaty obligations with a defeated neighbor than countless (broken) treaties guaranteeing Indian rights to their land. The territorial courts of New

Mexico, for example, did not recognize "community property" and refused to uphold the property rights of land held in common by Mexicans. Even more devastating was the enactment of the federal Land Act of 1851, which required that all holders of land granted under the Spanish or Mexican governments prove their ownership of the land.[61] Many Mexican landowners, however, could not produce titles to land grants issued under governments of Mexico or Spain, some of them hundreds of years old. Nor did they possess surveys of their land that would hold up in a U.S. court of law. Their "title" to the land was based on generations of communal knowledge of the geographical boundaries of each land grant, expressed in language that referenced a stream, or pile of rocks, or grove of trees as boundary markers. Mexican families knew the boundaries of the land they and other families owned, often for many generations, but Anglos demanded proof.

Under the American system of land ownership, Mexicans without titles had to hire surveyors and pay Anglo lawyers to draw up new titles and deeds of transfer. Many Mexican landowners were forced to pay lawyers with parcels of land rather than dollars, which most did not have. Over half a million square miles of Spanish and Mexican land grants were thus made available to Anglo-American settlers through laws like the Land Act. In New Mexico about 80 percent of all land grants eventually ended up in the hands of Anglo lawyers and settlers.[62] One Texas historian, who acknowledged that some Mexican landowners were robbed of their land by "force, intimidation, or chicanery," nevertheless claimed, without a trace of irony, that "what is usually ignored is the fact the [Mexican landowning] class was stripped of property perfectly legally, according to the highest traditions of U.S. law."[63]

After the loss of their land, and the economic status that accompanied ownership, resident Mexicans and Mexican immigrants became an indispensable component of the labor force in the burgeoning economy of the Southwest. They were recruited as unskilled laborers to work in the mines of Arizona and New Mexico, on large agribusiness farms in California and Texas, and on the railroads throughout the Southwest. Meanwhile, the Anglo-American race to the West continued unabated. To fill the vast expanse of the newly acquired land, developers and land speculators sent agents to Europe to recruit new immigrants, trumpeting cheap land and plentiful work. One historian argues that the "intimate tie between exterminating the Indians and dispossessing Mexicans, on the one hand, and bringing in Europeans on the other" represented a systematic attempt to transform the West into a region of European-American farmers, a process he calls "racial replacement."[64]

Of the territory acquired from Mexico, California became a state in record time, mainly because the discovery of gold in 1849 attracted tens of thousands of Anglo-American settlers and prospectors, outnumbering their primary competitors from Mexico, China, and Chile.[65] Despite the arrival of about twenty thousand Mexicans from the silver-mining regions of Sonora and Zacatecas, many with mining experience, the demographic balance tipped in favor of Anglo Americans, and California became a state in 1850, only two years after U.S.-Mexican War.[66] In one of the saddest historical ironies in the history of North America, Mexico—whose Spanish founding fathers had devoted themselves to discovering cities of gold since Cortez first arrived in 1519—lost California to the United States in 1848, exactly one year before the conquering Yankees struck it rich.

Many Mexicans in the newly acquired U.S. territories rebelled against Anglo rule and legal machinations to deprive them of their land, but the vast majority of them simply withdrew from contact with Anglos as best they could. In New Mexico, Hispano insurgents staged a short-lived rebellion in 1847 and killed the newly appointed territorial governor. In California, Angelenos initially resisted invading U.S. troops, but were no match for the U.S. Army. Over the next half century or more, some Mexican "bandits" sought to defend the rights of Mexicans and exact what revenge they could for violations of their citizenship rights, including the outright murder of Mexicans by law enforcement officials like the notorious Texas Rangers. In Texas Juan Cortina, and in California the legendary Joaquín Murieta and Tiburcio Vasquez, became the subject of numerous *corridos,* or ballads, for their exploits and acts of revenge against Anglos, while Anglos offered large rewards for their capture, dead or alive.[67]

Gregorio Cortez, who shot a Texas sheriff in self-defense in 1901, is perhaps one of the most celebrated Mexican "outlaws" of the Southwest as a result of a book-length study, *With His Pistol in His Hand,* by folklorist Américo Paredes. The Karnes County sheriff drew his pistol and shot Cortez's brother, Romaldo, over a mistranslation involving a stolen horse. In the confusion that followed, Cortez escaped. It took ten days and hundreds of men, including the Texas Rangers, before Cortez was caught trying to escape into Mexico. Cortez served more than a decade of a life sentence before being pardoned. Fifty years later, shortly after publishing the book in 1958, Paredes received a death threat from a retired Texas Ranger for having the temerity to suggest that the real outlaws were the police, especially the Texas Rangers.[68]

From the moments of first contact, even before the U.S.-Mexican War, Anglos regarded Mexicans as the bad guys—racially inferior, lazy, and criminal. But the era of Hispanophobia in the Southwest began gradually to wane as Anglo Americans consolidated their control over the area, and came to rely on Mexican labor for everything from clearing brush to building and maintaining railroads. In fact, Hispanophobia was giving way gradually to Hispanophilia, which included the Spanish colonizers but not Mexicans. Anglo writers began to celebrate the "Spanish heritage" of the Southwest, even though the English and their New World offspring had thought of the Spanish as inferior Europeans. For Anglo-Saxon Americans, the legacy of Spanish colonial rule was one of cruelty, barbarism, and superstition (i.e., Catholicism) and over time came to be called the *la leyenda negra* (the Black Legend). Ironically, the person most responsible for the evolution of this legend was a Spanish friar, Bartolomé de Las Casas, who published in 1552 the equivalent of an international bestseller, *Brevísima Relación de la Destrucción de las Indias (Brief History of the Destruction of the Indies),* that revealed in agonizing detail the torture techniques of Spanish friars and soldiers in commanding the loyalty, both spiritual and political, of the Indians. But by the 1880s, writers like Helen Hunt Jackson, Bret Harte, and later Charles Fletcher Lummis waxed nostalgic over the carefree pastoral society of "Spanish America" with its haciendas, caballeros, dueñas, and demure señoritas.[69] Swashbuckling conquistadors, self-sacrificing friars, and rugged Spanish settlers were Europeans, they seemed to recall—white people like Anglo-Saxon Americans, only Catholic and Spanish-speaking. In a letter to Santa Fe's leading citizens in 1883, Walt Whitman expressed his appreciation of the "splendor and sterling value" of Hispanic culture, which dressed up the "seething materialistic" ethos of the United States.[70]

What exactly was it about colonial Spain in the Southwest that Anglo Americans and elite Californios and Nuevomexicanos gradually came to find so attractive—and so different from the Spaniards of Black Legend fame? David J. Weber, the preeminent historian of Spanish North America, reminds us that "Anglo Americans inherited the view that Spaniards were unusually cruel, avaricious, treacherous, fanatical, superstitious, cowardly, corrupt, decadent, indolent, and authoritarian."[71] But as the nineteenth century drew to a close, Spaniards and their callous conquest faded into distant historical memory, even to the Mexicans who defeated them in their war for independence in 1821. The Spanish "Fantasy Heritage," writer and lawyer Carey McWilliams tells us, goes something like this:

Long, long ago the borderlands were settled by Spanish grandees and caballeros, a gentle people, accustomed to the luxurious softness of fine clothes, to well-trained servants, to all the amenities of civilized European living. Inured to suffering, kindly mission *padres* overcame the hostility of Indians by their saintly example and the force of a spiritual ideal, much in the manner of a gentle spring rain driving the harsh winds of winter from the skies. . . . There was none of the rough struggle for existence that beset the Puritans of New England. The climate was so mild, the soil so fertile, that Indians merely cast seeds on the ground, letting them fall where chance deposited them, and relaxed in the shade of the nearest tree while a provident and kindly nature took over. Occasionally one of the field hands would interrupt his siesta long enough to open one eye and lazily watch the corn stalks shooting up in the golden light.[72]

The celebration of Spanish culture in the Southwest represented a serious injustice to the Indians and Mexicans through whom—"and only through whom," McWilliams declares, "Spanish cultural influences survived in the region," reinforced by constant immigration.[73]

The Anglo-American rediscovery of Spanish America not only did not include Mexicans of Greater Mexico/the Southwest, it was never meant to. What did Mexicans have to do with the greatness of Spain and the exploits of its conquistadors, explorers, and missionaries—or the art, architecture, language, and culture that the Spanish and their descendants implanted in the New World from San Francisco to the southernmost tip of South America? The invention of Spanish America owed as much to Anglo-American desire for the exotic and picturesque—like Pueblo Indian culture—as it did to nostalgia for the pastoral community of "Spain-away-from-Spain" that the juggernaut of westward expansion helped extinguish. In his 1893 book, *Land of Poco Tiempo,* Charles Fletcher Lummis conjured an image of New Mexico that was both alluring and disquieting: "New Mexico . . . is a picture, a romance, a dream, all in one. . . . It is a land of quaint, swart faces, of Oriental dress and unspelled speech; a land where distance is lost, and the eye is a liar; a land of ineffable lights and sudden shadows; of polytheism and superstition, where the rattlesnake is demigod, and the cigarette a means of grace, and where Christians mangle and crucify themselves— the heart of Africa beating against the ribs of the Rockies."[74] For Lummis, the bizarre religious practices of New Mexican *penitentes,* a confraternity of Hispano Catholic men who flogged themselves while reenacting the scourging and crucifixion of Christ, evoked the primitiveness of Africa more than the high civilization of Spain. Despite the "mangled" culture the Spanish implanted in the New World, their pioneering of the Americas was, as Lummis exuberantly put it, the "largest and longest and most marvelous feat of manhood in all history."[75]

Celebrating all things Spanish had its advantages for New Mexicans, whose deepest anxiety was that Anglo Americans viewed them less as racial equals than as mixed-race kin of the Indians. Light-skinned and English-speaking New Mexicans took advantage of the Spanish Fantasy Heritage to identify themselves as Hispanos, or Spanish Americans, who traced their lineage to Spain. In this way they could escape the stigma of being "Mexican"—poor, uneducated, and racially mixed. From this lumpen mestizo population thus emerged a class of Mexican elites who were accorded a certain measure of equality with Anglo Americans. Unlike in California and Texas, where the population of Anglo Americans far exceeded the native Mexican population, in New Mexico Anglo Americans represented a distinct minority. New Mexico's population included approximately 60,000 native Mexicans and 15,000 Pueblo Indians, compared to only about 1,000 Anglo American settlers, who maintained power and control in the territorial government after 1848 by co-opting the Mexican elites as an intermediate white group between Anglo Americans above them and Indians and African Americans below.[76]

By the early twentieth century the transformation of many light-skinned Mexicans into Spanish Americans was largely complete. "These Spanish people of New Mexico," wrote a columnist for *Harper's Weekly* in 1914, "are not of the mixed breed one finds south of the Río Grande. . . . Indeed, it is probable that there is no purer Spanish stock in Old Spain itself."[77] That belief that the settlers of New Mexico were of "pure Spanish stock" attests to the power of the racial fantasy reimagined by Hispanos and Anglo Hispanophiles.[78]

The city of Los Angeles was founded in 1781 by the Spanish governor Felipe de Neve under the official name "El Pueblo de Nuestra Señora la Reina de los Ángeles de Porciúncula" (the Village of Our Lady, the Queen of the Angels of Porciúncula). Fueled by the mythology of its Spanish origin, parades and holidays celebrating the Spanish colonial heritage took place in many borderland cities, despite the fact that of the original settlers of Our Lady Queen of the Angels, only two were Spaniards. The rest were mixed-race *gente de color,* people of color. One was mestizo, two were afro-mestizos, eight were mulattos, and nine were Indians.[79] Although the vast majority of those who first settled the northern borderlands, including

California, were Indians and mestizos, the streets in Los Angeles, Santa Barbara, and other cities are named for prominent Californios with names like Sepúlveda, Pico, and Figueroa. As late as the 1940s, McWilliams notes, "Spanish" Californios occupied a social position in most communities that "might best be compared with that of the widow of a Confederate general in a small southern town."[80]

Through the celebration of Spanish Americans, the Southwest elevated European culture over indigenous "Mexicanness," thereby providing a powerful incentive for Mexicans to pass as "Spanish" and lay claim to a European lineage. "Old Spanish Days" festivals proliferated throughout the Southwest to celebrate Spain's heritage in America while ignoring the historical role played by Mexicans and Mexico in the formation of Southwestern culture. City officials throughout the West built monuments to Spanish America for tourists to marvel at and re-created Spanish plazas, like Balboa Park in San Diego, while Mexicans and Indians as well as Africans and Asians, whose labor helped to build the West, were marginalized as racial primitives, inassimilable foreigners, and "wetbacks."[81]

Maintaining the Fantasy Heritage of the Southwest served two important purposes: to Europeanize cities like Los Angeles, San Antonio, and Santa Fe to make them more attractive for tourists and investors; and to provide an opportunity for some Mexicans to become "Spanish." The Californios themselves provided the essential insight into the difference between being Mexican and Spanish: "one who achieves success in the borderlands is 'Spanish'; one who doesn't is 'Mexican.'"[82] Mexicans were "Mexicans" because they were too poor and too dark to become Spanish. Neither term identified one's nationality, but rather one's race and class position in the multiracial, mixed-race borderlands where Negroes, Japanese, Chinese, Indians, Filipinos, "Hindoos," and Mexicans found their social and economic niches in the Southwest—or were forced into them. Whites too fell along a racial continuum: at or near the top were the descendants of Protestant northern Europeans, and just below them the Irish and European Catholics; at the bottom, Indians, and not far above them, in ascending order, were the Chinese and Japanese, blacks, and Mexicans. Of these latter groups, only Mexicans had the remotest possibility of shedding the stigma of "color" by becoming "Spanish," which made them acceptable in small numbers to the Anglo ruling elites.[83]

Anglo Americans thus reproduced the Spanish colonial practice of allowing certain light-skinned mestizos to become español, or white, and erased the mixed-race reality of Indian and mestizo Mexicans. Over the centuries, diverse peoples, voluntarily or not, had shaped a Mexican nation whose borderlands extended deep into North America, but in 1848 the Mexican far north became the U.S. Southwest as a result of conquest. Despite the imposition of a border designed to separate them, in effect the two nations overlapped geographically and demographically, and subsequent relations between the two would continue to be problematic, and sometimes precarious, as Mexicans continued to move north across the border along well-trod corridors of migration. Mexicans and Mexican immigrants came to form a large reservoir of cheap labor for the development of agriculture and industries throughout the Southwest. Anglo efforts to curb massive Mexican immigration in the 1920s emerged as many Anglo Americans questioned whether dark-skinned Indian and mestizo Mexicans could ever become "true" Americans.

2

NO ESTÁS EN TU CASA

After 1848 Mexicans in the present-day states of California, Arizona, New Mexico, and Texas became strangers in their own land, foreigners who seemed not much different from the Indians of the Southwest. It was a bitter pill for Mexicans to contemplate maps of the northern half of their country lopped off by the United States in a war of aggression and the creation of a continent-wide border dividing Anglo North America from Mexican North America, the latter greatly reduced in size. What used to be the Mexican North had become the American Southwest, and successive generations of Mexican immigrants and Mexican Americans learned rather quickly that in the "Spanish" Southwest brown skin wasn't much better than being black or red. Citizenship bestowed about as many rights and privileges on Mexican Americans, Asian Americans, and Native Americans as it had on black Americans in the South after the Civil War. These groups—as well as Jews, Slavs, Italians, Irish, Poles and other not-quite-white immigrant groups—faced many decades of struggle to transform America into the kaleidoscopically ethnic nation it is today, to feel that they too were "at home" in their own country.

In the opening decades of the twentieth century, the surging economy of the Southwest created a massive demand for Mexican labor at a time when controls and regulations for entry at the border were lax or nonexistent, a time when many Anglo Americans warned that Mexican immigrants could just as easily destroy America as build it up. Nevertheless, Mexicans continued to migrate to the north as "immigrants," following the same paths their forebears took as migrant laborers, crossing and recrossing the border to work in mines, railroads, and agribusiness farms. While most returned to their homes in Mexico, many others stayed in El Otro Lado (the Other Side), joining many thousands of Mexican Americans and Mexican resident nationals in the border states.

The transborder migration of Mexicans to the United States can be divided into two periods: 1900 to 1930, when the Great Depression not only curtailed immigration but led to the mass deportation of Mexicans; and the period beginning with the demand for Mexican agricultural and railroad laborers in World War II and continuing, with periodic lulls from the late 1950s to the early 1970s, until the turn of the twenty-first century. The debate over restricting Mexican immigration began in earnest during the 1920s, an era of extreme xenophobia and animus toward all immigrants except those from northern Europe. When Congress failed to restrict immigration from Mexico (and the rest of the western hemisphere) in 1924, many Americans questioned whether the growing number of Mexicans in the United States and their U.S.-born children could ever become "true" Americans. The question had less to do with their assimilation—learning English, paying taxes, voting, and swearing to uphold the Constitution— than with the transcendent belief that Mexicans constituted a race of mongrelized Indians whose presence in large numbers threatened the core concept of what it meant to be "American." The border, they insisted, must be strictly controlled to limit the numbers of Mexicans crossing over.

Controlling the border proved much more difficult than marking it off on a map or erecting border monument markers in the desert between Tijuana and El Paso. In 1849, a year after the United States and Mexico concluded the Treaty of Guadalupe Hidalgo that ended the war and formalized the cession of Mexico's northern territory, the Joint United States and Mexico Boundary Commission began the difficult task of transferring onto the ground the actual placement of the international border as it appeared on the new map. Unlike the Rio Grande (Río Bravo as it is known in Mexico) that formed the border from the Gulf of Mexico to El Paso, the western half of the border had to be marked by scientists, surveyors, and sundry bureaucrats across vast stretches of desert and mountain ranges. Lingering boundary disputes over the western border resulted in the U.S. purchase, for $10 million, of additional Mexican land in present-day southern Arizona and New Mexico (the Gadsden Purchase of 1853) for the purpose of completing a southern route for a transcontinental railroad. By 1855 the U.S.-Mexico border had finally been surveyed and marked with 258 border monuments or obelisks from El Paso westward through 698 miles of desert to the Pacific Ocean. The not-so-mighty Rio Grande formed a natural boundary between El Paso and the Gulf of Mexico. Various joint boundary commissions have returned over the last 150 years to correct errors, make adjustments for the shifting channels of the Rio Grande, and to restore or replace boundary monuments.[1]

Rebuilding Monument 40 along the Mexican border west of the Rio Grande, 1892. Records of the Office of the Chief of Engineers, 1789–1988, AMWEST 013. Courtesy of National Archives.

Throughout the last two decades of the nineteenth century, Mexicans living in towns on the south side of the Rio Grande routinely crossed into New Mexico and Texas to work on farms and in the mines, and sometimes to settle permanently. There were no immigration officials to monitor the flow across the border before the 1890s (the border patrol was not established until 1924). From the American Civil War until the turn of the twentieth century, Mexicans frequently crossed the border into the United States, in some places wholly unaware that they had left their country. Before 1910 American immigration officials were less concerned with the relatively small number of Mexicans crossing the border than with the surreptitious entry from Mexico of Chinese immigrants, who had been banned from immigrating to the United States since the enactment of the Chinese Exclusion Act of 1882.[2]

Gradually, almost imperceptibly, both sides of the border came to form a single economic region with two-way, cyclical migration, especially when Mexican and American railroads linked up in the borderlands in the 1880s,

Mexican workers in an Arizona mine, 1900s. Arizona Historical Society, Mexican Heritage Project, 64323.

and Anglo investors opened mining operations in northern Mexico around the same time. Located just forty miles south of the Arizona border, the American-owned Cananea Consolidated Copper Company became the largest mining town in the entire border region, employing thousands of Mexicans, as well as smaller numbers of Anglo Americans, South Americans, and some Europeans.[3] In Arizona Mexicans established a pattern of traveling freely between northern Mexican mines and southern Arizona settlements like Nogales, Tuscon, Tubac, Tombstone, and Bisbee. Before the enactment of the 1917 Immigration Act, Anglo employers viewed the comings and goings of Mexicans across the Rio Grande and the largely invisible boundary west of El Paso less as immigrants than as seasonal transborder migrant workers.[4]

With the completion of railway links between Mexico and the Southwest, Mexican laborers began to move en masse from central Mexico across the hostile northern desert region to the border states, mainly Texas and California. Mexicans performed the arduous task of "grubbing" the land in south Texas, which consisted of removing the mesquite brush and thorny undergrowth prior to the cultivation of cotton. Many more Mexicans were needed to fulfill the labor demands of expanding cotton acreage in Texas after 1900. In southern California Mexicans joined Japanese and Chinese Americans in the cotton, fruit, and vegetable fields, where the development of irrigation projects revolutionized the scale and production of agricultural products.[5] Between 1915 and 1919 the number of Mexican workers in the California citrus industry tripled to 7,000 workers, comprising 30 percent of all citrus workers. According to a survey conducted by the United States Immigration Commission in 1909 (better known as the Dillingham Commission), Mexican immigrant farm workers averaged $1.42 per day, the lowest wage of any other immigrant group. They also worked in sugar beet factories, mines, on road construction, railroad maintenance, and irrigation projects—providing much of the unskilled labor in the cities and countryside of the Southwest. "The members of this race," the Dillingham Commission noted, "have always been the hewers of wood and the drawers of water."[6] A grower of sugar beets in northeastern Colorado explained what qualities he appreciated in Mexicans that made them ideal laborers, besides the fact that they could be paid low wages: "A Mexican is the best damn dog any white man ever had. He will do lot more for you than any white man would. If you are doing something heavy, he will come and help you. Of course you can't kick him and cuss him around any more than you would a dog. He's more loyal to you than any white friend."[7] Although most doubted that Mexicans could be made into bona fide Americans, few doubted they made ideal workers, not unlike sentiments expressed today.

While many came north in search of job opportunities and higher wages, many Mexicans were forced to leave their families and communities in Mexico as a result of extreme poverty. As many contemporary observers have noted, the majority of Mexican immigrants came from the "peon" class, mainly landless peasants driven from their land by the policies of General Porfirio Díaz (strongman president of Mexico from 1876 to 1911). During his thirty-five years in office, Porfirio Díaz enacted laws that concentrated community-held lands, or *ejidos,* into large holdings (haciendas) where a small class of wealthy owners held a large peasant workforce in semi-feudal bondage through debt peonage. Under this system the rural worker was unable to leave the hacienda until he paid the debt owed to the patrón for advances of food and other supplies on credit. Andrés Molina Enríque, a leading social critic on the eve of the 1910 Mexican Revolution, accused these large landholders of exercising "the absolute domination of a feudal lord" over their workers.[8] At no time before 1910 did the average wage of farm labor in Mexico exceed $0.25 per day in U.S. currency. With static wages and high credit prices for goods charged in the *tiendas de raya* (the owner-owned "company store"), peons were unable to pay their debts from year to year, and debts passed from fathers to sons for generations. By comparison, a migrant Mexican cotton picker in Texas or unskilled mine worker in Arizona could earn wages ten times higher than landless peasants in the densely populated Central Plateau of Mexico such as Guanajuato, Jalisco, Zacatecas, and San Luís Potosí.

With America's entry into World War I, growers in California, Arizona, and Texas became increasingly desperate for farm workers. As able-bodied Americans left the fields, drawn by higher wages in the manufacturing sector, such as shipbuilding, munitions, and other war industries, growers in the Southwest pressured the Labor Department to waive the requirements for Mexican migrant workers. Accordingly, in May 1917, the secretary of labor, William B. Wilson, suspended the literacy test, the head tax, and the contract labor clause forbidding labor contractors from signing up laborers in Mexico. Under the "temporary admissions" program, the border was essentially opened to tens of thousands of Mexican laborers seeking work in the United States.

The chairman of the House Immigration and Naturalization Committee and other congressional representatives initially objected to the opening of the border without congressional approval. Secretary Wilson had invoked a provision of the 1917 law that permitted the secretary of labor to grant entry to temporary workers who would otherwise not be eligible for admission—mainly those over the age of sixteen who could not read. Wilson explained to the chairman his reason for invoking the provision: "From many sources we were being pressed to encourage the migration of Filipinos, Hawaiians and other labor of similar character, and to secure the suspension of the Chinese Exclusion Law so that Chinese might be admitted . . . to supply the deficit of farm labor alleged to exist on the Pacific Coast and along the Mexican Border. Of course, we could not yield to importunities of that kind. We have all the race problems in the United States that it is advisable for us to undertake to deal with at the present time."[9] The advantage of admitting Mexicans rather than Asians on a temporary basis was that they could be more easily returned, or so many believed. And while many Anglo Americans worried about the "Mexican problem" in the Southwest, they mostly feared the Chinese and Japanese in their midst as the principal race problem.[10] Labor organizations strenuously opposed the program, arguing that "American labor be used before cheap labor is imported."[11] Nevertheless, influential farmers associations, as well as mining and railroad companies, persuaded the congressional leaders that the labor secretary had responded appropriately to a national emergency. Although the war ended in 1918, the temporary admissions program was extended to 1922, when it could no longer be justified as an emergency war measure.

The Mexican government was not informed, much less consulted, of the "temporary admissions" program at the border, and many Mexican government officials worried that the exodus of Mexican workers would leave Mexico with a labor shortage for its own agricultural sector.[12] Others worried about Mexico's own inability to provide adequate employment for its rapidly growing rural population. In a dispatch rarely seen in diplomatic correspondence, the Mexican consul in Kansas, L. G. Villalpando, wrote a blistering condemnation of Mexico's inability to feed and clothe its own poor, while at the same time the government discouraged the poorest Mexicans from leaving to work in the United States, implying that those who left were traitors to their country. The lowest-paid of these workers in the United States, Villalpando wrote the Mexican secretary of labor, work fewer hours and earn four times the salary than workers in Mexico. The poorest Mexicans in the United States "have fresh milk, ham, eggs, meat and fish— better even than our middle class in Mexico." Their children attend the public schools, and even the smallest towns have movie theaters with reduced prices on the weekends. In Mexico, by contrast, the poor work long hours in the fields, often with their children who never attend school—and the "only entertainment they can look forward to in their lives of perpetual misery is the patriotic display of fireworks each September 16 in the town squares." Villalpando blamed the "criminal selfishness of Mexican capitalism" that ignored the problem of hunger and poverty in Mexico.[13]

While most of the temporary Mexican laborers ended up on farms in the four border states of the Southwest, the Mexican government received requests for temporary workers in the shipyards of Newport News, Virginia; the sugar cane fields in Louisiana; the mines, quarries, and farms in central Georgia; sugar beet fields in Colorado; and the salmon fisheries of the Alaska Territory. The Mexican secretary of labor turned down many of the requests because the growing number of nationals seeking higher wages in the United States had caused a labor shortage in Mexico.[14] But the Mexican government also worried—as one consul put it in a section of his report titled *punta de alarma* (warning sign)—that Mexican workers in the United States ran the risk of becoming *desmexicanizados* (de-Mexicanized) at the very moment when Mexico was entering "a period of resurgence" and needed all of its workers to help develop Mexico's struggling economy. The consul worried that these workers would soon forget that they owed their allegiance to Mexico and not to the development of the United States.[15] Even the lowest-paid Mexican workers received considerably higher wages than what they were accustomed to in Mexico. In any case, no law prevented Mexicans from leaving the country, and since Mexican president Venustiano Carranza was powerless to prevent them from leaving, he issued an order in 1918 officially conceding the right of Mexicans to emigrate to the United States.[16]

Mexicans were not the only ones seeking new opportunities. Thousands of U.S. workers, including war veterans, had lost their jobs in the recession following World War I, many of whom traveled to Mexico, often illegally, to work for American oil companies. Others wrote to the Mexican government seeking jobs in industry, railroads, utilities, mining, and other occupations.[17] The Mexican consuls sent monthly reports to the Mexican Labor Department on the economic crisis in the United States, and especially the strikes that occurred across the country between 1919 and 1922, when between 600,000 and 700,000 of the 4.5 million veterans of the Great War were unemployed.[18] An unemployed American from Binger, Oklahoma, wrote to the Mexican secretary of labor: "I would like to have information concerning the demands for white labor in Mexico."[19] Numerous German Americans and resident German nationals in the United States also sought work in Mexico, some of whom frankly admitted that discrimination against Germans during World War I had made it difficult to find work. Mexican officials noted that many U.S. oil and mining companies in Mexico preferred to hire *peones Americanos* (unskilled American workers), whom they paid higher wages than the Mexicans they employed. These companies set up recruiting centers in Tampico, Mexico, and other cities and paid American workers' travel expenses, helped them find lodging, offered free medical services, and paid for them to return to the United States every six months for a visit.[20] An official of the Mexican Interior Ministry was outraged when he learned that the oil companies had created their own security force, called "Guardia Blanca," to police their workers, including Mexicans, thereby "exercising total sovereignty in our own country."[21] The interior minister recommended closing the border to American workers, but the secretary of labor opposed the idea, suggesting instead that Mexico close its borders to all immigrants from China as well as "Turks, Armenians, and Arabs because they carry contagious diseases." He warned that prohibiting the immigration of American workers into Mexico might damage Mexico's future, especially since, "in reality, we urgently need for other races to settle in Mexico."[22] The United States and Mexico faced similar dilemmas: Mexico did not want American immigrants taking jobs from Mexicans but at the same time desired "other races"—white ones—to settle in Mexico, while the United States did not want mixed-race Mexicans to pollute America's white "racial stock," but nonetheless wanted them as low-wage, temporary workers.

Three years after the end of the war, the Mexican government ordered that work visas no longer be issued to Americans and urged Mexican workers not to go to *al vecino país,* the neighboring country.[23] Governors also issued circulars enjoining the citizenry not to leave the country and forbade labor contractors from operating in their jurisdictions, unless they had permission from the government. Faced with the option of migrating to the United States to earn a living wage, or remaining in their villages where jobs were scarce, many Mexicans ignored official warnings and made the trek to the United States.[24]

In reality, the Mexican government was powerless to prevent the mass exodus of its citizens during and after the war. The mayor of Nuevo Laredo (Mexican "twin" city of Laredo, Texas) said he would do nothing to restrict the flow from his city across the border because that would mean feeding and housing thousands of workers who did not have the means to return to their homes in the interior states of San Luis Potosi, Guanajuato, and Michoacán where most of them came from.[25] To afford a minimum of protection to those who left, the Mexican government drafted an amendment to the migration law, Ley de Migración, that would require braceros to sign contracts. The contract spelled out the responsibilities of American companies and labor contractors regarding length of service, salaries, medical attention, indemnification in case of job-related accidents, and the costs of repatriation at the end of their contracts. No mention was made of involving the U.S. government or state governments in agreeing to oversee and enforce the contracts. Braceros were supposed to carry a copy of the contract and negotiate with employers on their own, as if a written contract were sufficient to oblige both parties to comply with the provisions of the contract.[26] No mention was made of the fact that many or most of the braceros could not read or write—nor of the fact that U.S. employers could simply decline to sign the contract or refuse to hire any bracero foolish enough to present a contract which obligated the employer to pay a certain salary and repatriation costs, offer medical services, guarantee length of employment, and so forth. And no personnel were made available, on either side of the border, to ensure that Mexicans received proper treatment, their contracts were honored, and that they were returned to Mexico after their contracts expired.

Much has been written of the exploitation of Mexican workers in the United States in the first half of the twentieth century, and with each wave of immigration from Mexico, a significant percentage of them returned to

Mexico no richer, although evidently wiser, than they left. Employers in the United States reaped all the benefits of low-cost braceros but were burdened with few responsibilities for their welfare. Nevertheless, of over 75,000 temporary workers admitted from 1917 to 1921, fewer than half of them returned to Mexico.[27] Perhaps for many who returned to Mexico the American Dream seemed just beyond their grasp, or not worth the hardship and separation from their families. But tens of thousands stayed, settled down, and raised families in towns and cities across America, proving the truth of the saying that there's nothing more permanent than temporary workers. While the U.S. Congress ended the program in 1921 and reimposed the provision of the 1917 Immigration Act, hundreds of thousands of Mexicans entered the United States during the 1920s, many illegally, when the demand for agricultural labor peaked. Many Mexicans also fled the turmoil of the "Cristero Rebellion" in which devout Catholics launched a massive armed revolt in 1926 against the government for its enforcement of the anticlerical provisions of the 1917 Constitution.[28] Many who became long-term resident nationals lived long enough to witness the Bracero Program of 1942, when their conationals were once again contracted by the U.S. government with the Mexican government's on-again, off-again approval until 1964, twenty-two years after the program began and nineteen years after the war emergency had ended.

The population surge of Mexican immigrants to the Southwest after World War I did not escape the notice of Anglo Americans in towns and cities from Los Angeles to San Antonio. Contemporary journalist and author Carey McWilliams noted that the "Readers Guide to Periodical Literature" listed fifty-one articles on the "Mexican Problem" in the 1920s, compared to only nineteen the previous decade. Most of the articles detailed the social consequences of Mexican immigration: delinquency, disease rates, illiteracy, low wages, poor housing conditions, and so forth.[29] Not everyone thought of Mexicans as a problem. Texas congressman John Nance Garner, who for forty years represented a district in south Texas on the border with Mexico, argued that Mexicans had been integrated into the south Texas economy for hundreds of years and that the entire economy of south Texas agriculture depended on cross-border Mexican migrants. He made the point that "They will do necessary labor that even a negro won't touch."[30] Texas representative John Box of north Texas, an ardent supporter of legislation restricting Mexican immigration, disagreed with his Texas colleague. Box cited a California immigration study that Mexican immigrants represented a dangerous "health hazard" and that, because of their tendency to rear large families, "in time American culture will be wiped out and the United

States will fall like Rome and ancient Greece if Mexican immigration is not restricted."[31] Box told the House Immigration Committee in 1930 that the Southwest must be preserved "as the future home of the white race" and not be used as a "dumping ground for the human hordes of poverty stricken peon Indians of Mexico."[32]

During the 1920s Americans feared that endless waves of poor eastern and southern Europeans as well as Mexicans would take American jobs and change American culture for the worst. The "tribal twenties," as one immigration historian dubbed the decade, was a time of Anglo Americans circling the wagons to safeguard America from being overrun by racially inferior immigrants.[33] In 1921 Congress passed the Emergency Quota Act, and a few years later the Johnson-Reed National Origins Act of 1924, which limited the number of immigrants who could be admitted from any country to 2 percent of the number of people from that country who were already living in the United States in 1890. Since the majority of the nation's population in 1890 were Protestant descendants of northern Europeans, the quota system based on national origins curtailed immigration from eastern and southern Europe from 45 percent to 15 percent. The Chinese Exclusion Act of 1882 and the Gentlemen's Agreement with Japan in 1908 had effectively ended most Chinese and Japanese immigration, but the 1924 law went a step further: it banned all immigration from Asia, declaring that only those eligible for citizenship under the amended 1790 Naturalization Act (free, white persons and persons of African origin) could immigrate to America.[34]

By restricting immigration from Europe and ending it from Asia, the 1924 law sought to preserve the economic, political, and cultural dominance of white Protestant Americans of northern European background. These "true" Americans devoutly believed that they, and only they, could save the republic from meeting the same fate as Greece and Rome. While there would always be barbarians at the gate, in small numbers they provided useful labor in the development of the nation's industrial and agricultural infrastructure, but their numbers needed to be carefully controlled. The problem, however, was that immigration from Mexico (and the rest of the hemisphere) was exempt from the quotas established in the 1924 Act. Some of the same Anglo Americans responsible for restricting immigration from Europe were strongly opposed to restricting immigration from Mexico. They reasoned that mining, manufacturing industries, agribusiness, and railroad construction and maintenance had so thoroughly relied on Mexican labor that any law to restrict Mexican immigration would mean nothing less than economic disaster for the entire region. Unchecked immigration from Mexico, others believed, would imperil American civilization, like a Trojan horse, from within America's borders.[35]

While the Congress was debating immigration restriction for Mexicans, the Bureau of the Census worried that it had no accurate way to count how many Mexican immigrants and Mexican Americans resided in the United States. Part of the problem had to do with the racial classification of Mexican people. From the first census in 1790 until 1930, persons of Mexican descent, whether citizens or not, were classified as "white." While the census included separate racial categories for Chinese, Negroes, Filipinos, American Indians, and other nonwhite groups, it classified Mexican-origin persons much as it did Italians, Germans, Irish, Dutch, Swedes, Arabs, Puerto Ricans, Poles, and Peruvians—"white." In an effort to secure an accurate count of the growing Mexican population in the United States, the census created the separate racial category "Mexican" and provided the census enumerators with guidelines for distinguishing between white Mexicans and nonwhite Mexicans: "Practically all Mexican laborers are of a racial mixture difficult to classify, though usually well recognized in the localities where they are found. In order to obtain separate figures for this racial group, it has been decided that all persons born in Mexico, or having parents born in Mexico, who are not definitely white, negro, Indian, Chinese, or Japanese, should be returned [classified] as Mexican." Census takers generally decided which Mexicans should be classified as "white" and which ones "Mexican" based on skin color, language, and economic status. Since most Mexican immigrants and Mexican Americans were poor and dark-skinned, the outcome, not surprisingly, was that over 1.4 million Mexican-origin persons were classified as racially "Mexican," while only 65,986 Mexicans, or 4 percent, met the subjective criteria for being classified as "white."[36] Many Mexican-American civil rights advocates loudly objected to being classified as racially "Mexican" because they fully understood the implications of being nonwhite in America. After 1930 the census abandoned the attempt to count Mexicans as a separate racial group until 1980, when the census classified Hispanics/Latinos as an ethnic group, but required them to choose which "race" they considered themselves to be.[37]

Regardless of how the census classified them, Anglo Americans rarely regarded Mexicans as belonging to the white race. Neither did most Mexicans— they identified themselves simply as *mexicanos,* a national identity that embraced the concept of *mestizaje,* or racial mixture. Writing in 1930 the sociologist Max Handman observed, "The American community has no social technique for handling partly colored races. We have a place for the Negro and a place for the white man: the Mexican is not a Negro, and the white man refuses him an equal status."[38] He further explained that "The Mexican presents shades of color ranging from that of the Negro, although with no Negro features, to that of the white. The result is confusion."[39] Some Mexicans, mainly upper-class Mexican nationals and middle-class Mexican Americans, looked undeniably Anglo-white, while others were darker than many light-skinned African Americans. "Such a situation cannot last for long," wrote Handman, "because the temptation of the white group is to push him down into the Negro group, while the efforts of the Mexican will be directed toward raising himself to the level of the white group." Mexicans would form a separate group, he surmised, "on the border line between the Negro and the white man."[40]

Many second-generation Mexican Americans, who by 1930 outnumbered Mexican immigrants in the Southwest, sought to have their status as whites recognized socially and politically in a region that had practiced Jim Crow segregation of Chinese, Japanese, Indians, African Americans, as well as Mexicans. They challenged attempts by state and federal governments to classify them as nonwhite and require them to attend segregated schools. But the dark skin of most Mexicans—the principal evidence of Indian ancestry—had not been lost upon Anglo Americans, who believed that Indians could not be expected to understand, much less practice, the principles of republican government. The idea of European superiority over Africans, Asians, and Indians was institutionalized in the first Congress of the United States when it passed the Naturalization Act of 1790 making only "free white" immigrants eligible for naturalization. American Indians were excluded from citizenship until 1925, and most Asian immigrants were ineligible for citizenship until after World War II. While the Fourteenth Amendment guaranteed automatic citizenship to anyone born in the United States, immigrants desiring to become naturalized citizens had first to demonstrate that they were white. What "white" meant, of course, was usually in the eye of the beholder, excluding those whose skin was many shades too dark—or in the case of Asians, whose skin was white but whose "race" was not.[41] For Mexican immigrants, the question of whether or not they could become citizens depended on whether or not they had too much "Indian blood" in them. For Mexican Americans, on the other hand, the worry was that Anglo Americans regarded them as "colored" and more racially kindred to Indians and African Americans than whites.

In the United States, one's citizenship status was rarely as important as one's racial status, and few Anglo Americans in the Southwest regarded Mexicans, Indians, Asians, and blacks as fellow white people. It was one thing for Mexican immigrants to fill jobs that few Americans wanted to do, but the idea of Mexican immigrants as worthy and deserving of U.S. citizenship was for many simply preposterous, a truly un-American proposition. From 1790 to 1952, U.S. naturalization law offered a "path to citizenship" to immigrants who were "free white persons" (and after the Civil War, persons of African ancestry). While many Mexican immigrants hoped to return to Mexico with their hard-earned savings, many also chose to settle in the United States where their U.S.-born children could take advantage of educational and employment opportunities. Some Mexican immigrants chose to become naturalized U.S. citizens, assuming they could meet the prerequisite for being a "free white person." But if immigrant Mexicans were part Indian, and most Mexicans themselves acknowledge their mixed-race heritage, were they eligible to become naturalized citizens under the law forbidding any but "free whites"?

On June 15, 1915, Timoteo Andrade, seventeen years old, crossed the Río Bravo at El Paso, Texas, where thousands of Mexicans and Spanish-Mestizos had crossed for centuries. Like tens of thousands of Mexicans, young Timoteo crossed the border before the establishment of the Border Patrol in 1924. In those days there were few immigration restrictions to prevent Mexicans from simply wading across the Rio Grande that joined Texas with Mexico, or walking across the unmarked border in the vast deserts that stretched from San Diego to El Paso.

When Timoteo was twenty he married Sara de la Cruz, a nineteen-year-old girl from Torreón, Mexico, who had also crossed the border at El Paso in 1915, two months after Timoteo. According to his naturalization record, he lived in Sara's hometown before immigrating, so it is likely they knew each other and planned to meet in El Paso where they married and started a family. They had three children—Michael, Maria, and Timoteo, Jr.—and lived for a number of years in Galesburg, Illinois, before settling in Buffalo, New York, where Timoteo worked as a waiter.[42]

Unlike most Mexican immigrants, then or now, Timoteo Andrade decided to become a naturalized citizen of the United States. In 1929, at age thirty-one, he submitted his Declaration of Intention to the Supreme Court of New York at Buffalo and listed his race as "Spanish," his nationality as "Mexican," and his "color" as "white" (the distinction between "color" and "race" was never very clear even to the naturalization officials).[43] Two Anglo-American men, salesman who had known him for five years, signed affidavits that Andrade was of good moral character and "attached to the principles of the Constitution of the United States." Andrade himself signed an oath that he was not an anarchist or "a believer in the practice of polygamy." He willingly renounced "absolutely and forever all allegiance and fidelity to any foreign prince, state, or sovereignty and particularly to the United States of Mexico," of which he was a citizen at the time of his petition.[44]

All that remained was the judge's approval of his petition before he could take the oath of allegiance to the United States, the final step in his journey, begun six years earlier, to become a U.S. citizen. Then the unexpected happened. The district director of immigration and naturalization, Arthur Karnuth, moved to dismiss his petition on the ground that Andrade was ineligible to citizenship by virtue of his race. Andrade had stated in an affidavit in response to a question about his racial background that he was half Indian and half Spanish. At one point he indicated he was probably 70 percent Indian. Andrade had no idea that under U.S. naturalization law, only "free white persons" and persons of African ancestry were eligible to become naturalized citizens. Moreover, numerous federal court cases, including Supreme Court cases, had determined that most racially mixed persons, like Andrade, were not "white" and were therefore ineligible for citizenship.[45]

When his case went before the federal District Court of New York in 1935, Judge John Knight rejected his application for citizenship, citing numerous court rulings denying citizenship to persons who were not white, or whose racial mixture rendered them nonwhite.[46] He cited a recent case on California's Alien Land Laws, *Morrison v. California* (1934), in which the judge reflected on the racial nature of Mexicans, even though the case involved an Asian national: "There is a strain of Indian blood in many of the inhabitants of Mexico as well as in the peoples of Central and South America. Whether persons of such descent may be naturalized in the United States is still an unsettled question." Knight intended to settle the question by denying Andrade citizenship for having considerably more than a "strain of Indian blood." He concluded that the Texas case of Ricardo Rodríguez in 1897, in which the judge ruled that all Mexican nationals were eligible for citizenship regardless of their racial mixture, "was not consistent with the later decisions of the Supreme Court."[47]

The Naturalization Act of 1790 purposefully excluded from citizenship all indentured servants, slaves, free blacks, Indians, and later Asians. The law said nothing about Mexicans—or Syrians, South-Asian Indians, Filipinos, and other dark-skinned peoples whose status as whites was accepted in some states and denied in others. Particularly confusing were cases that involved mixed-race applicants. Was a person who was half white and half Indian a white person? The district court of Oregon ruled in *In re Camille* (1880) that "half-breed Indians" were not considered white persons: "Indians have never, ethnologically, been considered white persons. . . . From the first our naturalization laws only applied to the people who had settled the country, the European or white race." In order to be considered a white person, the court ruled, a person would have to be at least three-quarters white.[48] Numerous other cases came to similar conclusions regarding mixed-race persons.

An American lawyer from Los Angeles, Walter E. Barry, who served as a consultant to the Los Angeles-based Latin American Chamber of Commerce, warned of another consequence of Judge Knight's ruling: Indo-mestizo Mexicans would be barred from owning property because of racial restrictions contained in the deeds to property in many subdivisions in California and the nation. The deeds for property owned by Mexicans, he wrote, contained the following provision: "No part of said premises shall ever be sold, leased, occupied by or conveyed to a person of any race except the Caucasian or White race." Knight's ruling, in other words, placed Mexicans "in the category of Negroes and Chinese" as far as property ownership was concerned. The deeds further provided that "upon violation of the covenant, the land shall revert to the original grantors." Once "racketeers" learned that Mexicans were not members of the "White race," they would "immediately pounce upon the . . . property belonging to poor Mexicans of the indigenous race."[49]

The case presented other legal challenges. If Mexicans were generally considered to be a mixture of Spanish and Indian, then how would the courts determine which Mexicans desiring U.S. citizenship were white and thus eligible, and those who were mainly Indian and thus ineligible? That very question arose in 1893 in San Antonio, Texas, when Ricardo Rodríguez filed his intention to become a naturalized citizen.[50] While courts had ruled on the ineligibility of Chinese, Hawaiians, and mixed-race Indians to become citizens, no court had ruled on the eligibility of Mexicans until the Rodríguez case in 1897.[51]

Ricardo Rodríguez immigrated from Guanajuato, Mexico, in 1883 when he was thirty-five years old and settled in San Antonio, Texas. His petition, like Andrade's, was denied on the grounds that he was not white. Rodríguez appealed the decision in the federal district court. One of the attorneys opposed to his becoming a U.S. citizen, Floyd McGown, described him as "a pure-blooded Mexican, having . . . dark eyes, straight, black hair, chocolate brown skin, and high cheek bones."[52] McGown hoped to persuade the court that Rodriguéz's skin color indicated that he was more Indian than Spanish.

Although there were no restrictions in the 1890s on the number of immigrants from Mexico, immigration inspectors on the U.S.-Mexico border were required to record the country of origin and race of all aliens entering the United States. They adopted the practice of listing light-skinned Mexicans as belonging to the "Spanish race" and those with dark skin (i.e., primarily Indian) as belonging to the "Mexican race."[53] Immigration inspectors understood that "Spanish" signified white, whereas the label "Mexican" indicated mixed-blood or Indian. Since Rodríguez described himself as a "full-blooded Mexican," naturalization inspectors naturally concluded that his race was Indian. In a similar manner, McGown concluded that Rodríguez's appearance—dark skin, straight black hair, and high cheekbones—clearly demonstrated that he was "not a white person . . . in the sense in which these words are commonly used and understood in the every-day life of our people."[54]

Jack Evans, a local San Antonio politician also opposed to Rodríguez's bid for citizenship, cited the 1884 Supreme Court case *Elk v. Wilkins,* in which John Elk, an Indian, sought to vote in a municipal election in Omaha. The local registrar denied him the right to vote on the grounds that Indians were not U.S. citizens. On appeal to the Supreme Court, Elk stressed that he had voluntarily separated himself from his tribe and had "taken up his residence among the white citizens of a state." But the Supreme Court was not persuaded that association with whites made Indians into white people. In fact, the court ruled, "Indian tribes, being within the territorial limits of the United States, were . . . alien nations . . . with whom the United States might . . . deal, as they saw fit, either through treaties . . . or through acts of congress." In short, tribal Indians were legal aliens in the United States, barred by law from citizenship.[55]

It did not look good for Rodríguez. No Indian had ever been granted citizenship, even those, like Camille, who were only half Indian. Even District Judge Thomas S. Maxey acknowledged that "if the strict scientific classification of the anthropologist should be adopted, [Rodríguez] would probably not be classed as white."[56] But after having studied the issue for almost a year, Judge Maxey determined that international treaties trumped naturalization law—that is, Article VIII of the Treaty of Guadalupe Hidalgo, which ended the U.S.-Mexican War in 1848, granted automatic citizenship to all Mexicans who chose to remain in the conquered territories of what had become the U.S. Southwest, unless they signaled their intention to remain citizens of Mexico. Maxey ignored the fact that the article's citizenship clause addressed only those Mexicans then living in the territory ceded to the United States, and not future immigrants to the United States. However, he cited a treaty between Mexico and the United States concluded in 1868 that required the United States to recognize the naturalization of

U.S. citizens in Mexico, and for Mexico to recognize the naturalization of Mexican citizens in the United States. Therefore, Maxey concluded, whatever might be the racial status of Rodríguez "from the standpoint of the ethnologist," Mexican citizens were "embraced within the spirit and intent of our laws upon naturalization."[57] Rodríguez had magically become, as one legal scholar put it, "white by treaty."[58]

The Rodríguez case was the only time in U.S. history that a Mexican immigrant desiring U.S. citizenship had been challenged on the basis of race—until thirty-eight years later, in 1935, when Timoteo Andrade's petition for citizenship was denied. Why had these two men—among the thousands of Mexican immigrants who had successfully become naturalized U.S. citizens from 1848 until 1935—been singled out as ineligible for citizenship on the grounds that they were not white? Surely, these were not the only dark-skinned Mexicans who had sought citizenship. Rarely were Mexicans in the Southwest, whether citizens or not, accorded the status of white people. As one might suspect, these two court cases occurred in political contexts that shed light on America's chronic fear of nonwhite immigrants, and particularly the potential of massive immigration from Mexico to overrun Anglo-Saxon culture and control in the American Southwest.[59]

Ricardo Rodríguez, for example, was singled out in 1896 San Antonio because Republicans, Populists, and other reformers believed—with some justification—that the Democratic Party perpetrated large-scale voter fraud by manipulating the votes of immigrants. Anglo politicians T. J. McMinn and Jack Evans, members of the Populist and Republican Parties respectively, challenged the right of Mexicans to become naturalized citizens on racial grounds, arguing that dark-skinned Mexicans were Indians and thus ineligible for naturalization under the nation's whites-only immigration laws. If Mexican immigrants could not become citizens, then they were also ineligible to vote, because the state's alien suffrage rule required a valid form certifying that the foreign-born voter had declared his intention to become a citizen. The case generated interest throughout the city and the state among Texas Mexicans, and over 200 men of Mexican descent met in San Antonio to condemn efforts to disenfranchise them.[60]

The case of Timoteo Andrade was far more controversial not only because it reversed the Texas *Rodríguez* ruling, but also because it threatened to damage U.S. relations with Mexico precisely at a moment in American history—just prior to the outbreak of World War II—when the United States sought to be "good neighbors" with Mexico and all of Latin America. President Roosevelt's Good Neighbor policy signaled an end to U.S. military intervention in Latin America and increased trade and cultural ties, particularly with Mexico.[61] The Good Neighbor policy followed a decade of fiercely anti-immigrant sentiment, culminating in the 1924 law establishing quotas on immigrants from southern and eastern Europe. Congress repeatedly failed to pass legislation restricting immigration from Mexico because the demand for low-wage Mexican workers outweighed the anti-immigrant demand for restriction.[62] During the Depression of the 1930s, however, when jobs were scarce, over half of all foreign-born Mexicans in the Southwest were repatriated to Mexico, many of them involuntarily.[63] Unlike most Mexican immigrants who worked jobs in the border states, Timoteo Andrade had migrated east to Illinois and later Buffalo, New York, a city that was not exactly a magnet for Mexican immigrants at the time. Unfortunately, the records do not reveal why Andrade moved to Buffalo, although he likely knew a friend or relative who already lived there and could help give him and his family a start.

Judge Knight's ruling denying citizenship to Andrade took the Mexican and U.S. governments by surprise. The Mexican consul general of New York, Enrique Elizondo, learned of the ruling from articles in the *Buffalo Courier-Express* and the *New York Times*.[64] He quickly sent a copy of the ruling to the Mexican ambassador, Francisco Castillo Nájera, and the foreign minister of Mexico, Eduardo Hay, asking them how best to "fight this insult to the nation."[65] Shocked at the implication of the ruling, Elizondo reminded the ambassador: "Only persons eligible for naturalization can be admitted as immigrants to the United States. If Mexicans are denied the right to become American citizens, practically the entire population [of Mexico] will be denied the right to immigrate to this country, which would place us in a similar status as that of Asian countries."[66] After conferring with the foreign minister by telephone, Ambassador Castillo Nájera instructed Elizondo "to protest against the spirit" of the court by filing an appeal against Knight's ruling.[67]

Knight's ruling, if allowed to stand, would be troubling for the U.S. State Department. Not a single Mexican immigrant had ever been denied citizenship on account of racial status. State Department officials nonetheless understood that Knight was merely following the letter of the naturalization law in denying Andrade's petition, since Andrade's declaration that he was "half Indian" automatically rendered him ineligible for citizenship. An appeal would likely fail to reverse Knight's ruling, which would provoke a frosty response from the Mexican government and virtually all other Latin-American nations whose indigenous populations were quite numerous. Rather than risk losing on appeal, Undersecretary of State Sumner Welles recommended that the State Department attempt to have Knight's ruling delayed until a strategy could be devised to have it reconsidered. Ambassador Castillo Nájera agreed, since in order to win on appeal, he acknowledged, "we would have to prove that persons of 'Indian blood' were of the 'white race,' which obviously would not succeed."[68] Since no American government had ever ordered naturalization inspectors to deny citizenship to Mexicans, much less under President Roosevelt, who was well-known in Mexico "for his spirit of friendly collaboration," Castillo Nájera reasoned that the United States was "actually more alarmed than are we by Judge Knight's inopportune ruling."[69]

After much consultation with the State Department and his own foreign minister, Castillo Nájera hired a preeminent immigration attorney, Frederick T. Devlin, who successfully petitioned Judge Knight to reopen the Andrade case based on new evidence of Andrade's true ancestry. Devlin's strategy was essentially to show that Andrade had virtually no idea what his racial makeup was, had never discussed his ancestry with his mother, and claimed to be of "Indian blood" mainly for political reasons:

Devlin:. . . you stated [in an affidavit] . . . that you had been told that you were about fifty percent Indian blood and about fifty percent Spanish blood. Will you now explain first of all why you claim to a large percentage of Indian blood?

Andrade: It happened this way. In Mexico, even if we have full Spanish blood, we say that we have Indian blood, because in Mexico we are all Mexicans. There is no distinction, no matter in what part of the country we are born, and I thought that it would put me in a better position.

Devlin: Is the having of Indian blood something that is to be boasted of? Is it something to be proud of? . . .

Andrade: Yes.[70]

Devlin sought to prove that Timoteo Andrade was actually of "Spanish blood" by introducing testimony from Andrade's mother, Maria Bera Andrade. Devlin questioned Andrade's mother closely about her own ancestry in order to establish that Andrade had misrepresented the amount of Indian blood in his ancestry. Bera Andrade claimed that her mother "came of Spanish blood" and her father "of Mexican blood." Devlin asked: "What does Mexican blood mean to you?" To which she responded: "To me, Mexican blood is the blood of the people living in Mexico." Devlin tried another tactic. He wanted to know how she could be sure that her ancestry was free of Indian blood. "Mexican blood" might mean part Indian, she confessed, but added: "I have heard that we were a mixture of Spanish and Mexican.

I never heard that we were mixed with Indian blood." How, Devlin wanted to know, did Maria Bera Andrade distinguish a "Mexican" from "a pure blooded Indian from the back country." She and her townsfolk in Jalisco knew exactly who the Indians were by what villages they lived in, the native languages they spoke, and other cultural markers, such as dress, traditions, food, and so forth. In her district, she told Devlin, "when the Indians come from the neighboring towns, the people say, 'Here come the little Indians.' They never say, 'Here come the little Mexicans.' "[71]

In the 1930s, Indians in Mexico had long since ceased being a racial group in the sense of being identified by distinctive somatic features. After centuries of *mestizaje,* the lines between Indian, Spaniard, and African had been blurred practically beyond recognition, and the caste system had gradually yielded to stratification based on culture, language, skin color, and social class rather than "race." For Maria Bera, as with most Mexicans in postrevolutionary Mexico, "Mexican blood" was an expression of nationality rather than race—"the blood of the people living in Mexico." Or as her son told Devlin, "in Mexico we are all Mexicans." It was understood that being Mexican meant being mestizo.[72]

Toward the end of the testimony, Devlin finally felt confident that he had extracted from Timoteo Andrade's mother more credible information about his "Mexican blood" than Andrade provided in his affidavit for citizenship. Based on the testimony of his mother, Judge Knight reconsidered his original ruling and approved Andrade's petition for citizenship.[73]

The outcome was no surprise. The secretary of state and the secretary of labor had spoken to Judge Knight about the importance of reconsidering his original ruling.[74] Devlin was a personal friend of Knight, and of the mayor of Buffalo and the local naturalization officials, including John Murff, who originally recommended against granting citizenship to Andrade. Knight also must have known that Devlin, a high-priced attorney, was not representing Andrade, a poor Mexican waiter, pro bono. In fact, Devlin's client, the Mexican ambassador, agreed to pay him $2,000 for his services. (Devlin told the ambassador that "the question of money was not important to him," although he originally requested $4,000 for his services.)[75]

In granting citizenship to Andrade, however, Knight reaffirmed his original opinion and numerous prior court decisions that "sustain the conclusion that where one is half Indian and half Spanish blood, he is not entitled to naturalization under provisions of . . . the U.S. Code."[76] Knight's opinion was a hollow victory as far as the Mexican chargé d'affaires Luis Quintanilla was concerned, since the law remained in force that would deny citizenship to Mexican immigrants of Indian ancestry—the very race, he wrote, that "formed the basis of our nationality." Mexicans, he warned, could be barred from immigrating, like the Japanese and Chinese.[77] Nevertheless, a State Department official told Ambassador Castillo Nájera that the American government could order, "discreetly and confidentially," that naturalization inspectors not question whether Mexicans desiring citizenship were Indian or not, and simply continue to recognize their right to naturalization.[78] Quintanilla was not convinced: even if all immigration officials received instructions not to oppose Mexicans seeking citizenship, federal judges could rule against the administration, he believed, and likely would do so, "given the political nature of judicial appointments and the fact that many federal judges did not belong to the same political party as Roosevelt."[79] Sooner or later, he concluded, the Supreme Court would have "to force the United States to find the means necessary, including changing the constitution, if it is to continue to co-exist, morally and materially, alongside its Latin-American neighbors."[80]

In fact, however, the Andrade case was soon forgotten and naturalization of Mexicans continued apace, without regard to whether Mexicans had "Indian blood" or not. Neither the Mexican government nor the U.S. government desired further publicity or court challenges to what had become accepted practice since the Rodríguez case in 1897: Mexicans were to be treated, for the purposes of naturalization, *as if* they were white. Not everyone agreed, however. In a 1929 article in the scholarly journal *Foreign Affairs,* eugenicist author Glenn Hoover argued that full- or mixed-blood Indian Mexicans should not be entitled to become citizens—that is, since they are not "free whites," the Naturalization Act forbids them from becoming U.S. citizens. The population of Mexico consisted primarily of Indians "with but a veneer of European culture," Hoover explained, but "It seems that there is a tacit understanding among all departments of the federal government that ... anyone born south of the Río Grande is a white person." If interbreeding between Indian Mexicans and Nordic whites could not be prevented, Hoover lamented, "his descendants will be our descendants, and the 'Gringo' and 'Greaser' will be one."[81]

Hoover was right in one respect: a "tacit understanding" between the State Department, the Labor Department, and the Foreign Ministry of Mexico had made it possible for Mexicans to be admitted to citizenship, notwithstanding the "free white" requirement of the Naturalization Act. That concession was resolutely defended in the Roosevelt administration, as the Andrade case makes clear. Under Roosevelt's Good Neighbor policy, the United States had become more conscious of its image in Latin America, particularly with respect to its closest neighbor, Mexico. The

United States shared a long, complicated history with Mexico, as well as a long, porous border. To deny citizenship to Mexican immigrants would damage relations with Mexico and other Latin-American nations, particularly at a time when the United States was growing wary of the extreme to which race-based laws, like the Naturalization Act and the sterilization laws of the 1920s, had become models for Hitler and the National Socialist Party in creating their own grim program of "racial hygiene."[82] For many, but certainly not all, the idea of limiting citizenship to "free white persons" was not compatible with democratic ideals, as they had come to be understood since 1790, particularly where Indians in the United States were concerned. With the passage of the Indian Citizenship Act of 1924, American Indians were made U.S citizens. Why then would Indo-mestizo Mexicans be any less eligible for citizenship than their Indian kin in the United States? As one Texas journalist observed of the Andrade case, "the law's position that an Indian is not fit to be an American is an absurdity itself."[83] Given the overwhelming preponderance of Mexicans of indigenous ancestry, and the size of the Mexican-origin population in the United States, it would not be entirely mistaken to suggest that mixed-race Indian Mexicans in the United States comprise the single largest tribe of North American Indians.[84]

Of course, most Mexicans did not identify themselves as "indios," although like Andrade and his mother, relatively few were willing to categorically deny their indigenous heritage. Some U.S. citizens of partial Indian ancestry simply did not know how to identify their race for official purposes. Sammy Howe, a racially-mixed New Yorker like Andrade, wrote the State Department that on numerous documents requiring him to identify his race, "we don't know what to put," which he said had caused him "a lot of embarrassment." "My mother is mixed with Cherokee Indian and French, and my father is mixed with Negro, and also Indian. What does that make us, their children?" The State Department did not know how to respond to Howe's question about his racial identity and referred his letter to the Office of Indian Affairs in the Department of the Interior, perhaps on the assumption that his Indian ancestry on both sides trumped his father's African ancestry. On the other hand, the State Department bureaucrat could just as easily have sent Howe's inquiry to the U.S. Division of Negro Affairs of the National Youth Administration or the National Association for the Advancement of Colored People, if he thought that partial Negro ancestry rendered him an African American. Where the tricky business of classifying racially mixed immigrants for citizenship is concerned, you are often, as Timoteo Andrade learned, what your mother says you are.[85]

In deciding who was white and who was not for the purpose of becoming a naturalized citizen of the United States, the Supreme Court came to rely on "common knowledge," or how the average white person viewed the racial identity of a person, rather than testimony from anthropologists who divided the world's populations into broad racial categories, such as Caucasian, Mongolian, Negro, and so forth. In twelve naturalization cases between 1878 and 1909 to determine whether a person seeking U.S. citizenship was white or not, the courts barred the naturalization of eleven applicants from China, Japan, Burma, and Hawai'i, as well as two mixed-race applicants. In each of the cases, the applicants sought to convince the court that they were "free white persons," but state courts, and sometimes the Supreme Court, decided who was white and who was not. Takao Ozawa, a Japanese citizen educated at the University of California at Berkeley and resident of the United States for twenty-eight years, petitioned the court to become a citizen on the grounds that his skin color made him a "white person." The court disagreed and denied him citizenship on the grounds that Japanese people belonged to the "Mongolian race." In the eyes of the law, white skin did not always make a person white.[86]

Months after ruling that Japanese were not of the "Caucasian race," the Supreme Court in *United States v. Bhagat Singh Thind* (1923) rejected its own equation that only Caucasians were white. Bhagat Singh Thind, one of a growing number of Asian Indians in the United States, applied for citizenship on the grounds that Asian Indians were Caucasian and not Mongolians, were therefore white, and therefore eligible for citizenship. The court agreed that Thind was Caucasian, but ruled that not all Caucasians were white despite the technical link between Europeans and South Asians. "It may be true," the court ruled, "that the blond Scandinavian and the brown Hindu have a common ancestor in the dim reaches of antiquity, but the average man knows perfectly well that there are unmistakable and profound differences between them today."[87] The Supreme Court thus ruled in the same year that Takao Ozawa was not white because, although he had white skin, he was not of the Caucasian race, whereas Bhagat Singh Thind was denied citizenship on the grounds that, although he was a Caucasian, he was not white. In the shifting eyes of the law neither white skin nor being classified Caucasian was sufficient to being accorded status as a "white person," particularly for immigrants from India, Japan, and other Asian nations.

Virtually the only groups that could not lay claim to white racial status were African Americans, Native Americans, Filipinos, Japanese, Chinese (and other Asians)—Americans, in other words, whom the census classified as separate and distinct from the white race. Therein lay the beauty of a word like "white" or "Caucasian": it was historically broad and flexible enough to include Jews, Italians, the Irish, Poles, Greeks, Arabs, Armenians, and other immigrant groups, so why not Mexicans as well? Assimilated Mexican Americans in the 1930s and 1940s wondered when their turn would come to be acceptable to—and be accepted as—whites.

The progress of civil rights for Mexican Americans and Mexican nationals was slow, as it was for most marginalized groups, especially African Americans and Asian Americans, but gradually cracks were beginning to show in the foundation of Jim Crow laws and practices across the Southwest. With the United States entry into World War II, and the global struggle against fascism and Nazism, maintaining structures of racial segregation and racial restrictions for citizenship became increasingly problematic for the United States. President Roosevelt's Good Neighbor policy with Latin America, which called for reciprocal economic, cultural, and political relations with the twenty other American republics in the hemisphere, could not be seriously invoked as long as the problem of racial discrimination in the United States between Anglos and Mexicans in the Southwest continued to make headlines in the Latin-American press, particularly in Mexico. America's entry into the war raised national security concerns over the Axis threat in Latin America, particularly along the U.S.-Mexico border, which motivated the United States to acknowledge the problem of racial discrimination and the need to apply the Good Neighbor policy in the Southwest as well as with Mexico other Latin-American countries. As Texas civil rights activist and educator George I. Sanchez prophesied in 1941, the Southwest would become the "frontier of inter-American relations and the proving ground for the hemispheric order of tomorrow."[88]

3

BECOMING GOOD NEIGHBORS

Since the 1848 U.S.-Mexico War, Mexico had harbored resentment toward its more powerful northern neighbor, not only for the loss of half its territory—the present-day states of California, Arizona, New Mexico, Texas, Nevada, Utah, and parts of several others—but also for repeated U.S. incursions into Mexican territory and interventions in its internal politics. Relations between the two countries had been cordial at best up until the turn of the twentieth century, but they gradually began to improve, particularly as the violent coups and counter coups of the decade-long Mexican Revolution (1910–1920) subsided. As the 1930s drew to a close, and war with Japan and Germany appeared on the horizon, the United States began to recognize the strategic importance of Mexico to its national security, as well as its economic importance.

The United States had enjoyed relative isolation from conflicts in Europe and Asia by vast stretches of the Atlantic and Pacific Oceans, but advances in aerial warfare made attacks on the homeland, including Hawai'i, a conceivable reality. The possibility of a land invasion in South America or Mexico, where the United States shared a 2,000-mile unprotected border, no longer seemed farfetched. Becoming Mexico's "good neighbor" thus became an important priority for President Franklin Roosevelt, who articulated his "Good Neighbor" policy in 1933, the same year that Hitler rose to power. Mexico, in turn, sought to leverage its newfound importance to the United States by increasing economic and cultural ties with its neighbor, as well as declaring war on the Axis Powers six months after the attack on Pearl Harbor. Mexican president Manuel Ávila Camacho (1940–1946), and his foreign minister, Ezequiel Padilla, encouraged Mexican resident nationals in the United States to join the U.S. Army, but they also pressured the United States to end discrimination against Mexicans in the American Southwest.

Being good neighbors, the Mexican government insisted, also meant respecting the rights of Mexican-descent people in the United States, whether U.S. citizens or resident foreign nationals.[1]

Shortly after America declared war on Japan in 1941, the Office of War Information (OWI), responsible for countering Axis propaganda against the United States, reported that the "existence of institutionalized discrimination against several million Latin-Americans in the American Southwest is a constant irritant in hemispheric relations, a mockery of the Good Neighbor policy, and open invitation to Axis propagandists to depict us as hypocrites to South and Central America."[2] At the same time Carey McWilliams, California director of the Division of Immigration and Housing, told Nelson Rockefeller, head of the Office of the Coordinator for Inter-American Affairs (OCIAA), "If we really want to demonstrate good will towards the Latin-American nations, then no more obvious tests of the sincerity of our policy could be suggested than our attitude toward resident nationals of these countries."[3] In other words, the United States government began to take an active interest in the "forgotten people" of the Southwest as an instrument of foreign policy during World War II.[4] That instrument was President Roosevelt's Good Neighbor policy.

In 1933 FDR declared in his first inaugural address: "In the field of world policy, I would dedicate this nation to the policy of the good neighbor— the neighbor who resolutely respects himself and, because he does so, respects the rights of others—the neighbor who respects his obligations and respects the sanctity of his agreements in and with a world of neighbors."[5] In December of that year, Secretary of State Cordell Hull traveled to Montevideo, Uruguay, to attend the Seventh International Conference of American States, the first time a secretary of state had ever participated at a Pan-American meeting. At that meeting he declared, to the surprise of many of the delegates, "The people of my country strongly feel the so-called right of conquest must forever be a banished from this hemisphere."[6] In the fifty years before 1933, the United States had intervened in Latin-American countries, particularly in the Caribbean, over sixty times. Skeptical delegates from the Dominican Republic, Haiti, and Nicaragua—all of whom had endured landings or occupation by the U.S. Marines—and Cuba, which at that moment was surrounded by U.S. warships, joined other countries in proposing a declaration that read: "No state has the right to intervene in the internal or external affairs of another." Cordell Hull not only signed the declaration, but also pledged that "no government need fear any intervention on the part of the United States under the Roosevelt Administration."[7] Three years later, at the Inter-American Conference for the Maintenance of

Peace in Buenos Aires, the United States and twenty other American nations signed a nonintervention protocol that became the cornerstone of FDR's commitment to a new era of good neighborliness and Pan-Americanism—cooperation between the United States and the other twenty American republics.[8]

For the first time in the long and troubled relations between the United States and Mexico, from the U.S. invasion of Mexico in 1846 to Mexico's controversial nationalization of the holdings of U.S. oil companies in 1938, the United States and Mexico sought to put their differences behind them and solidify their economic and political ties in the face of the Axis threat.[9] In a speech to the Mexican nation in 1941, President Ávila Camacho voiced his view of the changed nature of relations between Mexico and the United States: "Almost a century ago an unfortunate armed conflict divided us, but since then circumstances have brought us closer together. We look to the future not with memories of those hostilities, but rather with confidence and mutual respect and trust."[10] A year later the same Mexican ambassador who managed Timoteo Andrade's citizenship case, Francisco Castillo Nájera, was only slightly exaggerating when he said, "For the first time in history our ideals and our interests coincide with those of the United States. We face the same risks—but also the same glorious destiny."[11] And finally, in 1943, FDR himself met with President Ávila Camacho on Mexican soil and declared, "Our two countries owe their independence to the fact that your ancestors and mine held the same truths to be worth fighting for and dying for. Hidalgo and Juárez were men of the same stamp as Washington and Jefferson."[12] No longer the "Bolshevist" country that nationalized the property of British and U.S. oil corporations, Mexico now occupied the southern flank of a nation engaged in a two-front war in Europe and the Pacific.[13]

As the United States drew nearer to war with the Axis Powers, shoring up friendly relations with Mexico and other Latin-American nations became a vital national security priority. Between 1939 and 1940 the planning committees of the Navy, War, and State Departments met over a hundred times, and in all but six of the meetings Latin America topped the agenda.[14] The United States worried that one million Germans living in Brazil (one hundred thousand of whom were German citizens) and a third as many Japanese (two-thirds of whom were Japanese nationals) constituted a "menace of the first magnitude," mainly because they were concentrated in "self-contained colonies" and settled in areas where they could be useful in military maneuvers.[15] Military strategists considered the possibility, even the likelihood, that Germany might launch an airborne inva-

AMERICANOS TODOS
★
LUCHAMOS POR LA
VICTORIA

★ AMERICANS ALL ★
LET'S FIGHT FOR VICTORY

Americanos Todos, Luchamos por la Victoria (Americans All, Let's Fight for Victory). OWI Poster no. 65, Office of War Information, Washington, DC: GPO, 1943. Courtesy of University of North Texas Digital Library.

sion of the western hemisphere across the Atlantic Ocean at its narrowest point—between Dakar, in French West Africa, and Natal on the protruding eastern bulge of Brazil.[16] According to one military report, "Any Axis attack by bomber and parachute troops would probably begin at this point from Dakar base. Once in Nazi hands, the bulge region would provide a vital bridgehead for attack on the Panama Canal via bases in the Amazon

Valley."[17] Fearing just such an attack, Roosevelt ordered his military to draw up a plan—"Operation Pot of Gold"—to send one hundred thousand U.S. troops to Brazil.[18]

The eastern bulge of Brazil was not the only focus of attention in the years leading up to war with the Axis Powers. The 2,000-mile border between the United States and Mexico, the "Achilles heel of North America" according to one press account, presented an ideal opportunity for Axis agents to stir up trouble on both sides of the border.[19] The Mexican Interior Ministry estimated that approximately 6,500 Germans, 6,900 Italians, and 4,300 Japanese citizens were living in Mexico on the eve of the war, many of whom held important positions in business and were suspected of being pro-Axis.[20] Some military strategists believed that Japan planned to establish air bases in Baja California, Mexico, from which to launch air strikes on the mainland. Fearing a Japanese attack somewhere along the West Coast of North America, some edgy residents of San Francisco took up positions on the beach to scan the horizon for evidence of an invasion, while college athletic officials elected to change the venue of the Rose Bowl game from Pasadena to North Carolina just in case.[21]

As both countries sought to overcome almost a century of mistrust, misunderstanding, and U.S. territorial and economic imperialism, the Roosevelt administration voluntarily abrogated an embarrassing clause in the Gadsden Treaty (signed a few years after the Treaty of Guadalupe Hidalgo ending the U.S.-Mexican War in 1848), which gave U.S. investors the rights to build a strategic interoceanic railroad across the Tehuantepec Isthmus, the narrowest point in Mexico between the Pacific Ocean and the Gulf of Mexico. Other outstanding differences, such as Mexico's nationalization of the foreign-owned petroleum industry, its expropriation of American-owned agricultural property, and ongoing water and boundary disputes, continued to be settled through arbitration. Despite the history of U.S. military aggression in Mexico (including the landing of Marines in Veracruz in 1914), President Ávila Camacho signaled Mexico's willingness to sign an agreement with the United States in 1941 to allow reciprocal use of air bases and port facilities in both countries. Shortly afterward, the Mexican Congress passed a law allowing the troops of any American country, including the United States, to pass through Mexican territory in defense of their country or to contribute to the defense of the continent.[22] As a journalist for the *Christian Science Monitor* observed in 1942, "Mexico realizes today that her economy and destiny are tied irrevocably to those of the United States."[23]

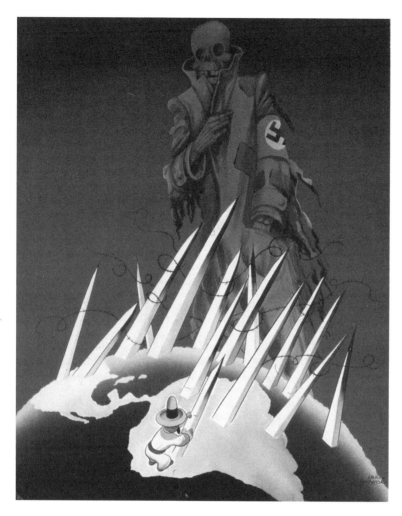

Enlisting Latin American republics in defending the hemisphere against Nazi aggression. Propaganda Materials, 1941–1945, U.S. Office of War Information, 229-PG-7–1. Courtesy of National Archives.

FDR's Good Neighbor policy with Mexico also forced the federal government to acknowledge the long-standing problem of discrimination against Mexican-origin people in the border states, especially Texas, and to find ways of addressing the problem to Mexico's satisfaction as well as to counter Axis propaganda that the United States routinely mistreated its dark-skinned citizens, whether of African, Asian, or Latin-American descent. Mexican American civil rights leaders and Mexican consuls throughout the Southwest took advantage of the wartime alliance with Mexico and nineteen other Latin-American countries to question how the United States could promote friendship and cooperation with Latin America when dark-skinned Latin-American citizens and Mexican Americans were routinely subjected to segregation and other indignities in the United States.[24] Nonetheless, relatively friendly relations during and since World War II have continued, with some minor challenges, to shape U.S.-Mexico relations.

Americans feared that millions of resident Mexican nationals in the four border states with Mexico might pose a threat to the nation's security potentially as great as that of the Japanese.[25] Many Anglo Americans felt that Mexicans on both sides of the border were susceptible to the propaganda efforts of Nazi agents and fascist groups in Mexico, in part because of their alleged resentment toward the United States for the loss of Mexican land after the U.S.-Mexican War. A similar fear had swept the country during World War I when the British Admiralty decoded a telegram—the so-called Zimmerman Note—from the German foreign secretary to the German ambassador in Mexico instructing him to propose an alliance with Mexico "to make war together, make peace together [with] an understanding on our part that Mexico is to re-conquer the lost territory in Texas, New Mexico and Arizona."[26] Oklahoma senator Josh Lee warned the House Un-American Activities Committee almost a year before the attack on Pearl Harbor that Mexico was "infested with Nazis" and communists, and added, "I don't think it is an accident that Leon Trotsky is in Mexico."[27] In this climate of fear citizens were encouraged to report any suspicious activity, no matter how implausible. A California public school teacher, for example, reported, "Axis agents are distributing marihuana to Mexican youths who do not have proper supervision and adequate recreational facilities."[28]

Mexico recognized that German resident nationals constituted a potential fifth column in Mexico, but concluded early on that removing them from the border area and military and industrial installations had reduced the threat considerably.[29] President Roosevelt, however, warned Congress in 1940 that a German airborne invasion from the Mexican port city of Tampico was "only two and a quarter hours to St. Louis, Kansas City, and Omaha." In his 1941 State of the Union address he cautioned that "the first phase of the invasion of this hemisphere would not be the landing of regular troops. The necessary strategic points would be occupied by secret agents and their dupes—and great numbers of them are already here."[30] Hitler's agents, he added, had already begun to build "footholds and bridgeheads in the New World, to be used as soon he has gained control of the oceans."[31] FBI director J. Edgar Hoover, directed by FDR to protect the United States from subversive movements in Latin America, reported that over four hundred Germans owned coffee plantations in Chiapas, Mexico, which he believed were centers of German espionage activity because of their easy access to Central America and the Pacific Ocean.[32]

Germany had long been a principal trading partner of Brazil, Argentina, and other South American countries, and had relied heavily on Latin-American nations for raw materials during its rearmament drive in the 1930s. During this time Germany had established close ties with the large number of German citizens living in Latin-American countries, including Mexico, and launched a massive propaganda campaign through its numerous banks, businesses, schools, cultural centers, and other venues.[33] Ernst Wilhelm Bohle, head of the Foreign Office of the National Socialist Party (the Nazi Party), called it the duty of all Germans living abroad "to act as agents of the Reich."[34] German diplomatic missions committed large sums of money to subsidize radio addresses, motion pictures, and print media that portrayed the United States and the Good Neighbor policy as "an iron fist in a silk glove."[35] In 1941 the Mexican Congress formed the Comité Contra la Penetración Nazi-Fascista (Committee against Nazi-Fascist Penetration) and like the United States, compiled *listas negras* (black lists) of companies that allegedly did business with Axis countries.[36]

Rumors of Axis penetration of Mexico and the United States had become widespread in government as well as civilian circles in both countries. In 1942 the California legislature appointed a committee to hold hearings on fifth-column activities in California. Rockefeller urged Governor-elect Earl Warren to hold closed hearings to avoid "possible international implications" with "an important neighboring country and ally."[37] Citing confidential sources in Mexico, FBI director Hoover informed the State Department that Mexican Army officers were "radically pro-German" who believed that Germany would "see to it that Texas, New Mexico, Arizona . . . will be returned to Mexico."[38] While no evidence has surfaced that the German government sought an alliance with the Mexican government as it did in World War I, still many Mexican officials worried that Germanophilia ran deep among many Mexican citizens who were, "frankly speaking, anti-Yanqui" and not at all hostile toward the Japanese or the Germans.[39] One Mexican citizen (anti-American and evidently anti-Semitic) criticized President Ávila Camacho for cooperating with "our eternal enemies, the North American Pirates" and asked, "Aren't you afraid, Mr. President, that the Mexican people might resist serving as canon fodder [*carne de canon*] for the interests of this Anglo-Jewish piracy which our history shows without a doubt is the bitter enemy of our country and our people?" Germany and Japan, he reminded the president, had "never seized any part of our territory, never humiliated us by intervening in our domestic politics, and never exploited us by fomenting domestic revolts as the Yanqui pirates have done on numerous occasions."[40] A widely distributed handbill of the Partido Nacional Socialista Mexicana warned that Latin America's cardinal enemy was the United States, not the Axis Powers.[41]

Despite some vocal opposition, the majority of Mexican people supported the Mexican government's close cooperation with the United States, and shortly after the latter entered the war, President Ávila Camacho appointed Ambassador Castillo Nájera as chief of the Mexican delegation for the bilateral Joint Mexican-United States Defense Commission to manage all aspects of collaboration between the armed forces of the United States and Mexico.[42] In April 1942 Foreign Minister Padilla met with FDR in Washington to review measures that the Mexican government had taken to aid the allies in the war effort, such as opening Mexican ports to ships of the Allies, preventing Axis countries from obtaining strategic materials from Mexico, and expelling Axis diplomats and others suspected of fifth-column activities. He told FDR, "The United States of America has only to fear the oceans. On land to the North and the South, this great country has only friends."[43]

One month later, German U-boats sank two Mexican ships, the *Potrero de Llano* and the *Faja de Oro,* and President Ávila Camacho immediately declared the nation in a "state of war" with the Axis Powers.[44] Having already severed diplomatic relations with Germany, Japan, and Italy days after the attack on Pearl Harbor, Ávila Camacho told a nationwide radio audience that Mexico would play its part in defending democracy, "not in the trenches but in the factories and fields." He also opened Mexican airspace to U.S. warplanes to fly from bases in the United States to the Panama Canal Zone.[45] Under the Lend-Lease Act, Mexico began receiving equipment from the United States for its army and air force shortly before it entered the war.[46] Mexico, on the other hand, had been supplying the United States with essential war matériel since 1938. In accordance with an agreement signed between the United States and Mexico, under the aegis of the Mexico-North American Commission for Economic Cooperation, Mexico agreed to provide the United States with minerals of vital importance to the war effort, especially lead and copper. From 1938 to 1941 Mexico supplied the United States with 238,900 tons of lead, 164,800 tons of copper, and 256,900 tons of zinc, as well as significant quantities of magnesium, mercury, and tungsten. By 1943 Mexico had shipped close to a million tons of lead and copper to the United States.[47]

Shortly after the attack on Pearl Harbor, FDR recognized the urgency of strengthening economic and cultural ties to Latin America and appointed the aforementioned Rockefeller, a young Republican with financial and cultural interests in Latin America, to head the newly created Office of the Coordinator for Inter-American Affairs (OCIAA).[48] A few months later he wished the Los Angeles-based El Congreso Nacional del Pueblos de Habla Española (Congress of Spanish-Speaking People) success in their efforts to "unite more effectively the Spanish speaking people of California," despite an OCIAA field representative's concern that the congress was a communist-front organization that in the late 1930s had "proved to be a disruptive force" and would continue to "serve as a disturbing factor in any effort to bring about organization in the interest of the Spanish speaking people."[49] The following year, in spring 1943, Rockefeller met with President Ávila Camacho and other members of his administration to discuss "mutual problems and plans for the great future of the Republic of México."[50] Rockefeller grasped the importance of working both sides of the border to demonstrate FDR's commitment to making the Good Neighbor policy apply at home as well as abroad.

The Mexican government had been complaining of mistreatment of Mexican laborers in the United States since the 1920s, but now the federal government recognized and worried about the international consequences of ignoring the problem. The Office of Facts and Figures prepared a confidential report that warned that the "submarginal" standard of living of over two million Mexicans in the border states might offer fertile ground for Axis propaganda, especially since "these people . . . are extremely susceptible to emotional propaganda appeals."[51] David Saposs, a special investigator for the OCIAA, reported that Mexicans were "probably the most submerged and destitute group in the United States—economically, intellectually and socially," with the possible exception of "poor whites and hillbillys."[52] As the picture of poverty and discrimination in the border states became more clear to the investigators, the OCIAA arranged for New Mexican senator Dennis Chavez to make a radio broadcast in Spanish to 130 stations in Latin America and the Southwest "to tell those people of our noble ideals and traditions and that this certainly is the land of opportunity." German propagandist Antonio Sorel responded with his own shortwave radio broadcast reminding Latin Americans that opportunities were routinely denied to Americans of Spanish descent throughout the Southwest, and that Mexicans were especially despised in California and Texas.[53]

In order to address the problem of discrimination against Latin Americans in the United States, Rockefeller established the Division of Inter-American Activities and appointed field representatives to Texas and California to investigate reports of racial prejudice in those states.[54] With little detailed information on conditions in the Southwest, however, the Division of Inter-American Activities got off to a slow start. Like the State Department, the OCIAA believed that the best way to end discrimination was through gentle and patient persuasion of local leaders, organizations, and state officials rather than by censure, public hearings, legislation, or other means of coercion. And rather than address the principal objection of Mexican workers in the Southwest—discrimination in hiring practices, differential wages based on race, and racial barriers to skilled and semiskilled positions in defense industries—the division focused its attention on attitudes and beliefs that were mainly offensive to middle-class Mexican Americans and Mexican nationals, especially the ever-vigilant Mexican consuls and members of the League of United Latin American Citizens (LULAC). One OCIAA official, for example, complained to the national director of the Boys Scouts of America when he learned that a Boy Scout skit in Washington, DC, was given the title "How our Marines beat up Pancho Villa and the rest of those Mexican bandits." While its title suggests the enduring stereotype of Mexicans as bandits and radical revolutionaries, the skit hardly seemed likely to knock the bottom out of the Good Neighbor policy. Nevertheless, the official duly noted that the "whole future of inter-American relations" would be advanced if Anglo Americans, including Boy Scout leaders, could be prevailed upon to take a more "constructive attitude" toward Mexicans.[55]

The Division of Inter-American Affairs within the United States hoped to change negative attitudes toward Mexicans by underwriting documentary motion pictures for distribution in the United States and Latin America. One such documentary on Mexican contract railroad workers "should play up the patriotism and good-will exhibited by [Mexican] workers in volunteering for urgent war work." Another film on the 5,000 Mexican American workers in Los Angeles shipyards should show them doing skilled work to avoid "the stereotyped idea that these people can only dig ditches or work on section gangs." But in countering the stereotype of Mexicans as unskilled cheap labor, the OCIAA reinforced the stereotype of Mexicans as essentially premodern sheep and cattle herders in mountain villages: "Sympathetic glimpses should be given of the ordinary life of the Spanish-speaking people. They might be shown, for instance, at work in one of the rural mountain villages of New Mexico, tilling their tiny irrigated fields, rounding up their cattle in the high mountain pastures, taking part in a [Catholic] mass, a procession through the village and the quiet renewing of old friendships afterward that feature the celebration of the village saint's day."[56]

The release of Walt Disney's animated film *Saludos Amigos* in 1942 accomplished more than the State Department in showing Americans modern Latin-American cities with skyscrapers and bustling crowds in Western dress. The film also featured the misadventures of Donald Duck as a tourist in Guatemala; and "el Gaucho Goofy" in the role of an American cowboy on the grassy plains (pampas) of Argentina, where he observes the cultural similarity between South American *gauchos* and North American cowboys.[57]

But neither Disney nor the State Department sought to portray Latinos in the United States as anything like Anglo Americans. Mexican consuls and Mexican-American civil rights leaders complained bitterly to the OCIAA and State Department about the persistence of discrimination against Mexicans in the Southwest, particularly in Texas, which one official of the War Manpower Commission called "the worst situation in the country."[58] Mexicans were segregated in separate schools, forced to sit apart from Anglo Americans in movie houses, refused service in restaurants and cafés, and denied entry to many public swimming pools, parks, and other public spaces. When a Mexican consul complained to the governor of Texas, Coke Stevenson, that many towns segregated Mexicans in movie theaters, the city attorney of one town, L. A. Wicks, told the governor that "our local theater requires Mexican citizens to see its attractions from points other than the main floor"—from the same point in the balcony where black Texans were forced to sit. As Wicks explained, "[Anglo] Texans are wont to accord but little distinction between Negroes and Mexicans, generally speaking; and, frankly, there is often very little to choose between them."[59]

The majority of complaints concerned discrimination of café and restaurant owners, followed by public parks and recreation centers, courthouses and jails, real estate subdivisions, and schools and universities.[60] In a strictly confidential memo, Under Secretary Sumner Welles wrote to the American consul general in Ciudad Juárez, William P. Blocker, instructing him to "survey the problem of racial discrimination against Mexican citizens and nationals of the other American Republics in Texas and New Mexico." Sumner Welles cautioned Blocker that "subversive elements" had exploited these difficulties for the purpose of injuring relations between the United States and Mexico.[61] Blocker was charged with the delicate task of urging Governor Stevenson and other Texas officials to end discrimination against Mexicans without infringing on "state rights" and to remind them that "Latin Americans . . . are staunchly behind us in defending democracy."[62]

Perhaps nothing was more embarrassing to the U.S. government and its Good Neighbor policy than repeated complaints from Mexican foreign minister Padilla and numerous Mexican consuls concerning the mistreatment of Mexican diplomats as well as resident Mexican nationals. Luis L. Duplan, consul of Mexico in Austin, Texas, asked Governor Stevenson to investigate the case of discrimination by the owners of Blue Moon Café near Houston who denied service to Adolfo G. Dominguez, consul of Mexico in Houston; John J. Herrera, an attorney in Houston; and J. V. Villarreal, an employee of Texas Gulf Sulphur Company. According to Duplan, the proprietor told Consul Dominguez that if he wanted service, he could be "served in the kitchen."[63] When a Mexican baseball team, Trueba-Elosua, came to the "City of the Alamo" to play their U.S. counterparts, the owner of a café asked them to eat their lunch in the kitchen" or outside.[64] Venezuelan Air Force pilots in uniform undergoing training at military bases in Texas were refused service in cafés and restaurants. When two Mexican officers of Aerial Squadron 201 were refused service, while in uniform, in a restaurant in Rockdale, Texas, Mexican consul Fidencio Soria complained to Governor Stevenson that "There is not the slightest justification . . . for humiliating Mexican nationals because of their racial extraction [especially] where Mexico has sent their very best youth to train in Texas that they may fight our common enemy and preserve the dignity of man and the principles of democracy."[65]

The refusal of service to the Mexican consul at the Blue Moon Café and other acts of discrimination were widely publicized in Mexico. An editorial in the Mexican newspaper *Mañana* was typical for comparing racism in Texas with Nazism: "The Nazis of Texas . . . are slaves of the same prejudices and superstitions [as Hitler]. Hitler hates the noses of the Jews, and his co-religionists in Texas view with the same profound aversion the black skin . . . of the descendants of the enslaved race. . . . Mexicans also become the victim of ignorant rabble who see in blond hair and blue eyes their pretended racial superiority. . . . While many thousands of bronze complexioned boys are fighting heroically in New Guinea and in Italy, their fathers and brothers who live under perpetual threat of receiving death notices [War Department "casualty telegrams"] cannot sit down to eat at the side of white people." The editorial praised Eleanor Roosevelt, the "dynamic wife" of President Roosevelt, for her principled stance against racism; and Secretary of State Hull and Governor Stevenson for their efforts to end the "idiotic vanity" of North American whites and their "fanaticism against brown skin." Commenting on the editorial, Guy Ray, second secretary of the American embassy in Mexico, put the matter squarely: "Discrimination must be stopped before there can be real understanding between Mexico and the United States."[66]

The ubiquity of "No Mexicans" signs in café and restaurant windows continued to be a source of embarrassment to both the U.S. and Mexican

Mexican sign ca. 1944. III-818–1, Archivo Histórico de la Secretaría de Relaciones Exteriores, Mexico City.

governments. Mexican consuls noted that signs forbidding Mexicans to enter or requiring them to use separate facilities were posted in most Texas towns with large Mexican communities.[67] *Time* magazine reported in 1944 that "'No Mexicans' signs can be found in other border states. But big, bumptious Texas is the most assertive in maintaining the doctrine that anyone with dark skin, however cultivated, industrious and well-behaved, is forever inferior to any light-skinned person. . . . This doctrine has not gone unnoticed in Mexico (or in other parts of Latin America)."[68] Even many Catholic churches that served the Mexican faithful were segregated or held segregated services. One Catholic church near the border excluded Mexicans from all services with a sign at the door reading "Whites Only."[69] Father Lockhart, secretary of the Bishopric of the Catholic Church in San Antonio, admitted "confidentially that frequently in the churches located in exclusive sections of the cities, the attendance of persons whose bodies were not clean or whose clothes were soiled were resented by the congregations, and that frequently they had received protests suggesting that the priests persuade such persons to attend churches provided for them."[70]

These signs could also be found in government buildings as well as privately owned businesses and public spaces. A sign above a public bathroom in the Wharton County courthouse read: "For Colored and Mexicans," and in the Cochran County Courthouse a sign over the bathroom read, "For Whites, Mexicans Keep Out."[71] The Mexican embassy reported in 1941 that the Cochran County Courthouse in Whiteface, Texas, a small town in West Texas, forbade Mexicans from using the "Whites Only" toilets.[72] One sign became evidence in a U.S. Supreme Court ruling, *Hernandez v. Texas,* in 1954 that Mexicans represented a "distinct class" historically excluded from jury duty. On the Jackson County Courthouse grounds, where the trial was originally held, were two men's toilets, one unmarked, and the other marked "Colored Men—and Hombres Aquí."[73] Chief Justice Earl Warren was so struck by the signage that he referred to it in his ruling as evidence suggesting that in certain Texas communities racial distinctions were made between Anglos and Mexicans in ways little different from Jim Crow segregation of whites and blacks throughout the South.

Signs served to warn Mexicans and African Americans where they were welcome and where they were not. However, the racial situation for Mexicans throughout Southwest was more ambiguous than it was for African Americans: some white restaurant owners served Mexican customers and some did not. Those who did not wish Mexican trade often put signs in their windows that read "No Mexicans" in order to remove any doubt.[74] When a Mexican consul complained that a sign in a public park in Brady, Texas, about a hundred miles northwest of Austin, read "For Whites Only—Mexicans Keep Out," local officials changed the sign to read "For Whites Only."[75] The consul general of Mexico, Carlos Calderón, noted that "if some Mexican citizen in Mexico City were to put a sign in front of a restaurant reading 'No Anglo-Americans Allowed,' the authorities would immediately tear down the sign as an offense to the dignity of the people of the United States" and an obstacle to friendly relations between the two countries.[76]

Sign on Tarrant County Courthouse, Fort Worth Texas, 1942.
Department of State, RG 59, Decimal File 811.4016/337. Courtesy
of National Archives.

The impact of discrimination in Texas on relations between the United
States and Mexico became clear in June 1943, at the height of U.S.-Mexico
cooperation during the war, when the Mexican foreign minister Padilla
banned Texas from receiving agricultural laborers "because of the number
of cases of extreme, intolerable racial discrimination."[77] Mexico and the
United States had signed the bilateral Mexican Farm Labor Program
Agreement (which became known informally as the Bracero Program) on
August 4, 1942, as an emergency measure to provide temporary Mexican

contract laborers to work in agriculture to offset the loss of U.S. workers to the armed forces and defense industries. The binational agreement called for written contracts; joint administration of the program and monitoring of contract compliance; the number of contracts to be based on domestic U.S. labor supply so that braceros would not replace domestic laborers or cause their wages to be lowered; employers or the U.S. government to pay for transportation costs from recruitment centers in Mexico to work sites; and mandatory return to Mexico of braceros after the expiration of their temporary contracts.[78]

Texas was the only state banned from receiving braceros. Padilla hoped that the ban would motivate the Texas legislature to pass a bill making it a civil offense to discriminate against Mexicans. However, the decision to ban braceros was not made simply in response to the failure of Texas to pass an antidiscrimination bill. Passing such a law would have *lifted* the ban, but the ban itself was imposed on Texas as a result of pressure from the Mexican press, Mexican consuls in the United States, and most importantly, the citizens of Mexico themselves.

For years prior to the ban and in the months leading up to it, Mexican nationals working in the United States had sent thousands of letters to the Mexican president, most of them handwritten and addressed simply to "Presidente de la República de México, Palacio Nacional, México." Letters touched on a wide range of subjects, including low wages, residential restrictions based on race, discrimination in public areas, school segregation, discrimination in hiring and promotion in defense industry jobs, and less frequently, problems involving Mexican men dating white women.[79] A Mexican resident of Minatare, Nebraska, wrote to President Ávila Camacho that the city council had approved a real estate ordinance forbidding "any person of Mexican blood or race" from purchasing property in white residential areas. A major newspaper in Mexico City, *Novedades,* editorialized, "Naturally being of such a pure and refined race, the inhabitants of Minatare [Nebraska] are loath to live among people, as the Nazis would say, who belong to an inferior race. . . . The sweet inhabitants of Minatare thus pass laws about where Mexicans can live, as if they were pointing out where to dump the trash."[80]

Mexican domestic politics were also at play in the enactment of the ban. Numerous Mexican labor groups, chambers of commerce, state governors, and farm owners strenuously opposed sending bracero workers to the United States, fearing a labor exodus would harm agricultural production in Mexico.[81] President Ávila Camacho's own cabinet member, Ignacio García Téllez, the secretary of labor and public welfare, also opposed the signing of the bilateral agreement with the United States. In a lengthy letter to Padilla, he cited the fact that in the United States there were already about 700,000 Mexican nationals engaged in migratory farm work in cotton, sugar beets, spinach, cabbage, green beans, onions, tomatoes, among other vegetables and fruits, and that their salaries, on average, were disgracefully low, ranging from $2.35 to no more than $7.00 per week. He cited numerous reports in the United States that detailed the low salaries, malnutrition, lack of adequate housing, sanitary facilities in the fields, and discrimination in public places. "The extreme poverty of Mexican workers in the U.S. will only get worse after the war," he continued, "when soldiers are released from military service and many workers in the defense industry are laid off, resulting in fewer job opportunities and higher unemployment rates for Mexicans."[82]

Mexican Americans and Mexican resident nationals from the border states sought to persuade the Mexican government not to agree to a binational emergency contract-labor program with the United States. A young Houston civil rights attorney, the aforementioned John J. Herrera, asked President Ávila Camacho to consider the widespread segregation of Mexicans in Texas before deciding to send braceros to the state.[83] When the Mexican press published rumors of a possible agreement between the United States and Mexico to allow 50,000 braceros to work in Texas, Mexicans on both sides of the border sent letters and telegrams to President Ávila Camacho imploring him to make Texas off limits for braceros.[84] Theodore G. Miles, who described himself as a "North American of color" from Washington, DC, read in *Time* magazine that President Ávila Camacho had banned braceros from Texas and wrote to him, in Spanish, to thank him for "demanding the civil rights that North Americans love to preach but rarely practice" and to express his conviction that millions of "personas de color" in the United States supported his efforts to end discrimination in Texas and other states.[85]

While Mexico stood firmly with the United States against the Axis Powers, and signed the Mexican Farm Labor Program Agreement in August 1942, many Mexican citizens and high-ranking Mexican officials continued to oppose the Bracero Program. In the spring of 1943, Padilla sent a high-ranking diplomat of the Foreign Ministry, Visitor General Adolfo de la Huerta, to tour the "South of the United States" from California to Texas (the "South" to Mexicans was the region of the United States that was formerly the "North" of Mexico) to report on the condition of the braceros with respect to housing, wages, medical services, and generally to monitor employer compliance with contracts. De la Huerta reported that braceros in California were generally paid wages set by the Farm Security Administration, whereas employers paid considerably lower wages in Arizona and Texas. He strongly recommended under no circumstances should workers be sent to Texas for "the countless abuses" *(el sinnúmero de atropellos)* suffered by Mexicans, including pervasive segregation.[86] As the honorary Mexican consul in Dallas, Jack Danciger, put it in a letter to California governor Earl Warren, Texas had become the "proving ground" of the Good Neighbor policy.[87]

Padilla's ban on braceros to Texas thus served mainly to placate domestic Mexican opposition to the program, including from his own ministry, by requiring that Texas pass a law punishing the practice of turning away Mexicans from "whites only" parks, pools, restaurants, cinemas, schools, and other public places.[88] Banning braceros from Texas was not an easy decision for Padilla, who had worked hard to mend differences between Mexico and the United States over the nationalization of the oil industry and to persuade other Latin-American countries to support the Allied war effort.[89] The *New York Herald Tribune* called him "Mexico's All-American Diplomat" and noted that Padilla proudly displayed photographs of FDR, Winston Churchill, and Undersecretary of State Sumner Welles along with one of President Ávila Camacho in his Mexico City office. Just months before the ban a journalist described him as a "spark plug of Pan-Americanism and the prophet of a hemispheric New Order . . . the United States of the Americas."[90] Padilla felt great affection for the United States, but not for Texas. For Padilla, as for most Mexicans, Texas represented the worst attributes of "Yanqui" racial arrogance and intolerance.

A month before the ban, in May 1943, the Texas state legislature passed House Concurrent Resolution 105, the so-called Caucasian Race Resolution, to demonstrate to the Mexican government that it was taking active steps to end discrimination against person of Latin-American descent. This nonbinding resolution stated that since "our neighbors to the South" were cooperating in the effort to "stamp out Nazism and preserve democracy" and in order to "assist the national policy of hemispherical solidarity," the state of Texas resolved that "all persons of the Caucasian Race . . . are entitled to the full and equal accommodations, advantages, facilities, and privileges of all public places of business or amusement."[91] The resolution made clear that "our neighbors to the South" were "Caucasians" and should be extended all the rights and privileges normally accorded to white people. While a concurrent resolution did not have the force of law, which would have levied fines for discrimination against Mexicans, the resolution did reflect the urgency of reaching an accommodation with the Mexican government to import braceros at a critical moment in the war effort when the United States faced labor shortages, particularly in agriculture. The Texas Good Neighbor Commission, established by Governor Stevenson shortly after the ban, reported that in Texas there were about 260,000 fewer people on the farms than there were in 1940, and "the farmers are being called upon to produce 37.5 percent more than in 1940."[92]

Unimpressed with the resolution, the Mexican government formally banned Texas from the Bracero Program. The ban sent shock waves through the Texas legislature and agribusiness community. It was clear that the Mexican government was not satisfied with a toothless resolution to end discrimination. Pressure mounted on both sides of the border to pass a law that would make it a civil offense to discriminate against persons of Latin-American descent. An antidiscrimination bill had been introduced two years earlier, in 1941, but the legislature failed to pass it. LULAC leaders Manuel C. Gonzales and Alonso S. Perales persuaded state representative Fagan Dickson and four other legislators to introduce House Bill 909—the Racial Equality Bill or the Equal Accommodations Bill—to "assure full and equal accommodations, rights, and privileges to all persons of the Caucasian Race in all public places of business or amusement in Texas, repealing all laws in conflict herewith and declaring an emergency." The bill called for a fine of $100 to be levied against any business found guilty of discriminating against "any person of the Caucasian Race."[93]

Perales likely got the idea for an antidiscrimination law from an antirace hatred law passed in New Jersey in 1934, which he alluded to in a radio interview. The New Jersey legislature adopted the law after violent confrontations in the state between Nazi and anti-Nazi groups. The law imposed criminal penalties for disseminating "propaganda or statements creating or tending to create prejudice, hostility, hatred, ridicule, disgrace or contempt of people . . . by reason of their race, color or creed or manner of worship."[94] Perales either did not know, or chose to ignore, that in 1941 the New Jersey Supreme Court overturned the conviction of August Klapprott and other members of a pro-Nazi German-American group for disseminating race-hatred propaganda on grounds that the law violated constitutional guarantees of free speech.[95]

Efforts to pass the Racial Equality Bill illustrate the growing importance in Texas and the nation of establishing pragmatic and mutually advantageous relations with Mexico during the war. The United States relied on imports of critical minerals and metals from Mexico as well as bracero labor, but it also hoped to improve its image among Latin-American nations that had long regarded the United States as unfriendly to dark-skinned peoples.

Not all Texans, however, were ready to accord Mexican Texans "racial equality" with whites.

When the Racial Equality Bill was first introduced, it was "met by laughs, murmurs of disapproval and a few shouts of dissent."[96] But Mexico's ban on braceros was no laughing matter. Industry and agribusiness leaders were concerned with the consequences of the ban on the state's economic health, and the State Department worried that discrimination in Texas and California compromised relations with Mexico and fueled Axis propaganda in Latin America. Support for antidiscrimination bills introduced in the Texas legislature from 1941 to 1945 came from both sides of the border as well as both sides of the aisle. *El Universal,* a major Mexico City newspaper, applauded the Texas legislature for attempting to pass the Racial Equality Bill, and urged it to include Mexicans in Texas who are "not only of pure Spanish ascendancy, but also . . . have in their veins the unmistakable signs of Nahoan [*sic*], Mixtec and Zapotec origin."[97] The State Department, perhaps recalling the embarrassment a few years earlier when Timoteo Andrade was denied citizenship because of his "Indian blood," also suggested that the bill be amended to include "Indian Mexicans" as well as Caucasians.[98] The Mexico City newspaper *El Nacional* viewed the introduction of the Racial Equality Bill as an expression of the Good Neighbor policy and the "doctrine of continental solidarity," as well as "a barrier to foreign ambitions" in the Americas.[99] Despite international support for the bill, it died when the legislature adjourned in 1941.

When the Texas biannual legislature met in 1943 a series of bills were introduced in the House and Senate practically identical to House Bill 909. The senate bill died in committee where senators puzzled over "just what is meant by the phrase 'Caucasian race,' to which the bill applies."[100] When the legislature opted to pass the Caucasian Race Resolution, which did not include sanctions or have the force of law, the Mexican government was deeply disappointed and refused to lift the ban on braceros. The Mexican consul in Austin sent a sixteen-page letter detailing cases of discrimination to major Texas newspapers explaining that the Mexican government would not lift the ban until legislation was enacted to protect the rights of Mexican citizens.[101]

A month after the Mexican foreign minister announced the ban, the Mexican ambassador to the United States, Castillo Nájera, met with Secretary of State Hull and presented him with a memorandum regarding "mistreatment and injustices suffered by Mexicans resident in this country, especially in the State of Texas." Castillo Nájera complained that while a world war was being waged "to destroy the ridiculous theory of the racial superiority of the German race," in the United States incidents of racial prejudice "not only continue to occur but are constantly increasing in number." He cited the recent race riots in Detroit, Los Angeles, and Beaumont, Texas, and expressed disappointment that the Texas state legislature failed to pass a law to end segregation and other forms of discrimination. Castillo Nájera seemed particularly incensed that one of the consular officials in Austin, Jorge Aquilera Camacho, was not permitted to have his child baptized at St. Mary's Catholic Church because of that church's policy of not providing religious services to Mexican Catholics.[102]

Two months after Castillo Nájera met with Hull, Diputado (Congressman) Franciso Jiménez, formerly a Mexican consul in El Paso, introduced a resolution on September 13, 1943, in the Mexican Chamber of Deputies (the equivalent of the U.S. House of Representatives) that called for the formation of the Comité pro México de Afuera (Committee for the Protection of Mexicans Living Abroad) because, as Jiménez put it, "The greatness of the State of Texas is due in large part to the effort of the Mexican worker and in payment of this work they discriminate against him, they segregate him and . . . deny him justice." Of the duties assigned the committee, one included "protest, by international representations, all acts of discrimination, segregation, or denial of justice to our nationals." The resolution passed unanimously in the Mexican Congress.[103]

The Mexican Congress also established the Comité Mexicano Contra el Racismo (Mexican Committee against Racism) to disseminate the principle of the "equality of races." Its monthly publication, *Fraternidad,* documented the long list of discriminatory practices in over 150 Texas communities and carried a regular column entitled "Texas, *Buen Vecino?*" (Texas, Good Neighbor?). The members included numerous senators and deputies in Mexico, as well as well-known labor leader Vicente Lombardo Toledano and Mexican poet, educator, and statesman Jamie Torres Bodet. Many were highly critical of the U.S. government's reluctance to intervene in Texas to end discrimination. The committee also sought to combat racism in other parts of the world, particularly in Nazi-occupied Europe, and asked President Ávila Camacho to establish a colony for Jews persecuted by the Nazis. Both committees favored the passage of a law in Texas with sanctions for those guilty of discrimination, but when Texas failed to pass an antidiscrimination bill, the Comité Mexicano Contra el Racismo compared Texans to the Nazis, calling Texas "a refuge for the henchmen of Goebbels and Himmler."[104]

The frequent comparisons of Texas to Nazi Germany by the Mexican press, consuls, and politicians did not go unnoticed, or unanswered, by some Anglo Texans. Chris Fox, vice president of the El Paso Chamber of Commerce, resigned his position on the Texas Good Neighbor Commission

Cover of *Fraternidad*, July 1, 1944, a monthly publication of the Comité Mexicano contral el Racismo (Mexican Committee against Racism). The headline
reads: "Fight the Nazi Eagle—Reject All Racial Prejudice." The monthly column
"Texas, Buen Vecino?" compared Texas racism against Mexicans to Nazi racism
against Jews. Archivo de Ávila Camacho, exp. 546.1/1, caja 789, Archivo General
de la Nación, Mexico City.

because he was fed up with the "cloistered do-gooders" on the faculty of the University of Texas, like George I. Sanchez and his Committee on Inter-American Relations, who Fox claimed had become the "tools of a particularly smelly bunch of Mexican politicians."[105] Another Texan, W. S. Gandy, wrote that "Texas is being discriminated against by Mexico. Mexico's consuls are trained and instructed to claim discrimination." She sent a newspaper clipping from the *Corpus Christi Caller* on which she typed the word "Discrimination?" The clipping showed a picture of Robert Sánchez, and the caption read: "Robert Sanchez, 19, son of Mr. and Mrs. C. A. Sanchez . . . has received his Bachelor of Arts degree from the University of Texas in Austin. He . . . is planning to return to the University . . . to begin work toward his M.A. degree."[106] Most middle-class, light-skinned Mexican Americans, like University of Texas graduate Robert Sanchez, rarely suffered the same degree of discrimination as dark-skinned, "peon" Mexicans, as this 1944 *Houston Post* editorial illustrates: "There is some discrimination against Mexicans in Texas, and it is reasonably subject to criticism. But in the main it is not, as in the case of negroes, a racial discrimination, for Texans regard Mexicans as being of the Caucasian race, though they are part Indian—many of them full-blooded. In candid truth, this prejudice is primarily a mere repugnance to the personal uncouthness of the peons [who] are ragged, filthy, ignorant and speak no English; almost as primitive as their savage Indian ancestors."[107]

When the Texas legislature failed to enact a bill prohibiting discrimination, Padilla informed the U.S. ambassador George Messersmith that the ban on braceros could not be lifted. But in the interests of maintaining good relations with Texas, Padilla unveiled his own plan: if Governor Stevenson would write a letter to all state and county officials, including police and other law enforcement officials, calling their attention to the importance of ending discrimination against Mexicans, then the foreign ministry was prepared to ignore any Mexican labor recruited by the Farm Security Administration that ended up in Texas. In other words, "The Mexican government would ignore the fact that labor . . . recruited for another area would be sent to Texas."[108] Padilla insisted, however, that proclamations and the nonbinding resolutions calling for equal accommodations for Caucasians would not be sufficient to have the ban lifted.[109] The Mexican government wanted to remain on friendly diplomatic terms with Texas, sharing as it did a 1,000-mile border with the state, but remained firm on the question of racial discrimination against Mexicans. Ambassador Messersmith reported to the State Department: "I think Dr. Padilla feels that if anything is ever to be accomplished with regard to discrimination it must be done during the war when our needs from Mexico are so great and so urgent."[110]

Nothing illustrated better the soundness of the Mexican government's position than when the antidiscrimination resolution was put to test in a court case in 1943 involving a Mexican American and LULAC member, Jacob I. Rodríguez, who was refused admittance to the Terrell Wells swimming pool near San Antonio. Rodríguez contended that discrimination against Latin Americans violated the Good Neighbor policy of the state as found in House Concurrent Resolution 105 and the governor's proclamation. The owner of the pool "whose healing waters flow from the earth, which not so long ago was Mexican soil," declared at the trial: "We will close our establishment before we will permit the entrance of Mexicans or persons of Mexican origin, regardless of their state of culture, either social or economic."[111] Citing House Concurrent Resolution 105, the district judge ordered the pool to open its doors to Mexicans. The Texas Court of Civil Appeals, however, held that "the proprietor of a place of amusement which is privately operated can refuse to sell a ticket to, and may thereby exclude, any person he desires from the use of his facilities for any reason sufficient to him, or for no reason whatever." The court further held that "a mere resolution by the legislature and a proclamation by the governor do not have the effect of a statute."[112]

In San Bernardino, California, a similar court case was brought against the owners of a swimming pool that denied admittance to Mexican-descent persons. In that case, tried at the same time as the Terrell Wells case, the court held that the owners' conduct was illegal and in violation of the petitioners' rights and privileges as guaranteed by the Constitution of the United States. The difference was that the pool in San Bernardino was a public pool and the one in Terrell Wells a private pool. Municipalities sometimes attempted to circumvent federal laws forbidding discrimination by leasing public pools to private agencies. In these cases defendants could argue that discrimination was not unconstitutional because it resulted from private rather than state action.[113]

The Texas legislature made one more attempt to introduce a bill before the end of the war. Texas senator J. Franklin Spears introduced Racial Discrimination Bill No. 1, the Spears Bill, which would fine anyone guilty of discrimination against "persons of Latin-American origin" of up to $500 or thirty days in jail, or both.[114] M. C. Gonzales and Alonso Perales spoke in favor of the Spears Bill, and it was successfully reported out of committee in March 1945.[115] The publisher of the *Laredo Times,* William Prescott Allen, wrote to President Ávila Camacho that the ban had "served it purpose . . .

but further punishment would only hurt your friends."[116] Mexican newspapers, politicians, and the Comité Mexicano Contra El Racismo lobbied for the passage of the bill, including the president of the Partido de la Revolución Mexicana (Party of the Mexican Revolution), Senator Antonio Villalobos, who submitted a communiqué to the Texas senate urging the senators to support the bill.[117]

U.S. ambassador Messersmith had little respect or tolerance for Mexican-American civil rights activists, like University of Texas professor Carlos Castañeda, who initially supported the bill: "He is just like some Germans . . . who live in the United States . . . their whole lives. They may be of the second and third generation. No matter how much they receive from their new country, their allegiances remain with the country of origin. The same, of course, is true of some Latins."[118] Messersmith was not alone in this assessment. A radio commentator called Castañeda, Gonzales, Perales, and George I. Sánchez—the most vocal supporters of antidiscrimination bills—"professional Mexicans."[119] Maury Maverick, the liberal mayor of San Antonio and former New Deal congressman, denounced Perales as "a nut" and "racial agitator."[120]

The Spears Bill was defeated in the House by a wide margin, 63 to 46. While legislators realized the importance of maintaining friendly relations with Mexico—and ending the ban on braceros—most believed that that legislation would not solve the problem of discrimination. The State Department had long argued that "a slow process of education is the only solution," and the Texas Good Neighbor Commission also preferred quiet persuasion and education to enacting laws.[121] The Mexican newsletter *Fraternidad,* published monthly by the Comité Mexicano Contra el Racismo, summed up the failure of education this way: "Will the [Mexican] victims have to wait, patiently suffering this oppression, until Texans are re-educated? Why do the legislators . . . say that they wish to reaffirm the friendship between American countries, and that they reject the principles of Nazism, among which is the belief that superior and inferior races exist, reject a law which would have helped in the reaffirmation of democratic unity between the peoples and would have banished the evidence of Fascism?"[122]

Jacob Rodríguez, the plaintiff in the case against segregated swimming pools, explained a few years later why it was important to challenge discrimination in the courts: "Time and time again, we have heard . . . 'you can't make people love you through legislation.' . . . We don't want anyone to love us who is not that way inclined. All we ask for, all we want, is respect for our rights as citizens of this country, guaranteed to us by its political Constitution and Laws."[123]

The failure to pass the bill reverberated throughout Mexico. Mexican state legislatures in Oaxaca, Sinaloa, Chihuahua, Tamaulipas, Guerrero, and Colima requested that the Mexican Chamber of Deputies formally protest the mistreatment of Mexicans in Texas.[124] Students of the National University in Puebla near Mexico City went on strike to protest the admission of forty-two summer students from Sam Houston State Teachers College in Texas. If Mexican citizens could not be educated in the same classrooms as Anglo Texans, the students reasoned, why should Anglo Texans be allowed to enroll in Mexican universities? The president of the teachers college, who accompanied the students, told the Mexican press that he regretted the failure of the Texas legislature to pass the antidiscrimination bill and that he and his students had never discriminated against Mexicans.[125] The students in Puebla were also angry at a news item reporting that fourteen Mexican youths in Los Angeles were denied admission to the main floor of a movie theater because they were "dirty Mexicans" *(mexicanos mugrosos)*.[126]

Of all the challenges to the Good Neighbor policy, none raised the level of international awareness over discrimination more than the Sleepy Lagoon trial in 1942 and the Zoot Suit Riots in Los Angeles in the summer of 1943. California, home to the second largest foreign-born population of Mexicans after Texas, had a similarly troubled history with its Mexican population; but unlike Texas, California also had a large population of Chinese, Japanese, and Native Americans who often received worse treatment than Mexicans.[127] State law, for example, sanctioned segregated schooling for Asian Americans and Native Americans in California, whereas Mexican Americans were placed in separate schools as a result of independent school district policy rather than state law. Before the Zoot Suit Riots, the Mexican government paid scant attention to California, and the U.S. government did its part to keep potentially embarrassing situations in California from undermining its Good Neighbor policy with Mexico.[128]

Californians, like Texans, worried about Axis influence among resident Mexican nationals, but after the attack on Pearl Harbor, they viewed the large number of Japanese in the state as a far greater threat than Mexican right-wing *sinarqistas* (pro-Axis, anticommunist Catholics), and so did the federal government. In 1942 President Roosevelt issued Executive Order 9066 authorizing the internment of tens of thousands of American citizens of Japanese descent and resident Japanese citizens. Californians breathed a sigh of relief at the federal government's prompt action to save California from the "Yellow Peril," but recurrent newspaper accounts of Mexican gang activity in Los Angeles rekindled their fear of Mexicans as un-American and a potential threat to the social order during time of war.

The Sleepy Lagoon murder case, which began the previous summer, set the stage for the Zoot Suit Riots. The streets of Los Angeles were not safe, the headlines frequently proclaimed, and the Los Angeles Police Department intended to crack down on Mexican gangs. Their opportunity came in the summer of 1942 when they began rounding up Mexican youths as potential suspects in the murder of José Diaz, whose body was found near the "Sleepy Lagoon," a popular hang-out for Mexican-American youths. Over six hundred youths were arrested, twenty-two were indicted, and seventeen were convicted, three of them for first-degree murder, even though virtually no evidence of their guilt was presented at the trial.[129] What was presented before and during the trial was testimony on the criminally inclined nature of Mexicans: Captain E. Duran Ayres, for example, chief of the Foreign Relations Bureau of the Los Angeles County Sheriff's Department, told the Grand Jury that the Mexican's "desire to kill, or at least let blood" was an "inborn characteristic that has come down through the ages."[130] A schoolteacher in a predominantly Mexican school in Los Angeles provided a more nuanced explanation of the "outbursts of gangsterism" among Mexican youth: "Many of our own pupils are exceedingly cynical regarding our recent attempts to 'buy favor south of the border' while we treat Mexicans in the United States worse than enemies. . . . Much of the resentment comes from our having educated the Mexican-American pupils regarding the privileges afforded by a democracy only to turn them out into a community that denies them most of the privileges and many of the rights of American citizenship."[131]

Civil rights activists as well as federal officials warned that that the arbitrary indictment of so many youths for a murder without any evidence of guilt provided further evidence to the Mexican government of anti-Mexican sentiment in the state. California civil rights activists Josefina Fierro de Bright and her husband John Bright warned the OCIAA's Division of American Republics: "The disastrous reaction to this 'cracking down' of the police and courts, to support a dubious theory of 'Mexican crime wave,' cannot be exaggerated."[132] Nelson Rockefeller seemed to agree. He held a meeting with officials of the OWI, the War Production Board, and other agencies to discuss the impact of the murder trial on the Good Neighbor policy with Mexico.[133] Alan Cranston of the OWI spoke to Los Angeles district attorney John F. Dockweiler about the international repercussions that would result if the trial were permitted "to turn into a Sacco-Vanzetti case—as it will if many of the kids are given stiff sentences."[134] Cranston worried that the newspapers were "convicting not only the boys but the whole race," as well as causing "greater friction and ill-feeling" throughout Latin America.[135]

He persuaded three Los Angeles newspapers (*Examiner, Herald,* and *Express News*) to stop using the term "Mexican" in connection with the murder trial inasmuch as the vast majority of the youths involved were Americans. The publishers agreed to write positive stories about Mexican-American participation in the war effort and to refer to them as "Americans of Mexican extraction."[136]

A federal official of completely different views, FBI director J. Edgar Hoover, had little use for the Good Neighbor policy or the Sleepy Lagoon Defense Committee (SLDC), which sought to publicize the injustice of the trial and raise funds for an appeal. The national chairman, the aforementioned Carey McWilliams, was a well-known and respected author, attorney, and civil rights activist, but to Hoover virtually all progressives were communists or communist sympathizers. After the Second District Court of Appeal unanimously overturned the second-degree murder convictions in 1944, Hoover informed the State Department that the SLDC had been since its origin in 1942 under the "consistent domination and control" of the Communist Party, and that members of the Los Angeles chapter of the National Lawyers Guild (of which McWilliams was a member) had attempted to persuade a Mexican senator at an Inter-American Bar Association meeting in Mexico City in 1944 to introduce a resolution in the senate calling upon President Roosevelt "to pardon or otherwise secure the release of the Mexican defendants imprisoned in the Sleepy Lagoon case."[137] Hoover viewed McWilliams's contact with a Mexican senator treasonous and put him on the FBI's "Security Index," a list of persons considered a security risk in case of a national emergency.[138]

Shortly after the Sleepy Lagoon trials, Harry F. Henderson, a member of the Los Angeles Grand Jury and chairman of the Special Mexican Relations Committee, wrote to Rockefeller that raising the social and economic level of Mexican Americans and promoting their full integration into American society was "no longer a reformist or humanitarian movement but a war-imposed necessity."[139] But when California legislator William H. Rosenthal asked the State Department to support an investigation of relations between Anglos and Mexicans in California, Undersecretary of State Sumner Wells feared that public hearings would create "widening circles of ill feeling."[140]

The Sleepy Lagoon trial did not widen the circle of ill feeling in Mexico nearly as much as the Zoot Suit Riots, in part because Mexico had just declared war on the Axis Powers in June 1942, just two months before José Diaz's body was found at the lagoon. With higher levels of binational economic and military cooperation at stake, both governments sought to view the trial as a matter of juvenile delinquency rather than a racially

motivated police crackdown. But the Zoot Suit Riots the following summer involved far more Mexican Americans and threatened to damage the
United States' image as a "good neighbor" in Latin America. Mexican-
American youth, called "pachucos" for their outlandish style of dress and
nonconformist attitudes, drew attention from sailors of the Naval Reserve
Armory who rampaged through the Mexican barrios of Los Angeles, beating up Mexican, African-American, and Filipino youths, cutting their
hair, and stripping them of their clothes in an attempt to humiliate them.
The Los Angeles Police Department usually arrived after the assaults and
then arrested the victims of the violence for disturbing the peace. Many
viewed pachucos and pachucas, the vast majority of them the children of
immigrants, as dangerous gang members who rejected their parents' culture as well as Anglo-white America.[141]

A month before the Zoot Suit Riots, Visitor General de la Huerta reported during his visit to Los Angeles that young U.S.-born Mexicans were
"misguided youth who had often provoked the police," but that the Mexican government needed to "acknowledge the racial basis of their persecution."[142] California civic leaders, the Los Angeles Police Department, and
the Hearst newspapers strenuously denied the racial basis of the riots and
characterized pachucos as unpatriotic Mexican hoodlums.[143] Pachucos
also faced scorn from certain sectors of Mexican society on both sides of the
border. The Mexican consul of Galveston, A. Cano del Castillo, told the Mexican Rotary Club of Monterrey, Mexico, that zoot suiters were the "scum
of the cities and [were] pool room hangers-on" that included "Anglo-Saxons"
as well as Negroes and Mexicans. A Mexican citizen in Los Angeles, Maria
Lorosco, told President Ávila Camacho that pachucos were "jovenes irresponsible" (irresponsible youths) influenced by "fifth columnists."[144] Mexican Nobel Prize-winner Octavio Paz, in his masterpiece on the Mexican
national character, *The Labyrinth of Solitude,* characterized pachucos as
rebels "ashamed of their origin" who did "not want to blend into the life of
North America." Like many Mexican nationals, Paz believed that pachucos,
and Mexican Americans more generally, had lost "their whole inheritance:
language, religion, customs, beliefs." Unlike Negroes who tried to "pass" as
whites in their effort "to be like other people," Paz observed approvingly,
the pachuco "flaunts his differences." While he did not ignore the fact that
"North American racism [had] vented its wrath on them more than once,"
Paz's characterization of pachucos was both unsympathetic and exaggerated.[145] Like other marginalized groups, particularly African Americans,
pachucos created their own youth culture where they could celebrate their
difference—and their marginality.

Not surprisingly, the Mexican press provided wide coverage of the Zoot Suit Riots. So did the U.S. press. The local press of Mexico City reproduced a *Time* magazine article entitled "California, Zoot-Suit War," which received extensive coverage throughout Mexico, making it difficult to claim that discrimination against Mexicans occurred mostly in rural areas of Texas. The article blamed the military authorities who were "notably lax" when they could have and should have canceled all shore leave for sailors. The police "apparently looked the other way . . . and Los Angeles, apparently unaware that it was spawning the ugliest brand of mob action since the coolie race riots of the 1870s, gave its tacit approval."[146] U.S. ambassador Messersmith reported, with wondrous understatement, that press coverage of the riot as "a war against Mexicans . . . with the tacit approval of the police and military authorities," was having "an unfortunate effect" on relations between Mexico and the United States.[147] California Democratic senator Sheridan Downey offered a more unsparing view of the riots when he told an audience in San Francisco: "Imagine what the probable reaction will be south of the border when the news reaches them that American servicemen attacked Mexican civilians."[148]

News of the anti-Mexican riots spread throughout Mexico. Between 500 and 600 law students marched from the National University of Mexico in Mexico City to the office of the Foreign Ministry to protest the mistreatment of Mexican citizens in Los Angeles. Several automobiles with U.S. license plates were damaged and several American women were allegedly "jostled." The rector of the university, Brito Foucher, addressed the crowd from the top of an automobile and urged the students to return to campus, defusing a "very embarrassing situation."[149] The Mexico City newspaper *Novedades* blamed Foreign Minister Padilla for not having more vigorously protested against the mistreatment of Mexicans in California.[150]

In a clumsy attempt at damage control, the U.S. embassy in Mexico insinuated that many Mexican newspapers were "almost certainly receiving money" to focus attention on the riots and characterized the publisher of *Novedades,* Ignacio Herrerias, as having "a pigmentation which is probably responsible for his personal racial inferiority complex."[151] Paying for favorable (or unfavorable) press coverage was not uncommon in Mexico, but it was hardly surprising that most newspapers carried stories on the riots highly critical of the U.S. government's tolerance of racial discrimination. One embassy official predicted that the sensation of the zoot-suit disturbance in Los Angeles would soon die down.[152] It didn't, and even the embassy was forced to conclude: "There is no doubt that the question of racial discrimination has done more harm during recent weeks to relations between Mexico and the United States than any event which has taken place since the expropriation of the petroleum properties of 1938."[153] Consul General Blocker, however, privately blamed the disturbances in Mexico and in Los Angeles on the Mexican consuls for seizing the "slightest pretext to charge racial discrimination." Blocker also blamed the immigrant parents of the two hundred pachucos arrested for having "failed to break away from the apron strings of their mother country."[154] "What the riots did," observed Carey McWilliams, was "to expose the rotten foundations upon which the City of Los Angeles had built a papier-mâché façade of 'Inter-American Good Will' made up of fine-sounding Cinco de Mayo proclamations."[155]

Despite the racial tensions that prevailed in Texas and California, Mexico and the United States nonetheless recognized the importance of maintaining neighborly relations as allies in the war against the Axis. More important for the future of U.S.-Mexico relations, World War II brought the domestic racial policies of the United States into the domain of international and transnational politics, particularly as Mexico leveraged its wartime alliance with the United States to secure better treatment of Mexican immigrants as well as their U.S.-born offspring. While Mexican consuls had been active in defending the rights of Mexican nationals in the United States since World War I, rarely had the U.S. government become directly involved, except in cases that could potentially harm relations between the two countries. The attempt of a New York federal court to deny U.S. citizenship in 1936 to "Indian" Mexicans—and therefore potentially making immigration of all mixed-race Mexicans illegal—was one such moment, as was Mexico's nationalization of U.S. holdings in Mexico's petroleum industry. The Zoot Suit Riots in Los Angeles and the ban on braceros in Texas also required delicate negotiations between the U.S. State Department and the Mexican Foreign Ministry.

These moments of tension and conflict threatened the viability and credibility of the Good Neighbor policy, as did problems that arose from the importation of tens of thousands of bracero workers who entered the United States on temporary work contracts, and the requirement that all Mexican immigrants between the age of twenty and forty-five were subject to induction in the U.S. armed forces beginning in June 1942. Both governments sought to sustain and build upon the growing economic advantages of "good neighbor" rapprochement despite the tensions that developed over drafting Mexican immigrants into the U.S. Army and the importation of hundreds of thousands of braceros in the 1940s and 1950s.

4

DEFENDING THE HEMISPHERE

Americans are most grateful in times of war when young men and women dutifully risk their lives to defend and protect the homeland. World War II was no exception. In all-out war, everyone serves the national interest, whether as soldiers fighting on the front, Rosie-the-Riveter women working in defense industries, or civilians selling war bonds and planting victory gardens. Men were drafted into the army regardless of their race or ethnicity, or even their citizenship status. For immigrants, serving in the army generally put them on the fast track to citizenship, should they desire it. During World War II the United States and Mexico worked closely as allies to ensure that the hemisphere would be safe from invasion, as well as to strengthen economic and political ties between them. The drafting of Mexican immigrants into the U.S. Army became a test of that relationship, owing as it did to the willingness of the United States to ensure fair treatment of Mexican nationals in the military. Slowly, the United States and Mexico were moving beyond the resentments of the past to a more stable, long-term, and pragmatic relationship based on trade, trust, and binational diplomatic agreements.

The problems that arose over the rights and obligations of Mexican citizens in the U.S. Army involved delicate diplomatic maneuvering among many branches of both governments: the Mexican Foreign Ministry, the Ministry of National Defense, and the president of Mexico, as well as the U.S. State Department, War Department, Immigration and Naturalization Service (INS), and the Selective Service System. In keeping with the goals of the Good Neighbor policy and increasing economic and military ties between Mexico and the United States, these government agencies sought to resolve conflicts and disagreements in a cooperative, if not always a mutually satisfactory way, to ensure fair and humane treatment of

Mexican servicemen in accordance with international law and binational military agreements.[1] Both governments sought to respect the laws and interests of the other and to minimize, as much as possible, the long history of mistrust, animosity, and outright hostility that had prevailed on both sides of the border. The fair treatment and protection of Mexican citizens' civil rights in the U.S. Army became an important test of that relationship, one that continued after the war with extensions to the Bracero Program (1942–1964) and bilateral trade agreements culminating in the signing, almost fifty years later, of the North American Free Trade Agreement in 1994.

During World War II approximately 500,000 men and women of Hispanic descent served in the U.S. armed forces, although some estimates range as high as one million. The War Department did not keep records of the ethnicity of Latino servicemen since they were integrated into white units, like Italians or Jews—and unlike African-American and Japanese-American GIs who served in segregated units. Nevertheless, Mexicans were by far the largest contingent of Hispanics in the armed forces, followed by about 65,000 Puerto Ricans.[2] Like other parents across the nation, Mexican resident nationals tearfully saw their U.S.-born children off to war and worried about their safe return. When their children failed to write home from the fronts for many months, they wrote to the War Department, usually in Spanish, to find out if their sons were safe, or asked Mexican consuls if it was possible to have their sons transferred from the U.S. Army to the Mexican Army, which became an option after Mexico joined the Allied Nations in 1942. And like thousands of parents all over the country, many received "casualty telegrams" from the War Department informing them that their son had been wounded, killed, or was missing in action.

Draft-age Mexican immigrant men volunteered or were drafted into the U.S. Army. In total, some 14,943 resident Mexican nationals, mainly immigrants residing in California, Arizona, New Mexico, and Texas, served in the U.S. Army during World War II.[3] While their numbers are small compared to the half million or so Mexican Americans, Puerto Ricans, and other Latinos who served in the war, their presence in the U.S. Army raised questions and concerns about the rights and obligations of Mexican nationals that challenged the diplomatic communities of both nations. Unlike the majority of Mexican Americans who fully expected to be drafted, many Mexican immigrants assumed they were exempt from military service because of their Mexican citizenship. Many Mexicans immigrated to the United States for the sole purpose of joining the U.S. Army, while other resident Mexican nationals fled across the border to Mexico (as did a number of American citizens) to escape induction into the army.[4] But most Mexican immigrants registered for the draft, as required by the Selective Training and Service Act of 1940, and showed up on their appointed day to be inducted into the U.S. Army. Many decided to become naturalized citizens, while others zealously clung to their Mexican citizenship. Some sought protection from Mexican consuls in the United States from *mal trato* (mistreatment) in the army, usually for unequal treatment with U.S. servicemen in matters of promotion and training, while others sought deferrals or exemptions because they were the sole support of their families.

On the eve of World War II the majority of Mexican immigrants—legal and illegal—lived in two states, California and Texas, where they came in the decades before World War II to work primarily as migrant laborers in agriculture. According to the census of 1940, more Mexican immigrants lived in Texas (159,266) than in California (134,312), but most contemporaries believed then, as now, that the census failed to obtain an accurate count of those who resided in these states illegally.[5] So numerous were Mexicans in these two states that the Mexican government regarded Los Angeles and San Antonio as the capitals of México de Afuera, or "Mexico Abroad," and the consul general of Mexico called San Antonio the "real center of Pan-Americanism."[6]

Many Mexican immigrants had been resident in the United States for decades, had married and raised children, and had made the transition from temporary sojourner to permanent resident. Often living in segregated neighborhoods, or *colonias,* with little contact with Anglo Americans, these Mexican immigrants continued to feel a strong sense of national pride and patriotism toward their homeland, remaining loyal to the *bandera tricolor* (three-colored flag), as they often referred to the Mexican flag, rather than to *las barras y estrellas,* the Stars and Stripes.[7] Since World War I Mexican consuls actively promoted Mexican nationalist sentiment among immigrant communities in the Southwest, often urging them to return to Mexico.[8] No matter how long Mexican nationals lived in the United States, many still maintained close ties to families and friends in Mexico and believed that they owed their loyalty and patriotism to *la madre patria* (the motherland). When they were required by law to register for the draft, many believed that serving in the U.S. Army would automatically strip them of their Mexican citizenship, a belief erroneously shared by many Mexican consuls themselves.

The United States needed men and women to fight the war, run the railroads, work in factories, and harvest the crops. Tens of thousands of Mexicans signed temporary work contracts as braceros to come to the United States to do their part to support the war effort as farm laborers and track workers.[9] Many Mexican immigrants and long-resident Mexican nationals also joined their coethnic Mexican Americans, many of them the offspring of immigrant parents, in enlisting in the U.S. Army to bring the fight to Japan, Germany, and Italy. The Mexican government, as a member of the Allied Nations, encouraged Mexicans on both sides of the border to defend the continent against the *nazifascista* threat. And they did. As one newspaper put it, "Our steadily mounting casualty lists . . . include Garcia, Guerra and Ramirez as well as Smith, Jones and White."[10] For a brief time Mexico's postrevolutionary nationalism aligned with American patriotism, as both governments sought to find pragmatic ways to resolve problems that developed between two nations of greatly unequal wealth and resources and sharing a 2,000-mile border.

When the United States declared war on Japan and Germany shortly after the attack on Pearl Harbor, thousands of Mexican immigrants and Mexican Americans rushed to enlist in the U.S. Army to fight for the triumph of the democracies over the Axis Powers. In Mexico, hundreds of citizens, like Tomás Oropeza Ramírez, wrote to President Ávila Camacho seeking permission to leave Mexico "para ir a Estados Unidos, en calidad de soldado voluntario, para defender las Democracias."[11] In California Marcos Gómez and other Mexican nationals petitioned the Mexican government for permission to join the California State Militia because "California . . . can be attacked at any moment."[12] Over 700 Mexican immigrants joined the United Mexican Reserve of the California State Militia. The commanding officer, Lieutenant R. L. Vásquez, asked President Ávila Camacho for official recognition in order to dispel the belief among many immigrants that joining the California State Militia would constitute an act of treason against Mexico.[13] Latino organizations throughout the Southwest, such as Alianza Hispano Americana, the League of United Latin American Citizens (LULAC), the League of Loyal Latin Americans, and the Congreso Nacional de Pueblos de Habla Española (National Spanish-Speaking People's Congress), encouraged full participation of Hispanics in the war effort.[14] Felipe Carvajal, secretary-general of the Confederación de Trabajadores Mexicanos en Norte América in Dallas, Texas, summed up the attitude of many Mexican immigrants and Mexican Americans in a letter to President Roosevelt: "We are being drafted and all of us are completely disposed and ready to lend our services in the armed forces of this Great Country, under the glorious flag of the stars and stripes, to defend justice, democracy, and human liberties."[15] Numerous Mexican nationals also joined the armed forces of Canada, England, and France after the Mexican government passed legislation in September 1942 that Mexican nationals in those countries would not lose their citizenship by enlisting in the armed forces.[16] A Mexican immigrant even served as General Eisenhower's private cook.[17] Mrs. Daniel Arias Sierras, a Mexican immigrant who settled with her family in Fresno County, California, saw seven of her eleven sons serve in the U.S. Army: "We mothers have our part to perform in this national emergency. This is the time of resignation as well as love. We must fortify our sons with our words and our prayers."[18]

Before the United States entered the war, the draft status of Mexican nationals was a source of confusion and contention not only for the immigrants but also for Mexican consuls seeking to defend their rights in the United States. When the U.S. Congress passed the Selective Training and Service Act in 1940, every male citizen residing in the United States between the ages of twenty and forty-five was liable for training and service in the "land or naval forces of the United States."[19] All resident foreign nationals were also required to register with Selective Service local boards, although resident aliens from neutral countries could claim exemption from military service.[20] Claiming an exemption, however, would permanently bar the foreign national from ever becoming a U.S. citizen. Nevertheless, after the United States entered the war, draft boards often ignored the neutral status of Mexico and made no distinction between foreign nationals of neutral countries and those of countries, like France and Great Britain, that were "co-belligerents" with the United States. Consuls protested, often in vain, that draft boards could not induct Mexican citizens as long as Mexico remained a neutral country.[21] But after Mexico declared war on the Axis Powers in May 1942, joining the United States and other allied nations as co-belligerents, Mexican nationals became subject to immediate induction into the armed forces.[22]

Although Mexican consuls had complained since the passage of the Selective Training and Service Act that local draft boards made little effort to distinguish between Mexican Americans and Mexican immigrants, or between foreign nationals of neutral countries and those of co-belligerent nations, the U.S. Selective Service System reported to the Mexican government that the first Mexican nationals were drafted into the army in September 1942, three months after Mexico became a cobelligerent. By October 1943, according to the report, 11,319 Mexican immigrants in the United States had been drafted into the U.S. Army.[23] Most Mexican immigrants, however, were wholly unaware of the provisions of the draft law and the obligation to serve in the armed forces.[24] Some petitioned the Mexican president to intervene with local draft boards to allow

MEXICANS IN THE MAKING OF AMERICA

them to return to Mexico to serve in the Mexican armed forces.[25] To add to the confusion, many consuls invoked Article 37 of the Mexican Constitution that "rendering voluntary services to a foreign government" without permission from the Mexican Congress would result in the loss of Mexican citizenship.[26]

The situation involving the U.S.-born children of Mexican immigrants presented a different set of problems. Growing up in a cultural borderland straddling two countries, they adapted elements of both national cultures in the process of becoming "Mexican American."[27] The ambiguity and contradictions of their ethnic and cultural identities were reflected in the legal confusion stemming from their dual nationality. According to Mexican law, children born to Mexican citizens living in foreign countries automatically acquired Mexican citizenship by Article 30, Section II, of the Mexican Constitution.[28] The Mexican Foreign Ministry was troubled by the "difficult situation" created by the *doble nacionalid* (dual nationality) of U.S.-born children of Mexican citizens, but acknowledged that *hijos de mexicanos* born in the United States were citizens of the United States and subject to all laws, including induction into the armed forces—they would not lose their dual citizenship status by enlisting in the U.S. Army, and they did not require the permission of the Mexican government to serve in the U.S. Army.[29]

Frequent disagreements between local draft boards and Mexican consuls over the induction of resident Mexican nationals prompted President Ávila Camacho to announce in October 1942: "All Mexicans resident in the United States are permitted to enlist in the North American Army. Mexico is a member of the Allied Nations and we are obligated to contribute decisively to the triumph of the Allies over Germany, Italy, and Japan." The Mexican government also published a pamphlet for distribution in the United States titled *Los Mexicanos en los Estados Unidos y la Guerra* that explained the obligation of Mexican nationals to register and serve in the armed forces of the United States.[30] Still some Mexican nationals insisted they could not be drafted into the military service of a foreign country. Victor Alvidrez of Alhambra, California, received this letter from his local board: "You are apparently under the impression that because you are a citizen of Mexico you do not have to recognize the Selective Service Laws. If you do not report for your physical exam we will be compelled to report you to the FBI as a last resort."[31] Alvidrez did not report for his physical, refused to serve, and was sentenced to a year in prison. His case was unusual, since those who felt strongly about not serving in the

U.S. Army had the option of returning to Mexico to fulfill their military obligation.

To avoid misunderstanding and diplomatic disputes, in January 1943 the United States and Mexico signed a Convenio Militar (Military Agreement) clarifying the rights and responsibilities of resident nationals in each country for the duration of the war. One of the articles of that agreement stipulated that resident nationals of each country in the territory of the other could be drafted into the armed forces of the resident country, except for *residentes fronterizos* (border residents) who commuted daily to work across the border.[32] Since the establishment of the border in 1848, many Mexicans had crossed daily to work in U.S. border cities and returned to their homes in Mexico at the end of the day. Transnational commuters, or "border crossers," lived in numerous twin border cities that included San Diego-Tijuana and Calexico-Mexicali on the border in California; and Nogales-Nogales and Douglas-Agua Prieta on the border in Arizona. Texas, with its 1,000-mile river border with Mexico, included the twin cities of El Paso-Ciudad Juárez, Eagle Pass-Piedras Negras, Laredo-Nuevo Laredo, McAllen-Reynosa, and Brownsville-Matamoros.

As a special case, transnational commuters were to be considered residents of the country in which they actually lived for purposes of military service. Many Mexican nationals took advantage of this clause to shift their residency from the United States to Mexico to avoid the U.S. draft, and consuls willingly, even eagerly, informed local draft boards that these nationals had "formally relinquished their residence in this country."[33] Upon establishing residency in Mexico they received "border crossing" permits that allowed them to continue working in the United States, as long as they returned to Mexico each day. To close this loophole, on February 16, 1942, the Selective Service System informed all lawful resident nationals of allied nations not willing to lend their services to the U.S. Army that they had three months in which to establish residency in a country other than the United States. Those leaving the country before May 16, 1942, or within three months of the date of entry, whichever was later, would not be subject to the draft.[34] Those seeking to establish residency elsewhere after May 16 would still be subject to the draft if they ever returned to the United States, even for a brief visit.[35] The director of the Selective Service System went a step further when he explained that "certain Mexicans who left the United States prior to May 16, 1942 might have left under such circumstances that the local board or reviewing authority might determine that it was not a bona fide departure and hold that they were still subject to the liabilities of the Selective Service Law."[36]

Mexican consuls frequently cited two of the articles of the 1943 bilateral Military Agreement in their dealings with the local draft boards and the War Department:

Article II: Resident nationals of each country resident in the other have the same rights and privileges as the citizens of the country of their residence.

Article VII: Nationals of either country serving in the armed forces of the other country shall receive the same treatment and have equal opportunities with respect to commissions and promotions . . . as are accorded by that country to its nationals in conformity with military law and practice.[37]

The agreement enabled Mexican consuls, the Foreign Ministry, and officials of the State Department and Justice Department to work together, mostly amicably, to resolve problems involving Mexican citizens in the armed forces. Mexican immigrants in the United States had the option, for example, of performing their military service in the Mexican armed forces, and if already serving in the U.S. armed forces, to apply for a transfer. Many Mexican nationals, however, were unaware of this option, and most draft boards rarely offered registrants a choice. Most nationals who wished to serve in the Mexican Army sought transfers after they were enlisted in the U.S. Army. In all, fewer than 1,000 Mexican draftees successfully transferred from the U.S. Army to the Mexican Army.[38] These nationals had "no objection to fighting for the cause of democracy" in the U.S. Army, according to one consul, but some complained that their Mexican citizenship and their inability to speak English prevented them from receiving promotions and certain kinds of advanced training. Having immigrated to the United States as young adults, these draftees spoke little or no English, while others joined the service with U.S. high school degrees and English-language skills that made them eligible for assignments in aviation mechanics, cavalry, artillery and medical corps.[39] The majority of them, like most recruits, were assigned to the infantry.

Manuel Narvaez Spíndola was a trained mechanic before joining the U.S. Army but claimed he was denied an assignment as a technician because of his Mexican citizenship. His commanding officer reportedly told him, in direct violation of Article VII of the Military Agreement, that he must take out "first papers" for U.S. citizenship in order to receive the technician assignment. Before the Mexican consul could intervene in his behalf, the

War Department reported that Private Narvaez Spíndola "was killed in action in Italy on May 12, 1944."[40] In another case of apparent discrimination based on Mexican citizenship, Rubén E. González, a graduate of McAllen High School in Texas, trained in the U.S. Army as a radio operator and technician but was denied a diploma from gunnery school because, he told the Mexican consul, his superior officer told him that only U.S. citizens could receive diplomas. A State Department investigation revealed that González was eliminated from the course in serial gunnery not because he was a citizen of Mexico, but "because of Air Firing deficiency."[41] Most consuls recognized that many nationals in the U.S. Army, like other American recruits, lacked the skills, training, or aptitude (like shooting straight) for some assignments, but poor English-language skills of many Mexican nationals left them vulnerable to charges of "draft delinquency" and, once recruited, to menial assignments that required few language skills.

Many Mexican immigrants could not read the English-language letters they received from draft boards informing them of the requirement to register for the draft. Those who failed to register were classified as "draft delinquents" and were subject to arrest and immediate induction or deportation. A number of Mexican nationals reported as delinquent had already enlisted in the armed forces without having notified their local draft boards. The Selective Service System estimated that about 50 percent of all Mexican draft delinquents had left the country. To better inform Mexican nationals in San Antonio, LULAC member Manuel C. Gonzales organized a meeting attended by 6,000 Mexican immigrants to explain—in Spanish and English—the legal requirement to register for the draft.[42]

Army recruiters often ignored the regulation that no registrant "will be inducted who cannot read or write the English language as commonly prescribed for the fourth grade in grammar schools." As a result, many Mexican recruits could not understand basic commands, learn military regulations and protocols, or apply for family allowances, transfers, promotions, or special training. The commanding officer at Camp Roberts, California, Colonel Moore, who was concerned that the inability of Mexican immigrants to speak or understand English could endanger lives, assigned Spanish-speaking recruits to five predominantly English-speaking training regiments, rather than segregate them in their own unit, in order to accelerate English language learning. When one recruit, Private Leandro Palomo, complained to the Mexican consul, Eugenio Aza, that he was required to attend English-language classes and was discouraged from speaking Spanish in the barracks, Aza bluntly informed Palomo: "The purpose of this order is for you to learn English, on which may depend your life and the lives of your comrades." Colonel Moore invited Consul Aza to Camp Roberts to visit with the 850 Mexican nationals who were learning English and in other ways adapting to life in the army. The vast majority of the recruits expressed satisfaction with the language classes, their training, and even "gringo" food. Aza told the recruits, including Palomo, to obey the English-language order for their own safety and the safety of others, and to make an effort to understand its importance.[43]

Older recruits who were often illiterate in both languages and physically unfit for assignments in the infantry frequently requested release from military service. Private Manuel Pineda, a thirty-seven-year-old former farm worker in basic training at Camp Roberts, told Aza he was assigned "odd jobs picking up papers and keeping the shower baths and rest rooms clean" because he could not read, write, speak, or understand English. Pineda told Aza that if he were released from the army, he could "be of more value and render better service to the prosecution of the war working in any agricultural activity."[44] In many cases army commanders cooperated with Mexican consuls and authorized the early release of older, often physically exhausted men who had spent most of their adult lives doing backbreaking labor on California and Texas farms.[45]

Although some army units were disproportionately Mexican or Spanish-speaking, the army made no attempt to form segregated units as it had for African-American and Japanese-American servicemen. Nevertheless, it occurred to a high-ranking Mexican diplomat, Visitor General Adolfo de La Huerta, that Mexicans in the U.S. armed forces would garner more prestige if they could serve in their own units with their own officers, as had some allied units composed only of Canadians, Australians, and other allied groups.[46] The only all-Mexican unit to serve in the war, Squadron 201, flew ground-cover missions in the Philippines (but under the American flag) in the final months of the war, which was the source of tremendous national pride among Mexicans after the war.[47]

When the Mexican consul at Austin, Luis Duplan, was asked if he could assist in establishing a company of Women's Army Corps (WAC) exclusively for Latin-American women, he worried that separate companies for Mexican WACs might be interpreted by some Mexican Americans as an act of discrimination on the part of the War Department, especially given the "animosity towards Mexicans in Texas."[48] The issue of forming all Mexican-origin military units was a sensitive one because the Mexican foreign minister would have vigorously protested any segregation of Mexican citizens

Private Benito Chávez Rivera (forty-three years old),
"físicamente agotado" (physically worn-out) from years
of strenuous physical labor as a street vendor, requested
release from the U.S. Army. III-806–2, folio 33.1, Archivo
Histórico de la Secretaría de Relaciones Exteriores,
Mexico City.

in the U.S. Army. Nevertheless, the issue surfaced when over a hundred
Mexican-American women recruits in the WAC of Texas requested permis-
sion to form the Escuadrón "Benito Juárez" del Cuerpo Militar Femenino
(Benito Juárez Squadron of the Women's Army Corps) to be stationed at
Kelley Air Field in San Antonio. Duplan decided that the formation of Air-
WACs did not imply segregation since the Mexican-American women
underwent six weeks of training in integrated WAC units.[49]

U.S. and Mexican military authorities approved the formation of Escuadrón Benito Juárez and organized a ceremony in front of city hall in San
Antonio to commemorate its founding on March 23, the birth date of the

Swearing-in ceremony of Mexican-American women in the "Benito Juárez" Squadron, Women's Army Corps, Municipal Auditorium, San Antonio, March 1944. III-803–1, 3ª pte, folio 148, Archivo Histórico de la Secretaría de Relaciones Exteriores, Mexico City.

revered ex-president of Mexico, Benito Juárez (1806–1872). Six thousand San Antonians attended the ceremony in which fifty Mexican American women were sworn into the special Air-WAC unit. The ceremony was carried internationally on shortwave radio and included patriotic speeches by the mayor of San Antonio, Gus B. Mauermann; Armando Arteaga Santoya, special representative of the Mexican governor of Nuevo León; Constancio Villarreal, the mayor of Monterrey; four U.S. Army generals; and consuls of Nicaragua and Honduras. The master of ceremonies, LULAC activist and honorary Mexican consul in San Antonio, Manuel C. Gonzales, introduced Colonel Walter White, commander of Randolph Field, who compared Benito Juárez to Abraham Lincoln because, he said, they both represented the democratic ideals of Mexico and the United States respectively. U.S. and Mexican military and civilian officials clearly viewed the formation of the Escuadrón Benito Juárez as an opportunity to recognize the contribution of Mexican-American women to the war effort, but they also took advantage of the occasion to affirm the shared history and heritage of two neighboring nations engaged, as Colonel White put it, in "the global war for democracy."[50]

Commemorative ceremonies and diplomatic decorum had become routine features of U.S.-Mexico relations during the war, but behind the scenes diplomats and military personnel on both sides of the border worked hard to eliminate potential conflicts. From the start diplomatic disputes arose as a result of the military regulation that all members of the U.S. Air Force and Navy be U.S. citizens for at least ten years prior to enlistment, which effectively barred all Mexican nationals from service in those forces. Mexican ambassador Castillo Nájera protested to U.S. Secretary of State Cordell Hull that numerous qualified Mexican citizens, including pilots, were not allowed to join the air force cadet training school or the navy because they were not U.S. citizens. He claimed that this was in violation of Article VII of the U.S.-Mexico Military Agreement that nationals of either country serving in the armed forces of the other country shall receive the same treatment and have equal opportunities with respect to commissions and promotions "in conformity with military law and practice."[51]

Undersecretary of State Sumner Welles replied that the ambassador's objection to the citizenship requirement was based on a misunderstanding of the agreement. The intent of Article VII, he explained, was "to assure that the nationals of neither country will be discriminated against when serving in the armed forces of the other country" and that Mexican nationals would have equal treatment and opportunity with U.S. nationals *"within the limits of military law and practice."*[52] The citizenship requirement did not violate the terms of the agreement with Mexico since it fell within "military law and practice." Sumner Welles acknowledged, however, that while the policy "may be a cause of apparent injustice in isolated cases, the War Department does not think it advisable to recommend any change in the law or the regulations."[53] The adjutant general of the War Department suggested that Mexican nationals could join the U.S. Army and complete their naturalization papers while in basic training and then request a waiver of the ten-year citizenship requirement for enlisting in aviation cadet training.[54]

The issue of the citizenship requirement of the U.S. Air Force and Navy proved somewhat embarrassing to Mexico when the undersecretary of the Mexican Foreign Ministry, Jaime Torres Bodet, acknowledged that Mexico's own navy and air force required its applicants to be Mexican citizens *"by birth,"* a requirement far more stringent than the ten-year citizenship rule for enlistment in the U.S. Air Force or Navy. Torres Bodet informed Ambassador Castillo Nájera that the U.S. War Department would be in violation of the spirit and letter of Article VII of the agreement only if the Air Force and Navy refused applicants "for the sole reason of being Mexicans."[55]

MEXICANS IN THE MAKING OF AMERICA

The citizenship requirement also affected qualified Mexican citizens who wanted to become army officers but were ineligible to receive Reserve Officers' Training Corps (ROTC) scholarships. According to Section 44 of the National Defense Act of 1916, membership in the ROTC was restricted to students who were citizens of the United States. But in practice the army often permitted qualified nationals of a cobelligerent country to enroll in ROTC training at their own expense and without a contract with the U.S. government. This "off-the-books" training did not qualify friendly foreign nationals for actual commissions in the army, but if they elected to undergo the three-month training course, and were otherwise eligible, noncitizen cadets could be appointed as "temporary Second Lieutenants" in the U.S. Army.[56]

Numerous conflicts arose between Mexican consuls and local draft boards over the proper classification of Mexican nationals who were the sole support of their families. Most Mexican immigrants who worked in the United States supported wives, children, grandparents, and other family members in Mexico.[57] As the sole supporters of families, they were eligible for a 3-A classification: "deferral because of hardship to dependents." Local draft boards often denied applicants for the "sole support" deferral because they lacked supporting documentation: marriage certificates, birth or baptismal certificates of children, and notarized testimony of other family members dependent on the applicant. Mexican consuls devoted much time and effort to obtain the documents, only to learn that the draft boards rejected the applications anyway.[58] As the state director of the Selective Service System explained to one consul, "it is the off-hand opinion of this headquarters that this [Mexican] family would benefit, to a far greater degree financially, if this registrant were inducted into the service than if he were deferred by reason of dependents."[59]

Whether or not a person might earn more in the U.S. Army, however, was not relevant to the provision of the Selective Training and Service Act that deferred men who were the sole supporters of their families. Nevertheless, the director was correct about the potential income of servicemen with families. According to the Servicemen's Dependents Allowance Act of 1942, all servicemen who were sole supporters of their families were entitled to receive a "family allowance" of $120 per month, more than double the earnings of performing farm labor. Many Mexican servicemen were often unaware of this allowance and failed to claim it. And those who sought the allowance faced the problem of obtaining documentation from Mexico. In response, the Mexican embassy developed a questionnaire that it administered to all Mexican inductees to inform them of the Servicemen's Dependents

Allowance Act and encourage them to take advantage of the family allow-ance to which they were entitled.[60]

Even more disturbing than the routine denial of 3-A classification for Mexican sole supporters of families was the denial of temporary border permits for resident Mexican nationals to visit their families in Mexico. Local draft boards routinely denied exit permits to any registrant, regard-less of citizenship, "whose age renders him liable for military service."[61] Draft boards believed that resident Mexican nationals would not return to the United States to fulfill their military service, although permission was readily granted to Canadian and other resident nationals who wished to leave. An official in the Office of the Coordinator of Inter-American Affairs (OCIAA), Jack Leighter, deplored the fact that a Mexican national "could not leave this country, not even for the purpose of enlisting in the Mexican Army. If he were a Canadian, or an Australian, or a New Zealander, he would be permitted to return to his native land to fight under his own flag, but as a Mexican he is subject to our draft laws without the rights granted to other allied aliens."[62] Ernesto Carrasco, a resident Mexican national in El Paso drafted into the army, was denied a permit to cross the border to visit his family in Ciudad Juárez. Carrasco had been a longtime resident national with permanent work in El Paso, had been married since 1933, and had three sons.[63] The INS instructed border agents to detain all Mexi-can nationals without passes until their draft status could be determined.[64] Mexican consuls vigorously protested the practice of detaining Mexican nationals at the border who simply wished to spend time with their fami-lies, including family members who were seriously ill or dying, before be-ing sent to the war fronts.[65] Private Miguel Meza, another El Paso resident national denied permission to cross the border, decided to risk crossing "illegally" into his own country. He drowned while trying to cross the Rio Grande at El Paso to see is mother, wife, and children in Juárez.[66]

A particularly sensitive issue for both governments involved the num-ber of resident Mexican nationals seeking to "self-repatriate" to Mexico rather serve in the U.S. Army. Foreign Minister Padilla instructed his con-suls to convince Mexican nationals in the United States "not to attempt to cross the border . . . to elude military service, but to fulfill their military obligation in the United States."[67] Two weeks earlier Padilla had issued a strongly worded circular that those who attempted to avoid military service in the United States "not only commit an act of ingratitude but also lack manhood (falta de hombría)." Mexicans, he said, needed to share with Americans the "hardships as well as the prosperity." His words did not go unchallenged. A Mexican citizen in Laredo, Texas, Serapio Martínez Pérez,

Guadalupe Hernández (age thirty-three, born in Mexico City) and his younger brother Ramón (age eighteen, born in Redlands, California), both living in Patterson, California, were denied permission by the local draft board to leave the United States to visit their parents and younger sister in Mexico after they were drafted into the U.S. Army. Though citizens of different nations, the brothers expressed their loyalty to both: "Victoria! Para las naciones unidas. Viva Mexico y vivan los Estados Unidos de Norte America!" III-804–1, 2ª pte, folio 117.1, Archivo Histórico de la Secretaría de Relaciones Exteriores, Mexico City.

wrote Padilla: "You do not have the right to doubt the manhood of Mexicans who have sought the protection of the Mexican government against arbitrary acts of discrimination against us." As far as "gratitude and prosperity are concerned," he wrote, "we have never been 'ungrateful' for the simple reason that we have never experienced the 'prosperity' you speak of." He reminded Padilla that Mexican citizenship barred them from obtaining employment in defense industries, which offered much higher salaries than agricultural work, and called Padilla's attack on Mexicans returning to Mexico "servile and indecent."[68] Padilla's announcement that Mexican nationals in the United States "should fight for the United States" had angered many nationals who wished to return to Mexico to serve in the Mexican Army.[69] As one Mexican national, Pedro Mena, put it, in the United States "we are denied employment practically everywhere, except in the military service."[70]

Most of the complaints regarding discrimination came from Mexican nationals in Texas where Anglo Americans had long refused to extend basic civil rights to Texas Mexicans.[71] Some army units in Texas, in fact, permitted the slogan "Remember the Alamo" to be stitched onto their company uniforms, in violation of army regulations regarding proper uniform attire. The Mexican consul objected that requiring nationals to wear the slogan as part of their uniform was an insult to all Mexicans in the army, especially when they were sacrificing their lives to defend Texas and the United States.[72] José Infante, a Mexican national from Minatare, Nebraska, where the city council passed an ordinance forbidding Mexicans to rent in white neighborhoods, wondered why he should fight to defend the territory that once belonged to Mexico before it was seized by the United States.[73] Marciano M. Zamarripa of Calvert, Texas, wrote to President Ávila Camacho that he did not think it was fair that Mexicans should be required to serve in the U.S. Army because *americanos* "don't let us Mexicans eat with them or get our hair cut in their barbershops, but still they want us to die like *americanos*." Zamarripa was also upset that most of the skilled jobs in defense were "only for the white race."[74]

Some Mexican parents in Mexico voiced their opposition to their children having to serve in the U.S. military. A father in Culiacán, Sinaloa, wanted President Roosevelt to release his son from a training camp in California because "I don't want my son to be cannon fodder" *(carne de canon).*[75] Amada Valles Macias, the mother of two sons in the army, pleaded to the Mexican president "with the tears of a Mexican mother" to have her sons transferred to the Mexican Army because, she frankly admitted, "Mexico doesn't send its soldiers outside of the country."[76] The president and foreign minister responded to these citizens that is was the obligation of all Mexican nationals in the United States to serve in the U.S. Army in "defense of the continent" and "our hemisphere."[77] In this way the Mexican government adroitly sought to portray service in the U.S. Army as no different from the obligation to serve in the Mexican Army, insofar as both nations together sought to defend "our hemisphere" against the Axis threat.

Some problems were brought to the attention of Mexican consuls by the parents of Mexican nationals in the army. Mexican soldiers wrote home, and if their letters contained information about mistreatment, their parents sometimes took the letters to the Mexican consulates or wrote to the foreign minister or president of the republic to see if they could intervene in their children's behalf. One Mexican national, Felipe Ramírez, wrote to his parents that he was not receiving adequate medical attention in a hospital in England and felt like killing all "gringos" as well as Germans.[78]

Jesús José Holguin Rentería, a Mexican national stationed at Deming Army Airfield in New Mexico, wrote his parents (in Spanish): "The only difficulty I have here is that I can't go places where other soldiers go because I am Mexican. On June 3rd I went to the Deming swimming pool where I was asked my nationality. I said I was Mexican and they told me that Mexicans couldn't swim here. Naturally this hurt me a lot, because even colored people have a day to swim at the pool."[79] That African Americans and Mexicans could not "go places" because of their race was well understood by Mexicans on the U.S. side of the border, but often came as a shock to Mexican immigrants accustomed to going any place they wanted in Mexico.

The mother of Hermino Garibaldi appeared at the Mexican consulate in San Antonio with a letter, in Spanish, from her son, a Mexican citizen in the U.S. Army stationed at Camp Carson, Colorado: "Mamá, I don't have a lot to say, but I'm going to tell you what happened to me last Wednesday. I went to do my laundry at a laundromat in Colorado Springs and ran into an American friend who said, 'Let's go get a beer.' So we went to Diana Café and my friend ordered two beers. The waitress said to me, 'We can't serve you because you are Mexican.' I said, 'you don't serve any Mexicans?' and she said 'no.' I asked to talk to the manager and asked him why I could not be served a beer, and he said, 'because you are a Mexican.' I got so mad I went to tell the military police what happened. They said they couldn't do anything. So I said, 'this uniform isn't worth anything, because we have fewer rights here than Negroes.'"[80]

At the request of the State Department and the Mexican consul, the district attorney in Colorado Springs conducted an investigation and reported that the "bartender refused him service because he believed Mr. Garibaldi "to be an Indian." The police had warned café owners, according to the district attorney, "that it was a criminal offense to serve liquor of any kind to an Indian . . . because of the presence in a nearby military camp of a large number of Indian soldiers." The Diana Café "does not discriminate against persons of Mexican descent or nationality," the district attorney added, "and has served them on numerous occasions."[81]

As a further irony, Native Americans in California objected to the state Selective Service System's practice of classifying Mexican immigrants and Mexican Americans as "Indians." The adjutant general and state director of the California Selective Service System, R. E. Mittelstaedt, informed county clerks throughout the state to have Selective Service registration clerks classify all Mexicans as members of "the Indian race." Like many state and municipal officials during the first half of the twentieth century, Mittelstaedt probably did not think it appropriate or accurate to classify Mexicans as "white." However, the racial categories used by the Selective Service System—White, Negro, Oriental, Indian, and Filipino—left him little choice, so he decided that Mexicans more appropriately belonged to the "Indian" than "White" category.

The Mexican consul in San Diego, Manuel Aguilar, registered an official protest with the county clerk of San Diego. So did California reservation Indians who protested "that Mexicans were not Indians" and that "only Indians should be registered as Indians."[82] Mittelstaedt, reacting promptly to the complaints, sent the county clerks a telegram telling them that in the case of registration of Mexicans, "strike out the word Indian and substitute Mexican." The Mexican consul of Los Angeles, however, had argued repeatedly that "there is no such thing as a Mexican race, as the Mexican people belong to the Caucasian or White race, regardless of their complexion."[83] In addition to five categories of race, draft board forms included the following categories of description: "Eyes" (blue, grey, hazel, brown, black); "Hair" (blonde, red, brown, black, gray, bald); and "Complexion" (sallow, light, ruddy, dark, freckled, light brown, dark brown, and black).[84] On many forms Mexicans were described as having brown or black eyes, brown or black hair, and dark brown complexion, which hardly fit the contemporary understanding of "white." Nevertheless, Mittelstaedt complied with the Mexican consul's objection to classifying Mexicans as members of the "Mexican race" and promptly telegraphed the San Diego county clerk, "All registrars should show Mexican registrants as [belonging to] the white race."[85]

Classifying Mexicans as "white" rather than "Indian" or "Mexican" had less to do with changing Anglo perceptions of Mexicans than with the growing awareness that good relations with Mexico and other Latin-American nations depended in part on ending discrimination against persons of Latin-American descent. The OCIAA called the practice of using the term "'Mexican" to denote American citizens of Mexican ancestry in Selective Service System records "ill-advised . . . because it is not only a misnomer but is also frequently regarded as an epithet and carries the unfounded implication that an individual so labeled is inferior." Furthermore, the OCIAA pointed out, the practice "prevents many qualified Spanish speaking youths from obtaining officer's training, and it apparently often happens that when such men are proposed as candidates for officer's training, the entry 'Mexican' is assumed to mean that the individual is a citizen of Mexico and is therefore ineligible to become an officer." When Mexican consuls in Texas complained of the practice, Brigadier General J. Watt Page, Texas state director of the Selective Service System, informed all local boards that all "persons of Mexican descent in the United States are enumerated and classified as white unless they are distinctly of Indian origin, in which case they are classified by the Census Bureau as Indians." He instructed all Texas draft boards not to use the term "Mexican" on inductees' papers "unless the individual is actually a citizen of Mexico."[86]

Although Mexican consuls could not intervene on behalf of U.S. citizens of Mexican descent who faced discrimination, they kept up a steady stream of newspaper clippings to the foreign minister on the problems faced by Mexican Americans. One Mexican American, José Frausto, a twenty-five-year-old veteran who was awarded the Bronze Star for valor and the Purple Heart for injuries sustained in Germany, was denied service at a restaurant in Fort Worth because he was a "Spaniard." "I felt like I was in a foreign country. I wasn't bitter. I wondered why these things happen." He reported the incident to the newspaper because he and his wife were expecting their first child: "I don't want the same things to happen to my kids." When the owner, Mrs. Losewitz, was asked why she refused to serve a Mexican American war veteran, she replied: "I'll tell you what . . . you run that *Star-Telegram* [newspaper] . . . and I'll run the Kentucky Grill."[87]

Many resident Mexican nationals sought jobs in defense industries, such as shipbuilding, but were denied employment because of their Mexican citizenship. In 1926 Congress passed a law requiring U.S. citizenship for jobs in industries with federal contracts from the navy and air force. The purpose of the law was to prevent noncitizens from potentially engaging in sabotage of defense-related industries. Employers wishing to hire alien workers first had to seek permission from the War Department, a process that was both cumbersome and slow.[88] A War Department official acknowledged that he had received reports from a number of sources "of wholesale discharges of aliens employed in plants holding defense contracts" and the practice of many companies of "specifying citizenship as a prerequisite for employment."[89] Mexican nationals complained bitterly that they and their children were expected to fight and die in the war but were not permitted to work in jobs created by the war—except in low-paying agricultural jobs. Atilano Venegas, the forty-eight-year-old father of five children, one of whom was serving in the U.S. Army, wrote to the president of Mexico that employers refused to hire him because of his Mexican citizenship and that many resident nationals in the United States "suffer from prejudice now more than ever, especially those of us who look 'Indian' and cannot pass as whites."[90] A Mexican from Dallas wrote to FDR: "Many Mexicans have already given their lives for this great cause of justice and equality, and we feel we should respectfully ask of you to concede the Mexican Citizens living in this Country the right to be granted work in Defense Industries and civil services."[91]

The Mexican government became directly involved in attempting to remove the citizen restriction. The problem, according to a memorandum from the Mexican ambassador, was that the War Department stipulated that only contract-holding companies could petition the secretary of war for approval to employ noncitizen workers. Aliens themselves could not petition on their own behalf. "As a result, the alien is at the mercy of the companies desiring to employ him." Companies desirous of hiring qualified alien workers were often reluctant to invest the time and resources necessary to obtain clearance from the War Department. The statute forbidding the hiring of aliens in defense industries was enacted over a decade before the war and could not have anticipated the urgent manpower demands the war created. The exclusion of Mexican nationals from war-production employment, especially in California's aircraft and shipbuilding industries, threatened "to create a very serious morale situation" among the thousands of Mexican nationals in the Los Angeles area. "Suburban Mexicans," the ambassador asserted, "are no more suited to agricultural occupations than are other suburban population groups."[92]

As a direct result of pressure from the Mexican Foreign Ministry, the War Department and other agencies issued a joint statement in 1943: Contractors must obtain written consent to employ aliens only in work involving aeronautical contracts and classified contracts. Otherwise, "contractors and subcontractors may employ aliens as freely as American citizens." Failure to request consent for the employment of aliens, or refusal to hire them once consent had been granted, constituted "a breach of the antidiscrimination clause of the [federal] contract and is contrary to national policy as expressed in the [Fair Employment Practices Committee] Executive Order."[93]

After the war ended, the Mexican government gave its approval and support to numerous Mexican nationals who opted to become naturalized American citizens. Some had taken out "first papers" during the war because they believed, correctly, that they would receive better treatment in the army, including opportunities for advanced training and promotions.[94] Many others hoped to take advantage of the G.I. Bill, passed by Congress in 1944, to provide college education for returning veterans, as well as unemployment benefits and low-cost loans to purchase houses or start businesses. The G.I. Bill, according to the Mexican government, had provided a "powerful incentive" for Mexican servicemen to become U.S. citizens and avail themselves of opportunities that would virtually "assure their future." In fact, the Mexican Foreign Ministry affirmed that citizenship had become "una necesidad moral" (a moral necessity) for many Mexicans who served in the U.S. Army.[95] However, Mexican veterans who could not demonstrate that they had entered the United States lawfully were barred from naturalization, even after having served honorably in the U.S. Army. Many Mexican veterans felt betrayed by this sudden application of the immigration laws, since the draft boards largely ignored the illegal status of Mexican immigrants when registering and drafting them into the army.[96] Suddenly honorably discharged veterans had reverted to "illegal aliens" who faced deportation after the war.

The demotion of Mexican veterans to the status of "wetbacks" and their summary deportation began to affect the conscience of the American people. Throughout the war newspapers in towns and cities across the nation published lists of casualties that included the surnames of thousands of Hispanic Americans, including numerous stories of Mexican Americans who had won special citations for gallantry.[97] California congressman Jerry Voorhis made a plea for respect and simple justice on the floor of the U.S. House of Representatives: "As I read the casualty lists from my own state, I find anywhere from one-fourth to one-third of those names are names such as Gonzalez or Sanchez, names indicating that the very lifeblood of our citizens of Latin-American descent in the uniform of the armed forces of the United States is being poured out to win victory in the war. We ought not to forget that."[98] Indeed citizens of the United States and Mexico expressed deep pride in the eleven Mexican Americans who were awarded the nation's highest medal for heroism, the Medal of Honor.[99] One of the recipients, Cleto Rodríguez, grew up in San Antonio, where officials of both governments, including President Harry Truman, honored him after the war for his heroism. Other Mexican-American Medal of Honor recipients from California, Arizona, and Oklahoma were similarly honored, most posthumously. It did not matter to the Mexican government that most of these war heroes were Mexican Americans, not Mexican nationals, because they regarded Mexican Americans as compatriots of dual nationality and transnationals of common Mexican ancestry. But if the United States could not claim the exclusive privilege of honoring these national heroes, neither could Mexico. "Today is a day of pride for Mexico," the Mexican consul general, Gustavo Ortiz Hernán, said at a ceremony in San Antonio to honor Cleto Rodríguez, "but our nation cannot claim as its own and exclusive honor, the honor conquered by this champion born in the plains of Texas. Neither can San Antonio, nor a flag, nor a race demand his name as their own . . . because his heroism was given to the highest cause—the freedom and dignity of man upon the earth."[100]

Cleto Rodríguez being honored at a dinner in San Antonio after being awarded the Medal of Honor at the White House by President Harry Truman. III-802-1, folio 59, Archivo Histórico de la Secretaría de Relaciones Exteriores, Mexico City.

World War II was not the first time soldiers of Mexican ancestry fought in defense of the United States.[101] They have been fighting in U.S. wars for over 150 years—the Civil War, the Spanish-American War, World Wars I and II, the Korean War, the Vietnam War, and more recently the wars in Iraq and Afghanistan. Mexican nationals and Mexican Americans, like other Americans, fought in the Civil War on both sides: Hispanos in New Mexico fought mainly in the Union Army, while Mexican Texans were deeply divided, with brother often fighting brother. Over 2,500 Mexican

Texans, or *tejanos*, fought on the side of the Confederacy, mainly out of fear of being sent out of the state and away from their families, while many New Mexicans, or *nuevomexicanos*, joined the Union Army, in part because they detested Texans for having invaded New Mexico in 1842. The federal government also authorized the military governor of California to raise four cavalry companies of Californios, Mexican Californians, because of their reputation for outstanding horsemanship. Some of these troops participated in defending New Mexico against invading Confederate troops. Mexican Americans even fought against the Spanish in the Spanish-American War of 1898, serving in four volunteer units including Lieutenant Colonel Theodore Roosevelt's "Rough Riders." In 1900, Private France Silva, a U.S. Marine, was the first Hispanic American to win the Medal of Honor, which he received for "meritorious conduct" during the Boxer Rebellion in China.[102]

Around 200,000 Hispanics, mostly of Mexican origin, served in the War to End All Wars, World War I, including 18,000 Puerto Ricans who served in segregated infantry units to protect key installations in Puerto Rico (newly acquired territory of the United States) and the Panama Canal Zone. David Barkley, son of an Anglo father and Mexican mother from Laredo, Texas, was the U.S. Army's first Hispanic Medal of Honor recipient, awarded seventy-one years after he gave his life for a reconnaissance mission behind enemy lines near Pouilly, France, in 1918. In addition to the Medal of Honor, Barkley was also posthumously awarded the Croix de Guerre by France and the Croce Merito de Guerra by Italy.[103] One Mexican veteran of World War I, José de la Luz Sáenz, published his diary in which he recorded his experiences defending democracy and justice abroad while being denied them in his home state of Texas.[104]

There is nothing exceptional about foreign nationals of cobelligerent nations voluntarily enlisting or being drafted into the U.S. Army, which was the case in World Wars I and II, Korea, and Vietnam. U.S. citizens of all ethnoracial backgrounds have served in these wars (including the current wars in Iraq and Afghanistan), as have foreign nationals from many different allied countries. What makes the World War II case unusual, however, is the extraordinary effort expended by the Selective Service System, the War Department, and other agencies to ensure that no Mexican nationals escaped service in the army, even to the point of denying many of them waivers to return to Mexico or release from service because of being the sole supporters of their families. Manpower shortages were a major concern during the war, to be sure, but it is difficult to believe that of the approximately 16 million men and women who served in the armed forces during the war, including over half a million U.S. Latinos, that 15,000 Mexican nationals drafted into the U.S. Army would have made much difference to the war's outcome. Why then was so much bureaucratic energy and diplomatic capital expended on a relatively small number of Mexican immigrants and resident nationals drafted in the United States?

Let us first consider the matter from the Mexican perspective. Diplomatic historians and historians of Mexico have often remarked that the government of Ávila Camacho (1940–1946) sought to leverage the alliance between Mexico and the United States during the war to advance its agenda of modernization and industrialization, particularly through favorable trade agreements.[105] Mexico hoped to be a player in postwar agreements among Latin-American nations, and requiring its citizen soldiers to serve (and die) in the war effort would ensure Mexico's place at the table, like Brazil's, in any postwar negotiations. For this reason, the Mexican government successfully lobbied to have its own 300-man Fighter Squadron 201 participate in securing the Philippine Islands from the Japanese in the closing months of the war. Around the same time, in the spring of 1945, Mexico hosted the Inter-American Conference on War and Peace in Mexico City, which produced the important Act of Chapultepec. This act was essentially a hemispheric security agreement, which stipulated that an attack against any state would constitute an attack against all participating states. In a sense, the hemispheric agreement represented an attempt to subvert the Monroe Doctrine, which had been frequently invoked by the United States as a pretext for military intervention in Mexico and other Latin-American countries.[106]

Mexico's willingness to sanction the drafting of its own citizens into the U.S. Army lined up well with its nation- and state-building project: Mexico enacted its own conscription law in August 1942, shortly after declaring a "state of war" with the Axis powers, with the twin goals of enhancing its national defense capability and advancing its drive for industrialization. Ávila Camacho stressed how conscription could cement internal order, professionalize the army, and, according to one historian, "provide a necessary school of discipline, sobriety, cleanliness and patriotism for Mexico's unruly men-folk." Despite the unpopularity of the draft (conducted by lottery) in Mexico and widespread resistance to it, Ávila Camacho nevertheless supported it at home as well as in the United States, and used the war "to extract credit, training and equipment from the USA with which to modernize its armed forces."[107]

After the bombing of Pearl Harbor, Americans overwhelmingly supported the war and the draft. In the most obvious sense, drafting Mexican nationals was what the Selective Training and Service Act of 1940 required, and state and local draft boards were obligated to fulfill the mandate of the law. The conscription of Mexican nationals was thus somewhat less problematic in the United States than in Mexico since conscription laws in the United States were not deeply contested as they were in Mexico since before the Mexican Revolution. Nevertheless, it is impossible to discount the role of race and racism in the draft boards' selective treatment of Mexican nationals, just as one cannot ignore the fact that of the more than 2.5 million African Americans registered during the war, only about 50,000 were allowed to serve in combat units.[108] The motivation, even the enthusiasm, evinced by draft boards for preventing Mexican nationals from leaving the United States before being drafted and inducted, but allowing nationals of Canada and other allied nations to leave, suggests the endurance of unequal treatment for racialized conscripts and soldiers. Ample evidence suggests that discrimination against Mexican nationals in the armed forces as well as in defense industries was pervasive enough to engage the sustained diplomatic attention of both Mexico and the United States.

The conscription of Mexican nationals in the United States did more than raise questions about bilateral military agreements and diplomatic efforts to resolve conflicts. Serving in the army affected Mexican Americans and Mexican nationals in similar ways: it brought them, many for the first time, into close contact with Anglo Americans as barriers that had long separated them broke down in army camps and on the front lines of combat. Opportunities to learn new skills in the armed forces as well as in the defense industry opened up for them, and they came into contact with new opinions and currents of thought. Many Mexican Americans began to express deep pride in their American citizenship and their collective contribution to winning the war against Nazism and fascism. Having lived and worked in the shadows for so long as a "forgotten people," Mexican-American men and women came forward after the war, proud of their service to their country and determined to fight for equal rights as passionately as they had devoted themselves to winning the war.

But Mexico's most significant contribution to the war effort, more crucial than the thousands of Mexican nationals who served in the U.S. Army, was the vast army of braceros—"soldiers on the farm front," as one Mexican consul called them—who played a decisive role in fulfilling America's wartime need for agricultural labor.[109] Despite the tensions created over the Mexican nationalization of the oil industry in 1938, FDR and Ávila Camacho agreed to the "Global Settlement" of 1941, followed a year later by the signing of the wartime emergency Bracero Program (1942–1964), which in its twenty-two-year history allowed over 4.5 million Mexicans to take temporary jobs in the United States, mainly on agribusiness farms.[110] Tens of thousands of bracero workers were repatriated to Mexico after the war, some with bitter memories of mistreatment, but many others with the goal of returning to the United States to earn a decent living and provide their children with opportunities for advancement that were—and in many ways still are—unavailable to large segments of the Mexican population. To this day many Mexicans earning less than $10 per day dream of coming to the United States where work is more plentiful and wages for unskilled labor are over ten times higher than in Mexico. The postwar era would see a growing ambivalence of Anglo Americans who worried that Mexican immigrants were overrunning America—ruining it—at the same time that their labor was needed to keep food on the table at prices Americans could afford.

5

BRACEROS AND THE "WETBACK" INVASION

W hile Allied soldiers, including Mexican immigrants in the U.S. Army, fought and died to end the global ambition of the Axis Powers, many women and men on the home front worked in the factories and fields. "Rosie the Riveter" posters blanketed America to encourage women to work in the factories to take the place of men in uniform. But who was going to take the place of men doing the backbreaking labor in the mass production of America's fruits and vegetables? Mexican resident nationals and Mexican Americans had been providing this labor in the Southwest since the late nineteenth century, and especially after 1910, but many more were needed than were available during the war. The United States turned once more to its neighbor to the south, as it had during World War I, to supply the cheap labor necessary to keep food on the table, and to feed the fighting forces abroad. And Mexico, having hitched its economic wagon to the United States during the war, continued to provide agricultural workers, or braceros, to the United States as part of both countries' long-term goal of economic development through binational trade and labor agreements.

Between 1942 and 1964, Mexico provided much of the agricultural labor in the United States—4.5 million workers—but many Americans worried that undocumented workers, referred to as "wetbacks"—would settle in and gradually overwhelm Anglos by their sheer numbers. In response, the U.S. Justice Department authorized a massive roundup of unauthorized Mexican immigrants in the summer of 1954, called "Operation Wetback"— the precursor of a series of quasi-military operations along the border in the 1990s with names like Operation Gatekeeper (California, 1994), Operation Hold-the-Line (Texas, 1994), and Operation Safeguard (Arizona, 1999). The fear of a wetback invasion in the 1950s echoed the fear in the 1940s that the Axis Powers might invade the hemisphere through Mexico and prefigured the immigration backlash of the 1990s and border fence security measure after 9/11. Despite growing ties of bilateral cooperation and trade, our strongest ally and closest neighbor in the hemisphere continued to represent a threat on multiple fronts: racial, cultural, political, economic, and national security.

After the World War II, braceros continued to migrate to the United States to work for wages many times higher than in Mexico. Begun as a bilateral emergency war program between Mexico and the United States in 1942, and continued until 1964, the Bracero Program provided temporary Mexican contract laborers to work in agriculture to offset the loss of U.S. workers to the armed forces and defense industries. Those unable or unwilling to sign six-month temporary work contracts under the Bracero Program crossed the border illegally as *mojados* (literally, "wet people"), particularly in Texas where braceros had been banned until 1947 because of anti-Mexican discrimination. Five years after the war the *New York Times* featured an article titled "Mexicans Convert Border into Sieve," and an immigration official characterized the mass movement of Mexicans across the border as "perhaps the greatest peacetime invasion ever complacently suffered by any country under open, flagrant, contemptuous violation of its laws."[1] In 1953 the Border Patrol apprehended a record one million Mexicans entering the country illegally. The equivalent of 10 percent of the population of Mexico had crossed the border into the United States since the end of World War II, according to one immigration official, who candidly admitted that "there is nothing to stop the whole nation moving into the United States if it wants to."[2]

Border tensions and incidents tried the patience of government officials on both sides of the border. The U.S. Immigration and Naturalization Service (INS), Employment Service, and State Department blamed Mexico for the "wetback problem" for not increasing its border force in an effort to prevent workers from leaving Mexico. Mexican officials, on the other hand, believed that the problem of illegal entry was mainly the responsibility of the United States, since it had failed to impose sanctions on employers of undocumented workers. Those employers formed a powerful farm bloc in American politics, with support on Capitol Hill, and few politicians wanted to risk arousing the wrath of American farmers. Rather than confront the problem at its source—the employer—the United States concentrated its efforts instead on cat-and-mouse apprehensions and deportations, often of the same wetbacks. Border Patrol agents sometimes joked that "deportees beat them back into the U.S."[3] The joke was often not far from the truth. After a raid on his farm to deport wetback laborers, a carrot farmer in southern California loaned his own trucks to the INS to help Border Patrol agents transport 310 of his 345-man carrot-harvesting crew to the border for deportation to Mexicali. "The sooner they get to Mexicali," the field foreman reasoned, "the sooner they can re-cross the border and start back to work."[4] The INS maintained that any kind of *cordon sanitaire* along the 2,000-mile border with only 600 Border Patrol agents was impossible and therefore the agency had resorted to a strategy of "mobile defense in depth"— that is, rounding up illegal entrants on farms extending back hundreds of miles from the border.[5] "Economic conditions in Mexico are so bad," observed farm labor activist Ernesto Galarza, "that I doubt that the entire Mexican Army could stem the tide of wetbacks."[6]

The United States was caught in a tough bind: growers continued to rely on Mexican laborers, while others worried that wetbacks lowered wages for American agricultural workers and were subject to almost inhuman exploitation. Still others, concerned that the porous border provided easy access to communist infiltrators, demanded that the border be tightly controlled. "As Congress haggles over admitting even a thin trickle of refugees from Europe," editorialized the *Washington Post* in 1953, "it is worth remembering that a torrential stream of immigration pours continuously across the southern frontier of the United States" and provides "a sluiceway for spies and saboteurs." Rather than "strive so zealously to shut the portals of America in the faces of those fleeing from Communist territory and tyranny in Europe," the editor urged members of Congress to "devote some of their zeal to closing the enormous loopholes along the Rio Grande."[7] When President Dwight Eisenhower announced the decision to launch Operation Wetback, which Attorney General Herbert Brownell called "the greatest anti-alien drive in the history of the Southwest," the *Los Angeles Times* called it a "war on wetbacks." With the "wetback influx" averaging about 75,000 a month and steadily increasing, Brownell worried that "large numbers of subversives . . . may be entering the country under the guise of farm laborers."[8]

The historical truth is that the United States had relied heavily on Mexican labor in the Southwest since the late nineteenth century, before any immigration laws were in place to control the flow of immigrants from Europe or the Western Hemisphere. In fact, both the U.S. and Mexican governments regarded the entry of Mexicans into the United States until World War I mainly as cross-border "labor migration" rather than immigration.[9] The Immigration Act of 1917 erected for the first time barriers to the immigration of Mexican migrant laborers. According to this law, all aliens were assessed an $8 head tax and were required to pass a literacy test in one language in order to gain admittance into the United States. "Not surprisingly," wrote one historian, "these new legal barriers to immigration encouraged Mexican workers badly in need of employment to attempt to enter the United States illegally."[10] From World War I to the post–World War II era, the United States and Mexico have sought ways to legitimate what they could not effectively control, namely the overwhelming numbers of Mexicans crossing the border to work in the United States.

When the Mexican Farm Labor Program Agreement (which became known informally as the Bracero Program) between Mexico and the United States was signed in August 1942 to provide temporary contract workers from Mexico, few could have predicted that this emergency war measure would be renewed repeatedly until the mid-1960s. The brainchild of agricultural interests whose profits depended on a massive mobile and low-cost labor force, the agreement included guarantees as to wage rates, living conditions, and repatriation for the Mexican workers, while specifying that they were not to be employed to replace other workers or to reduce those workers' current wages. Shortly after the agreement was signed by both governments, the State Department announced, "The enrollment of men in the armed services, the movement of farm workers into industry, and the Government's program to increase agricultural production to meet wartime needs were causing a shortage of agricultural labor which could not be met by the recruiting of workers in the United States."[11]

American labor leaders did not agree. Whether or not a labor shortage existed was a subject of intense debate between farmers associations and agricultural unions, such as the National Farm Labor Union (NFLU) and the Confederación de Trabajadores Mexicanos en Norte América. Labor leaders like H. L. Mitchell, president of the NFLU, and labor advocate Ernesto Galarza, at the time head of the Office of Labor and Welfare Information of the Pan-American Union, argued that the purpose of guest worker programs was to flood the labor market to drive down wages for American workers and increase profits for the growers. Growers claimed that if they paid higher wages, their farms would fail to make a profit. But a study conducted by sociologists at the University of Texas reported that while agricultural workers in south Texas earned $2.25 per day, workers 150 miles north in Corpus Christi were getting $3 per day, and those 400 miles further north in the Texas Plains were getting $5.25 per day. South Texas growers, the report calculated, realized an extra $5,000,000 profit by using "alien and illegal labor" from across the border.[12] Farmer associations used braceros as a "mobile striking force" to head off unionization of farm workers, Mitchell argued, while farmers

Braceros waiting in line for contracts, Mexico City, ca. 1942. Archivo Fotográfico Fondo Hermanos Mayo, Archivo General de la Nación, Mexico City.

maintained that if they could not rely on an abundant and mobile workforce, entire harvests would rot in the fields.[13] But rather than raise wages high enough to attract American farm workers, growers preferred to hire wetback laborers. These unauthorized immigrants worked for whatever wages they could get and under any conditions because, as one journalist put it, "legally they are as much fugitives from justice as anyone who 'crashes' the immigration barriers at the Port of New York."[14]

When the call for braceros was announced in Mexican newspapers, thousands of Mexicans from Jalisco, Ciudad México, Tamaulipas, Baja California, Chihuahua, Zacatecas, Guanajuato, Michoacan, and Veracruz wrote to their local government to find out how to get jobs in California and other states as braceros.[15] Many more—tens of thousands—journeyed to Tijuana, Mexicali, and Ciudad Juárez, where most of them crossed the border without contracts.[16] The Mexican government sought to avoid the congestion at the border by establishing only one recruitment center located in Mexico City. One of the first braceros to come to work in California during the war returned home broke and disillusioned with the program. In Greeley, California, he was idle for days before receiving wages, which were barely sufficient to pay for his meals. In Yuba City, California, he

Bracero boarding train in Mexico City, ca. 1940s. Archivo Fotográfico Fondo Hermanos Mayo, Archivo General de la Nación, Mexico City.

worked in peach orchards but left because the cost of food was deducted from his wages whether he ate on the farm or not, making it difficult to save money. But news of mistreatment in the Mexican press did little to slow the wholesale emigration of Mexican workers to the United States.[17]

The Mexican government had authorized the United States to recruit a maximum of 20,000 track workers and 75,000 agricultural workers in

MEXICANS IN THE MAKING OF AMERICA

1943.[18] However, since braceros were banned from entering Texas after 1943, Texas growers relied on wetback labor, often with the willing cooperation of U.S. immigration officials and the Border Patrol, who with a nod and wink let thousands of Mexicans cross into Texas during the critical harvest periods. When Texas growers complained that the Border Patrol was rounding up and deporting "illegals," INS officials instructed the Border Patrol to deport only those wetbacks "not engaged in the harvesting of perishable crops." A token few "repeaters" were jailed for short periods of time before being deported.[19] In a futile effort to seal the border, President Manuel Ávila Camacho instructed the secretary of national defense to commission a contingent of military forces to cooperate with U.S. immigration authorities to prevent the illegal exodus of Mexicans. The U.S. government subsequently signed a bilateral agreement with Mexico in which it also promised to strengthen its border security forces. Meanwhile the INS continued to complain that the Mexican government had not done enough to seal the border, while the Mexican government accused the INS of relaxing border surveillance in order to provide Texas growers with wetback labor.[20]

With so many Mexicans crossing the 1,000-mile Texas-Mexico border, Texas at the end of 1944 had become a net exporter of labor to other regions of the United States. The Mexican consul in Austin reported that the clamor for Mexican bracero labor in Texas proved that what growers most wanted were "trabajadores baratos" (cheap workers)—and that with the cooperation of U.S. and Mexican border authorities, had turned a blind eye to the "clandestine immigration" of more than 30,000 undocumented Mexican workers in Texas.[21]

When the ban on braceros was temporarily lifted in April 1947, some 20,000 braceros entered Texas before the ban was reinstated in October over a dispute involving wages in the El Paso area. Of those, 15,000 returned to Mexico at the end of their six-month contracts, and 5,000 remained. "Where are they? What has become of them?" asked one journalist. He suggested that they joined other wetback laborers on farms that did not hire braceros: "As long as illegal workers are available to employers, why should they undertake the expense and trouble of contracting legal workers? But until the 'wetback' problem is solved with legality and human dignity," he concluded, "it seems useless to attempt a labor contracting program for the border zone."[22] Despite the army of wetbacks entering Texas each year, Texas governor Beauford Jester, alarmed by the prospect of a labor shortage for the critically important Texas cotton industry, asked Secretary of State George C. Marshall to intercede with the Mexican government to lift the ban on braceros put in place because of the long history in Texas of mistreatment of Mexican immigrant workers. Jester publicly apologized to President Miguel Alemán for the "unfortunate incidents of discrimination" in Texas. The Mexican government refused to lift the ban and added counties in Mississippi and Arkansas to the list of regions banned from receiving braceros.[23]

In 1948, about 40,000 braceros were recruited to work in fifteen states. Arkansas farms employed the most with 11,496, followed by California (10,711) and Mississippi (5,065).[24] During the war Arkansas cotton farmers relied on the labor of Italian and German prisoners of war because many African Americans had left to work in factories in northern cities. After the war the governor of Arkansas requested 30,000 braceros for the state.[25] Shortly after the first few thousand began to arrive, hundreds of braceros petitioned their government to be immediately repatriated because of poor living conditions. They were housed in shacks with no electricity, plumbing, toilets or kitchen facilities (the same shacks abandoned by the African-American workers), paid low wages, no medical services— in short, according to one Mexican official, 2,000 braceros in Pine Bluff, Arkansas, were living in "a state of semi-slavery." The Mexican government immediately canceled the Bracero Program for the Jefferson County Farmers Association of Arkansas for having violated no fewer than five articles of the agreement.[26]

Braceros, for example, were entitled to medical services, according to the contract, although at their own expense, unless the injury or illness was job-related. Employers sometimes contracted with insurance companies to provide medical services. One insurance company charged each bracero 13 cents per day for medical coverage from their weekly earnings of $25, although it provided for only one unlicensed person with no training, Elvira Ruiz, to provide medical services for over 600 braceros in Brawley, California. One of the braceros she treated, Ezequiel Arismendi, suffered a severe case of influenza and had to be hospitalized. The doctor who admitted him to the hospital, Benjamin Yellen, helped Arismendi file a lawsuit against the Mid Continent Casualty Insurance Company and the Pan-American Underwriters for using unlicensed medical personnel to treat braceros and for refusing to pay for his hospitalization. Yellen said Arismendi was given "pills and injections without being given a physical examination." Elvira Ruiz claimed to have acted under the supervision of a doctor. After a heated trial, the court ruled that it was not illegal for a person without training or license to provide medical services "if acting under the direction of a doctor." Nevertheless, the judge told Ruiz's lawyer that he held his client "morally responsible for the worst medical abuse I've ever heard of." Although it had won its case, the insurance company sued Dr. Yellen for helping Arismendi file his suit, claiming that Yellen was "practicing law without a license."[27] Helping Mexicans file lawsuits for medical malpractice was an offense the insurance company could not ignore. Such unethical and unprofessional practices plagued the health and well-being of braceros, thousands of whom from all over the United States—California, Wyoming, Montana, New Mexico, Arizona, Arkansas, Mississippi, Michigan, Illinois, and Pennsylvania—wrote letters to the Mexican president about injuries, accidents, breaches of contract, and poor working conditions.[28]

The most serious instances of mistreatment often involved braceros recruited under the Railroad Bracero Program of 1943, mainly involving wages and working conditions.[29] Workers were often not provided adequate winter clothing for the "cold zones," like Ohio and Illinois in the dead of winter. An Ohio merchant saw fifteen Mexicans who had just arrived in Elyria, Ohio, for work on the railroads with no winter clothes when the temperature was 10 degrees Fahrenheit.[30] About fifty braceros were transported to the tiny town of Beaver Dams in upstate New York in the dead of winter where they were housed in a row of unheated crew cars. Fortunately for them, the townspeople and railroad officials provided them with winter clothes, and soon afterward organized English classes, birthday parties, and a small "orchestra" of braceros who had brought along simple musical instruments. "They came to help us win the war," said one of the residents of Beaver Dams, "Now they're going home as good-will ambassadors."[31]

Most braceros did not fare as well because to house and feed them properly, and to pay them living wages, would have been to defeat the purpose of hiring cheap labor. But there were some notable exceptions. One bracero in Arizona, Lazar Bautista, wrote to the superintendent of the Southern Pacific railway to thank him for the opportunity to aid in the war effort: "I am a not a bracero who came just to earn money, no, I want to help so that the democracies are victorious . . . and I am thankful for the way in which you have treated us."[32] Three other Mexican track workers of Southern Pacific Railway in California wrote A. T. Mercier, president of the Southern Pacific Railway in the United States, "In spite of the severe circumstances of the war we are going through, the Southern Pacific has not neglected or abandoned us for one minute, and we are completely satisfied and proud to have been of service to you."[33]

Many other railroad workers were not as lucky. An investigation of over 175 bracero railroad camps in New York, New Jersey, and Connecticut revealed that workers, ignorant of the English language or their rights as workers, signed away their compensation rights when injured on the job. Medical care was rarely provided, and always at the worker's expense. In one camp in New Jersey, two braceros for the Pennsylvania Railroad went on a hunger strike to protest the fact that they were required to pay for emergency appendectomies that would have cost them their total wages for the length of their contracts, leaving nothing for themselves or their families. The railway braceros were particularly incensed that they were required to pay 3.25 percent of their wages to the Railroad Retirement Fund, which would pay off in minute pensions when they reached the age of sixty-five. The life expectancy of Mexican track laborers at the time was thirty-four, and it would have been almost impossible for their families in Mexico to understand how to apply for and collect the pensions when the workers died. Murray W. Lattimer, chairman of the Railroad Retirement Fund, suggested that Congress enact a law to permit the funds to be transferred to the accounts of individuals in Mexico's social security fund.[34]

At the end of their six-month contracts, braceros were to return to the border where the Mexican government was required by the terms of the Bracero Program to provide transportation to the interior of Mexico, hundreds of miles from the border where most of them lived. The Mexican government's slow response to providing adequate train service to the interior forced many braceros to remain in border cities like Ciudad Juárez, waiting for transportation home. Both governments agreed to let braceros work beyond the period of their six-month contracts until more trains and buses could be arranged to transport them from the border. The Mexican government put more trains in service after the war—six trains that ran continually between the border and Mexico City, with a capacity of transporting 20,000 workers a month—and the U.S. Army assisted in Texas by transporting braceros, with the Mexican government's approval, to Ciudad Juárez where trains could take them to Mexico City.[35]

The original Bracero Program, amended three times from 1942 to 1947, terminated on December 31, 1947. A new agreement was signed on February 21, 1948, that required the INS and the U.S. Employment Service to certify that a labor shortage actually existed in the region where employers were requesting braceros and that the temporary admission of Mexican nationals would not result in the displacement of American farm workers "or otherwise detrimentally affect such labor in this country."[36] Other articles guaranteed return transportation at a cost to the employer, medical services, salaries set according to the prevailing wage of the region, and "hygienic lodgings." In addition, Mexican consuls were granted free access to all places of employment to ensure the protection of bracero workers.

Article 29 called for both governments to "take all proper measures to prevent the illegal migration of Mexican agricultural workers to the United States and to insure the prompt repatriation of Mexican workers illegally in the U.S."[37]

The Mexican government took the opportunity to draw up a list of instructions for braceros to remind them of all that their government had done to protect their interests. The first instruction tellingly reminded the workers never to forget that their loyalty was to Mexico, where they were born, where the people spoke their language, and where their families continued to live. They were reminded to preserve their traditions, which "had shaped your spirit and where your race [raza] is the guardian of your destiny." The document reminded them to learn as much as they could from their work in order to contribute to the development and progress of Mexico when they returned, and never to forget the great sacrifice their wives and children were making in their absence, and therefore to save as much of their earnings as possible to establish a small patrimony for their families. And finally, they were told that their absence from Mexico would teach them to appreciate better the opportunities their country offered them "if you exercise the same ambition, strength of character and aspirations for a better life that now impels you to seek those opportunities in a foreign country."[38]

The Mexican government had further informed the braceros that it had obtained assurances from the U.S. government that they would be treated with "human dignity and justice," and that they would not be subjected to social or economic discrimination on account of their race, beliefs, color, or nationality. The guarantees of fair treatment, the government added, extended only to those whose good conduct, honesty, and decency rendered them "worthy of the protection of the Mexican government." Braceros must obey all the laws and customs of their host country "in order to demonstrate that Mexico is a civilized nation." Personal hygiene—showers, clean clothes, grooming—was not only important for maintaining their general health, they were told, but also to avoid the humiliation of being denied admittance to restaurants, movie houses, stores, and other public places. They were even reminded of the dire consequences of crossing a state line in the United States "with a woman who is not family."[39]

Like the original agreement, the new Bracero Program of 1948 accomplished little more than ratify and renew a guest worker program that could not guarantee employer compliance with contracts, or prevent their hiring wetback labor. But that did not prevent both governments from signing an International Executive Agreement in 1949 requiring employers of braceros to sign an oath not to employ illegal workers and to provide all hospital and medical costs "necessitated by occupational accidents and/or diseases suffered or incurred by Mexican agricultural workers."[40] The worst that could happen to employers who violated the terms of the contract was to have their contracts canceled. No fines were levied against employers of undocumented workers, and those whose contracts were canceled, especially employers in the four border states, generally had little difficulty hiring undocumented immigrants who were willing to work for wages below those guaranteed in the bracero agreement.[41] Farmers claimed that the cost of hiring braceros was simply too high: they had to pay workers' transportation back to Mexico; they had to provide adequate housing and pay the workers on days when there was no work. As one California farmer put it, "To use this labor legally, we've got to have a . . . contract that farmers can afford."[42]

Tensions developed between the State Department and the Mexican government over the latter's refusal to allow braceros to be recruited from its northern state of Chihuahua, bordering on New Mexico and Texas, for employment in New Mexico, Arizona, and the mountain states in the west. Mexico worried that the congestion of unemployed braceros in the north would overwhelm the limited resources of cities to care for them. The State Department argued that if these workers were not formally recruited at the border, it would be "impossible to prevent their entry as wetbacks," in which case their salaries would be only one-third of the amount they would have received had they been legally recruited.[43] Meanwhile, thousands of Mexicans headed for the border at Ciudad Juárez-El Paso because they had lost hope of receiving contracts at recruitment centers located in the northern cities of Monterrey (Nuevo León) and Guaymas (Sonora)—neither city on the border—and there was no recruitment center at all in the northern state of Chihuahua, which bordered west Texas and New Mexico.[44]

In an unprecedented move that took the U.S. government by surprise and stunned the Mexican government, the INS opened the border on October 13, 1948, to thousands of braceros and turned them over to American farmers. Over 4,000 dashed across the border at El Paso in two days where they were put under "technical arrest" and then "paroled" to the Texas Employment Commission to be transported to cotton fields in west Texas and New Mexico. The unilateral opening of the border by the INS made headlines in both countries.[45] Grover Wilmoth, district INS director, claimed that he received instructions from Washington to "use his own judgment" in meeting the "critical and urgent need for farm laborers." Wilmoth denied that he allowed Mexicans to enter the United States illegally; rather, he said, "we endeavored to take into custody all Mexican farm laborers who effected illegal entry." However, instead of deporting them immediately to Mexico, he "paroled them to certain farmers shown to be in immediate need of farm laborers."[46]

The consul general of El Paso, Raúl Michel, fired off a letter to Wilmoth demanding to know why he had given the order to let Mexicans into the United States in absolute violation of the Bracero Program. Infuriated by the flagrant violation of the agreement, Michel demanded that Wilmoth "rectify or ratify, whichever the case may be, the absolute refusal of cooperation given to this Consulate by your [Immigration] Service."[47] President Miguel Alemán canceled the Bracero Program signed with the United States in February 1948 and immediately ordered the Mexican Army to the border to prevent Mexicans from leaving the country illegally.[48] The Mexican chargé d'affaires, Rafael de la Colina, delivered a formal protest, described as a "stemwinder" by U.S. diplomats, informing the State Department that the Mexican government had terminated the agreement as a direct consequence of the INS "permitting and, in fact, facilitating the illegal entry of Mexican farm workers into Texas." The State Department apologized for the "lamentable action" of the INS and promised to take corrective action. The chargé d'affaires further pointed out that the uncontrolled exodus of so many workers from northern Mexico represented a "serious economic loss to the agricultural production of that area" and suggested that the U.S. government punish the INS officials responsible for the action in order for both governments to "find a quick and satisfactory solution to this disagreeable matter."[49]

After an investigation, Paul Daniels, head of the Division of American Republics at the State Department, reported to the Mexican government that having permitted the entry of Mexican nationals "was indeed illegal and they were not, as required by Article 29 of the Agreement, immediately deported to Mexico." Daniels apologized for the "serious instance of noncompliance" and issued an order to the INS that all Mexicans who had been allowed to enter illegally be promptly returned to Ciudad Juárez.[50] During the five days in which the border was opened, an estimated eight to ten thousand Mexicans were "arrested" to work on America's farms. The chastened Wilmoth dutifully informed the Mexican consul in El Paso that the 8,173 braceros, whom he had "paroled for employment" from October 13 to 18, had been returned to Mexico.[51] At the same time, H. P. Brady, chief of the "alien control section" of the INS, announced that thirty-five new Border Patrol agents had been added to the 175 already on the Texas-Mexico border. The total number of wetbacks apprehended in a few months in 1947, he said, exceeded the totals for a whole year prior to World War II.[52] The following year the INS pulled twenty Border Patrol agents from the Vermont border with Canada and assigned them to temporary duty on the U.S.-Mexico border to halt the "terrific influx" of Mexicans.[53]

With so many unauthorized immigrants entering the United States, whole villages in Mexico were emptied of their able-bodied men. Fields lay fallow, as Mexican farmers could not maintain their level of operation without the labor of village men. From a small village in Durango, Carmen Gallegos González told the Mexican president that the Bracero Program had plunged her village into "a time of true poverty"—that the farmers had been abandoned by their government, just as their village men had abandoned their fields to work on el Otro Lado. She asked him to listen to "the voice of defenseless children" left behind and feel the "pain and misery of the suffering people" of her village.[54] José Hernández Serrano, one of the thousands of husbands and fathers who left his family behind, implored the Mexican president, Manuel Ávila Camacho, to modernize agricultural production in Mexico so that families who are unable to make a decent living on their farms are not forced to leave Mexico.[55]

The unprecedented numbers of Mexicans crossing the border in the decade following the war, whether as braceros or wetbacks, aroused the concern of many Americans who feared that the cost of cheap Mexican labor was simply too high. A popular radio broadcaster in Los Angeles, B. Tarkington Dowlen, noted that over half a million Mexicans labored in southern California counties and worried that they would change the economy and the culture of the region for the worse. His main concern was that Mexico itself was "sick physically," claiming that 70 percent of all Mexicans were "afflicted with syphilis," were "inherently dishonest," seldom took a bath, and were "practically illiterate." On the bright side, he concluded, the United States had already "established a precedent for the rounding up and concentration of undesirables, for if we as a people could ride rough shod over the property rights of the American-born Japanese, over their citizenship and their constitutional rights, and intern them solely because of their race and nationality, then with this precedent established we can do it again and again to any group or nationality who threaten our economic structure, our peace, our security or our happiness."[56] Others felt differently. The owner of a construction company who employed many Mexican workers wrote the president of Mexico that he should "restrict all Mexicans from leaving Mexico to help harvest the crops here" because as far as the farmers were concerned, "as soon as the harvest is over they are Greasers and Wet Backs." He added, "I cannot see why Puerto Ricans, negroes, and Filipinos are more welcome than our next door neighbor."[57] Whether we like it or not, a journalist from the border city of Brownsville wrote, "These people are going to sink roots in our soil."[58]

While the debate on Mexican immigration continued to be waged in the Congress, the press, and in the diplomatic corps of Mexico and the United States, the presidents of both nations insisted that nothing could stand in the way of their friendship and growing economic and political ties. President Harry Truman, the first U.S. president to visit Mexico City, ignored the problem of illegal immigration but pledged his commitment to the Good Neighbor policy and the doctrine of nonintervention, declaring "that a strong nation does not have the right to impose its will by reason of its strength on a weaker nation."[59] Alemán also side-stepped the issue, but acknowledged that "if prejudices have been an obstacle" for both nations to overcome for the sake of inter-American friendship, "then let us make the education of our children and of our youth a liberation from that inexcusable obstacle." He added: "Our reciprocal needs are so deep, so numerous and so varied that I deem it superfluous to rehearse at this moment" and concluded that Mexico and the United States "are bound to live together and to prosper together."[60] The junior senator from Minnesota, Hubert Humphrey, hoped that the "friendly relationship" between the United States and Mexico would "always continue to exist."[61]

The Mexican government was particularly encouraged by Truman's emphasis on securing human rights for its citizens who were "still denied equal opportunity for education, for jobs and economic advancement, and the expression of their views at the polls. . . . Any denial of human rights is a denial of the basic beliefs of democracy and of our regard for the worth of each individual."[62] The government also took note of the findings of the President's Commission on Migratory Labor, which reported in 1951 that the U.S. government contributed to the problem of illegal immigration by ignoring violations of the immigration laws and caving into political pressure from agricultural interests who were the main employers of wetback labor. The report was especially critical of the INS, the U.S. Employment Service, and the State Department.[63] The commission's recommendations were largely ignored, in part because of the war in Korea and the rapidly growing fear of global communism.

Nevertheless, Truman sent his administrative assistant, David H. Stowe, and other officials to Mexico City to negotiate a new Bracero Program that would address the concerns of the Mexican government over full compliance with the terms of bracero contracts. Truman stressed that improved working conditions and living standards for U.S. citizens and Mexican contract workers required that both governments "take steps to shut off the stream of Mexican citizens immigrating illegally into the United States."[64] The following year Truman proposed legislation to the Congress of imposing a fine of $2,000 and/or prison sentences of five years for employers of illegal Mexican immigrants, but legislators representing the interests of agribusiness farming in the Southwest defeated Truman's proposal.[65]

Once again the U.S. government was torn in two directions. While the Korean War made it necessary to increase agricultural production, which could only be achieved with the assistance of Mexican laborers, Congress was coming under increasing pressure from American citizens to do something about "the invasion of the wetbacks." Emanuel Celler, chairman of the House Judiciary Committee, became alarmed when he learned that immigration authorities had arrested 579,000 Mexicans for illegally entering the United States in 1950: "While we keep tightly closed our Atlantic and Pacific coasts to the entrance of subversives, our Southern border is open to their infiltration." The subcommittee's objective was to work out an amendment to the Immigration Law making "it a crime to harbor and employ illegal immigrants."[66] The legislation passed in 1952 made it a crime to *harbor* deportable aliens, but the Texas congressional delegation inserted the so-called "Texas Proviso" explicitly exempting employers from any penalties for *employing* undocumented workers.[67] Only those "harboring" undocumented workers faced penalties, such as "coyotes" and other human traffickers, whose very livelihood depended on their ignoring national and international laws.

The periodic increase in the number of Border Patrol agents, including reassigning agents from the Canadian border, reflected the penny-pinching sums the Congress appropriated for border security. "With the purse half shut," labor leader Ernesto Galarza observed, "the gate could remain half open."[68] And it did, except when the INS chose to open it all the way as it did in 1917 and again in 1948. In testimony before Congress in 1951, one INS official brashly explained how the INS managed the gate: "We do feel we have the authority to permit to remain in the United States aliens who are here as agricultural workers whether they are here legally or not."[69] This was hardly news. Immigration officials on the border for decades viewed their role as managing the flow of undocumented migration across the border, particularly the Texas segment, to ensure that farmers had an abundant supply of low-wage workers during the harvest season.

At the same time the Border Patrol was engaged in deporting undocumented immigrants, the U.S. travel industry was stepping up its efforts to lure travelers to Mexico. American Airlines created a full-page color advertisement of a young, white middle-class couple examining a silver serving set in Taxco. The text read: "Mexico—Silver Treasures for a Song. Quaint, old Taxco, the Silver City, is loaded with tempting 'buys' and dreamlike prices too. (Dollars really travel in Mexico!) When you've had your shopping spree . . . go down to beautiful Acapulco for some carefree sunning and swimming."[70] Mexico's single greatest export item was fantasy vacations for free-spending gringos. While tourists left behind millions of dollars in return for goods and services, braceros, Mexico's second largest export, sent back millions of dollars in savings to support families, build homes, and start small businesses.

When the Bracero Program expired on December 31, 1953, negotiations between the two governments continued for its renewal.[71] In the interim, the Mexican government stationed "armed guards" at some border points to prevent nationals from crossing the border, but withdrew the guards after a few days when the effort proved wholly ineffective.[72] During the House Committee on Agriculture hearings, the Congress of Industrial Organizations president, Walter Reuther, opposed renewing the Bracero Program on the grounds that "thousands of American farm workers are unemployed and available for work," to which Representative Leroy Johnson, Republican of California, replied, "we would be delighted to use American workers, but they just aren't available." Americans, he said, "just don't want to work at stoop labor." More ominously, he added, "consumers in the East, Midwest and South faced the prospect of higher prices for fruits and vegetables" unless a new agreement with Mexico was reached soon, or else crops "would be unharvested or have to be destroyed."[73]

Mexico and the United States signed a new two-year labor agreement in March 1954 that made changes to the bilateral contract.[74] Among other things, Mexico agreed to open recruiting stations closer to the border. In the past recruiting stations were only in the interior, a practice that encouraged laborers living close to the border to cross illegally as wetbacks.[75] For its part, the United States, through the Labor Department, once again agreed to certify and publicize the prevailing wage for U.S. workers performing the same work.[76] Ernesto Galarza pointed out that since 1942 the bracero agreements had lacked a mechanism for determining what were prevailing wages in a given region—that "the prevailing wage tends to be what the growers say it is."[77] Once more, however, farmer associations and their congressional supporters won the day over the objections of numerous labor unions, as well as Mexican-American civil rights organizations, such as the League of United Latin American Citizens and the American G.I. Forum. As with prior bilateral agreements, the stipulations about wages, medical services, and working conditions were hardly worth the paper they were printed on since most farmers regarded the agreement "only as a sop for Mexico" and ignored the provisions with virtual impunity.[78]

During the period from 1947 until 1955 the United States witnessed two distinct responses to undocumented migration. The first, which lasted from 1947 to 1951, involved mass legalization; the second, from 1954 to 1955, mass expulsion. The first process was called "drying out the wetbacks." The second, "Operation Wetback."[79]

In the first process—mass legalization—undocumented workers already in the United States were, under an agreement with the Mexican government, given bracero contracts without having to return to Mexico where braceros were recruited and processed. As a result, more undocumented workers were legalized in the United States in the five years following the war than were braceros contracted in Mexico. It is difficult to imagine how legalizing undocumented workers was intended to reduce the number of illegal entrants, since legalization of wetbacks already in the United States became an incentive for Mexicans to enter the United States without going through the trouble of obtaining bracero contracts. And it was trouble. Mexican authorities denied contracts to all females and those who were too old, too young, too sick, or too poor to pay bribes. Each bracero applicant was first required to obtain a "tarjeta de precontratación," a precontract card, from city officials who could only issue a limited number. The Mexican government established bracero quotas for each state, and the state for each municipality. Municipal authorities immediately saw an opportunity to earn some extra money and sold the precontract cards to would-be braceros at prices that often plunged them and their families into considerable debt before they even left town. Some officials received as much as 19,000 pesos in bribes for issuing bracero precontracts. Although the Mexican government was thoroughly apprised of the practice by the numerous letters demanding action, only a token few officials were indicted for fraud or given prison sentences.[80]

The second stage, Operation Wetback, had been planned at least six months in advance by order of Attorney General Herbert Brownell, who told a group of delegates from labor and church organizations that the Justice Department was "developing a program to control more effectively the flow of 'wetbacks' from Mexico into the United States."[81] Public pressure had been mounting across America since the end of World War II for the government to do something to seal the border. Only six months before, thousands of braceros stormed the border fence at Calexico, California. According to one newspaper account, Border Patrol agents, deputy sheriffs

Mexican workers storm the fence at the United States-Mexico border, Mexicali (Mexico). Courtesy of Los Angeles Times Photographic Archive, Department of Special Collections, Charles E. Young Research Library, UCLA.

and city police "crouched in a football stance, repulsed three determined assaults" of 7,500 Mexicans "trying to break into California for work on the farm harvests," after immigration officials refused to admit more than 500 braceros. The Border Patrol lined up trucks from the Fire Department to barricade the border, while firemen stood "ready to loose high pressure streams on the Mexican horde." The 16-foot-high tempered steel fence, according to one observer, "swayed perilously under the onslaught of the massed Mexican humanity." Six border guards were knocked down and trampled. A harvest of carrots and lettuce worth $20 million lay just beyond the fence, but immigration officials closed the border because of the high number of undocumented workers who had already broken into the region.[82]

Operation Wetback, a quasi-military campaign headed by INS commissioner General Joseph Swing, a veteran of the 101st Airborne and personal friend of President Eisenhower, began in June in southern California and moved to Texas by mid-July. State, county, and municipal police, as well as the military, worked with the Border Patrol to round up hundreds of thousands of undocumented workers who were deported by land, sea, and air to the border and often to the interior of Mexico. On the first day of the operation, the Border Patrol apprehended and deported 4,800 undocumented workers. Roadblocks were set up in the Rio Grande Valley of Texas to prevent wetbacks from fleeing north, while additional Border Patrol agents were brought in from the Canadian border to help out.[83] The INS claimed that it had deported over a million illegal entrants, but that number likely included Mexicans who voluntarily repatriated themselves rather than be apprehended and forcibly deported. In the San Antonio district of the INS, which included all of Texas but El Paso and some western counties, the Border Patrol apprehended over 80,000 Mexicans, while the INS estimated that over 500,000 had fled to Mexico before the operation began.[84]

The Mexican government had given its approval to Operation Wetback (Operación Espaldas Mojadas), providing transportation costs for deportees to reach the interior of Mexico, but the Mexican press, ever willing and ready to document the mistreatment of Mexican nationals in the United States, published little about the operation, relying mainly on United Press reports published in McAllen, Texas, and other border cities on the U.S. side.[85] Mexican nationals in Chicago, many of them former braceros, were infuriated by the Mexican government's quiet support for the operation, and together with the Comité de Habla Hispana of the United Packinghouse Workers of America, condemned the Mexican government for its failure to protect the rights of the deportees.[86]

American public opinion generally supported Operation Wetback, except in some places in California, Arizona, and Texas where farmers and other citizens strenuously objected to the operation.[87] The *Laredo Times* featured an article titled "Wetback Trek May Become Death March," with photographs of Mexicans deported into the desert to begin "the skin-shriveling trek" to a Mexican town 40 miles away.[88] David Moore, an American in Yuma, Arizona, outraged over the rounding up of Mexicans as if they were stray cattle and the abandoning of them at the border, wrote directly to Mexican president Ruiz Cortines: "Thousands of Mexicans in these and other border towns are without food and shelter, and no one seems to be doing anything about it. These are some of the finest men and women in the world . . . and never have I been approached by one asking for charity. Always it is a request for work. . . . These men have helped to clear and level the deserts of the Great Southwest and brought into being one of the most fruitful gardens man has ever created [and] they have helped to build an agricultural empire in Arizona."[89]

Moore attributed Operation Wetback to the fear of communism raised by the McCarthy hearings. Attorney General Brownell, who ordered Operation Wetback, justified the action on the grounds that subversives entered the country "disguised" as farm laborers.[90] One journalist reported that "Mexico has become a center of undercover Soviet activity. All this because the Mexican-American border is wide open." *Time* magazine featured an article on the operation called "Keeping the Communists Out."[91] Nevada Democratic senator Pat McCarran, who according to a *New York Times* editorial seemed "to be frightened to death by every foreigner except General Franco," fought hard in the Congress to erect an "Iron Curtain about the borders of the United States" and warned that among the millions of aliens illegally in the United States, a number of them were "militant Communists, Sicilian bandits, and other criminals."[92]

Most Latin-American countries, including Mexico, were mainly concerned with economic development and did not support U.S. anticommunist activity in Latin America, much less in the United States. Mexico opposed the anticommunist resolution proposed by the United States at the Tenth Inter-American Conference in Caracas that "domination or control of the political institutions of any American state by the international Communist movement . . . would constitute a threat . . . and call for appropriate action." Most delegates from Latin America reluctantly voted for the resolution, worried that opposing the United States would result in higher tariffs and fewer development loans. As one delegate put it, "You don't always see the sun, but you know it's there." Argentina and Mexico chose not to vote at all on the proposal, fearing a return to U.S. policy of military and political intervention in Latin America.[93]

While many Americans worried about the threat of communist infiltration at the border, the main impetus behind Operation Wetback was to crack down on the flow of undocumented Mexicans over the border. The Congress and the public generally regarded the operation as a success, in part because anti-wetback public opinion had begun to affect the attitude of employers toward the illegal status of their workers—though not their reliance on Mexican workers. The INS put out the word that Mexicans attempting to enter the country illegally would be subject to prosecution and jail terms, and employers were warned that frequent INS raids would interrupt their farm operations if they continued to rely on wetback labor. The success in reducing the volume of illegal immigration led INS commissioner Swing to report a year later that "The so-called 'wetback' problem no longer exists. . . . The border has been secured."[94] The border, of course, had not been secured, then or at any time up to the time of writing, but the flow of undocumented migration slowed considerably in the years after 1954.

The substitution of bracero labor for undocumented workers came at a huge cost, as both the Mexican and U.S. governments generally abandoned the protections afforded bracero workers. Mexico feared canceling the program because it could not risk ending an important safety valve for its rapidly growing population and the inability of the Mexican economy to provide adequate employment for it.[95] Moreover, the uncontrolled exodus of Mexican farm workers pointed out the failure of the Mexican government's efforts at land reform and therefore became a volatile issue in Mexican domestic politics. Mario Lasso, former consul general of Chicago during World War II, suggested to President Ruiz Cortines that he inaugurate a national recolonization program—Comisión Nacional de Colonización—to bring back tens of thousands of Mexican farm laborers to help them find land in Mexico to buy.[96] The United States, on the other hand, was not about to shut down the transnational labor force that kept America's farms running, but it did need to control the flow of undocumented workers to avoid the growing concern of the citizenry that Mexicans were invading the country. In other words, as one historian aptly put it, "after 1954 the bracero program became little more than a formally sanctioned recruitment system for the employment of 'wetbacks' in U.S. agriculture."[97]

Even INS officials couldn't resist the temptation of hiring their own Mexican workers. The practice came to light when Texas senator Lyndon Johnson asked Commissioner Swing during a public senate hearing in 1956 on immigration appropriations if he had a Mexican maid. Swing replied, "I certainly do." Johnson asked if the maid had been recruited through the INS. Swing explained that while he was on an inspection tour of El Paso he told the INS district director: "It is hard to get a maid in Washington. I wonder if there is any little Mexican girl over in Juarez who would like to emigrate . . . to work for me." Realizing the implication of his admission, Swing immediately asked that his comments be "off the record," to which Senator Johnson promptly replied, "General, I want to warn you that it is pretty difficult to keep it off the record when you have a bunch of newspapermen here." An INS career employee had tipped off Johnson of the practice and of the many man hours expended by INS employees in obtaining maids for INS officials in Washington. Johnson, who won his senate seat with the help of the Mexican-American vote, told Swing, on the record: "If the Immigration Service is out soliciting maids for officials in Washington, we ought to know about it."[98]

The Bracero Program continued to have its critics until its eventual termination in 1964. Labor groups maintained unrelenting pressure on Congress to end the program. Local health officials worried that braceros and un-documented workers aggravated community health problems and over-taxed health facilities. Local school officials found themselves swamped at the beginning or end of the school year, depending on harvest cycles, and social workers complained of the absence of facilities for the proper care of children and the inadequate housing in which they were required to live. Many Mexican-American agricultural workers were forced to leave their homes in South Texas to harvest crops farther north to avoid competition with braceros and unauthorized immigrants in Texas. For these workers, whether U.S. citizens or Mexican nationals, hoeing sugar beets, picking cotton, and harvesting all manner of vegetables was the only kind of work available to them—work that had no seniority, no security, no employment rights, and no experience or skills required.[99]

For many Americans, wetbacks and braceros had become a menace to American society, having quickly forgotten how much they depended on their labor during World War II when braceros were hailed as the "rear-guard" and "soldiers on the farm front." In the years immediately after the war, politicians, farmers, railroad executives, chambers of commerce, mayors, governors, and ordinary citizens had nothing but praise for braceros. The Inter-American Council of Ohio wrote to President Manuel Ávila Camacho: "It is well known now that one of the decisive factors in our victory was the efficient and almost super-human performance of our foundries, our farms and our railroads, which produced and moved raw materials, arms, ammunition and men. The service of the men from Mexico in keeping our trains rolling deserves the special gratitude of both Mexicans and Americans. The destinies of our two great countries have never been more closely fused."[100] In an open letter to bracero workers, the presidents of the Southern Pacific Company, the Northwest Pacific Railroad Company, and the San Diego and Arizona Eastern Railway Company wrote: "As good soldiers of democracy, you responded patriotically and with magnificent spirit. Without your help, I don't know how we could have kept our Victory Trains running without interruption."[101] The governor of Arizona, Sidney Osborn, acknowledged that "our state owes much in its settlement and development to citizens of Mexican derivation."[102] The Associated Farmers of California expressed "heartfelt appreciation to the Republic of Mexico and its loyal citizens for their great contribution to the successful prosecution of the war, and the cause of world freedom."[103]

If the long history of Mexican undocumented workers to the United States has made a mockery of U.S. immigration laws, much of the blame must be placed with powerful agricultural interests and our government's refusal to enact tough laws with stiff penalties for employers hiring workers who come to the U.S. illegally. Throughout the era of the Bracero Program the Mexican government pleaded with the United States to enforce sanctions against employers hiring unauthorized immigrants, but the U.S. government consistently sided with the agribusiness growers of cotton, fruit, and vegetables who had become addicted to cheap, nonunionized Mexican labor. "Sure we use wetback labor," reported one farm foreman in California's Imperial Valley. "So does almost everybody here. We have to. Americans won't do this kind of work. They can't. It gets too hot to kneel out here and tie carrots—too hot for everybody but these Mexicans."[104] George I. Sánchez, director of the University of Texas Study of Spanish-Speaking People, noted with an exemplary grasp of the obvious that measures taken to stop the flow of illegal immigration were "wholly inadequate—and I strongly suspect that they are purposefully so."[105]

Agribusiness farms have regularly relied on Mexican labor—in fact, they owe their very existence to Mexican workers. If employers could not hire Mexicans, they would not resort to hiring American workers. They would close down and move their business to where the labor is cheap, which in fact is what many agribusiness owners have done: they now rent land in Mexico to raise their crops. In 2007 Steve Scaroni, owner of a $50 million business growing lettuce and broccoli in California, moved his operation to Celaya, Mexico, where there's no shortage of labor, the wages are lower than in the United States, and he doesn't have to worry about having his workforce deported for being illegal. In Mexico he pays his workers $11 a day, more than double the minimum wage in Mexico. In California he paid his Mexican workers $9 per hour. Scaroni is not alone. Twelve large agribusiness firms in California and Arizona have moved part of their operations to central Mexico where they employ over 11,000 Mexican laborers. The Mexican consul in Boston, Carlos Rico Ferrat, also commented on the mistaken idea that "if [Mexicans] were not there, someone else could take their places." Rather, he observed, "if there are no Mexican migrants, that part of the production goes elsewhere, outside the United States. There is no way to retain it."[106] In other words, unemployed American workers are not available to replace fired or deported illegal immigrants because very few unemployed American workers are engaged in agricultural labor.[107] As for domestic work, "if all Mexican maids disappeared suddenly from U.S. homes," asked one immigration scholar, "would they be replaced by American maids? Or would the American homes go maidless?"[108] More recently, the 2004 film *A Day without a Mexican* takes a satirical look at California's economy when Mexican workers mysteriously disappear for a day. Food is left cooking on the stove, cars are abandoned in the street—a politician's maid doesn't show up for work, and a farm owner's entire harvest is at risk of rotting in the field. As the state's economy grinds to a halt, Californians are left confused and wondering where all the Mexicans have gone.

Carey McWilliams in 1948 put it most aptly: "Not only is the movement 'North from Mexico' older in point of time than the westward movement, but it has remained constant through the years; it is continuing now and is likely to continue indefinitely."[109] Today, almost a half century after the termination of the Bracero Program in 1964, and periodic crackdowns on illegal immigration from Mexico—Operations Wetback (1954), Gatekeeper (1994), Hold-the-Line (1994), and Safeguard (1999)—the Department of Homeland Security has yet to complete construction of a 700-mile fence along parts of the sinewy 1,952-mile border in a bootless attempt to stop the northward migration of Mexicans. If past history of the border is any guide, Mexicans will continue to find ways to enter the United States illegally, whether by land, sea, or air. As former Arizona governor Janet Napolitano put it before becoming secretary of homeland security, "You show me a 50-foot wall and I'll show you a 51-foot ladder."[110] Meanwhile, Homeland Security's 18,516 Border Patrol agents in the "Southwest Border Sector" continue to shovel sand against the historical tide of Mexicans migrating north from Mexico.[111]

U.S.-born Mexican Americans in the postwar era, like Cesar Chavez, founder of the United Farm Workers Union, and many who were the descendants of bracero workers, unauthorized immigrants, and resident Mexican nationals, increasingly demanded their full citizenship rights in a country that for over a century regarded them as "foreigners" and "wetbacks" insufficiently European to be considered authentic Americans, forgetting that Mexicans had longer and stronger ties to North America than did the late-arriving British colonists. Many Anglo Americans nonetheless believed that Mexicans came from the wrong side of the border dividing mostly white North America from Mexico and its mostly dark-skinned progeny of indigenous origin. But as Chicano activists of the 1960s reminded non-Hispanic Americans, alluding to the U.S.-Mexican War that resulted in the loss of half of Mexico's territory: "We didn't cross the border, the border crossed us."

6

THE CHICANO MOVEMENT

In the post–World War II decades of the 1950s and 1960s the persistence of segregation of African Americans in the South and discrimination against Asian Americans and Mexican Americans in the West seemed increasingly at odds with the ideals of freedom and equal rights for all Americans. Latin-American countries were sensitive to the affront to their national dignity by the perception in the United States that citizens of Latin-American descent did not deserve the same rights as white citizens.[1] The Mexican government quietly continued to pressure the United States to end segregation and discrimination against immigrants, braceros, and Mexican Americans, while increasing numbers of Americans and local and state officials in the Southwest also began to exert pressure on local businesses that discriminated against Mexicans. Not all non-Hispanic Americans were ready to open their hearts—or their schools and public parks—to Mexicans. When it was proposed that Mexicans deserved better treatment in Texas, one old-timer responded, "Why, we ain't even stopped hating the Yankees yet!"[2]

Throughout the Southwest Mexican Americans fought in the courts to end discrimination and segregation, and took to the streets and rural roads to protest low wages and intolerable working conditions on agribusiness farms. In those troubled decades of Cold War anxieties and African-American civil rights struggles, Cesar Chavez's United Farm Workers Union (UFW) in California and the Chicano Movement throughout the Southwest emerged as regional and transnational movements that brought national attention to one of the nation's least understood and fastest-growing populations. Already the World War II generation of Mexican Americans, many of them veterans, had grown weary of patiently waiting for democracy to take root in the Southwest and joined Mexican-American civil rights organizations in record numbers, particularly in Texas and California.[3]

The massive wave of U.S.-born, second and later generations of Mexican Americans constantly battled the barriers of racism that remained in schooling, housing, and employment, as well as the perception that all Mexicans were immigrants and "foreigners": criminal, lazy, and diseased. Like other racialized groups, Mexican Americans knew where they stood relative to Anglo Americans, and they resolved not to be defined by them. They would decide what being American meant from their perspective, and they would show "Anglo-Protestant America" that there would be no peace until America recognized their needs and aspirations. The struggles of Latinos and other marginalized groups to enjoy full citizenship rights in the postwar era thus set multicultural America on a path to redefining what it means to be a nation that could no longer ignore, or exploit, its "brown" citizens in the Southwest. But the roots of Chicano Movement militancy in the 1960s and 1970s began with the rise of second-generation, U.S.-born Mexican Americans who came of age during World War II and sought to leverage their patriotism and military service for inclusion and belonging in white America.[4]

After the war Dr. Hector P. García, a decorated veteran and founder of the American G.I. Forum, came home to Texas a changed man, as had so many other Mexican-American veterans. Dr. García forcefully denounced all forms of discrimination—segregation of Mexicans in schools, parks, pools, movie houses, and cemeteries. Born in Tamaulipas, Mexico, but brought to Mercedes, Texas, by his parents to escape the turmoil of the Mexican Revolution (1910–1917), García attended the segregated high school in Mercedes where he was named valedictorian of his graduating class. He obtained his baccalaureate and medical degrees at the University of Texas during the 1930s at a time when few Mexican Americans were enrolled in public universities. Following his two-year residency at St. Joseph's Hospital in Omaha, Nebraska, he joined the U.S. Army as an infantry officer and later as a Medical Corps officer. He saw combat in North Africa and Italy and was awarded a Bronze Star. He and his wife, Wanda Fusilla (a war bride from Naples, Italy), settled in Corpus Christi where he opened a medical practice to serve war veterans and others at low cost, offering free services to many, including farm workers, who could not pay.[5]

García was on a mission to squarely confront the long legacy of anti-Mexican discrimination, but officials in the State Department worried that continually calling attention to racial discrimination in the Southwest might undermine relations between Mexico and the United States.[6] The problem

Dr. Hector P. García, World War II veteran and founder
of the American G.I. Forum. Dr. Hector P. García Papers,
Special Collections & Archives, Corpus Christi Bell Library,
Texas A&M University.

was most prevalent in Texas where hotels and cafés routinely refused to
serve Mexican Americans as well as Mexican immigrants. The owner of a
café in Sinton, Texas, told Sergeant First Class Ysaias Morales, an army
recruiter in Corpus Christi who fought in Europe and Korea—and had
been decorated with five Purple Hearts, the Distinguished Service Cross,
the Bronze Star, and three Presidential Citations—that they did not serve
"Spanish" people.[7] Jose Maldonado, a lieutenant colonel in World War II
and a surgeon with a degree from Northwestern Medical School, was told
by a hotel owner in Brady, Texas, that he and his wife would have to seek
lodging elsewhere because he didn't allow "a Mexican, Spanish or Latin
American" in his hotel.[8] Incidents like these caused García's blood to boil.

One of his associates risked understatement when he described García's personality as "generosity mixed with impatience."[9]

The problem of discrimination against Mexican Americans in the Southwest received national attention in 1948 when the wife of a Mexican-American soldier, Beatrice Longoria, attempted to hold a funeral service for her deceased husband, Private Felix Longoria, in a small town near San Antonio called Three Rivers. Longoria had been in uniform only a year when he was shot and killed by a Japanese sniper on the Philippine island of Luzon just months before the Japanese were forced to surrender. His body, like many others, was not recovered for years after the war had ended.[10] When the government informed Mrs. Longoria that his remains would soon be returned to Texas, she contacted the local mortuary to hold a service in the chapel for her decorated husband. The manager, however, refused, explaining to Mrs. Longoria that "other white people object to the use of the funeral home by people of Mexican origin."[11] Mrs. Longoria complained to Dr. García, who immediately called a meeting of the American G.I. Forum, sent press releases to the *New York Times* and other newspapers, and telegrams to state and federal elected officials, including the newly elected junior senator of Texas, Lyndon Baines Johnson. Johnson immediately responded to García with a telegram of his own: "I deeply regret to learn that the prejudice of some individuals extends even beyond this life," and made arrangements for Private Longoria to be buried in Arlington National Cemetery with military honors. Mrs. Longoria thanked Senator Johnson for his kindness in her "hour of suffering and humiliation."[12]

News of the "whites only" policy of the Rice Funeral Home spread fast and reaction came from veterans and citizens from Texas and other parts of the country. World War II veteran Gale Harris wrote: "Is this Justice? Is this what we fought and died for? If it is, I can't help but feel that we fought in vain."[13] Twenty-three Mexican fathers and "Gold Star Mothers" of Corpus Christi petitioned Texas governor Beauford Jester to "prevent such humiliating and ignominious treatment of our dead sons as occurred at the Rice Funeral Home." Texas resident James Green wrote the governor that the Longoria Affair "will forever remain a monument of shame in the annals of Texas."[14] Governor Jester, who led a delegation of 250 Texans to the inauguration of Mexican president Miguel Alemán just two years earlier, was worried about the impact the Longoria Affair would have on Texas-Mexico relations and did not want to give credibility to the persistence of discrimination in his state.[15] One governor's assistant called the incident "exaggerated" and thought "It might be best to just to let the whole thing die out."[16] Three months after the Longoria incident Governor Jester met with

President Alemán in Matamoros on the border across from Brownsville, Texas, and publicly expressed regret for the numerous incidents of discrimination in Texas. He also promised Alemán he would visit every state in Mexico in an effort to "erase differences . . . between Mexico and Texas."[17] Jester's good intentions were never realized—he died a few months after his meeting with the Mexican president.

Diplomats on both sides of the border were troubled by the damage Texas seemed uniquely capable of inflicting on the spirit of friendly cooperation that had developed between Mexico and the United States. The Mexican foreign minister authorized the first secretary of the Mexican Embassy in Washington to place a floral wreath on Longoria's gravesite at Arlington National Cemetery as a symbol of the Mexican government's desire to respect the deaths of all allied soldiers as well as to publicize the international implications of this particularly shameful incident, which had been widely reported in the Mexican press.[18] The State Department was at the time engaged in delicate negotiations over the renewal of the Bracero Program, in spite of growing opposition from labor leaders on both sides of the border.[19] The Longoria Affair threatened to complicate those negotiations. Texas representative Lloyd Bentsen cautioned against "dodging or white-washing the facts," as Governor Jester's staff had tried to do. "The only way we can retain the respect and confidence of our Latin-American friends and Latin-American countries," he explained, was to "face the issue squarely and honestly and do what we can to discourage further acts of discrimination."[20] Not everyone was convinced that the United States deserved the "respect and confidence" of Mexico.

The Longoria incident made national news in the United States and Mexico because it seemed terribly wrong that a soldier who had given his life for his country should be denied full citizenship rights, even in death, solely because of his Mexican ancestry. As L. M. Granados, a Texan from El Paso, bluntly put it: "Here is why Mexico doesn't want to send people to work in Texas. [If] this is what they do to dead people, what about live ones?"[21] In some ways Longoria's Mexican ancestry was hardly the point. Over 400,000 U.S. soldiers gave their lives in World War II. The majority of the American people, including millions of grieving families and friends of the deceased, were in no mood in 1949 to tolerate petty acts of discrimination against the family of a fallen soldier.

America was not yet prepared to erase the color line between black and white, but the line between white and brown had always been porous, like the U.S.-Mexico border, and Mexican Americans had been slowly winning their rights as "Caucasians" since the 1930s. Many Anglo Americans with deep roots in the Southwest recognized that Mexican immigrants, who were poor, non-English-speaking, uneducated, or illiterate, and often dark-skinned, were not to be confused with the next generations of Mexican Americans, who were English-speaking, educated, and often, but not always, light-skinned. This small class of Mexican Americans, or *tejanos* as they were called in Texas, exercised certain rights and privileges extended to Anglo Americans, such as voting, holding public office, sending their children to white schools, and even allowing for intermarriage. These Mexican Americans had early on decided that the best strategy for extending full citizenship rights to all Mexican Americans was to end their segregation in public schools.

"Mexican schools," as school officials called them, were established throughout the Southwest from the late nineteenth century because, school officials claimed, Mexican-descent children had special language needs that could only be met in segregated classrooms, and that Mexican children fell behind Anglo children because of the migratory agricultural work of their parents. They denied that race played any role in the creation of separate Mexican schools. In practice, school officials arbitrarily assigned all Mexican children to these schools even though many Mexican-American children spoke little Spanish, if any, and some spoke English better than the children from whom they were segregated.[22] And no children of migratory white families were ever placed in the Mexican schools. In Texas separate schools for Mexicans were maintained in 122 school districts in 59 counties across the state.[23] According to the scholastic census of Texas in 1942, 38,857 pupils of Mexican descent were enrolled in the first grade, but only 19,214, about half, attended the second grade, and only 1,725—4.4 percent—were enrolled in the last year of high school. Fewer than half of all Mexican children of school age attended school at all.[24] School officials thus resorted to the shrewd but devious strategy of claiming special language needs and absenteeism due to migratory farm work as the main reasons for providing separate schools for Mexican children.[25]

In the nation's first desegregation case involving Mexican-descent children, *Independent School District v. Salvatierra* (1930), Mexican-American parents charged school officials with enacting policies designed to accomplish "the complete segregation of the school children of Mexican and Spanish descent . . . from the school children of all other white races in the same grade."[26] The parents did not seek a schoolhouse that was "separate but equal" to the "white" schoolhouse, as had been the strategy of African-American lawsuits. Rather, their suit was aimed exclusively at the school district's policy of denying Mexican Americans the equal protection of the law under the Fourteenth Amendment by separating Mexican American children from Anglo children. The district superintendent made the usual argument that segregation was necessary because of their English-language deficiency and not "by reason of race or color." In fact, he continued, "Spanish speaking children are unusually gifted in music" and possessed "special facilities" for art and handicrafts, talents he believed were best developed in segregated schools. The superintendent was careful not to refer to Mexican-descent children as "Mexicans," a word that carried strong racial connotations in Texas, and instead referred to them as "Latin Americans" and "children of Spanish descent."[27]

The Texas Court of Civil Appeals upheld the lower court ruling that "school authorities have no power to arbitrarily segregate Mexican children, assign them to separate schools, or exclude them from schools maintained for children of other white races, merely or solely because they are Mexicans." The arbitrary exclusion of Mexican-American children from "other whites," the court ruled, constituted "unlawful racial discrimination."[28] However, it was a Pyrrhic victory for Mexicans because the court also affirmed the principle that children could indeed be segregated if they had language difficulties or if as migrant workers they started school late. Nonetheless, the judge required that school officials demonstrate, through testing, which students lacked English-language skills necessary to compete with English-speaking students, and that separation for language instruction be applied with equal force to Anglo Americans as well as "Mexican race" students.

A year later Mexican-American parents in Lemon Grove, a suburb of San Diego, sued the school board when Jerome T. Green, the principal of the Lemon Grove Grammar School, barred about seventy-five Mexican children from entering the school. The school board had set aside a two-room "Americanization" school for the children, over 95 percent of whom were U.S.-born citizens. The parents, most of them Mexican immigrants, formed the Comité de Vecinos de Lemon Grove (The Lemon Grove Neighbors Committee) and sought legal advice from Enrique Ferreira, the former Mexican consul in San Diego. The children, with the support of their parents, refused to attend the Mexican school, which they called "la Caballeriza" (the horse stable) because of its ramshackle appearance and neglected state of repair. In that case, *Alvarez v. Lemon Grove School District* (1931), school officials once again explained that the separate school was designed to help Mexican children learn English and become Americanized. But Judge Claude Chambers could not understand the logic behind isolating Mexican-American children from Anglo children in order to "Americanize" them. He ruled that California law permitted the segregation of American-

Indian and Asian-American students but not those of Mexican ancestry: they were entitled to receive the same instruction in the same school on the basis of equality with all other "white" children. The idea that mixed-race Mexicans should be awarded white racial status by the courts did not sit well with one southern California assemblyman. George Bliss introduced a bill to segregate Mexicans "whether from the United States or not" in an obvious attempt to have Mexican children classified as nonwhite. When the bill failed to pass, Bliss established an "Indian School" for Mexicans in Carpenteria where he was a member of the school board.[29]

The Lemon Grove case was a precursor to a much more important California school desegregation case involving Mexican-descent children, *Mendez v. Westminster* (1946). For nearly two generations, from 1911 to 1947, Orange County school districts in California maintained separate schools for Mexicans and white students—until Gonzalo Mendez and other Mexican parents from four school districts filed suit in 1946 in the federal district court of southern California on behalf of 5,000 Mexican-descent children forced to attend separate schools. As in other desegregation cases, school officials claimed that Mexicans were segregated because of language deficiencies. The parents claimed that school segregation was a violation of their rights as citizens and that no California law sanctioned the segregation of Mexicans, as it had the segregation of Native Americans and Asian Americans. Public education, they claimed, was a public right that could not be abridged on account of race, color, creed, or national origin. In that case, which many scholars believe struck a major blow to segregated schooling eight years before *Brown v. Board of Education,* District Court Judge McCormick ruled: " 'Equal protection of the laws' pertaining to . . . California [public schools] is not provided by furnishing in separate schools the same technical facilities, text books and courses of instruction to children of Mexican ancestry. A paramount requisite in the American system of public education is social equality. It must be open to all children by unified school associations regardless of lineage."[30] In essence, the California district court had ruled that racially segregated schooling was unconstitutional, despite the fact that the U.S. Supreme Court had upheld the doctrine of "separate but equal" segregation since 1896.[31]

A year later, the U.S. Ninth Circuit Court of Appeals upheld Judge McCormick's ruling, although not on the ground that separate-but-equal schooling was unconstitutional, but rather that there was no California statute that mandated the segregation of Mexicans. In other words, in order to segregate Mexican children the California State Assembly first had to pass a law making it legal. But the attitude of Californians toward racial segregation had slowly begun to change after World War II. Shortly after the *Mendez* ruling, Governor Earl Warren signed an Assembly bill to repeal sections of the California Education Code that allowed school boards to establish separate schools for Native Americans and students of Asian descent. Six years later, in 1953, Warren was appointed by President Eisenhower to become the fourteenth chief justice of the Supreme Court. The following year Chief Justice Warren made history in *Brown v. Board of Education,* in which he ruled, echoing the words of Judge McCormick in the *Mendez* case eight years earlier, that "separate educational facilities are inherently unequal."[32]

Mendez was an important case, not only because the lower court ruling paved the way to *Brown,* but also because it exemplified how various civil rights groups crossed regional, racial, and ethnic lines to end racial discrimination at home only a few years after winning the war against Nazi racism abroad. The brief submitted by the American Jewish Congress (AJC) noted that no discrimination "is so vicious as the humiliation of innocent, trusting children, American children full of faith in life."[33] The Japanese American Citizenship League (JACL) mounted an attack in its brief on the California Education Code that required separate schools for Japanese and Chinese students. Like the AJC, the JACL linked California's racial and ethnic policies to those of Nazi Germany.[34] Other civil rights organizations also filed briefs in the case: the National Association for the Advancement of Colored People (NAACP), the American Civil Liberties Union (ACLU), and the National Lawyers Guild (NLG). For civil rights activists and organizations, *Mendez* held out the hope that the time had finally come to end segregation throughout the United States for all Americans regardless of race, creed, color, or national origin.

Meanwhile in Texas Mexican Americans, with support from League of United Latin American Citizens (LULAC) and the American G.I. Forum, prepared their first desegregation case since the *Salvatierra* case in 1930. Minerva Delgado and twenty other parents of Mexican-American children filed suit against the Bastrop Independent School District and three other districts alleging that they had "prohibited, barred and excluded" children "from attending the certain regular schools and classes [with] other white school children" and that segregation was "unjust, capricious, and arbitrary and in violation of the Constitution . . . and denies them the equal protection of laws . . . as guaranteed by the Fourteenth Amendment."[35] In *Delgado v. Bastrop Independent School District,* Judge Ben H. Rice ruled on June 15, 1948, that the school district was "permanently restrained and enjoined from . . . segregating pupils of Mexican or other Latin American descent in separate schools or classes."[36] Like judges in other cases, however, Rice allowed segregation for "language handicap," if it was not done in an arbitrary and discriminatory fashion.

In the last of the Texas desegregation cases until the late 1960s, and the first one to be litigated after *Brown v. Board of Education,* Mexican parents once again objected to the segregation of their children in the first and second grades and especially the practice of requiring many of them to spend three years in the second grade before being promoted to the third—on the ground that they could not speak English well enough to be put in classes with Anglo children. As in the *Salvatierra* and *Delgado* cases, the judge in *Hernandez v. Driscoll CISD* ruled in 1957 that arbitrary segregation of Mexican-American children on account of language handicap was illegal, but that linguistic segregation was permissible so long as school officials administered language tests to each child, which the district had not done. The courts never addressed the reasoning of school officials that isolating Spanish-speaking Mexican children from English-speaking schoolmates might somehow help them learn English, or that separate schools and classrooms might not be the best way to meet the special educational needs of Mexican-American children. Nor did the courts address the clear evidence that school officials had long used the "language handicap" excuse as a pretext for continuing to segregate Mexican children, even when they could not speak Spanish.

The first Mexican-American civil rights case to reach the Supreme Court occurred a few years after the school desegregation cases of the late 1940s when Mexican-American attorneys James DeAnda, John Herrera, Gus García and Carlos Cadena challenged the court conviction of Pete Hernández on the grounds that Mexican Americans had been systematically excluded from jury service in Jackson County, Texas. Hernández was indicted for the murder of Joe Espinosa by a grand jury in Jackson County, Texas, in 1951. No person of Hispanic surname had ever served on a jury in Jackson County in over twenty-five years, although roughly 14 percent of the county's population was of Mexican origin. An all-Anglo jury convicted Hernandez of murder.[37]

The appeals court upheld the lower court ruling that Mexican Americans were members of the "white race" as were members of the jury, and therefore no cause for discrimination existed.[38] The court basically reasoned that Mexican Americans could not have it both ways: they could not insist that they were white and, at the same time, that an all-white jury constituted a violation of the "equal protection" clause of the Fourteenth Amendment forbidding discrimination on the basis of race. In an earlier case involving discrimination in jury selection, a Texas judge ruled that

Mexican people "are not a separate race but are white people of Spanish descent" and found "no ground for discussing the question further."[39] Cadena and García, with the support of LULAC and the American G.I. Forum, appealed the decision to the Supreme Court. In their brief they strenuously objected to the appeals court judge's ruling and concluded that "For all practical purposes, about the only time that . . . Mexicans—many of them Texans for seven generations—are covered with the Caucasian cloak is when the use of that protective mantle serves the ends of those who would shamelessly deny to this large segment of the Texas population the fundamental right to serve as . . . jurors."[40]

The Supreme Court agreed in a decision announced on May 3, 1954, two weeks before its epic ruling in *Brown v. Board of Education*. In overruling the lower courts, it rejected the view that there were only two classes—white and Negro—within the contemplation of the Fourteenth Amendment. Chief Justice Warren, writing for the unanimous court, reflected: "Throughout our history differences in race and color have defined easily identifiable groups which have at times required the aid of the courts in securing equal treatment under the laws." He further noted that "community prejudices are not static, and from time to time other differences from the community norm may define other groups which need the same protection." In other words, "race" was not the only norm by which groups could be excluded from exercising their rights. The exclusion of Jews, Mormons, and Catholics from jury service, for example, would also be a violation of the equal protection clause of the Fourteenth Amendment.[41] The court did not conclude that Latinos deserved protection as a nonwhite group, but rather recognized Mexican Americans as a "distinct class" that had been singled out for different treatment in segregated schools and exclusion from restaurants, parks, and "white only" bathrooms (including one in the Jackson County courthouse where the original trial was held).[42] Recognizing prior court rulings that Mexicans were members of the "white race," the Supreme Court ruled that Mexicans had been wrongfully segregated from "other whites"—*by* other whites—solely because they were of Mexican descent.

By 1954, almost a decade after the war ended, Mexican-American civil rights advocates had scored important court victories in extending full citizenship rights to Mexican Americans. African-American civil rights attorney Thurgood Marshall and the NAACP Legal Defense Fund had also scored numerous court victories and could be justly proud of having laid the legal groundwork for *Brown v. Board of Education*, arguably the most important Supreme Court decision of the twentieth century. Many, though certainly not all, Americans were gradually warming to the idea that racial discrimination could not be reconciled with the principles on which the nation was founded and for which hundreds of thousands of Americans had died in the recent war.

At the same time, however, the Army-McCarthy Senate hearings underscored the nation's obsessive hunt for communists in government, Hollywood, the military, and academia, while the Soviet Union called attention to America's long history of racial discrimination and ridiculed its stained-glass attitude as the paragon of freedom and equality in the world. If Alabama and Mississippi represented the worst extreme of hostility toward African Americans in the South, Texas was renowned throughout Latin America for its segregation of Mexicans regardless of citizenship status. An editorial in a Texas newspaper in 1952 addressed the challenge Americans faced in these words: "It is paradoxical that the American people, so fundamentally decent, want desperately to be liked and respected abroad but are unwilling to do consistently the things which would make us liked and respected. There is one thing of which we may be certain, as we strive to rally the free world: We cannot operate two kinds of democracy and inspire confidence in our sincerity."[43] A veteran of World War II asked less charitably: "What kind of country is this anyway? Remember . . . lots of the so-called 'dirty Mexicans' are getting killed in Korea."[44] Latino casualties in the Korean War, mostly Mexican Americans, far exceeded their percentage of the population: in Arizona Mexican Americans were 20 percent of the population and 44 percent of the casualties. The ratio of population to casualties in Texas was 17 to 30 percent, in Colorado 10 to 28 percent, and in New Mexico, 49 to 56 percent.[45] Nine Hispanics, including one Puerto Rican, received the Medal of Honor for heroism during the Korean War, all but two of them awarded posthumously.[46]

Despite the slow pace of racial liberalism in the Southwest, many Latino veterans who served in World War II and the Korean War did take advantage of the G.I. Bill of Rights, which provided low-interest loans to start businesses and provided stipends for tuition and living expenses to attend college or vocational schools. They also used the Veterans Administration low-cost mortgages to buy homes, which facilitated their passage into the middle class in increasing numbers. Whether as homeowners or renters in their communities, Mexican Americans increasingly sought to participate actively in organizations to address local concerns and needs, including voting and running for office. As one Mexican-American veteran proclaimed: "I'm glad I'm going to have a flock of foliage [oak-leaf cluster military medals] . . . to put on my uniform for Armistice Day parades. I'm going into politics. There's seven or eight of us, all from Southern California, who've talked it over. Things are going to happen in these colonies [neighborhoods], and we're going to see that they do."[47] Things did begin to happen. Mexican Americans ran for political office, sometimes winning local and statewide elections in major cities of the Southwest. In 1953 Henry B. Gonzalez of San Antonio was elected to the San Antonio City Council and in 1961 to the U.S. Congress. In Los Angeles Edward "Ed" Roybal, with support of the city's chapter of the Community Service Organization (CSO) he helped to found, won election to the city council in 1949 and to the U.S. Congress in 1962 where he authored the National Bilingual Education Act to meet the needs of children from non-English-speaking homes and founded the National Association of Latino Elected and Appointed Officials (NALEO).

But while Mexican Americans were entering the political arena in greater numbers than ever before, another struggle for Mexican-American equality captured the attention of the nation. The strikes and boycotts organized by Cesar Chavez, a third-generation Mexican American from Arizona and U.S. Navy veteran, who founded the UFW with Dolores Huerta, became headline news. Born in Yuma, Arizona, in 1927, the second of five children, Cesar Chavez spent his childhood years on his family's small farm where his parents also ran a country store. "Our family farm was started three years before Arizona became a state," Chavez once reminisced. "Yet, sometimes I get crank letters . . . telling me to 'go back' to Mexico!"[48] His parents lost the farm at the height of the Depression and the drought of the 1930s that drove many rural families, including the Chavez family, to migrate to California in search of work. Chavez was ten years old when his family moved to California. Like the Joad family in Steinbeck's *The Grapes of Wrath,* the Chavez family moved from farm to farm picking crops and living on roadsides until they finally settled in Delano, a small farming community in California's San Joaquin Valley.

Chavez worked in the fields from an early age, having attended thirty-eight different schools before finishing the eighth grade, the last year of his formal education. He enlisted in the navy in 1947 at age seventeen, returning to Delano after his enlistment to marry his high school sweetheart, Helen Favela. They moved to San Jose, California, where Chavez met Fred Ross, founder of the CSO, who trained Chavez in community organizing, skills that served him well years later when he founded the UFW. Chavez left the CSO when it voted against his proposal to organize farm workers and returned to the fields where he organized farm workers under the banner of his own organization, the National Farm Workers Association (NFWA).[49] When a mostly Filipino union struck the Delano

Cesar Chavez in the U.S. Navy. TM/© 2013 the Cesar
Chavez Foundation, www.chavezfoundation.org.

grape growers in 1965 for cutting wages during the harvest, NFWA farm
workers voted to join *la huelga* (the strike), which Chavez gradually transformed into a broad-based, nonviolent crusade for human dignity and
civil rights. Chavez reached out to students, religious leaders, labor activists, and farm workers everywhere to form an army of volunteers nationwide to picket stores in major cities from New York to San Francisco that
sold table grapes grown by the DiGiorgio fruit-growing corporation and
other California growers. With the support of labor unions, civil rights
groups, and state and national political leaders, Chavez and the UFW asked
consumers to aid the cause of farm workers by refusing to buy grapes.
Chavez reasoned that the strike stood a good chance of success since the
United States and Mexico had agreed to end the Bracero Program in
1964, thereby reducing the supply of farm workers available to growers
and providing leverage for Mexican-American farm workers to strike for
higher wages and humane working conditions.[50]

The Delano Grape Strike marked the beginning of a long struggle for union recognition, contracts, living wages, and safe working conditions. In 1966 Chavez led farm workers on a 250-mile *peregrinación* (pilgrimage) from Delano to Sacramento, the capital of California, to present a list of their demands. Chavez chose the "Aztec eagle" as the union's symbol, and the image of the Nuestra Señora de Guadalupe (Our Lady of Guadalupe)—the dark-skinned patroness of the Mexican people—as the movement's inspiration. He recruited Luis Valdez, founder of El Teatro Campesino, the farm workers' theater troupe, to educate and organize farm workers, and to draft "El Plan de Delano" to articulate the reasons for the strike and the goals of the farm workers movement. At the beginning of the pilgrimage, Chavez issued a call to social justice: "Our men, women, and children have suffered not only the basic brutality of stoop labor, and the most obvious injustices of the system; they have also suffered the desperation of knowing that that system caters to the greed of callous men and not to our needs. Now we will suffer for the purpose of ending the poverty, the misery, and the injustice, with the hope that our children will not be exploited as we have been. They have imposed hungers on us, and now we hunger for justice."[51] What began as a labor strike gradually turned into a broad-based social movement, or *la causa* (the cause), as it became widely known.

In 1968 Chavez began a twenty-five-day fast for justice that marked his emergence as a national figure of nonviolent change who, like Martin Luther King, Jr., had been inspired by the writings of Mahatma Ghandi on active nonviolent resistance. Presidential candidate Robert Kennedy demonstrated his support when he came to Delano to break bread with Chavez at the end of his fast and declare his continued support for striking farm workers: "This is a historic occasion. We have come here out of respect for . . . Cesar Chavez. But I have also come to congratulate all of you . . . locked with Cesar in the struggle for . . . justice for the Spanish-speaking American. . . . The world must know, from this time forward, that the migrant farm worker, the Mexican-American, is coming into his own rights. You are winning a special kind of citizenship . . . you are winning it for yourselves—and therefore no one can ever take it away."[52] Chavez and the UFW reciprocated, pledging their support for Kennedy's campaign for president. The UFW continued to receive national support for their boycott when farm workers marched to the Mexican border at Calexico where they were met by a busload of Hollywood movie and television entertainers, the press, and Senators Walter Mondale, Ralph Yarborough, and Edward Kennedy, of the Senate Committee on Migratory Labor.[53]

Helen Chavez, presidential candidate Robert Kennedy, and Cesar Chavez, breaking bread at end of his twenty-five-day fast, 1968. Courtesy of the Walter Reuther Library, Wayne State University.

California growers had spent almost $10 million on anti-farm-worker publicity campaigns, while Governor Ronald Reagan called farm workers "barbarians" and labeled the strike "scandalous and illegal." Nonetheless, Chavez and the farm workers had won the support of millions of Americans in cities and towns across the nation and even in a few European cities. After years of boycotts and strikes, most Central Valley table-grape growers grudgingly agreed to sign three-year contracts with the UFW, representing over forty thousand farm workers—whereupon the UFW immediately launched a lettuce boycott to force those growers to the negotiating table. The boycott movement would endure into the 1990s when it would ultimately succumb to expanding mechanization, the ongoing demographic shift from rural to urban communities, and growing discontent and dissension within the union.[54]

The farm workers movement began in the 1960s when other social and political movements were in the offing, namely, the antiwar movement, the American Indian Movement, the Chicano Movement, and overshadowing them all, the African-American freedom struggle. A decade after the Supreme Court ended segregated schooling in 1954, not much had changed for black Americans: most continued to live in impoverished neighborhoods where their children attended dilapidated schools, and worked in the same low-wage, low-skill jobs they had occupied for a half century or longer. The passage of the Civil Rights Act in 1964 and the Voting Rights Act a year later, while important civil rights successes, did not materially change the lives of most poverty-stricken Americans, whatever their race. Those who worked in agriculture, whether as migrants, farm workers, or sharecroppers, were among the poorest of the poor. Most middle-class Americans could not see, much less understand, the impoverished conditions of those who felt left behind in the muscular postwar economy that gave rise to what Harvard economist John Galbraith in 1958 called "unprecedented affluence."[55] Four years later Michael Harrington would write about the "other America"—"the America of poverty" that is invisible to most Americans: "Poverty is off the beaten track. . . . The poor . . . are increasingly isolated from contact with, or sight of, anybody else. . . . The failures, the unskilled, the disabled, the aged, and the minorities are right there, across the tracks, where they have always been. But hardly anyone else is. . . . Living out in the suburbs, it is easy to assume that ours is, indeed, an affluent society." Galbraith at least acknowledged that there were enough poor people in the United States to constitute a "subculture of misery," but not enough of them apparently "to challenge the conscience and the imagination of the nation."[56]

But that was changing as more and more African Americans and Mexican Americans did more than just challenge the conscience of the nation. Whether on a pilgrimage for dignity and justice in Delano, California, or sit-ins against segregation in Birmingham, Alabama, poor folks were tired of not being seen and heard. African Americans especially had lost patience with politicians telling them to be patient. From his jail cell in Birmingham, Martin Luther King wrote that "wait" almost always meant "never": "We have waited for more than 340 years for our constitutional and God given rights. The nations of Asia and Africa are moving with jet-like speed toward gaining political independence, but we still creep at horse and buggy pace toward gaining a cup of coffee at a lunch counter." He reminded Americans that "freedom is never voluntarily given by the oppressor; it must be demanded by the oppressed."[57]

Before the war in Vietnam consumed his presidency, President Johnson declared "an unconditional war on poverty" in his first State of the Union address in 1964. Like President Kennedy before him, LBJ was troubled that poverty rates in some parts of the nation were often double the national rate. He experienced firsthand the poor living conditions of Mexicans in South Texas, when as a young man he was a school teacher in the Welhau-

MEXICANS IN THE MAKING OF AMERICA

sen "Mexican" school in Cotulla, a small town about 70 miles from the border with Mexico. He recalled "the Mexican children going through a garbage pile, shaking the coffee grounds from the grapefruit rinds and sucking the rinds for the juice that was left." Johnson grew up in the 1920s and 1930s with poverty all around him. As president he ushered legislation through Congress that included the establishment of migrant worker programs, local health care centers, Head Start, Job Corps, and many other programs, including remedial education, small business loans, and a college work-study program. His unavailing hope was that history would remember him more for his war on poverty than the war in Vietnam.[58]

The way out of poverty for African Americans and Mexican Americans often meant securing jobs that paid decent wages. Whether as urban sanitation workers or farm workers, their main concerns were wages and working conditions, and they marched, protested, and went to jail to force state and federal governments to address their needs and aspirations for a better life for themselves and their children. Economic power, as Cesar Chavez and Black Power advocates like Stokely Carmichael understood, was the source of political power. But not all disenfranchised groups believed that good-paying jobs were the only solution to their problems, which often were cultural and political as much as economic. The American Indian Movement, for example, was less about jobs or civil rights than broken treaties and the desire for genuine tribal sovereignty on the reservations to which they had been consigned by treaties with Euro-American settlers.[59]

A similar kind of movement took place in northern New Mexico in the 1960s among the "Hispano" descendants of the original holders of Spanish and Mexican land grants. Calling themselves "Indohispanos," or Indian Mexicans in recognition of their indigenous ancestry, Mexican Americans in New Mexico, the poorest state outside of the South, sought to reclaim land taken from their ancestors after the 1848 U.S.-Mexican War. Their Texas-born leader, Reies Tijerina, an itinerant evangelical preacher, told his followers: "The world ignored completely what the United States government had done to the millions of Indohispanos who lived in the Southwest." He was alluding to the theft of their land. The Treaty of Guadalupe Hidalgo guaranteed the defeated Mexicans their claims to community-held *ejidos,* or large tracts of land used for grazing sheep and other purposes, but Anglos and their Hispano collaborators of the so-called Santa Fe Ring wheedled, defrauded, and deceived the claimants into signing away their water, forest, and grazing rights, while legions of lawyers and surveyors collected fees in parcels of land for their efforts on behalf of the Santa Fe Ring. "From today on," Tijerina told his followers, "I am going to fight for the lands of my people. I am going to confront the Anglos that stole them from my people."[60]

Tijerina believed that the poverty of Mexicans, and the problems that stemmed from it, could be traced to the loss of their land. The problem was that few people outside northern New Mexico knew the history of the land grant theft, or cared. Tijerina told reporters that "Americans want nothing to do with anything Spanish and hope to keep Spanish-Americans in a second-class category of citizenship, worse than that of the Negroes, for at least the Negro problems are talked of, while the Spanish-Americans are regarded only as potential soldiers to be sent to fight in other countries."[61] (Tijerina sometimes used the phrase "Spanish Americans" or "Hispanos" when talking with reporters, but he more often referred to the Indian-Mexican origin people of New Mexico as "Indohispanos.")

In 1963 Tijerina founded the Alianza Federal de Mercedes (Federal Land Grant Alliance) whose membership he claimed exceeded 20,000 members in four Southwestern states. After spending time in Mexico and Spain studying laws issued by the Spanish Crown for regulating social, political, and economic life in the New World (Leyes de Indias), as well as the articles of the Treaty of Guadalupe Hidalgo, Tijerina began a long series of petitions to the United States and Mexican governments to investigate treaty violations, while the Alianza issued pamphlets that read: "The U.S. is trespassing in New Mexico" and "All trespassers must get out of New Mexico now!" But the U.S. government ignored Tijerina's petitions, as it had ignored similar pleas from the American Indian Movement for the reclamation of tribal lands. Tijerina also sought an audience with the Mexican government, which he hoped would be sympathetic to the cause of land dispossession in territory that once belonged to Mexico. But the Mexican government, which had recently concluded the bilateral Border Industrialization Program with the United States in 1964 to establish *maquiladoras* (factories) in a free trade zone on the Mexican side of the border, was hardly interested in siding with an "Indohispano" radical ostensibly demanding that President Johnson return the bulk of the Southwest to Chicanos. On the contrary, shortly after Tijerina's car caravan to Mexico City crossed the border, the Mexican secretary of the interior (Gobernación), Gustavo Díaz Ordaz (later president of Mexico), ordered Tijerina and his *aliancistas* deported, and issued directives to Mexican consulates in the United States to deny Tijerina permission to enter Mexico "on any kind of immigration status," in effect banning him from Mexico.[62]

Frustrated with Mexico's hostility toward him and his own government's indifference, and the patronizing deference of New Mexico politicians,

Tijerina and his supporters took action in the fall of 1966 when over 350 land-grant heirs occupied Echo Amphitheater, located in a section of the Kit Carson National Forest that had once been part of the Spanish land grant, San Joaquín del Río de Chama. Their goal—mostly an act of political theater—was to reestablish the township as the independent Republic of San Joaquín under the terms of the Treaty of Guadalupe Hidalgo. They elected a direct descendant of the original land grant as mayor, and when Forest Service rangers appeared on the scene, they were told, after an impromptu trial at a picnic table, that they were trespassing on private land and were escorted off the property. Tijerina pledged that the occupation would continue, while the Forest Service considered what would be an appropriate response to hundreds of New Mexicans attempting to establish a sovereign nation in a picnic area of the Carson National Forest. To stall for time, the forest supervisor announced that he regarded the camped Hispanos "as just visitors to the National Forest which always has been open to the public."[63]

The Alianza occupation was not as pointless or absurd as it may have appeared to many. Tijerina and the Alianza purposefully challenged the authority of the federal government in the hope of forcing the issue of the disputed land grants and treaty violations into federal court. Instead, the federal government charged Tijerina and four other Alianza members with assault against the forest rangers. Not to be outdone, Tijerina issued a warrant for the "citizen's arrest" of Rio Arriba County district attorney Alfonso Sánchez, who had ordered the arrest of Alianza members for "unlawful assembly" at Coyote, a small town on the edge of the Rio de Chama land grant, for what was supposed to have been a lawful meeting of land grant descendants.[64]

Tijerina felt his brand of active confrontation with federal authorities was needed to focus attention on the injustice of poverty and other problems that stemmed from the theft of native lands in violation of treaty agreements. Poverty in Rio Arriba, a county the size of Connecticut where two-thirds of the people were of Mexican descent, was shocking for its sheer pervasiveness: 74 percent had no flush toilets, 70 percent had no gas or electric stoves, 87 percent had no phone, and half the residents were on relief. While unemployment nationwide in 1968 was 3.3 percent, in Rio Arriba it was 28 percent.[65] Tijerina was keenly aware of the choices he and the Alianza faced. The headlines nationally were filled with the marches, sit-ins, and urban riots of African Americans, including the Los Angeles Watts Riot in the summer of 1965 that lasted six days and took the lives of thirty-four people; at the same time, not far from Los Angeles in the San Joaquin Valley, Cesar Chavez and thousands of mostly Mexican farm workers were striking peacefully, despite strikebreakers and grower-provoked violence, and making pilgrimages under the banner of Nuestra Señora de Guadalupe. For Tijerina and his followers, as one chronicler noted, these examples were symbolic of the "urgent choice" they faced in northern New Mexico: "Was it to be the benign patience of Our Lady of Guadalupe, symbol of the Delano strikers, or was it to be 'Burn, Baby, Burn!'?"[66]

What happened next was far from the "benign patience" of the farm workers. Tijerina decided to escalate the conflict between *aliancistas* and the politicians who ignored them or, in the case of District Attorney Alfonso Sánchez, sought to arrest them. On June 5, 1967, Tijerina and his followers stormed the Tierra Amarilla courthouse to arrest Sánchez, who happened not to be there at the time, and in the mayhem that ensued, wounded a jailer and a sheriff's deputy. They took two hostages and fled to the mountains of nearby Canjilón, touching off a massive manhunt involving planes, tanks, and helicopters of the New Mexico National Guard, the FBI, and New Mexico State Police. Not long afterward, Tijerina and a few of his confederates were caught, arraigned, and charged with kidnapping and armed assault. The courthouse raid, as it came to be called, brought the cause of the Alianza to the attention of the nation, even in a decade when violent opposition to actions of the federal government, including the Vietnam War, was hardly exceptional.[67]

Tijerina's daring courthouse raid and prophetic zeal as the deliverer of Indohispanos from sell-out politicians like Alfonso Sánchez and Senator Joseph Montoya (who called Tijerina a "damned liar," a "creature of darkness," and an "enemy of the United States") also caught the attention of Black Power radicals and Chicano activists, including Rodolfo "Corky" Gonzales, leader of the Chicano community in Denver, and California labor activist Bert Corona, founder of the Mexican American Political Association (MAPA).[68] Even the revered but reticent Cesar Chavez came to New Mexico where he publicly embraced Tijerina and announced that if he were a New Mexican, he too would join their struggle against "the cruel injustices of which they have been subjected."[69] Others, however, deplored the land-grant movement. District Attorney Sánchez claimed that *aliancistas* were communists being trained in "guerilla warfare tactics" to take over northern New Mexico "in the same manner Fidel Castro took over Cuba."[70] But by the late 1960s the bugaboo of communist conspiracies was beginning to lose its power to frighten citizens into conformity. As one New Mexican, Eddie Chávez, put it, "I'm not sure what a Communist is, but I get a feeling that a lot of the time it's anybody who causes trouble for the people in charge."[71] That certainly described Tijerina, who told the Associated Press that "the real conspiracy to take over northern New Mexico" was not hatched by communists but by "bankers and lawyers"—the ranchers, politicians, and descendants of the Santa Fe Ring who took offense when poor people spoke out.[72]

Tijerina's single-minded drive to seek redress for impoverished, landless New Mexicans gave Chicanos across the Southwest a renewed sense that they were not "Spanish American" or white, but rather "Indohispano" and brown, a recognition and rejuvenation of Chicanos' indigenous heritage. "We are," Tijerina proclaimed, "the people the Indians call their 'lost brothers.'" Like all native peoples in conquered lands, including Chicanos, Tijerina reasoned, "We have been forced by destiny to adopt two languages; we will be the future ambassadors and envoys to Latin America. At home, I believe that the Southwest is breeding a special kind of people that will bridge the color-gap between black and white."[73] Perhaps it was this belief, in part, that prompted Tijerina to journey first to Chicago to the New Politics Convention in fall 1967 and the following summer to Washington, DC, to participate in the multiracial Poor People's March, where he sought to build closer relations with African Americans, sympathetic whites, Native Americans and other Latinos, especially Puerto Ricans.[74] Tijerina acknowledged the difficulty and the urgency of many different groups with different grievances attempting to work together: "The situation of the Mexicans and Puerto Ricans is similar to that of the Negro people, but it is not the same. We have to fight for the right to speak our language. Even the demand of the Puerto Rican for independence is different from the Mexican's demands. But we must unite all these with the Negro, the Indian, and the 'good Anglos,' in order to change our condition."[75]

The Mexican's demands, it became increasingly clear to Chicanos across the Southwest, could not be addressed without recognizing the entire Southwest, which they called Aztlán, as stolen land and their poverty the result of being a conquered people, like their Indian brothers. Popularized in the "Plan Espiritual de Aztlán" at the First National Chicano Youth Liberation Conference in Denver, Aztlán was the presumed ancestral home of the Aztecs, the "occupied America" of the Mexican Southwest. Chicanos declared their difference from Anglo Americans: "We are a Bronze People with a Bronze Culture." The person most responsible for promulgating the Plan Espiritual de Aztlán was Rodolfo Gonzales, founder of the community-based Crusade for Justice, whose ambition was to establish a broad-based Chicano movement throughout the Southwest. Born in Denver, Colorado, and raised in the Mexican barrio, Gonzales was a Golden Gloves boxer, served as the chairman of the War on Poverty's youth program, ran the

Viva Kennedy campaign, and led a large contingent of Chicanos from the Southwest to Martin Luther King's Poor People's Campaign in Washington.[76] The Crusade for Justice, as the name implies, was less a movement to reclaim stolen land than to establish a degree of political and economic autonomy. To that end Gonzales organized young Chicanos from the barrios and raised funds to open their own child care center, an art gallery, a bookstore, a community center, and provide employment and housing assistance. They also fought against employment discrimination and particularly police brutality in their communities. For Gonzales, like many Mexican Americans, fighting for basic rights stemmed from a renewed pride in his indigenous ancestry—*Chicanismo*—that made Anglos the uninvited settlers in their ancestral homeland: "With our heart in our hands and our hands in the soil, we declare the independence of our mestizo nation. . . . We are a nation, we are a union of free pueblos, we are Aztlán."[77] The cultural pride expressed in the Plan Espiritual de Aztlán represented, according to one scholar, a "symbolic act of defiance, rather than a formal declaration of secession from American society."[78] Nonetheless, Gonzales, like Tijerina, recognized that Chicanos, or "Indohispanos," were native to the Southwest because their Indian ancestors had lived in the region for thousands of years before the Spanish settled the land, and long before Anglo Americans began their westward march across the continent in the early nineteenth century.[79]

In practical terms it mattered little that many Indian Mexicans were native to the Southwest before it was northern Mexico or a colony of Spain. Most conquered land rarely reverts back to the conquered, as all indigenous peoples of the Western Hemisphere can attest to. But conquered peoples often become incorporated into new polities over time, though rarely with full citizenship rights and privileges. Peoples long subordinated in the Southwest—Chinese, Japanese, Indians, African Americans, and Mexicans—have had to fight an uphill battle to exercise rights denied them because of prior conquest, slavery, racial discrimination, and in the case of Indians, broken treaties. While Tijerina wanted the United States to return land to its rightful owners, most Mexican Americans understood that the Southwest would never revert back to Mexico, Spain, or native peoples. Their rights would have to be won within the framework of courts and local, state, and national government, and on the economic front, in labor unions.

Mexican Americans began running for office in the Southwest in large numbers in the 1970s, and some of them were elected to the U.S. Congress after serving on city councils or in state legislatures. In addition to high-profile politicians like the aforementioned Ed Roybal, a U.S. representative from Los Angeles who traced his New Mexican roots back hundreds of years, and the Texas representative Henry B. Gonzalez, native of San Antonio elected to Congress in 1961, many Mexican Americans ran in races for city councils and school boards across the Southwest. But those beginning their careers as politicians in the late 1960s were a younger generation less patient and willing to strike deals with Anglos. Many were Chicano nationalists who often referred to Anglos as "gringos" and portrayed them as implacably racist and unwilling to share power with "Mexicans." The only way to obtain a measure of economic power, many believed, was to defeat Anglo politicians at the polls. Anglo-dominated school boards, for example, ran the school systems, which were among the largest employers in rural areas.[80] In Texas, Chicano student activists, including José Angel Gutiérrez, Mario Compean, and others, founded the Mexican American Youth Organization (MAYO) in 1967 that proposed the formation of a third political party, La Raza Unida Party (LRUP), and in 1970 fielded candidates for nonpartisan school board and city council races in South Texas towns where Anglos held virtually all of the elected offices, although Mexican Americans greatly outnumbered them.

In all, LRUP candidates won fifteen elections in races for mayor, school boards, and city councils in three cities—Crystal City, Cotulla (where LBJ once taught in the "Mexican school"), and Carrizo Springs. Flushed with success, LRUP nominated Ramsey Muñiz for the Texas gubernatorial election in 1972 (gaining 10 percent of the vote), as well as a slate of "raza" candidates for other state offices.[81] The head of LRUP, José Angel Gutiérrez, had become highly controversial for his anti-gringo rhetoric. At a rally in Del Rio, Texas, to protest the cancelation of the antipoverty program VISTA, Gutiérrez said, "We are fed up. We are going to move to do away with the injustices to the Chicano and if the 'gringo' doesn't get out of our way, we will stampede over him."[82] While LRUP survived in Texas from its founding until the late 1970s, its influence, such as it was for a brief time in South Texas, waned rapidly as a result of internal dissension, and as a more pragmatic breed of Mexican Americans, like San Antonio mayor Henry Cisneros, emerged who recoiled from the harsh separatist and anti-gringo rhetoric of Gutiérrez and LRUP.[83]

A major stumbling block to winning elections under the LRUP banner was the fact that the vast majority of Mexican Americans in the Southwest had been wedded to the Democratic Party and were reluctant to vote for third-party candidates. In the late 1950s they had participated in Viva Kennedy clubs to give JFK the edge in the close 1960 presidential election.[84] Cesar Chavez and the UFW were also closely aligned with the Democratic

Party, as were older Mexican-American civil rights organizations in Texas, like LULAC, the American G.I. Forum, and MAPA in California, despite their professed nonpartisan stance.[85] But the militancy of Chicanos in Texas and New Mexico, as well as the assertiveness of the farm workers movement in California, was having its desired effect. Like African Americans in the South, Mexican Americans were making their voices heard outside of their ancestral homeland in the states that once belonged to Mexico. Even some mainstream Mexican-American politicians, opposed to Chicano Brown Power radicalism, were forced to acknowledge the grievances of many urban Chicanos, frustrated with the slow pace of change in their communities.

Throughout the 1960s and 1970s, Mexican Americans enrolled in community colleges and universities in greater numbers than at any time in the past, as had many young Americans of the postwar "sixties" generation. The militancy of Chicano student organizations that proliferated on campuses in the Southwest stemmed from their core belief in Aztlán, that the Southwest was their homeland and that no Anglo American was going to tell them to "go back to Mexico." In 1969 the members of these student organizations, such as MAYO, the Mexican American Student Association, the United Mexican American Students, the Chicano Associated Student Organization, and many others, met at the University of California at Santa Barbara, where they formed a single umbrella organization called the Movimiento Estudiantil Chicano de Aztlán (MEChA), which deliberately rejected the appellation "Mexican American" and the conformist agenda of traditional, middle-class organizations like LULAC. They drew up the Plan de Santa Barbara, which called for the development of Chicano studies programs, hiring Chicana/o professors, increased enrollment and retention of Chicana/o students, and other changes. In Texas, MAYO Chicanos issued the Del Rio Manifesto, affirming their new identity, the "basic ingredient" of which was the "brownhood of our Aztec and Mayan heritage" and suggested that if the United States could not address poverty in their communities, then it should bring the Peace Corps volunteers home to do it.[86] Not surprisingly, older, integrationist Mexican Americans, including political leaders like Congressman Henry B. González, criticized militant Chicanos as being "orators of race and hate," whose organizations had "fallen into the spell and trap of reverse-racism."[87] Unlike mainstream black and brown elected officials, Chicanos, like Black Power advocates, based their agendas on political and economic self-determination, not accommodation to white society.

While Chicano college students were joining forces with community organizers and founding an impressive array of activist organizations, high school students were themselves beginning to take matters into their own hands. The practice of establishing separate schools for "Mexicans" in California and Texas was ended in the late 1940s, as a result of the influential Ninth Circuit court decision, *Mendez v. Westminster,* in California and the *Delgado* ruling in Texas, but schools were only as good as their neighborhoods and the tax base that supported them. Most Mexicans, whether in Los Angeles or San Antonio, attended high schools that were seriously underfunded, understaffed, and substandard educationally. School boards had failed utterly to provide trained and caring teachers, new and current textbooks, upgraded facilities, and other kinds of support that schools in white neighborhoods enjoyed. In 1968 thousands of students from East Los Angeles high schools, led by a Lincoln High School teacher, Sal Castro, walked out of several local high schools in what was at the time the largest school district in the country. The unprecedented walkouts in East Los Angeles received national attention and set in motion walkouts in other schools across the Southwest, particularly in Denver and San Antonio where Chicanos had strong networks of activist organizations. In San Antonio, hundreds of high schools students walked out to demand more classes in science, math, and physics as well as qualified teachers. Between 1968 and 1970 young Chicano activists led walkouts in over thirty-nine high schools in Texas.[88]

At the same time a disproportionate percentage of young Mexican Americans were fighting and dying in Vietnam. Mexican Americans had been willing to die for *la patria* in virtually every war the United States had fought. Even throughout the turbulent years of the antiwar movement, the Mexican cultural tradition of "warrior patriotism," as one scholar called it, remained strong in Mexican-American communities and organizations like the American G.I. Forum and LULAC.[89] Numerous Mexican-American men held cultural values that equated military service with *machismo* (manhood). Private First Class Silvestre Herrera, awarded the Medal of Honor for attacking the enemy through a minefield in World War II, explained his actions fifty years after his feet were blown off: "I am a Mexican American and we have a tradition. We are supposed to be men, not sissies."[90] Others, like Lance Corporal Patrick Vasquez, Jr., a Mexican-American Marine in Vietnam, believed, like so many Americans, that the "fate of the Free World" was at stake. Vasquez wrote his father, "if we don't stop the Red Empire somewhere, it'll never end."[91] He was killed in action three months later.

The American G.I. Forum, always the defender of the Mexican-American military tradition, staunchly supported the war. One forum member who attended Vasquez's funeral wrote to President Johnson to remind him that "Mexican Americans have died in many wars in our fight to preserve freedom."[92] Traditional Mexican Americans criticized Chicanos who protested the war, or worse, burned their draft cards, as *desgraciados* (ingrates) and *sinvergüezas* (indecent, shameless). The highest-ranking Mexican-American elected official, U.S. senator Joseph Montoya, Democrat of New Mexico, denounced antiwar protest as bordering on "the thin edge of treason."[93]

But a growing number of Chicanos saw little reason to abandon the struggle for equal rights at home to kill Vietnamese in a war that, win or lose, would not change the condition of their lives in their communities. Stopping the Red empire was not as urgent to them as stopping the indiscriminate brutality of the police in their neighborhoods and opposing a government that required blind patriotism but ignored demands for educational reform, political representation, and antipoverty programs. While Muhammad Ali's refusal to be drafted into the army sounded like treason to many Americans, Chicanos were likely to agree with him when he told the press, "I ain't got no quarrel with them Vietcong" and "No, I am not going 10,000 miles to help murder, kill and burn other people to simply help continue the domination of white slave masters over dark people the world over."[94] David Sanchez, one of the founders of the Los Angeles Brown Berets, an organization of Chicano and Chicana activists from barrios across the Southwest, went a step further when he declared over the radio that those "other people"—the Vietnamese—were in fact the biological "brothers" of Chicanos: "We figure that since [the ancestors of] Chicanos came down through the Bering Straits part Oriental, and that honkie, what's his name? Cortés, came across . . . and raped our women, so we're half mongoloid and half caucasoid, that makes the Viet Cong our brothers."[95]

Chicanos, antiwar Anglos, and Black Power advocates were not the only ones voicing opposition to the war. Martin Luther King, who in the last year of his life broke his silence on the question of the war, accused the government of decrying violence in the ghettos while perpetrating violence at home and abroad: "I knew that I could never again raise my voice against the violence of the oppressed in the ghettos without having first spoken clearly to the greatest purveyor of violence in the world today—my own government."[96] For Chicanos in East Los Angeles, the main purveyors of violence were the men in blue of the Los Angeles Police Department. Chicanos in cities across the Southwest could relate to King when he said, "Here we spend thirty-five billion dollars a year to fight this terrible war in

Vietnam and . . . Congress refused to vote forty-four million to get rid of rats in the slums and ghettos of our country."[97]

Like many African Americans, Mexican Americans were torn along generational lines, with older, more conservative Mexican Americans worried that Chicanos' growing opposition to the draft and the war in Vietnam would call into question the loyalty and patriotism of all Mexican Americans. Many working-class Mexican Americans were particularly inclined to view long-haired college protesters as "spoiled rich kids"—Anglos who did not love their country as much as Mexicans. Had Chicano antiwar protesters spoken out against the war in the barrios, one activist recalled, they "would have been run out immediately."[98] But gradually, as the number of Mexican-American soldiers coming home in body bags increased with the war's escalation, even some hard-line supporters of the war began to have their doubts. Congressman Henry B. Gonzalez, for example, was disturbed by the data on the casualty rates of Mexican Americans: according to the 1960 census, the population of Spanish-surnamed people in the Southwest was 11.8 percent, whereas between 1967 and 1969 Spanish-surnamed casualties from Texas represented a disproportionate 25.2 percent of the total, and in San Antonio in 1966, 62.5 percent of the casualties were Spanish-surnamed, although Mexican Americans made up only 41 percent of the city's population.[99] Rather than as evidence of Mexican-American patriotism and willingness to die for their country, many began to view these disproportionate casualty figures as yet another sign of the government's exploitation of Mexicans, even as some Chicanos continued to view military service as a manly obligation, a macho rite of passage, as well as a path to higher social and economic mobility.

The last hurrah for the Chicano antiwar movement came to a tragic end on August 29, 1970, just months after the National Guard shot and killed four students at an antiwar rally at Kent State University in Ohio. Seven months earlier, on October 15, 1969, over 2 million Americans in cities and towns across the country, young and old, middle-class and middle-aged, took part in the October Peace Moratorium to protest the war. Many wore black armbands to signify their dissent and mourn the deaths of over 45,000 American soldiers and many times that number of Vietnamese. The following month, on November 15, 1969, over half a million mostly liberal Anglo Americans joined a massive moratorium march in Washington, DC. Meanwhile on the West Coast, Chicanos were organizing their own antiwar moratorium, in part because they recognized that the predominantly white peace movement on the East Coast was unaware of, or unconcerned about, the disproportionate percentage of black and brown people dying in the war. Nonetheless, Chicanos had abandoned the earlier view that the conflict in Vietnam was not relevant to Chicanos—"the barrios are our Vietnam," as one Mexican-American politician asserted—and that the conflict was essentially "a gringo war."[100] Like Black Power African Americans, Chicanos could not ignore violence abroad while working for change at home, where police departments had all but declared war on Chicano "gangs," especially when Chicanos were dying in record numbers in Vietnam. As Brown Beret David Sanchez put it, antiwar protest was "a national trend and we just made it into a Chicano trend. . . . We realized . . . that the main thing the white peace groups were doing was keeping whites out of the service," which for Sanchez meant more Chicanos having to serve in their place.[101]

The Brown Berets and other groups, especially MEChA, formed the National Chicano Moratorium Committee in 1969 and over the next year planned numerous moratoria in the Southwest, culminating with the national moratorium in Los Angeles. The atmosphere was festive, as the streams of mainly Mexican-American marchers, between twenty and thirty thousand, congregated in Laguna Park (now Ruben F. Salazar Park) to listen to speeches, music, and generally enjoy the feeling of solidarity with so many antiwar Angelenos. Unbeknownst to the folks picnicking in the park, Los Angeles County sheriff deputies had converged on a liquor store about a block away where the owner believed some teenagers had pilfered a few soft drinks. A skirmish broke out between deputies and spectators when a phalanx of deputies descended on Laguna Park swinging their clubs indiscriminately, injuring men, women, and children who were unable to scramble to safety, and firing tear gas canisters into the fleeing crowd. Within a short time, over five hundred deputies arrived on the scene as well as hundreds of Los Angeles police. Eventually over twelve hundred officers occupied the park and nearby Whittier Boulevard. Over 150 people were arrested and three Mexicans were killed, including a fifteen-year-old boy from an exploding tear gas canister, and a journalist for the *Los Angeles Times*, Rubén Salazar. Salazar was sitting in the Silver Dollar Bar with some friends a few blocks from the park when a deputy sheriff, thinking there was a gunman inside, shot a high-velocity, tear gas canister into the bar, striking Salazar in the head and killing him instantly.[102]

By the mid-to-late 1970s the country had grown weary of riots in the cities, antiwar demonstrations, and college students shutting down campuses. The antiwar, Black Power, American Indian, and Chicano movements lost steam as a result of internal dissension and police repression. Cesar Chavez and the farm workers movement no longer commanded the attention of the media. Tijerina and the Alianza's land grant struggle ceased to exist after 1970. LRUP lingered for a few years but deeply divided along personal and ideological lines. The "silent majority" of the American people, who put Richard Nixon in the White House by a slim margin in 1968, frowned on radical politics, whether Chicanos demanding the return of stolen land, Black Power separatism, or the growing demand of women for equal rights with men—and certainly on lesbian and gay demands for equality, including the right to same-sex marriage. Mexican Americans increasingly distanced themselves from the confrontational tactics of Chicanos and sought greater influence in shaping policy that would benefit them and other "minorities" materially. Well-known Mexican-American civil rights leaders, including Ernesto Galarza and Julian Samora, for example, formed a nonpartisan advocacy organization, the Southwest Council of La Raza, in 1968, which in 1973 became the National Council of La Raza, the largest national Hispanic civil rights organization in the United States today. Also in 1968, the Mexican American Legal Defense and Educational Fund was founded in San Antonio, a national civil rights organization modeled after the NAACP Legal Defense Fund, which was the organization headed by Thurgood Marshall that succeeded in overturning the "separate but equal" doctrine in *Brown v. Board of Education*. And Texas UFW organizer William Velasquez founded the Southwest Voter Registration and Education Project. These mainstream organizations, still active today, were born in the tumult of the sixties and continue to champion civil and human rights in the United States.

Mexican Americans increasingly entered the arenas of politics, policy, and courts to achieve what marching in the streets or school walkouts had failed to accomplish. This newer, more pragmatic approach to change rested on a politics of pressure and prosecution rather than confrontation or supplication. Mexican Americans would get the constitutional rights they were entitled to from the Anglo "power structure"—not by asking humbly with hat in hand, nor by denouncing gringos as oppressors, but by working with like-minded Americans of all backgrounds who believed deeply and unselfconsciously in the promise of democracy and equality.

The federal government had evolved a more pragmatic approach, deciding it was time to learn more about these non-Anglo, non-black people— "Hispanics"—because, mirabile dictu, they were not all immigrants. Democrats and Republicans increasingly began to see them as voters and potential converts to their national parties, although before the 1970s, Mexicans, Puerto Ricans, and Cubans existed as separate nationalities rather than as a panethnic national constituency as they do today. By 1980, the so-called Decade of the Hispanic, they had become a newly invented "ethnic" group that would, by the turn of the century, make up 12.5 percent of the population and become the nation's largest and fastest-growing ethnic minority. The rapid growth of the Mexican-origin population, particularly in the Southwest and its dispersal throughout the Midwest and the South, caused many Americans to call for immigration reform and more "security" on the border for fear that Hispanics would take over—their jobs, schools, neighborhoods, and hospitals. The Hispanics who were "a minority nobody knows" in 1967 had arrived on the national scene by the 1980s as a potential voting bloc—a so-called sleeping giant—that politicians began to court and businesses recognized as a vast untapped market.[103]

7

BRAVE NEW MUNDO

The national news media dubbed the 1980s the "Decade of the Hispanic," recognizing Latinos' rapid population growth and potential influence in American mainstream life, economically, culturally, and politically.[1] While the Latino population had not made exceptional economic, educational, or political headway in the 1980s, politicians and businesses nevertheless read the demographic writing on the wall: Latinos were the fastest-growing population and were predicted to outnumber African Americans by the turn of the century, if not sooner, and hasten the "tipping point" in the twenty-first century when whites would no longer be a majority of the population. And Mexicans, whose struggles as farm workers in California came to the attention of the nation in the 1960s, began to appear in increasing numbers in cities and suburbs in major metropolitan areas from coast to coast.

It was also the decade when Latino subgroups—mainly Mexicans, Puerto Ricans, Cubans, and Central Americans—officially became "Hispanic": the panethnic identification the U.S. Census Bureau created to collect data on all "Spanish-origin" people in the United States. At the same time, immigration restrictionists worried about the growing number of immigrants, legal and illegal, who they argued competed with American workers and changed American (Anglo) culture into something foreign and inimical to the American Way. Beginning in the early 1980s Congress sought ways to reform the Immigration and Nationality Act of 1965, reinforce border security, deter illegal immigration by penalizing employers who hired unauthorized immigrants, and provide legal status (amnesty) to the millions of undocumented immigrants residing in the United States. In short, the decade represented both the promise and the anxiety of a country torn between taking advantage of the political and economic potential of the

Hispanic population, and fearing that the "job magnet" of American industry was attracting more immigrants than the economy or the culture could safely incorporate.

By the end of the 1970s, the federal government began to consider the political and economic implications of ignoring the growing Mexican-American population in the Southwest (which had nearly doubled since 1970) and their demands to be accorded full citizenship rights, including the right to seek redress for inferior and de facto segregated schooling, municipal neglect of Mexican neighborhoods, employment discrimination, and a host of other problems. Latinos had long complained that the census significantly undercounted them, which governed the amount of federal funding for programs that served poor communities, as well as the apportionment of political representation based on population size. The U.S. Commission on Civil Rights reported in 1974 that persons of Spanish-speaking background were probably undercounted by more than 7.7 percent as a result of the severe underemployment of bilingual census takers and confusing questionnaires, and warned: "If the [Census] Bureau does not make its programs and procedures for the 1980 census more responsive to the need for accurate and detailed information on the Nation's second largest minority population, this minority group will continue to remain uncounted and forgotten."[2] Accordingly, the Office of Management and Budget (OMB) issued a directive to all federal agencies, including the Census Bureau, to adopt the category "Hispanic" for all data collection and reporting on Mexicans, Puerto Ricans, Cubans, and other Latino groups. The directive defined Hispanic as "a person of Cuban, Mexican, Puerto Rican, South or Central American, or other Spanish culture or origin regardless of race."[3] With one stroke of a government pen in 1977, a new census category was born that carried little of the negative baggage historically attached to the appellation "Mexican" as brown-skinned "wetbacks," unassimilable and forever alien to the American way of life. As a panethnic identification, "Hispanic" was the least offensive label to Latino subgroups and did not imply fundamental unfitness for inclusion in the broader—and whiter—American polity.[4]

The creation of the Hispanic label solved the problem of how to categorize what the census and other bureaucracies variously called Spanish-surname, Spanish-origin, and Spanish-speaking peoples, but it also raised many questions. Chicanos in particular rejected "Hispanic" as much too Eurocentric and Hispanophilic, with no subtext to suggest their New World indigenous ancestry. Many preferred "Latino," a word derived from the Latin word for ancient Romans that hardly embodies the idea of indigenous peoples, but at least conjures images of "Latin" America rather than Europe.

Other debates center on the absurdity of homogenizing all Latino subgroups, who trace their ancestry to twenty different Spanish-speaking countries, rather than identifying them by their ethnonational affiliations, for example, as Paraguayans, Peruvians, and Puerto Ricans. Of course, few question the academic use of "Euro-American" or European American to describe unhyphenated, panethnic whites (as opposed to, say, Italian Americans), who trace their ancestry to multiple nationalities in Europe, from cultures and language groups as varied as those from Ireland to Greece.[5]

Nonetheless, beginning in 1980 the Census Bureau sought to distinguish Americans of Latin-American origin from European-descent Americans, without creating a new racial category. Hispanics, many of whom identify as racially white, nevertheless often view themselves as culturally different from European whites: Hispanic whites, as opposed to non-Hispanic whites. And to complicate matters, about half of all Latinos choose nationality rather than race in the census as a marker of identity, suggesting that a growing number of Hispanics/Latinos reject the idea of racial categories altogether, or at least the racial options the census currently limits them to.[6] Nonetheless, many came to accept the identity of "Latino" or "Hispanic" regardless of their country of origin, in part because identifying as Hispanic was a mark of assimilation into American society. "Today," the author Richard Rodríguez reminds us, "white Cubans describe themselves as Hispanic, not white; and there are black Dominicans who describe themselves as Hispanic, not black. . . . The immigrant may refuse the label. But with time, the experience of America forces it."[7]

The creation of the Hispanic census category served not simply to "provide for the collection and use of compatible, non-duplicated, exchangeable racial and ethnic data by Federal agencies," as OMB Directive 15 states, but also to systematically map the rapid increase in the diverse, multigenerational native-born and immigrant Latino population, particularly those of Mexican origin. During the 1970s and the 1980s, immigration from Mexico and other countries increased dramatically as a result of the enactment of the Immigration and Nationality Act of 1965, passed at the height of the black civil rights movement.

Immigration was hardly a hot topic in the 1960s, a decade dominated by the Vietnam War and the African-American civil rights struggle, but the passage of the Immigration and Nationality Act was viewed as a long overdue reform of the 1924 immigration law—the National Origins Quota Act—which favored "Nordic" northern Europeans over "swarthy" southern and eastern Europeans. In the opening decades of the twentieth century, Americans had felt that Slavic peoples, east European Jews, and immigrants from southern and southeastern Europe (mainly Italy, Greece, Albania, Bulgaria, and other countries of the Balkan Peninsula), were too different to assimilate into American culture. The 1924 law also barred all immigration from Asia, including China and Japan, on the grounds that only those eligible to become naturalized citizens (free "white persons" and those of African ancestry) should be allowed entry into the United States. It was this racial dimension to the 1924 immigration law that did not sit well with many Americans after World War II, especially during the civil rights movement. The 1965 Immigration Act eliminated quotas based on national origin and replaced them with a race-neutral system of quotas and "preferences," such as favoring immigrants with certain occupational skills. But top priority for visas was given to "family reunification" so that U.S. citizens and permanent residents could sponsor children, spouses, married children over twenty-one, as well as siblings and their spouses, to come to the United States. Once here, and after obtaining permanent residence, they could sponsor other family members to immigrate. Few realized that the family reunification provision of the law would set off a chain migration that resulted in the exponential increase of immigrants from Asia and Latin America, and especially from Mexico. In less than two decades, almost two out of every three immigrants came from Asia and Latin America, a large percentage of them from a single country—Mexico.[8] Leonel Castillo, the former commissioner of the Immigration and Naturalization Service (INS), suggested that the Statue of Liberty was "facing the wrong way" and "should be turned around" to face Asia and Latin America, not Europe.[9]

Shortly after the enactment of the law, key advisors in the Nixon administration began to perceive Latinos as "potential key members of the Nixon coalition—they were numerous, their votes were winnable, and they lived in key electoral states."[10] Nixon understood early on that attempting to curry favor openly with African Americans might alienate the white vote, particularly in the South, but Latinos, while generally regarded as "foreign," mostly poor, and Catholic, did not arouse the same degree of white racial hostility as did blacks. They were a safer bet, which led to Republican support for minority "set-aside" programs for Latinos as well as African Americans—the affirmative action practice of setting aside a fixed percentage, or quota, of federal contracts for companies owned by minorities and women. Nixon also became a supporter of the 1968 Bilingual Education Act, passed in the aftermath of the civil rights movement, that provided millions of dollars in federal funds for school districts to develop programs for children with limited English proficiency (LEP). The government declared that failure to accommodate the language needs of LEP children in public schools constituted a form of discrimination under Title VI of the Civil Rights Act of 1964, and since the vast majority of LEP children were from Spanish-speaking families, bilingual education became a litmus test for politicians seeking to win favor with Latinos. "These people are watching us," Senator Barry Goldwater told President Nixon, "to see if we will treat them the way the Democrats have."[11]

As Nixon and other politicians recognized the potential of Latinos as voters on a national level, a new Latino civil rights organization emerged in 1973, the National Council of La Raza (NCLR), whose primary goal initially was to represent "Hispanics" as a national panethnic constituency, like African Americans. Originally founded in 1968 as the Southwest Council of La Raza (SWCLR) by Mexican-American leaders Herman Gallegos, Dr. Julian Samora, and Dr. Ernesto Galarza (and funded by the Ford Foundation), the NCLR sought to become a national organization equivalent to the National Association of Colored People (NAACP). The black civil rights movement had always overshadowed Mexican Americans' civil rights struggles, in part because of the geographical isolation of Mexicans in the Southwest. As the "invisible minority," Latinos faced the uphill battle of having the antidiscrimination clauses of the Civil Rights Act applied to them, as well as federal funding for programs that served Latino communities.[12]

Unlike traditional Mexican-American civil rights organizations with headquarters mainly in California and Texas, the NCLR set up its main office in Washington, DC, to emphasize its national reach—and also to cultivate ties to politicians and private-sector funding sources. Its publications also reflected the changed nature of the organization by including other Latino subgroups in addition to Mexican Americans. In 1979 the board of directors officially approved the organization's role as an advocate for all Latino subgroups and produced a magazine, *Agenda,* dedicated to "Hispanic issues." It also launched a television series called *Latin Tiempo*— produced in English to reach younger, bilingual Latinos—to provide program content that "reflects the multiplicity of national groups within the Hispanic community—Mexican, Puerto Rican, Cuban, Colombian, Nicaraguan, El Salvadoran [and] emphasizes the importance of unifying these various nationalities into a single force that will be felt on the political and economic fronts."[13] An episode that aired in 1984, for example, featured a Cuban-American cigar-maker family in Tampa, Florida; a Mexican artist; a Puerto Rican boxer, and the Chicano band Los Lobos.[14] Hispanics, the NCLR argued, represented diverse customs and cultures but shared similar experiences of migration as well as a common language. In its efforts to appeal to all Latino subgroups, the NCLR purged itself of any trace of Chicano nationalism, such as references to Aztlán or the suggestion that the "La Raza" in its name meant "race" and specifically people of Mexican descent. Instead, the organization insisted that it meant "the Hispanic people of the New World" and reflected the fact that Latin Americans "are a mixture of many of the world's races, cultures, and religions."[15] In fact, Columbus Day is celebrated in many Latin-American countries as Día de la Raza or Día de las Américas. Thus by providing a pan-Hispanic perspective on a range of issues central to the well-being of Hispanic communities, such as immigration, criminal justice reform, housing, health, and employment, the NCLR purposefully promoted the idea of Hispanics as a national panethnic group with growing political importance, while simultaneously trumpeting the commercial implications of marketing products to the nation's fastest-growing minority.

Businesses hardly needed to be persuaded to tap the Hispanic market, which tipped the demographic scale at over 20 million in 1980 and was growing six times the national average. McDonald's developed its own "Hispanic marketing plan" and signed the pop group Menudo for promotional tours. Coors Brewing Company dubbed the eighties the "Decade of the Hispanic" on billboards in the Southwest to get Latinos to drink more beer, and the Coca-Cola Company allocated more than $10 million to reach the Hispanic market.[16] But selling to Mexican Americans, if not exactly hiring them, was a learning experience for numerous businesses largely ignorant of Latino culture. One such company, Frito-Lay, badly miscalculated the response to its national promotion and advertising campaign when it featured an animated character—the "Frito Bandito"—a friendly but wily Mexican who relieved unsuspecting Anglos of their corn chips, usually at gunpoint. Outfitted in a bullet-riddled sombrero, bandolier, and brace of pistols, the Frito Bandito appeared in a full-page wanted poster ad in *Look* magazine: he will stop at nothing to get your "cronchy" Frito corn chips, the poster warns, and "what's more, he's cunning, clever . . . and sneaky!"[17] One television commercial features the Apollo astronauts taking their tentative first steps on the moon, when they discover that the Frito Bandito has already taken the "one giant leap" for mankind: "Welcome to the moon, señor." He is the "moon parking lot attendant," he tells them with a grin, and kindly asks them to hand over a bag of corn chips, good for one hour.[18] Liggett & Myers promoted its L&M cigarettes with an ad featuring a shiftless Mexican revolutionary, "Paco," who never "feenishes" anything, not even the revolution (for the smoker who will get to it mañana?). Not to be outdone, Bristol-Myers decided that an amusing way to sell its underarm deodorant "Mum" was to feature a gang of Mexican-style bandits whose leader pauses during an attack to spray on the product, while the announcer intones: "If it works for him, it will work for you."[19]

The American G.I. Forum, the National Mexican-American Anti-Defamation Committee (NMAADC), Nosotros (a Latino arts advocacy group founded by the actor Ricardo Montalban) and other organizations protested against the Frito Bandito ads and the hundreds of television affiliates that aired them.[20] The general counsel for three Mexican-American organizations asked the Federal Communication Commission (FCC) for "equal time" to answer commercials featuring the Frito Bandito and "any other 'Stepin Fechits with Spanish accents.' "[21] In response, the company agreed to remove the gold tooth and beard, eliminate his "leer," soften his voice, and in other ways domesticate the bandito to have an overall friendlier face. But Frito-Lay was "sticking to its 'pistolas,'" according to one account, stressing again and again that the bandito was "a cute, loveable cartoon character." The company explained that its market surveys of Mexican-American families in five southwestern cities indicated that 93 percent of those who viewed the ad liked it. The company's vice president for public affairs, John R. McCarty, wrote Vicente Ximenes, the head of the Equal Employment Opportunity Commission: "our company would never intentionally defame or degrade any race or nationality, and even though leaders such as you feel quite strongly about this advertising, the valid research facts simply do not justify your concern."[22]

Richard Hernandez, legal counsel for Nosotros, suggested that Frito-Lay's ad agency create a "Frito Amigo" who *gave away* corn chips, but the company did not take the suggestion seriously.[23] As opposition to the ad grew and was featured in articles in the *New York Times* and *Los Angeles Times,* the company instructed its ad agency to develop another ad, "Munch-a-Bunch," to replace the bandito; but when it failed to bring in high-volume sales, Frito-Lay ditched the ad and resurrected the bandito. American G.I. Forum founder Dr. Hector P. García grew impatient with the company's repeated promises to replace or euthanize the bandito and spearheaded a nationwide boycott of all Frito-Lay products.[24] At the same time the NMAADC filed a $610 million suit in federal court "for the malicious defamation of the character of 6.1 million Mexican Americans in the United States."[25] NMAADC argued that negative stereotypes of Latinos had damaging psychological effects on Mexican-American children who viewed the commercials on television and were sometimes singled out in schoolyards as "banditos" by their Anglo classmates. The Chicano newspaper *La Raza* put the matter more bluntly: "Chicanos have become the media's new nigger."[26]

On the East Coast, where most people had little contact with Mexican Americans or their culture (except perhaps through the cartoon character Speedy Gonzalez), a well-known African-American columnist for the *Washington Post*, William Raspberry, was aghast by the undisguised racism of the ad: "You just can't imagine a fried-chicken restaurant chain trying to sell its product with advertisements featuring a drawling head-scratching Negro chicken thief. . . . Then how in heaven's name does the Frito-Lay Corp. keep getting away with its Frito Bandito ads?" Raspberry argued that the ad reinforced cultural myths that Mexicans were "comical, lazy, and thieving," adding: "You don't have to be a super-militant Brown Power advocate to be offended by the mustachioed little cartoon character. It's offensive, or should be, to anyone with the slightest degree of sensitivity to minority issues."[27] Representative John Murphy (D-NY), who introduced a resolution to have the FCC look into the matter, counted himself among those sensitive to ethnic stereotypes: he told the House Subcommittee on Communications and Power, which was holding hearings on defamation of ethnic, racial, and religious groups in television and film, that not all "Spanish Americans" were thieves and "drug pushers," just as "All fat cops stealing apples are not Irish, and all Orientals are not conniving 'murderous sneaks.'"[28] With local and national politicians speaking out against the ad, Frito-Lay reluctantly retired the bandito for good in 1971.

Not long after the Frito-Lay marketing debacle, Mexican Americans spearheaded a boycott of Coors beer. In the early seventies Coors had grown from a local Rocky Mountain brewer to one of the fastest-growing and most profitable breweries in the nation—at the time the fifth largest. As Coors expanded its operations, the American G.I. Forum received numerous complaints of hiring discrimination against Mexican Americans, African Americans, and women in the Coors brewery in Golden, Colorado. When Coors executives refused to meet with forum and other Latino leaders, or disclose information on their hiring practices, the forum launched a boycott that lasted throughout the 1970s. The Colorado Civil Rights Commission investigated the complaints and found Coors in violation of nondiscriminatory hiring practices. Out of a total of 1,330 workers in the Coors plant, only twenty-seven were Mexican Americans. At the time more than 120,000 Latinos, mainly Mexicans and Mexican Americans, lived in the Denver metropolitan area. The American G.I. Forum appealed to other groups that pledged their support of the boycott, including the League of United Latin American Citizens, Movimiento Estudiantil Chicano de Aztlán, the Mexican American Legal Defense and Educational Fund (MALDEF), the Denver Crusade for Justice, and the National Student Association.[29]

The boycott expanded to fourteen states throughout the 1970s and brought together an unanticipated alliance of opponents with grievances against the either the Coors family or the beer company they operated: the American Federation of Labor and Congress of Industrial Organizations (AFL-CIO), women's rights groups, gay and lesbian rights groups, the NAACP, the Anti-Defamation League of B'nai B'rith, and numerous Mexican-American civil rights groups from California to Texas. When Coors began using its trucks to haul lettuce and grapes during the United Farm Workers Union (UFW) strikes in California, for example, seventeen labor unions went on strike against Coors.[30] Shortly after the Equal Employment Opportunity Commission filed a complaint in 1975 for "unlawful employment practices," including employment tests and interview questions that tended to have "adverse impact on employment opportunities of Negroes, females, and Spanish-surnamed Americans," the AFL-CIO launched its own boycott: 1,500 members of Local 366 of the Brewery Workers Union walked off the job when talks stalled over seniority and other nonwage issues, as well as the company's plan to subject its employees to lie-detector tests to check the veracity of employees' responses to lengthy questionnaires that included questions about sexual preferences and political affiliations.[31] In California the National Organization of Women (NOW) joined the boycott against Coors because of the Coors family's efforts to defeat the Equal Rights Amendment guaranteeing that equality of rights under the law "shall not be denied or abridged by the United States or by any state on account of sex."[32] As a measure of the boycott's effectiveness, "Boycott Coors" stickers were ubiquitous from New York to California, and in Washington, DC, an enormous "BOYCOTT COORS" sign sat atop the city's AFL-CIO headquarters.[33]

The Coors family's support of right-wing causes deserves much of the credit for bringing together women, Latinos, blacks, and gays and lesbians in a nationwide boycott that catalyzed wide support among white liberals as well. In 1973, Joseph Coors helped found the Heritage Foundation, a conservative think tank whose theorists played a major role in laying the probusiness, antigovernment groundwork for the Reagan era (he was a member of President Reagan's "kitchen cabinet"). He was also a principal benefactor of the Committee for the Survival of a Free Congress (CSFC), a probusiness lobbying group that Joseph Coors touted as opposed to "anti-business legislation . . . written largely by professional politicians, political science professors and labor union bosses." He asked donors to contribute to CSFC to "help stop our nation's decline toward socialism."[34] His brother, chairman and CEO William Coors, held racial views that like-minded public figures at least tried to keep under wraps: at a business seminar in

Denver, he told the predominantly black audience that Africa's economic problems stemmed from "a lack of intellectual capacity." Ignoring the muffled gasps in the room, he added, alluding to slave traders: "One of the best things they did for you is to drag your ancestors over here in chains." He was vilified in the press for his remarks, although Coors spokesman Ron Kirkpatrick insisted that the remarks were "taken out of context" and that the speech was well received, until, he admitted, Chairman Coors "did some talking off the cuff."[35] William Coors promptly apologized and as a sign of the company's goodwill toward black Americans signed an agreement with the Los Angeles chapter of the NAACP to promote blacks into executive-level positions and spend more money on black-consumer advertising and black-owned businesses.[36]

The boycott hit Coors where it hurt the most: their bottom line. Sales were down in its core market in the Southwest as well as in newly opened markets in the East, where minority consumer acceptance was crucial. But the decline was most noticeable in the Latino community where Coors' share of the Latino beer sales declined from over 40 percent to 17 percent in less than a decade. In the early 1970s Coors commanded the top market share in California, but "You just can't be No. 1 in California," a Coors spokesman acknowledged, "without the support of Hispanics."[37] From 1977 to 1984 profits had declined from $67.7 million to $44.7 million, even as Coors expanded its operation to virtually every state in the country. The decline came as Anheuser-Busch and Miller, the nation's first- and second-largest breweries, increased their national advertising campaigns and market share, but Coors conceded the boycott had sharply reduced its share of the Latino market and sought to repair the damage.[38]

Coors initiated an affirmative action program to hire more Latinos and develop more minority beer distributors. They produced in-house radio spots in Spanish, instituted a Christmas "food basket" program, hired its first Hispanic ad agency, and began to sponsor Latino events and programs throughout the western states.[39] The results were mixed: after much debate and dissension among Latino organizations, the American G.I. Forum voted to end the boycott, but many Latino organizations as well as the AFL-CIO continued the boycott against the antiunion brewery until the mid-1980s. Finally, in 1984, Raul Yzaguirre, president of the Washington-based NCLR, brokered a "trade covenant" with Coors to end the Latino boycott once and for all. Six Hispanic groups signed the pact, including the U.S. Hispanic Chamber of Commerce and the American G.I. Forum: Coors pledged $350 million over five years to hire more Latinos, provide distributorships to Latinos, and increase the number of contracts with Hispanic-owned banks, suppliers, and insurance companies. The brewery also agreed to spend $8.9 million on advertising and promotion aimed at projecting a "positive image of Hispanics."[40] Grassroots Latino organizations in California rejected the agreement, as did the AFL-CIO. "We will aggressively pursue the boycott," vowed Dolores Huerta, vice president of the UFW, "because Coors represents the worst of American business. . . . On the one hand they talk about giving to the Hispanic community under this agreement, and on the other, they donate to causes that cut loans to Hispanic students, that weaken unions and that promote right-wing causes."[41] The gay community also elected to continue the boycott. "Coors has cost us too many lives," lamented the coordinator for the northern California boycott, "by their support of antigay groups."[42] The pragmatic great grandson of the company's founders and head of the brewery division, Peter Coors, admitted: "We have a generation of attitudes about our company that will be hard to change," ignoring the generations of attitudes *in* the company that were unyieldingly slow to change.[43]

The covenant with Coors ending the boycott represented an odd alliance between the conservative Republican owners of Coors and Latino activists, many of them prolabor and left-leaning Democrats. This marriage of convenience could only have happened in the "Decade of the Hispanic," when Latino activism left the streets and entered electoral politics in record numbers ("tu voto es tu voz"—your vote is your voice). Between 1974 and 1984 the number of elected Latino/a officials more than doubled (from 1,539 to 3,128), and from 1983 to 1993 their numbers increased about 41 percent, with California, Texas, and New Mexico accounting for 80 percent of those elected. Henry G. Cisneros became the first Mexican-American mayor of San Antonio in over 140 years, a city that was founded over a hundred years before the 1836 Texas revolt. Two years later Denver elected its first Mexican-American mayor, Federico Peña, since its founding in 1858, and Toney Anaya was elected governor of New Mexico, only one of a handful of Mexican Americans to be elected governor in a state in which Anglos have been a minority since New Mexico became a state in 1912. Gloria Molina, elected to the California State Assembly in 1982 and the Los Angeles City Council in 1987, became the first Mexican-American woman to be elected to the Los Angeles County Board of Supervisors in 1991.[44]

Successful Latino/a candidates appealed to voters across ethnic and racial divisions, but also sought to address national and international policy issues affecting the Hispanic community and to integrate Latinos into American political society. As one journalist wrote in 1980, "The Hispanic giant in the United States is awakening and coming out of his labyrinth of solitude." The journalist was alluding to the national social and political potential of the Latino population—the "sleeping giant"—once it emerges from its slumber and draws itself up to its full height.[45] "The silent minority of Hispanics," declared the secretary for Hispanic affairs of the National Conference of Catholic Bishops, "is becoming a very vocal [ethnic] minority."[46]

The engine driving the rapid growth of the Hispanic population in the 1980s was immigration from Mexico, both legal and illegal, and when Cuban president Fidel Castro allowed 125,000 "marielitos" (refugees, including 2,000 prisoners and mental patients) to immigrate to the United States in 1980, Congress began to take seriously the need for comprehensive immigration reform. In all, the foreign-born population increased from 9.6 million in 1970 to 14.1 million in 1980 (including over 400,000 refugees from Vietnam and Cambodia) and to 19.8 million in 1990, an increase of over 100 percent in two decades, and accounting for one-third of America's population growth. In the same two decades the percentage of the Hispanic population almost doubled: from 4.7 percent in 1970 to 9 percent in 1990, partly as a result of native Hispanic births but mainly as a result of legal and illegal immigration from Mexico.[47] While Mexico had been a source of cheap labor in the Southwest for over a century, by the last two decades of the twentieth century Mexico had become, as two immigration scholars correctly observed, "the de facto low-skilled labor reservoir for the American economy."[48]

Although there was growing recognition throughout the 1970s that illegal immigration from Mexico needed to be addressed in Washington, it was hardly a priority for President Jimmy Carter, whose hapless administration was in its final death throes after two years of double-digit inflation, high unemployment, and the year-long crippling hostage crisis in Iran at the decade's end. A month before the crisis, however, President Carter met with President José López Portillo in Mexico City to discuss oil and gas purchases, and when the issue of illegal immigration came up, Carter told López Portillo he would enforce U.S. immigration laws "as fairly and humanely as I can" and would "protect the basic human rights of all people within the borders of my country."[49] Earlier President Carter and Congress created the Select Commission on Immigration and Refugee Policy (SCIRP) to review the nation's immigration and refugee laws and make recommendations to Congress because, as Carter announced, illegal aliens "had breached [the] Nation's immigration laws, displaced many American citizens from jobs, and placed an increased financial burden on many state and local governments."[50] SCRIP executive director Lawrence Fuchs put it more tersely: "We found growing anxiety, even outrage over an immigration policy that is out of control."[51] Fuchs and the select commission chair, University of Notre Dame president Theodore Hesburgh, were committed to examining immigration without the eugenic assumptions about racial hierarchies that informed previous immigration commissions, most notably the Progressive-era Dillingham Commission, which over fifty years earlier concluded that immigration from southern and eastern Europe posed a serious threat to America and needed to be restricted. As Fuchs put it, "the central strategy was to take xenophobia, race, and even economic conflict out of the debate."[52] Commission members included Rose Ochi, whose Japanese-American parents were interned during World War II, and Judge Cruz Reynosa, whose father was deported during the massive Mexican repatriation drive of the 1930s.[53] The fundamental conclusion of the SCIRP report was that immigration in general continued to be beneficial to the nation, but that rising levels of illegal immigration was creating a shadow population of residents living outside the law. "We think the front door to America . . . should be opened a bit wider," Hesburgh said, "and the back door, the illegal one, closed."[54]

The national print media featured articles, many of them front-page news, with headlines such as "Los Angeles Swells with Aliens," and interviews with Border Patrol and INS officials who warned that the "brown horde" had grown rapidly in the last decade and that Los Angeles was already "infested" with Mexicans. The INS had conducted numerous raids on Los Angeles' mushrooming garment industry, which employed about 80,000 workers, 50 to 75 percent of whom the INS estimated were undocumented.[55] The Latino population of Los Angeles County had grown to 27.6 percent in 1980, up from 18.3 percent in 1970, and reached the "tipping point" when their children surpassed Anglos as the majority group in the schools. Mexican immigrants were also swelling the Hispanic population of Chicago, which had for decades been a popular destination for Puerto Ricans as well as Mexicans. The Hispanic population increased dramatically in other cities outside of the border states: St. Paul, Newark, New Orleans, Kansas City, and Miami— the destination of many Central Americans as well as Cubans and Puerto Ricans. But two-thirds of all legal immigrants, over 50 percent of whom came from Mexico, settled in just six states: California, New York, Texas, Florida, New Jersey, and Illinois.[56]

The Census Bureau estimated in 1980 that there were fewer than 5 million illegal aliens in the United States, a number far below the number of six to ten million that some government officials had offered and that drove Congress to introduce bills in the House and Senate to address the problem of illegal immigration. The executive director of one immigration restriction organization criticized the census estimate as too low and "practically snatched out of the air," while an official with Zero Population Growth said "all those figures are pretty squishy." But the higher estimates were also challenged. An official with MALDEF argued that the INS estimate of six to ten million was "far too high" and was responsible for creating hysteria among the American people: "They think they're being swamped by brown hordes."[57] Nonetheless, the higher estimates played a significant role in the ongoing political debate over the need for immigration reform and explain in part why an overwhelming majority of those interviewed in a Roper poll in 1981 urged an "all-out effort" against illegal immigration.[58] At the same time, however, a sizable portion of the American public strongly believed that immigration had always been in America's best economic, cultural, and even defense interests—that the outrage over undocumented immigrants might better be channeled into overhauling the 1965 Immigration Act which, according to executive director of the SCIRP, was "loaded with anachronisms, ambiguities, and inequities."[59]

Like Carter, President Reagan rarely offered any commentary on immigration, even as governor of California. As the star of the "New Right," Reagan's popularity rested on his vision for America—less government, lower taxes, traditional values; but he could not ignore the growing chorus of voices, including from his own party, to enact comprehensive immigration reform. Shortly before his meeting with President López Portillo in Ciudad Juárez in 1981, Reagan told CBS news anchorman Walter Cronkite that he was "intrigued" with the idea of legalizing cross-border workers to provide an adequate workforce for employers and a controllable "safety valve" for Mexico's troubled economy, which included large numbers of unemployed and underemployed workers. He was also intrigued with the idea of tapping Mexico's huge oil reserves to help the United States during a period of uncertainty over energy sources. "It is in our interest also that the safety valve is not shut off," he told Cronkite, which might result in "a breaking of the stability south of the border." Republican senator Harrison Schmitt of New Mexico, who authored one of the guest worker bills, put it more straightforwardly: "The desirability and mutual benefit of having a close-by source of imported energy for the United States . . . is obvious to all. . . . It serves our interests to preserve and strengthen Mexico as a nation and our good relations with that nation."[60] Republican Texas governor William Clements and Republican senators from California and Arizona also favored some form of guest worker program to legalize at least a small percentage of undocumented workers from Mexico—and protect the "safety valve."

After SCIRP issued its final report on the question of immigration reform, the Reagan administration's interagency Task Force on Immigration and Refugee Policy, headed by Attorney General William French Smith, submitted its carrot-and-stick recommendations that included penalties against employers who knowingly hired illegal aliens; legal status ("amnesty") for undocumented immigrants who had lived and worked in the country since January 1, 1982; and a pilot program to allow 50,000 Mexican "guest workers" each year for two years—in effect, a renewal of the Bracero Program begun in World War II and ended in 1964. The task force also recommended an increase in the annual immigration quota for Mexico and Canada from 20,000 to 40,000 each, as well as an increase in the total allowable from all countries from 230,000 to 310,000 (not counting refugees).[61] The proposal recognized that limiting immigration from Mexico to the same quota allotted to other countries—20,000—ignored the special relationship of the United States with Mexico and Canada, and the history of Mexicans crossing and recrossing the 2,000-mile border to work in the Southwest long before the first immigration restrictions were enacted in 1921. The imposition of a visa quota on Mexico in 1976 led to a massive backlog of Mexicans seeking visas who, unable or unwilling to wait, crossed illegally into the United States. In effect, the small quota produced—created— "illegal aliens." But by doubling Canada's quota as well as Mexico's, it became possible to allow Mexicans to fill any slots left over from the Canadian quota. Senator Walter Huddleston (D-NY) called the increase in Canada's quota a "charade" to allow more Mexicans into the country "because the Canadians never use their full quota."[62] But of course that was precisely the idea.

The bipartisan Simpson-Mazolli Bill (after Republican senator Alan K. Simpson of Wyoming and Democratic Representative Romano L. Mazzoli of Kentucky) was introduced in the Senate in 1982, where many Republicans and Democrats opposed either employer sanctions or amnesty for distinct ideological reasons. Although in general both parties remained enthusiastic about legal immigration as beneficial to America's prosperity, a bipartisan group of fifty-one senators (including thirty-three Republicans and eighteen Democrats) wrote to President Reagan supporting employer sanctions and amnesty, but also urging him to consider a reduction in the overall number of immigrants as both legal as well as illegal immigration had risen to unsustainable levels. The letter noted Attorney General Smith's pronouncement that the United States "has lost control of [its] own borders" and that illegal immigration was creating "a fugitive class living outside society's laws and protections." Others, like former ambassador to Mexico Robert H. McBride, worried that imposing harsh penalties on undocumented

Mexicans (who made up over half of the undocumented immigrants in the United States) would seriously impair relations with Mexico, as would imposing ironclad restrictions on legal immigration that would prevent Mexicans from reuniting with their families in the United States. He wrote to Reagan's assistant for policy development, Martin Anderson, that immigration reform bills "that fail to take into account the growing economic and social interdependence between the United States and Mexico will have a negative impact upon both governmental and business relations between our two countries."[63]

The Reagan administration remained committed to the bill's amnesty provision for undocumented immigrants and defied House Republicans who insisted that "illegal aliens" should be punished, not rewarded, for breaking the law. In a televised debate with Democratic presidential nominee Walter Mondale in 1984, Reagan said: "I believe in the idea of amnesty for those who have put down roots and lived here, even though sometime back they may have entered illegally."[64] As a former governor of California, Reagan was firmly on the side of growers in their struggles with unionized farm workers, but he also endorsed the idea of a North American free trade zone in which products, services, and capital as well as workers could move freely across U.S., Mexican, and Canadian borders. Like other conservative advocates of the free market unfettered by immigration restrictions and government regulation, Reagan parted ways with those calling for reduction in legal immigration but joined with others who supported "earned citizenship"—amnesty—for those here illegally, although without extending broad civil, social, or political rights to them.

Reagan also knew that without the amnesty provision, the House would never pass the Immigration Reform and Control Act (IRCA): liberal Democrats in Congress opposed employer sanctions but would be willing to accept them as a Faustian bargain only if they were linked to granting amnesty to unauthorized immigrants. They opposed sanctions because they believed that employers, fearing federal fines, would discriminate against "brown-skinned" people, mostly of Mexican descent, or anyone else who looked "foreign."[65] As one scholar put it: "The public identification of 'illegal aliens' with persons of Mexican ancestry is so strong that many Mexican Americans and other Latino citizens are presumed to be foreign and illegal."[66] Senator Edward Kennedy, and early supporter of immigration reform, opposed the employer-sanction provision of the bill because it "threatens new discrimination against those who have already suffered too much discrimination."[67] The American Civil Liberties Union (ACLU), MALDEF, NCLR, and other civil rights groups also expressed their concern that Latinos, including U.S.-born American citizens, might be passed over for jobs because of the suspicion they might be illegal aliens. Vilma Martinez, president of MALDEF and an outspoken opponent of employer sanctions, issued a statement at the joint hearings of the immigration subcommittees: "Well-meaning employers, fearful of government sanctions, will shy away from persons who appear 'foreign.' Racist or biased employers will simply use the 'fear' of sanctions as an excuse to avoid hiring qualified minorities."[68] MALDEF representative Antonia Hernandez simply called the bill "anti-alien and anti-Hispanic."[69] Even the AFL-CIO, an early advocate of employer sanctions, joined civil rights groups in lobbying for stronger antidiscrimination protections for Latinos, Asians, and others who might be suspected of being in the country illegally.[70]

Many politicians in Congress supported the guest worker program to ensure that employers continued to have an adequate supply of cheap labor. They argued that temporary workers would return to Mexico after their contract expired, but many labor and civil rights groups, including the ACLU, MALDEF, NCLR, U.S. Chamber of Commerce, and Roman Catholic Bishops opposed the guest worker provision. A task force issued a statement opposing the program on the ground that it would exploit Mexican workers: "Even if the administration devises a somewhat less exploitative program than the old bracero program, temporary foreign worker programs worldwide tend to provide less than equal rights for workers. . . . That certainly has been the European experience with 'guest workers.'"[71] The Reverend Allan Deck of the Orange County, California, Hispanic ministry opposed the temporary worker program for essentially the same reason as labor organizations: "[It] will not control the flow of illegal aliens across the borders but will enrich the coffers of business by providing cheap labor."[72] Others worried that the final bill might include the Justice Department's task force recommendation to establish "detention camps" on remote military bases "to hold people whose only crime is their nationality, ethnicity, race or citizenship status."[73]

After years of congressional wrangling over the details of amnesty, employer sanctions, and limited guest worker program, IRCA was signed into law by President Reagan in November 1986, although congressional conservatives, both Democrats and Republicans, objected to granting amnesty to law breakers, but supported employer sanctions, a guest worker program, and increased enforcement at the border. Liberal Democrats opposed guest worker programs (as they had since World War II) and argued that employer sanctions would lead to discrimination against "foreign-looking" residents. And while some conservative Republicans worried that immigrants took American jobs and increased social welfare costs, others, like Congressman

Jack Kemp (R-NY), argued: "Immigrants don't take jobs and wealth away from Americans. Immigrants create jobs and wealth, as consumers of American goods and services and entrepreneurs beginning small businesses, which are the major source of new jobs for all Americans." And not all Democrats supported amnesty. Conservative Texas congressman Kent Hance opposed amnesty because it would "legalize the theft of American jobs."[74] Many had begun to view the question of immigration reform as the "Vietnam of domestic politics," as one scholar put it, "an arena of bitter, protracted warfare from which no one emerged unharmed."[75]

IRCA marked the first time in our nation's history that a law made it illegal for employers to hire undocumented workers. These workers could be arrested and deported, of course, but neither they nor their employers faced penalties under labor and employment laws.[76] But by the 1980s the number of unauthorized immigrants from Mexico was reaching historic proportions. To add to those numbers, nearly three million unauthorized immigrants received amnesty, or temporary legal status, shortly after the passage of IRCA in 1986. The problem, as it soon became clear, was that the employer sanctions provision of the bill had failed almost entirely to accomplish its twin goals: to deter illegal immigration and protect U.S. workers.[77]

In the long run sanctions failed because the Reagan and George H. W. Bush administrations fundamentally opposed government regulation and intervention in the marketplace: they reduced federal funding for enforcing employer sanctions and cut the number of INS agents tasked with investigating violations by half between 1989 and 1990. Sanctions also failed because employers argued that they should not be held accountable for verifying the legitimacy of an immigrant's documents and Congress agreed, stipulating that fines would be levied against only those employers who *knowingly* hired undocumented workers. The law called for employers to complete Form I-9, indicating that they had examined their employees' work authorization documents, such as visas, birth certificates, social security cards, rent receipts, and driver's licenses. Employers were required to accept documents that appeared to be genuine, relieving them of the obligation to verify their authenticity. Naturally, this led to widespread document fraud, as undocumented workers purchased black market documents to satisfy I-9 reporting requirements. Thus while many employers satisfied the law by keeping document records of their employees, regardless of their authenticity, others refused to hire "foreign-looking" workers to avoid the risk of incurring penalties. In 1990 the Government Accounting Office issued a report that confirmed what many Latinos and others had feared: that there was "widespread discrimination" against immigrant workers and that a "substantial amount" of the discrimination occurred as a result of employer sanctions. The report also blamed the government for not providing employers with a "simpler and more reliable verification system."[78]

With no simple and cost-effective way to verify the authenticity of documents, employers could avoid federal fines by arguing that they had not knowingly hired workers with fraudulent documents. This worked to the employer's benefit in other ways: if workers complained to the Occupational Safety and Health Administration about safety violations, or to the Labor Department about violations of the minimum wage law, or supported a union organizing campaign, the employer could conveniently "discover" the unlawful status of the workers and terminate them.[79] The solution proposed by many was to issue a fraud-proof national identity card in conjunction with a computerized national registry that could be used to verify one's legal status, but the Reagan administration shared the widespread public view that such a requirement would violate individual privacy rights. Jesse Jackson even crossed the border into Tijuana to tell an audience at the Center of North American Border Studies that enactment of the Simpson-Mazzoli Bill would require Americans to carry "pass books as South Africans do."[80]

By 1990 it became clear that IRCA had been a stopgap measure at best. A fraud-resistant identification card failed to win traction with the public or Congress; employers could only be penalized if they knowingly hired undocumented workers; and the guest worker program represented a compromise between grower interests and liberal demands for worker protection. IRCA did little in the long run to deter illegal immigration: border apprehensions dropped for three years after its enactment, but by 1990 apprehensions shot up by 27 percent over the previous year. In addition, about three million undocumented Mexicans made legal under IRCA could now sponsor spouses and children from Mexico, who suddenly qualified for visas under the family preference program. Designed to curtail illegal immigration, IRCA succeeded mainly in making immigration policy more liberal, more expansive, especially for guest workers and the millions who qualified for amnesty. Roger Connor, president of the Federation for American Immigration Reform (FAIR), an organization in the forefront of immigration restriction and border enforcement, described IRCA as a major defeat for the restrictionist movement: "We wanted a Cadillac, we were promised a Chevy, and we got a wreck."[81]

With legal and illegal immigration on the rise again, Congress deliberated over a new immigration bill (Immigration Act of 1990) to adjust the annual number of visas for legal immigrants, including funding for hiring an additional one thousand Border Patrol agents, tightening employer sanctions, streamlining deportation procedures, and reducing the number of certain family-preference visas granted in a single year.[82] Yet the law also increased the ceiling on legal immigration by 40 percent, including higher "point" values for immigrants with desired job skills, education, and "source-country diversity" (visas for immigrants from underrepresented countries, like Ireland, who did not benefit as greatly as Asians and Latin Americans from family-based visas). While it took almost five years for conservatives and liberals to hammer out their differences over sanctions and amnesty in the Simpson-Mazolli Bill to deter illegal immigration from Mexico and other countries, a strong bipartisan majority in Congress approved the 1990 Immigration Act that significantly increased legal immigration from 290,000 to 675,000, with higher caps on both family-based and employment-based visas. Both sides hailed the bill as a triumph for "cultural diversity," "family unity," and "job creation."[83]

The beginning years of the 1990s saw record numbers of illegal immigration, about 60 percent of it from Mexico. As the United States, Mexico, and Canada sought closer integration of their markets for capital, commodities, and goods—a borderless North American economy—the United States was simultaneously barricading—militarizing—the border. "This sort of schizophrenia toward Mexico is nothing new," some immigration scholars have noted. "Throughout the twentieth century the United States regularly encouraged or welcomed the entry of Mexican workers while publicly pretending not to do so."[84] From the time of Mexico's entry into the General Agreement on Tariffs and Trade (GATT) in 1986 and its membership in the trinational North American Free Trade Agreement (NAFTA) in 1994, the U.S.-Mexico border would be closed to the free movement of migrating workers, while capital flows and goods would pass through the border in both directions with little hindrance.

In response to the growing outcry of the public over illegal immigration in the border states, Congress appropriated record levels of funding to the INS to stanch the flow of unauthorized immigrants at the border by doubling the number of border patrol agents, building fences at key crossing points in San Diego and El Paso from Mexico, and in some cases using the National Guard to assist in various short-term border "operations," such as Operation Gatekeeper in San Diego.[85] Governors of California, Texas, Florida, and New York began threatening lawsuits unless the federal government took action to halt illegal immigration. They complained that unauthorized immigrants were draining billions of dollars in state welfare funds, taking jobs, committing crimes, crowding hospital emergency rooms, and overwhelming the public schools with their "anchor baby" children. Like

Reagan and Bush before him, President Bill Clinton did not place illegal immigration and increased border security high on his list of priorities, but widespread public frustration over the failure of IRCA to stem the flow of undocumented immigrants could not be ignored. Clinton authorized $540 million to add 1,010 new Border Patrol agents and erect miles of corrugated steel walls and high-power stadium lighting along the border in the San Diego and El Paso sectors.[86]

The Mexican government was none too happy over the militarization of a shared international border and was annoyed that it was not consulted when the United States constructed a 14-mile, 10-foot-high wall spanning the Tijuana-San Ysidro border crossing in California, just months after signing the trilateral NAFTA to eliminate trade barriers between Canada, the United States, and Mexico. "These walls don't do anything," said Mexico's foreign minister, Manuel Tello: "Mexicans are specialists in making holes. . . . There's no way a wall . . . will stop a Mexican from entering the U.S. if he wants to." Even more worrisome, Tello noted, was the predictable xenophobic response of Californians when the economy takes a nosedive to "blame everything that goes wrong there on the Mexicans."[87]

If the 1980s was the "Decade of the Hispanic" that saw the rise of the "illegal alien" in an era of expansive immigration reform, the 1990s saw an end to the almost genteel give-and-take between liberal and conservatives as they worked through a series of compromises to pass IRCA and the 1990 Immigration Act. The public, it seemed, was not nearly as liberal-minded as congressional policymakers where immigration in general was concerned, particularly illegal immigration from Mexico. Citizens in the border states came increasingly to resent Mexicans coming to the United States to take advantage of liberal welfare policies. They resented the Supreme Court ruling in *Plyler v. Doe* (1982) that prevented Texas from denying public education to the undocumented school-age children. They believed that many undocumented immigrants served as drug couriers for the Mexican cartels, spreading their poison to the nation's youth. And they resented undocumented Mexican mothers who crossed the border to give birth to—to "drop"—"anchor babies." The media often fanned the flames of xenophobia with stories on gang warfare, crime, blighted neighborhoods, identity theft, and the "secret" agenda of immigrants to reconquer the Southwest for Mexico. The opening salvo in the backlash decade of the 1990s began, to no one's surprise, in California, where the majority of undocumented Mexican immigrants resided, and where the Republican Party hoped to capitalize on the state's—and the nation's—growing hostility to immigration in general, and Mexican "illegal aliens" in particular.

8

FORTRESS AMERICA

Throughout the 1980s many Americans clamored for stricter border controls and immigration reform at the same time that they recognized the cultural, political, and economic impact of the fast-growing Hispanic population. When the Immigration Reform and Control Act (IRCA) failed to curtail illegal immigration, California, Arizona, and many other states began to take matters into their own hands. If the federal government was unwilling or unable to deter unauthorized entry from Mexico, the states would pass laws to make life harder for undocumented immigrants and their children. The backlash against the growing numbers of "illegal aliens" dominated the last decade of the twentieth century and began in California, which led the nation as a destination for undocumented immigrants. The Immigration and Naturalization Service (INS) estimated that almost half of the undocumented immigrant population in the United States resided in California in the 1990s. The state's population surged nearly 26 percent in the 1980s, adding about 6 million new residents fueled by the booming aerospace and other industries that made the Golden State a magnet for both U.S. and immigrant job seekers, as well as ground zero for mounting xenophobia toward "alien immigrants" who Anglos feared were changing California—and America—into something foreign, strange, and "third world."[1]

In less than a decade the nation went from granting amnesty to 3 million undocumented immigrants during the "Decade of the Hispanic" to the backlash 1990s and post-9/11 era when states, fueled by popular fears and uncertainty, passed harsh laws against unsanctioned immigrants, like California's Proposition 187 to deny unauthorized aliens state welfare, education, and medical services, and Arizona's SB 1070, which allows police officers to arrest unauthorized immigrants under the state's trespassing law.

Under pressure from the states and the public nationally, Congress and the Clinton administration began a program of fence building and quasi-military operations to barricade the border in areas of heaviest illicit border crossing. Many states passed resolutions to make English the official language and took steps to end bilingual education. The decade of the 1990s was not openly anti-Latino, but aggressive local and state policies against unauthorized immigrants from Mexico, the movement to suppress the use of Spanish, and the growing obsession with "border security" all contributed to a growing sense among many Latinos that they were being targeted.

In the years leading up to Proposition 187 in 1994, California had led the country in efforts to establish English as the official language of the nation. "English First" and "U.S. English" advocates, like former California senator S. I. Hayakawa, who unsuccessfully sought to have the U.S. Congress declare English the official national language in 1981, and Texas representative James Horn, worried that the "dangerous spread of 'bilingualism' in our society" threatened to divide the nation into different linguistic camps, much like francophone Quebec in Canada. Bilingual education in public schools was inaugurated as part of the Great Society of the late 1960s to help school-age immigrant children make the transition to English in public schools by providing limited instruction in their native languages. The success rate of these programs has been the source of much heated debate for decades, but the dominance of English in the United States—indeed in the world—has yet to face a serious challenge. The ascendancy of English globally as the language of technology and finance has grown steadily since World War II, as has the influence of the English-language media—from Hollywood movies to music videos—on youth cultures of the world. One Latino journalist wondered why so many Californians got so "worked up" about people in cities like Los Angeles speaking Spanish. "That has always been the case with new immigrants," he wrote. "Wait a few years and their children will be listening to rock 'n roll like their peers."[2] Indeed a Rand Corporation survey in 1985 found that more than 95 percent of U.S.-born, second-generation Latinos were proficient in English, and that over half of all third-generation Latinos spoke no Spanish at all. "The plain fact is that making English the official language of the United States," wrote one linguist, "is about as urgently called for as making hot-dogs the official food at baseball games."[3] Nevertheless, Proposition 63, the referendum making English California's official language, passed with a lopsided 73 percent of the vote.[4]

Within a few years, Arizona, Colorado, and Florida also voted to designate English as their official language and to restrict the use of other tongues in official government business. Opponents called the movement for "English only" thinly veiled nativism—linguistic bigotry—aimed primarily at the large population of Mexican immigrants in the Southwest and Cubans in Florida, where Miami had already become a bilingual city owing to its large population of Cuban refugees and their descendants.[5] These state laws were not intended to challenge federal laws, like the use of foreign languages in bilingual education programs, public health, or safety, or bilingual ballots as mandated by the 1965 Voting Rights Act where 5 percent or more of voters lacked English-language proficiency (at the time of writing 248 counties in 30 states). The ordinances were mainly symbolic and were as innocuous as the wording of the congressional resolution proposing an amendment to the constitution: "The English language shall be the official language of the United States." Most advocates understood that the passage of such ordinances would not silence the immigrants speaking in their native tongues. As one lobbyist for U.S. English put it: "These laws only aim to preserve English as a common language, to serve as a bridge across the language barriers that are present in our country." But many Latino/a language activists were not buying the view that these laws were mostly symbolic. For Martha Jimenez of the Mexican American Legal Defense and Education Fund, the laws "prevent people from having meaningful access to the government to which they pay taxes." She added that in the United States, "no one is more aware of the social, political and economic importance of learning English than those who cannot speak it."[6] One journalist satirized the "officialization of English" in California by alluding to the problem of the governor's name: "Does anybody here think 'Deukmejian' sounds English enough to be official? Hardly suggests a cottage in Sussex with dear old Nanny slicing into a steaming plum pudding while grumbling to the upstairs maid about poachers in the grouse patch, does it?"[7]

The chairman of the U.S. English national campaign, John Tanton, a retired Michigan eye doctor, blamed "self-serving ethnic politicians" for promoting bilingual education, bilingual ballots, and other multilingual services that had created "language ghettos" of non-English-speaking people. But making the English language "official" was not his principal goal: Tanton believed, like many white nativists, that Anglo America and all it stood for was in imminent danger of being overrun by dark, dangerous alien immigrants, particularly from Mexico, because of their high fertility, low education, and Catholic religion. Tanton, who also founded the the Federation for American Immigration Reform (FAIR), an immigration restriction organization, and a host of other immigration restrictionist organizations (NumbersUSA, Center for Immigration Studies, and U.S. English, among others), had written a memo in 1986 in which he railed against the "non-economic" consequences of the "Latino onslaught" because of their "greater reproductive powers," abetted by the Catholic Church's opposition to contraception. The low fertility of Anglo Americans coupled with hyperreproductive Mexican immigrants would have disastrous consequences for America's future: "Can homo contraceptivus compete with homo progenitiva if borders aren't controlled? . . . Perhaps this is the first instance in which those with their pants up are going to get caught by those with their pants down."[8]

Demographic predictions that whites would be a minority in California before the turn of the century and a minority of the nation's population in the twenty-first century deeply troubled Tanton: "In California of 2030, the non-Hispanic Whites and Asians will own the property, have the good jobs and education, speak one language and be mostly Protestant," while blacks and Latinos will own little property, lack good jobs and education, speak different languages, and be "mainly Catholic." Unless the United States could stop or reverse the browning of America, Tanton asked rhetorically, will the "present majority [whites] peacefully hand over its political power to a group that is simply more fertile?"[9] Several years later, Tanton told a colleague: "I've come to the point of view that for European-American society and culture to persist requires a European-American majority and a clear one at that."[10]

While many saw California's Proposition 63 as an expression of linguistic chauvinism and nativist animus against the 1.6 million undocumented immigrants residing in the state, a majority of Californians had more practical concerns about taxes, the dire budget deficit, an overgrown social welfare system, jobs, crime, and border security, and they blamed undocumented immigrants for economic problems afflicting the state. The failure of IRCA in 1986 to stanch the flow of unsanctioned migrants from Mexico led California and four other states—Texas, Arizona, Florida, and New Jersey—to sue the federal government to recover billions of dollars expended on unauthorized immigrants who they argued were the federal government's responsibility. Pete Wilson, a two-term Republican senator elected as governor of California in 1990, struggled for reelection as the state's sluggish economy was slow to come out of the recession and his polls showed him trailing by twenty points. But all that changed when he lent his support to a ballot initiative, Proposition 187 ("Save Our State"), and made it the centerpiece of his reelection campaign, blaming "illegal aliens" for costing the state an estimated $3 billion annually in public services and bankrupting the state. The initiative, if passed, would bar undocumented immigrants from receiving welfare, education, nonemergency medical care, and other services paid for by the state—and require teachers and health care workers to report suspected "illegal aliens" to immigration authorities.[11]

Wilson took out full-page newspaper ads of an "open letter" to President Clinton "on behalf of the people of California," in which he asked: "Why even have a Border Patrol and I.N.S. if we are going to continue the insanity of providing [government-funded] incentives to illegal immigrants to violate U.S. immigration laws?" One of Wilson's TV ads featured a clip from grainy Border Patrol infrared film footage showing the dark outlines of immigrants dodging traffic across the I-5 freeway in southern California with the menacing line: "They keep coming."[12] Wilson's hard line against undocumented workers contrasted with the legislation he authored previously as a U.S. senator (with a large agribusiness constituency) that advocated a generous guest worker program and that forbade the INS from conducting raids on farm fields without a judge's warrant.[13] Wilson went a step further than Proposition 187 and called for the repeal of the clause in the Fourteenth Amendment granting citizenship to persons born in the United States because of the growing number of "emergency alien deliveries" in California hospitals to mothers residing in the state illegally. As native-born American citizens, these "anchor babies" would be entitled to a full range of social services, including preferential treatment for family members who wish to enter the country as legal immigrants.[14]

Proposition 187 would create a state-mandated screening process to verify the legal status of all persons seeking public education, health care, and other public services. It also would make it a felony offense to use, make, or distribute false documents to obtain public services. Many Californians who supported the initiative felt that the future of the state was at stake: Would it remain an economically viable state with a strong Anglo-Saxon Protestant culture, or would Mexicans fundamentally change the character of the state into an extension of northern Mexico—"Mexifornia"? One proponent of 187 believed that a cultural showdown between Anglos and Latinos was inevitable: "They've never merged into the culture . . . it's kind of an island of English-speaking people surrounded by . . . lots of Mexicans." Another supporter, an advertising executive, feared the power of the Latino vote as the Mexican-American population continued to grow: "Hispanics could take over . . . They are going to do it legislatively. And there are already radical forces within the Latino community that promote that." Another proponent believed Latinos were a favored minority and that the federal government had turned a "blind eye" to immigration from Mexico: "I've often wondered how we would have reacted if China were on our border instead of Mexico . . .

Yes, I think it would be much different. We'd have tanks and everything at our border."[15]

Opponents of 187 included doctors and health care workers who worried about the medical consequences of people untreated for communicable illnesses and diseases that would put whole communities at risk. Teachers and school principals objected to being turned into immigration agents responsible for investigating the legal status of school children and their families and reporting suspected "illegals" to the authorities. Police departments also objected to taking on the added burden of enforcing federal immigration laws. A commander with the Los Angeles Police Department, who worried that his force barely had enough detectives to work on murder cases, called 187's directive to track down unauthorized immigrants "administrative lunacy."[16] Ironically, the initiative would not have made it a crime for employers to hire undocumented workers or penalize them as required by the provisions of the IRCA of 1986.

Californians engaged in a fierce debate between those who opposed the measure—unions, religious leaders, educators, students, health professionals, and law-enforcement officials—and those in favor, 80 percent of whom described themselves in exit polls as Republicans or conservatives. Certainly not all Democrats opposed 187 or Republicans favored it. Ron Unz, a Republican who opposed 187 and Pete Wilson in the 1994 primary, but who also supported the official English campaign, argued that the overwhelming majority of immigrants were "self-reliant and entrepreneurial, with strong families and low welfare-dependency and crime rates." Illegal immigrants were California's "unwanted house guests," he acknowledged, but 187's solution to driving them away—"set your own house on fire and burn it to the ground"—was over the top. "It would be a financial and social disaster for California," he warned, "and the worst moral disaster for our state since the internment of the Japanese-Americans."[17] Two other staunch Republican conservatives opposed the initiative: former U.S. secretary of education William Bennett and former U.S. representative Jack Kemp. They issued a statement through a proimmigration think tank they cofounded, Empower America: "We urge Republicans not to support an anti-immigration movement which we consider in the long run to be politically unwise and . . . would help contribute to a nativist, anti-immigrant climate. . . . It seems to us that some of the most vocal and prominent voices in the anti-immigration movement fail to recognize the valuable contribution immigrants continue to make to this nation; unfairly blame immigrants for being the source of America's social and moral decline; and mistakenly assume that immigrants are a net economic liability."[18]

Others opposed 187 irrespective of party affiliation because of the direct effects it would have on their occupations. Teachers, for example, did not want to run interference for the INS and students did not want their class-mates pulled from the schools and summarily deported. In Los Angeles, over ten thousand students walked out of thirty-two middle and high schools in protest against the initiative, which had attracted national and international media attention. President Clinton weighed in against passage of the initiative, although he confessed that the federal government "should do more to help to stop illegal immigration and to help California bear the costs of the illegal immigrants who are there." But the majority of Californians had grown weary of a succession of presidents since Ronald Reagan promising to enact effective immigration reform and secure the southern border.[19] The proposition passed handily, with 59 percent of the voters approving the measure, although District Judge Mariana Pfaelzer granted an injunction blocking 187 on the ground that it was in conflict with federal immigration authority. Nonetheless, 187's symbolic message was clear: many were tired of the hypocrisy of the federal government promising to do something about illegal immigration while supporting big business that benefitted most from cheap immigrant labor. Wilson, who had been trailing his opponent Kathleen Brown just months before the election, won reelection by a comfortable margin, as did other Republican candidates who supported the initiative.

Mexican immigrants began to realize that, even as legal residents, they had few rights or protections that could not be curtailed by anti-immigrant initiatives. Their only fail-safe protection against the erosion of their rights and privileges was to become naturalized citizens of the United States, a status that bestowed the full panoply of rights and obligations that accrued to natural-born citizens, as well as the singular right to exercise the vote in determining who should represent them and their interests in local, state, and national elections. As nativist sentiments took hold in California, Mexican immigrants rushed to take out citizenship papers, even though Mexicans historically have had the lowest rate of naturalization of any major immigrant group and constituted the single largest population of non-citizen legal residents in the United States. But the number of naturalized citizens from Mexico rose by 144 percent from 1995 to 2005, the sharpest increase in naturalization among immigrants from any major sending country.[20] As tens of thousands of legal Mexican nationals took out naturalization papers to become citizens, they "marched out the doors," as one journalist put it, "into the welcoming arms of the Democrats, who just as quickly registered them as new voters." "In California," he concluded, "the GOP never recovered from 'they keep coming.'"[21]

In Mexico, politicians and the press roundly condemned the California initiative as racist and xenophobic, as did many leaders of Latin-American countries who argued that such legislation, if acted upon, would severely damage U.S. relations with Latin America. Many were simply appalled by the provision to deny education to school-age undocumented immigrants. Upon his arrival at the first Summit of the Americas, convened in Miami in 1994 and attended by representatives from thirty-four nations of North, Central, and South America to discuss the formation of trade blocs and open markets, Guatemalan president Ramiro de León Carpio attacked Proposition 187 as "a flagrant and massive violation of human rights, especially to children." El Salvadoran president Armando Calderon Sol said it was "inconceivable in the United States that a state could vote for something which violates . . . international children's rights."[22] Mexican president Carlos Salinas de Gortari declared that the vote "tramples and ignores" the basic human rights of migrant workers in California. Of the undocumented residents of California who would be denied educational and medical services, Salinas asked: "What will happen to the children? Will they return to Mexico? Wash windshields in California? Sell newspapers on the streets or beg?" Salinas reminded Mexicans that Proposition 187 did not represent the will of all American citizens or the federal government, and that he was bound by principle and hemispheric agreements not to interfere in the internal affairs of other countries. In Mexico City, however, two thousand Mexican citizens marched to the U.S. embassy under the banner of the Convención Nacional Democrática (National Democratic Convention) to protest California's ballot initiative and denounce "Wilson culeeeeero" (asshole Wilson); they also called President Salinas's response to 187 "tibia y tardía" (too little too late). After 187 was passed, some vandalized the McDonald's in Mexico City's Zona Rosa tourist district, and in San Diego, Mexican consul general Ramón Xilotl warned that progress toward implementing the North American Free Trade Agreement (NAFTA) could be jeopardized if California's "sentimiento antimexicano" spread to the rest of the United States.[23]

Supporters of 187 steadfastly denied any racist intent toward unlawful Mexican residents. While they worried that Mexicans might be taking some kinds of work that deservedly should go to citizens and legal residents, what terrified many middle-class white Californians was the formation of a criminal underclass of "illegals" in their midst. Unlawfully crossing the border or overstaying one's visa became in the eyes of many Californians evidence not just of illegality but of criminal behavior. The trope of Mexicans as criminals and "bandits" had a long history in California as elsewhere in the Southwest. In the 1990s, Californians hoped to save their state from the lawlessness of Mexico by those who broke U.S. laws to come to the country to deceive employers with false documents and "steal" taxpayer money by availing themselves of public services and education for their children. A *Los Angeles Times* poll in Orange County, the birthplace of 187, reported that more than half the residents viewed Latinos as "more inclined to violence" than others.[24] Throughout the twentieth century, Mexico was portrayed in countless novels, movies, and the print media as a country in perpetual turmoil, a place of violence and aggression, where the figure of the *bandido* lives on as "urban bandits"—gang members—in films like *Boulevard Nights* (1979), *Colors* (1988), *American Me* (1992), *Blood In Blood Out* (1993) and *Mi Vida Loca* (1994) that depict the violence of Mexican gang members in East Los Angeles.[25] The increasing violence along the border between rival drug cartels abetted the perception of Mexico as a place of lawlessness and corruption.

The passage of 187 was aimed at unauthorized immigrants already present in California and was intended to make illegal immigration a central issue in state and national politics. Augmenting the number of Border Patrol agents had predictably resulted in increased apprehensions, but did little to prevent those apprehended from returning shortly after they were deported, much less reduce the total number of illicit border-crossers.[26] In response to the growing demand for the federal government to secure the border, the Clinton administration shifted from a policy of apprehending unauthorized immigrants to preventing them from crossing the border in the first place—"prevention through deterrence"—by quasi-military operations to barricade the border.[27] The militarization of the border began in earnest in 1994, the same year as California's Proposition 187, when Attorney General Janet Reno announced "Operation Gatekeeper." Modeled after a similar program—Operation Blockade (renamed "Hold the Line")—along the Texas-Mexico border at El Paso, Operation Gatekeeper added 1,000 immigration agents, new surveillance tactics, and two parallel fences and lighting to the stretch of border between urban Tijuana, Mexico's third-largest city, and San Diego, the eighth-largest city in the United States.[28]

Other operations were launched at key border points: Operation Safeguard in Arizona (1996) and Operation Rio Grande in Brownsville, Texas (1997). In the first year of Operation Gatekeeper Border Patrol agents apprehended almost a half million unsanctioned immigrants, surpassing apprehensions in other heavily traveled corridors of illegal entry at Tuscon, Arizona, and El Paso, Texas. With ten-foot-high walls made of corrugated steel landing mats left over from the Vietnam War, buried seismic sensors, and Border Patrol all-terrain jeeps and helicopters with high-tech surveillance equipment, Operation Gatekeeper succeeded in barricading the border at San Diego/Tijuana but experienced a corresponding increase of illicit border crossing and drug smuggling to the east in the Imperial Valley Desert where summer temperatures reached 120 degrees. Between 1994 and 1998, over three hundred migrants along the border east of San Diego died of dehydration, hypothermia, or heat stroke, and 115 slipped into the fast-rushing water of the All-American Canal and drowned. Operations like Gatekeeper and Hold the Line at historically popular border-crossing points near cities like San Diego, Tuscon, and El Paso forced migrants to attempt crossings at less traveled but more remote and dangerous desert areas. By 2000 nearly seventeen hundred migrants had died along the U.S.-Mexico border, the majority of them in the deserts of Sonora and Arizona, the so-called "Devil's Highway," or drowned in the Rio Grande. Some froze to death in the Laguna Mountains east of San Diego. In the first six years of Operation Gatekeeper and Hold the Line, the Border Patrol apprehended 88,000 fewer unsanctioned migrants at the California border, but 564,409 more at the Arizona border and 188,168 more crossing into Texas. As one immigration official put it, "It's like squeezing a balloon. The air has got to go somewhere."[29]

The deaths of hapless migrants drowning in canals and rivers or dying from heat stroke and dehydration in the desert represented the dark side of U.S. border policy and its quasi-military approach to barricading the border, but there were other consequences, less tragic to be sure, which nonetheless illustrated the long-term ineffectiveness of border barriers. Smuggling rings, for example, benefitted enormously from "prevention through deterrence" immigration policies. As crossing became more difficult and dangerous, migrants increasingly came to rely on "coyotes" or "polleros"—human traffickers—to smuggle them across the border at highly inflated prices that left migrants and their families deeply in debt for the passage. Migrants who successfully made the journey were less inclined to make the return trip to Mexico to visit family, as many had been accustomed to doing, because of the high cost of coyotes and the often life-threatening dangers of returning on the Devil's Highway. Operation Gatekeeper thus turned many unsanctioned temporary workers into long-term or permanent residents.[30]

The prospect of earning more than ten times their wages for a day's work in Mexico in the United States outweighed the risks and the costs of migrating. As one journalist put it, "there is an unlucky man in the Sonoran Desert today who will die for a chance to pluck dead chickens in Georgia or change diapers in a rest home in Nevada."[31] Mexico's entry into NAFTA in 1994 was supposed to create enough jobs that would reduce the need for the increasingly hazardous "safety valve" of Mexicans risking their lives to find good-paying jobs in the United States. But the results were mixed. The surge in direct foreign investment in Mexico led to an increase of 500,000 jobs in manufacturing from 1994 to 2002, but the agricultural sector, where almost a fifth of Mexicans worked, lost 1.3 million jobs. Corn, the crop upon which the pre-Hispanic Mayan civilization was built over eight centuries ago and to which 60 percent of Mexico's farmland was devoted, could be grown more cheaply on heavily subsidized agribusiness farms in the United States. As Mexico's protective tariffs were lowered each year during a fifteen-year transition period, U.S. corn imports increased by 400 percent. Displaced corn farmers in the rural reaches of southern Mexico—Yucatan, Veracruz, Oaxaca—were forced to join migrant streams from central and northern Mexico to the United States to earn a living wage. Mexico's assistant agriculture secretary, José Luis Solis, admitted that NAFTA "would have a significant effect of massive unemployment in the Mexican countryside," but that cheap corn would benefit the majority of Mexicans since 75 percent of the population was urban.[32] A decade after its ratification, according to a Carnegie Endowment report, "NAFTA has not helped the Mexican economy keep pace with the growing demand for jobs." With the number of visas allotted for Mexican workers grossly inadequate to meet demand, unsanctioned migration continued to increase after NAFTA, as did apprehensions along the border, which increased from 700,000 in 1994 to more than 1.3 million by 2001. During the same period the number of undocumented immigrants increased from 3.5 million to 9.3 million, despite Operation Gatekeeper and INS raids.[33] NAFTA, in short, resulted in the free flow of capital and goods across the border at the same time that the United States was building border fences to keep Mexicans out—a borderless economy and a barricaded border—that, according to Mexico's former president, Carlos Salinas, was supposed to empower a richer, more prosperous Mexico "to export goods, not people."[34] Faith in the free market had been eclipsed in the United States by fear of immigrants. Salvador Reza, an organizer of Mexican day laborers in Phoenix, many of them undocumented immigrants, said he couldn't understand why America accepts global flows of companies, money, and jobs but not workers. "They actually are people with a work ethic that would make the Puritans proud," he said.[35]

In 1994, during the midterm elections in President Clinton's first term in office, the Republican Party won control of both houses of Congress for the first time in forty years and saw an opportunity to legislatively fix the ongoing problem of illegal immigration. Republican senator Alan Simpson of

Wisconsin and Republican representative Lamar Smith of Texas, sensing a strong national consensus, introduced bills calling for stricter enforcement measures to deter illegal immigration, since virtually all sides of the immigration issue agreed that IRCA had fundamentally failed to deter illegal immigration by penalizing employers who hired undocumented workers. Although begun in California, the groundswell against illegal immigration caught on nationally and crested in 1996 with the passage of a landmark immigration reform law that included some of the toughest provisions ever enacted against unauthorized immigrants: the Illegal Immigration Reform and Immigrant Responsibility Act (IIRIRA). Like Proposition 187 before it, IIRIRA sought to remove the lure of welfare benefits and public services for undocumented immigrants, but it went a step further by limiting benefits for legal immigrants, who would be ineligible for social services for their first five years in the country, and their sponsors would have to sign an affidavit of financial support for the first five years.[36]

But the main objective of IIRIRA was to crack down on illegal immigration: it doubled the number of Border Patrol agents to ten thousand over a period of five years and authorized the construction of a 14-mile fence on the border stretching eastward from the Pacific Ocean; enacted harsh penalties for smuggling and document fraud; streamlined procedures for expediting deportation without appeal to the courts; and inaugurated pilot programs to test electronic verification of workers' documents and work status. Unauthorized immigrants who stayed for six months after the law went into effect, and were caught, would be deported and banned from returning for three years, even if they obtained a legal visa. Those in the country illegally for a year or more faced ten-year bans. If deported immigrants disregarded the ban and entered the United States illegally, they would face stiff federal prison sentences. This provision applied to undocumented immigrants regardless of whether they had a spouse or children who were U.S. citizens. Finally, unauthorized immigrants with misdemeanor arrest records, such as theft of baby clothes from a department store, could be deported without judicial review. Three years after the passing of IIRIRA, the INS had placed 16,000 immigrants in detention centers, triple the number it had before IIRIRA, which required all citizens convicted of crimes to be detained for deportation. In addition to expanded border security measures, IIRIRA created a memorandum of understanding, called 287(g), that empowered local police to cooperate with federal immigration agencies in identifying and deporting unauthorized immigrants. Critics denounced the new law as the most draconian legislation since the immigration restriction acts of the 1920s.[37]

Two years after the passage of IIRIRA, in 1998, the anti-immigrant forces of California expressed themselves yet again in another statewide proposition, this time to end bilingual education—Proposition 227. Bilingual education, mandated by the federal government in 1968, provided funding for school districts to teach English to non-English-speaking school-age immigrants without losing their first language. Opponents of bilingual education, like former California senator S. I. Hayakawa and Silicon Valley businessman Ron Unz, argued that Americans should speak "English only." Unz, head of the California chapter of U.S. English, spearheaded Proposition 227, which required that "English immersion" programs be implemented in place of bilingual programs in so-called sheltered English classrooms, followed by immersion in English-only classrooms. Despite research showing that learning a new language is facilitated by a transitional period of simultaneous English-language and native-language instruction, many Californians worried that record numbers of Mexican immigrants would cling to Spanish and reject "Americanization." Proposition 227 passed with 61 percent of the vote, reflecting deeper fears about the rapidly changing "face" of California as a direct result of illegal immigration from Mexico. Flushed with success, Unz took the antibilingual education campaign to Arizona where a referendum there, Proposition 203, passed in 2000 with 63 percent of the vote.[38] The enactment of Proposition 227, like Propositions 63 (official English) and 187 (denial of public services to undocumented immigrants), reflected fears that California, at least southern California, was becoming less like the rest of the country and more like Mexico.

The election of George W. Bush in 2000 continued the pattern of formulating immigration reform and greater integration with Mexico under NAFTA at the same time that the administration presided over the massive buildup of border security and enforcement begun almost a decade earlier. Bush announced his interest in reviving a guest worker program with Mexico, similar to the Bracero Program that ended in 1964, that would give legal status to laborers from Mexico to work in the United States on temporary work contracts. Mexican president Vicente Fox also supported the idea of a guest worker program that included amnesty of the kind granted by Congress in 1986, which gave legal status to an estimated 3 million undocumented immigrants.[39] But talks about immigration reform came to a complete standstill after the terrorist attacks on September 11, 2001, as the administration's War on Terror reframed immigration reform as a national security issue.

Before 9/11 immigration restrictionists worried mainly about the effects of an impoverished Global South on the American economy and culture:

immigrants taking American jobs and the mushrooming cost of providing social, medical, and educational services to undocumented immigrants. Others worried about the ominous cultural and linguistic consequences of the "browning of America." After 9/11 Americans were principally preoccupied with their safety and security: immigrants, legal and illegal, became suspected "fifth columnists" for terrorist organizations like Al-Qaeda. Immigrants don't just "take our jobs"—they take our lives. America would never be safe until the federal government sealed the U.S.-Mexico border from surreptitious entry by dangerous terrorist aliens. "We can't protect ourselves from terrorism," declared Steven Camarota, director of research for the Center for Immigration Studies, "without dealing with illegal immigration."[40] Mexican president Fox, while sensitive to the United States' need to feel secure from terrorism, reminded Americans of the distinction between anti-American foreign terrorists who flew hijacked planes into buildings and impoverished Mexicans who entered the United States illegally to fill jobs as construction workers and nannies. The scapegoating of unauthorized immigrants as potential terrorists ignores the fact, then and now, that most acts of domestic terror in the last two decades have been carried out by domestic terrorists: the Unabomber, Timothy McVeigh, who blew up the Oklahoma federal building killing 168 people, the 2001 anthrax attacks, and numerous school, church, and workplace shooter rampages.

But unlike most domestic attacks, the surprise attacks on September 11, 2001, that took thousands of lives in the middle of the nation's largest city shocked America so deeply that news reporters and television commentators likened the aerial strikes on the Twin Towers and the Pentagon to the Japanese attack on Pearl Harbor on December 7, 1941.[41] Within days of the attack President Bush announced that he would create an Office of Homeland Security that would oversee and coordinate a national strategy to safeguard the country against any future terrorist attacks. The new cabinet-level Department of Homeland Security (DHS), which combined twenty-two different federal agencies and departments, was charged with preventing attacks within the United States, reducing America's vulnerability to terrorism, and recovering from attacks that do occur. When the Democratic governors of Arizona (Janet Reno) and New Mexico (Bill Richardson) declared an immigration "emergency" in their states because the federal government had failed to prevent illicit border-crossing, DHS secretary Michael Chertoff announced that the problem of illegal immigration across the U.S.-Mexico border was a national security issue that had to be solved "once and for all."[42] The deputy secretary of DHS, James Loy, testified before Congress that "Al Qaeda leaders believe operatives can pay their way into the country through Mexico and also believe illegal entry is more advantageous than legal entry for operational security reasons." After 9/11, "the fear one heard in America," one journalist wrote, "was that agents of violence from the Middle East might easily disguise themselves as Latin American peasants and trespass into our midst."[43]

Immigration reform and border security had become flip sides of the same policy coin. Increasingly political discourse conflated unlawful entry with the potential for more terrorist acts. The largest component of DHS, U.S. Customs and Border Protection, which includes the Border Patrol, was created "with a priority mission," according to its webpage, "of keeping terrorists and their weapons out of the U.S."[44] The ranking Republican on the House Armed Services Committee, Duncan Hunter, made it clear what was needed to keep out terrorists and their weapons: "Our nation's security rests on the security of our borders. We know what we need to do. All we have to do is act." The solution, Duncan argued, was "more enforceable . . . border security fencing."[45] To make the border more secure from illegal immigrants, drug smugglers, and foreign terrorists, the House Homeland Security chairman Peter King urged DHS to deploy more unmanned aerial vehicles—drones—along the border because, he said, "We need to treat the border as a quasi-war zone."[46] By conflating illegal immigration with terrorism, border enforcement merged with the War on Terror and the War on Drugs to create, as one critic put it, "what can only be described as a permanent state of low-intensity warfare along the U.S.-Mexican border."[47]

President Bush believed in keeping the border with Mexico as open as possible, in keeping with his desire to work with Mexico on a guest worker policy. In 2000, his first year in office, he made his position on immigration clear: "Latinos have come to the U.S. to seek the same dreams that have inspired millions of others: they want a better life for their children. Family values do not stop at the Rio Grande River. Latinos enrich our country with faith in God, a strong ethic of work and community and responsibility. . . . New Americans are not to be feared as strangers; they are to be welcomed as neighbors."[48] After 9/11, however, he realized he could not make progress on his plan for comprehensive immigration reform without acceding to Republicans' demand to "secure the border." In Congress supporters of Bush's immigration reform, led by Republican senator John McCain and Democratic senator Ted Kennedy, introduced legislation to create a guest worker program and offer a "path to citizenship" for undocumented immigrants, which was essentially the agreement Bush and Mexican president Fox had negotiated in the months before 9/11. But House Judiciary Committee chairman Jim Sensenbrenner was fiercely opposed to the bipartisan bill because it did not include provisions to secure the border against illegal immigration before other initiatives, like a guest worker program or amnesty, could be considered. House Republicans agreed and flatly rejected the McCain-Kennedy Bill, which later failed in the Senate to come to a vote. Senator Kennedy, discouraged by the defeat, lashed out at those who opposed the bill: "What are they going to do with the 12 million who are undocumented here? Send them back to countries around the world? Develop a type of Gestapo here to seek out these people that are in the shadows? What's their alternative?"[49]

Sensenbrenner's bill, H.R. 4437, the "Border Protection, Anti-Terrorism and Illegal Immigration Control Act," called for the construction of a 700-mile reinforced fence along the border, and included two provisions that were so shockingly punitive that millions of Americans took to the streets to protest: the bill made "illegal presence" in the United States an "aggravated felony" instead of a civil offense—in other words, unauthorized immigrants could be subject to the sentencing guidelines similar to those for murder, rape, and sexual abuse of a minor. The bill would also subject any person found guilty of assisting an undocumented immigrant to a prison sentence of up to five years. It included no guest worker or legalization provisions. Nonetheless, the Sensenbrenner Bill, the most draconian anti-immigrant legislation ever seriously proposed, easily passed in the Republican-dominated House, 239 to 182, with the majority of members voting along party lines (92 percent of Republicans in favor and 82 percent of Democrats opposed). Sensenbrenner said the bill would "help restore the integrity of our nation's borders and re-establish respect for our laws by holding violators accountable, including . . . employers who hire illegal aliens and alien gang members who terrorize communities."[50]

In response to the bill, 3.5 million immigrants and native-born Americans organized peaceful marches in 120 cities from March to May 1, 2006, including Los Angeles, Chicago, New York, San Antonio, Houston, Dallas, Phoenix, San Francisco, Detroit, Atlanta, and many others, according to the Mexico Institute at the Woodrow Wilson International Center for Scholars. The marchers objected to making it an "aggravated felony" to be in the country without proper authorization. Many carried signs, reading "We Are Not Criminals," and "Hoy Marchamos, Mañana Votamos" (Today We March, Tomorrow We Vote). Church groups and nonprofit organizations also objected to being threatened with prison sentences for aiding undocumented immigrants by offering them legal aid, social welfare, or sanctuary to those about to be deported.[51] By their numbers and sheer presence, millions of marchers across the nation rendered themselves visible, and "by simply

Illegal-alien "babies" at a march in Los Angeles for comprehensive immigration reform, May 1, 2010. Their T-shirts read: "I don't want to keep being an alien. I want to be legal." Courtesy of Camilo Bernal.

appearing," observed journalist Roberto Suro, "they made an existential statement, powerful for its simplicity: 'We are here. We are human, flesh and blood, parents and children . . . and we are many.'"[52] Another journalist, Richard Rodriguez, wrote: "It was the first time I had seen the children of illegality demanding that the United States show respect for their parents. It was the first time I had seen illegal parents, standing fearlessly in public with their children. I tell you it was a momentous time in the history of the Americas."[53] Senator Kennedy, addressing 200,000 people at a rally in Washington, DC, told those gathered: "I look across this historic gathering and I see the future of America. You are what this debate is about. It is about good people who come to America to work, to raise their families, to contribute to their communities, and to reach for the American dream. This debate goes to the heart of who we are as Americans. It will determine who can earn the privilege of citizenship. It will determine our strength in separating those who would harm us from those who contribute to our values."[54] Despite pleas across the nation for a kinder and gentler immigration policy, raids and deportations authorized by the DHS continued unabated. The president of the National Council of La Raza, Janet Murguía, declared at its annual convention in 2008, "Our nation's immigration laws need to be enforced. But what is happening today with these raids is an assault on civil rights, common decency and basic human dignity."[55]

With the House and Senate divided over immigration reform, both parties managed to agree on a bill that both houses could support: the construction of a reinforced fence along the border. A week before the midterm elections in 2006, Bush signed the Secure Fence Act authorizing the construction of a 700-mile border fence. "Unfortunately, the United States has not been in complete control of its borders for decades," Bush conceded, "and therefore illegal immigration has been on the rise. . . . We have a responsibility to secure our borders." The construction of a 700-mile reinforced fence, at a cost of $3 million per mile, was supposed to be the solution. Mexican president Fox was even less pleased than Bush with the construction of a border wall and issued a statement, signed by nearly every Central and South American member state of the Organization of American States, calling the "secure fence" legislation a unilateral measure that "goes against the spirit of understanding . . . between neighboring countries" and that undermines "cooperation in the hemisphere."[56]

Bush continued to argue that border enforcement ought to be accompanied by a guest worker program because, as he put it, "Willing workers ought to be matched with willing employers." He also hoped that with the passage of the Secure Fence Act Congress might pass the Development, Relief and Education for Alien Minors (DREAM) Act, which would grant legal residence to any undocumented minor brought to the United States as a child, provided they attended college or served in the military. The DREAM Act had already failed to pass three times as separate bills or attachments to omnibus bills between 2003 and 2005. Adversaries of the Act, calling it the Nightmare Act, warned that passage would lead to even more immigration under family reunification provisions, and that amnesty—even for children brought to the United States illegally through no fault of their own—would offer continued incentive to Mexican migrants to enter the United States unlawfully.[57] It began to look as if the threat to America had less to do with "illegal aliens" from Asia and Latin America per se than with the growing population of Latinos in the United States, especially Mexicans.

Domestic pressure to fence part of the border had simply become too great for either political party to ignore. California governor and former resident alien Arnold Schwarzenegger, who declared it was "just unfair to have all these people coming across," advanced an even more radical solution: "Close the borders in California and all across, between Mexico and the United States." Republicans, according to one writer, could not turn unauthorized

Protest against the Sensenbrenner Bill at the U.S. Capitol, March 2006, to make it a felony offense to be in the United States illegally. Courtesy of Rick Reinhard.

immigrants into felons, "prevent gays and lesbians from marrying, or capture Osama bin Laden, but at least they could build a border fence." *Time* magazine cynically alluded to the fence as "The Great Wall of America" and questioned whether any border barrier could "stop the tide of illegal aliens." The Mexican press was no less skeptical, as were leaders in Mexico and Central America who sometimes called the fence the "Wall of Shame" (Muro de la Vegüenza). Jorge Hernández, leader of the popular cross-over Mexican band Los Tigres del Norte, called the wall "a separation not only between our country and the United States, but also the rest of Latin America."[58]

Advocates of the border fence had argued for the urgent need to curb drug smuggling and contain the growing level of drug-related violence along the border, which was fueled by demand for drugs in the United States and competition among Mexican drug cartels fighting for territorial dominance. Drug smuggling across the U.S.-Mexico border historically involved regionally produced heroin and marijuana. In the 1980s, however, U.S. interdiction of cocaine trafficking routes from Colombia to the United States through the Caribbean and Florida resulted in a strategic alliance between Colombian cocaine exporters and Mexico's drug cartels. By the early 1990s over half of cocaine exports were routed through Mexico, elevating Mexico's position in the global drug trade as well as the wealth and influence of its warring drug cartels.[59] Successive Mexican governments have tried, with limited success, to curb the power and influence of the cartels that continue to smuggle drugs into the United States despite decades of increased border surveillance and control. Richard Rodriguez, son of Mexican immigrant parents, sees drugs, death, and decadence on both sides of the border that have less to do with fences and "security" than cultures in decline:

> On the Mexican side, if you stand with your back to the wall, you will see the poorest neighborhoods . . . weedy streets [that] have become the killing fields in an international drug war . . . where police kill federal soldiers who kill police who kill drug gangsters who kill other gangsters of the sort who did kill, apparently with impunity, at least 15 teenagers celebrating a soccer victory. . . . On the American side, if you stand with your back to the wall, you will see . . . suburban streets laid out in uniform blocks, and cul-de-sacs where Mexican gardeners are the only ambulatory human life. The suburban grid belies America's disorder. Grandma's knockoff Louis Vuitton handbag is so full of meds it sounds like a snake rattle. Grandma shares a secret addiction with her drug-addled dude of a grandson, whose dad prowls the Home Depot parking lot in his Japanese pickup, looking to hire a couple of Mexicans to clear out some dry scrub.[60]

Drug smuggling had always been a concern of those advocating stricter border enforcement and the construction of a fence, but it was only part of a larger complex of fears and anxieties that affected those living in the border states, as well as many Americans in cities across the country where "minorities" outnumbered whites. In 2004, two years before construction of the 700-mile border fence began, a loose network of mostly white men calling themselves the "Minutemen," including founders Jim Gilchrist (Minuteman Project) and Chris Simcox (Civil Homeland Defense), converged on the border to defend the sovereignty of the nation against the Brown Peril, doing what they claimed the government had failed to do, namely, enforce immigration laws at the U.S.-Mexico border.[61]

Armed with lawn chairs, binoculars, and in some instances, weapons, many Minutemen expressed concern that "illegal aliens" were not simply ignoring immigration laws, damaging property, transporting drugs, and taking jobs from U.S. citizens, they were also changing America in ways they did not like—and they aimed "to take America back." Minutemen saw themselves as patriots committed to protecting America from legions of "illegal aliens," the "enemy within" and the advance guard of an invading army. A sociologist who spent years on the border conducting interviews in Minutemen camps narrates a conversation with "Earl," a veteran of the first Gulf War and gun store owner in his mid-forties, who explains, "What's happening is nothing less than invasion. . . . We have already lost California. I walk around parts of Los Angeles and no one speaks English, all the signs are in Spanish. I feel like a complete outsider in my own country." Their goal, the interviewer tells us, "is deceptively simple: to prevent the collapse of America."[62] Earl loves America and worries about its future. He and others like him rarely encountered "José Sánchez," the collective name they used for "the enemy"; mostly, they spent long stretches of time together, drank beer, and swapped war stories about their tours of duty in the military.

Border volunteer groups like the Minuteman Project and Civil Homeland Defense were careful to warn racist groups advocating "white supremacy" that their members were not welcome at Minutemen camps, but the distinction between nativists, which described virtually all Minutemen volunteers, and racist white supremacists was often not very clear. When Simcox launched his Civil Homeland Defense volunteer border militia, the white supremacist blog Stormfront—calling itself a "White Nationalist Community"—enthusiastically supported his patriotic effort "to stop the Mexican invasion" and his call for "all White men to the front lines to do battle!" These "Aryan warriors," the blog continues, "seek nothing less than an end to the Browning of America."[63]

For most Minutemen, patrolling the border was less about catching "José"—or even spotting him—than it was about "reclaiming a lost masculinity, reliving the camaraderie and bravado from their service in the military."[64] "What brings them to the border is less a set of beliefs about Mexicans than a sense of nostalgia for days long past when . . . they felt like they were participating in the making of this country."[65] They were the older, white, retired, and often divorced working-class men who had been left behind by America's rapidly changing economy and made to feel increasingly powerless and unimportant, like a minority, which they were rapidly becoming, and who had begun to feel like strangers in their own land. "If José didn't exist," the sociologist writes, "the Minutemen would invent him."[66] But not all Minutemen were as peacefully patriotic and nostalgic for an older and whiter America as Earl. At one Minutemen encampment, a sixty-nine-year-old Special Forces veteran, Carl, declared, "It should be legal to kill illegals. . . . Just shoot'em on sight. That's my immigration policy recommendation. You break into my country, you die."[67] Another Minuteman in Arizona ready "to hunt Mexicans" sported a T-shirt that read: "Some people are alive simply because it's illegal to kill them."[68] At a summit meeting in Waco, Texas, with Mexican president Fox and Canadian prime minister Paul Martin, President Bush characterized the Minutemen as "vigilantes" that had no place in America.[69] Nonetheless, most Minutemen viewed themselves as border "soldiers" and patriots doing their part to prevent "José" from turning America into Mexico.

By the end of the first decade of the twenty-first century, Congress had failed to pass comprehensive immigration reform, failed to complete the border fence for lack of adequate funding, and had reduced funding for DHS's "Secure Border Initiative" to provide a "virtual fence" of surveillance technology along the border. But the murder of Arizona rancher Robert Krentz near the border, allegedly by an undocumented immigrant (no suspects have been arrested), sparked a firestorm of protest that led to Arizona politicians taking matters into their own hands: in spring 2010 the Arizona senate passed one of the most controversial anti-illegal immigration bills on record: SB 1070, "Support Our Law Enforcement and Safe Neighborhoods Act." The bill institutionalized racial profiling by requiring that police check the legal status of those they have a "reasonable suspicion" of being in the country illegally during "any lawful stop, detention or arrest" in the enforcement of local or state laws. In effect, Arizona would become the first state to demand that immigrants—or anyone who "looked like" one—carry documents demonstrating that they are in the country legally. SB 1070 would also set the standard for "states' rights" immigration enforcement that other states could follow.[70]

Although SB 1070 was mainly a nativist response to the bottleneck of illegal immigration along Arizona's 368-mile border with Mexico and the mistaken belief that crime was on the rise in in the state (crime rates were falling), the attacks of 9/11 had stoked fears of terrorists living in Arizonans' midst when it was found that one of the terrorists who crashed the plane into the Pentagon, Hanji Hanjoor, lived in Phoenix and received his flight training instruction in Scottsdale, while another terrorist, Lotfi Raissi, who lived in North Phoenix, provided flight training to four of the 9/11 terrorists. Some investigators and scholars began to suggest that metropolitan Phoenix had become a "sleeper cell" of Al-Qaeda.[71] Even though the 9/11 terrorists crossed the U.S.-Mexico border by air and not by land, some worried that post-9/11 terrorists ran fewer risks of surveillance once in the country, if they entered illegally across the border with Mexico or Canada. Few Arizonans seemed to focus on the more credible terrorist threat represented by unauthorized immigrants, say, from Saudi Arabia receiving flight instruction than the ubiquity of Mexican nationals in their midst, the majority of whom worked in construction and service industries.

Like California's Proposition 187, Arizona's harsh anti-illegal immigration law was in large part a reaction to economic hard times that aroused latent resentment over the supposed disproportionate use of state educational and medical services by the relatively young and poor Latino population, which had almost doubled in two decades. Arizona's fiscal crisis was worse than most states—staggering budget deficits, rising unemployment, and the massive collapse of the "real estate-industrial complex"—at the same time that it was dealing with a steady flow of unauthorized Mexicans crossing the border. After the housing bust in 2007, Arizona was ranked the fourteenth-poorest state, but by 2010 it was second only to Mississippi. Before the global financial crisis, Arizona benefitted from migration from the Midwest, retirees and others seeking its sunny climate, and from Mexicans from south of the border, who built the suburban homes of the mostly white transplants. In just three decades, from 1980 to 2010, the Latino population increased 180 percent, while the white population declined from 72 percent to 58 percent, and the white school-age population dropped to 43 percent, compared to 83 percent of the seniors. Like California and Texas, Arizona was on the fast track to becoming a majority-minority state. The backlash against immigrants, combined with low rates of Latino electoral participation, contributed to a resurgence of the Republican Party championed by law-and-order sheriffs and others who blamed unauthorized immigrants—"undocumented Democrats," as Rush Limbaugh called them—for Arizona's declining fortunes.[72]

Arizona had replaced the California border with Mexico as the leading magnet for illegal crossings, mainly as a result of the massive buildup of border enforcement along the 66-mile San Diego sector, beginning with the construction of reinforced border fences in the early 1990s and fast-tracked in 1994 with Operation Gatekeeper. Mexican migrants, forced to go around heavily fortified sectors, found less fortified areas along the border in the deserts of Sonora and Arizona. For years Arizona politicians had been complaining to the federal government that its failure to control the border was costing the states millions of dollars in public services. Part of the problem was the difficulty of constructing a continuous fence in the mountainous region of the border, as well as opposition from Arizona's Native Americans on the Tohono O'odham Indian Reservation, who complained that fence construction was desecrating sacred burial grounds and dividing their transnational homeland. SB 1070 was aimed at identifying and arresting unauthorized immigrants already living in Arizona and turning them over to U.S. Immigration and Customs Enforcement for deportation, or in some cases, detention and criminal prosecution. Governor Jan Brewer, whose election campaign was floundering until she signed SB 1070 and fueled immigration panic with stories about drug-related beheadings in the desert, hailed the law as "another tool for our state to use as we worked to solve a crisis we did not create and the federal government has refused to fix."[73]

Shortly after passing SB 1070, Arizona banned the teaching of ethnic studies courses in the Tucson Unified School District, especially courses on Mexican-American culture and history. The bill states that no school district shall include in its program of instruction any classes that "promote the overthrow of the United States Government, promote resentment toward a race or class of people, are designed primarily for pupils of a particular ethnic group, or advocate ethnic solidarity."[74] Unlike SB 1070's logic of "papers please" requiring all immigrants to carry proof of legal residence, HB 2281 aimed at denying one group of U.S. citizens—Mexican Americans—the right to study and explore their own history. These classes were developed in the wake of civil rights struggles of the 1960s and 1970s to expose young Latinos and Latinas to the struggles of their immigrant ancestors for inclusion and fair treatment in a country they helped build and defend in time of war. But Arizona superintendent of public instruction Tom Horne (and attorney general-elect) claimed that these classes promoted "ethnic chauvinism." Like many who believe Mexicans want to "reconquer" the Southwest, Horne told the *New York Times*: "They are teaching a radical ideology in Raza [Chicano/a studies], including that Arizona and other states were stolen from Mexico and should be given back." Phoenix journalist and playwright James E. Garcia summed up the reason behind the padlocking of Chicano/a studies: "It happened because the state's Latino population has nearly doubled in the past 20 years and the right wing is angry and afraid that it is helpless to stop it. In one generation, Latinos will be 50 percent of the state's population and, short of declaring martial law and deporting everyone with brown skin, there's nothing anyone can do to prevent that."[75]

Alabama, Georgia, Indiana, South Carolina, and Utah, inspired by SB 1070, passed copycat laws that invited rampant racial profiling in states, mainly in the South, that had experienced record growth in the Latino population since 1990. Eight other states have taken steps toward passing similar legislation: Florida, Kentucky, Mississippi, Missouri, Oklahoma, North Carolina, Tennessee, and Virginia. In the first half of 2013, according to the National Council of State Legislatures, forty-three states and the

District of Columbia passed a total of 377 laws and resolutions related to immigration, an 83 percent increase from the 206 laws and resolutions enacted in the first half of 2012. Not all laws were designed to make life uncomfortable for undocumented persons. Since 2001 fifteen states have passed laws allowing undocumented students (DREAMers) to be considered in-state residents for tuition purposes, while other states allowed undocumented students to be eligible for scholarships and financial aid.[76]

While undisguised xenophobia coupled with economic hardship were the driving forces behind the illegal immigration backlash, the proliferation of state-level laws pertaining to immigration represents a new twist in the periodic recrudescence of anti-immigrant fears in the nineteenth and early twentieth centuries. At the turn of the twenty-first century states continue to face deep fiscal deficits, and many believe the presence of undocumented immigrants adds an additional financial burden and drain on already limited public services. State legislatures blame Congress, with good reason, for failing to pass a comprehensive immigration reform bill that will address the problem of what to do with over 11 million undocumented immigrants already living in the United States, as well as the ongoing debate about how much to fund border fence-building and enforcement. But larger questions continue to percolate just below the surface of the controversy over immigration and the flurry of backlash laws and resolutions that have been passed across the country. The American public—like Congress—is deeply divided over the issue of whether immigrants are a burden or a benefit, of whether they will assimilate into American culture or remain culturally apart in ethnic and linguistic "enclaves." The vast majority of Latino youths (over 90 percent) are U.S.-born citizens and will automatically become eligible to vote once they turn eighteen. Today, approximately 800,000 U.S. Latinos turn eighteen every year. This number is expected to grow to one million per year by 2030, according to the Pew Research Center, adding a potential electorate of more than 16 million new Latino voters.[77] As the percentage of white non-Hispanics in the population continues to decline, many worry about America's future when by midcentury nearly one in three Americans will be of Hispanic descent. Whether one is optimistic or pessimistic about the rapid changes wrought by unprecedented immigration from Mexico and other Latin-American countries, Latinos will be central to ensuring the future health and well-being of the nation.

EPILOGUE

"We Are America"

What will the United States be like when whites are no longer the majority? This was the question posed on the cover of *Time* magazine under the headline "America's Changing Colors" almost twenty-five years ago, when demographers began speculating at the close of the "Decade of the Hispanic" about the inevitable "browning of America"—when Latinos, blacks, and Asians would outnumber non-Hispanic whites by the mid-twenty-first century, if not before. "Long before that day arrives," *Time* noted, "the presumption that the 'typical' U.S. citizen is someone who traces his or her descent in a direct line to Europe will be part of the past." That time has already come, particularly among the younger generation, by far the most diverse generation in the history of the country, the majority of whom trace their ancestry to Africa, Asia, and Latin America. Although the largest wave of immigration from a single country—Mexico—has recently dropped to zero, according to the Pew Research Center, and may even have begun to reverse itself, many European-descent Americans fear that these mostly nonwhite immigrants and their descendants will hasten America's decline and turn it into a "third world" country.[1] Peter Brimelow, an immigrant from England and naturalized U.S. citizen, put it starkly in his 1996 national bestseller *Alien Nation*: "America will become a freak among the world's nations because of the unprecedented demographic mutation it is inflicting on itself."[2] But for over 150 years Anglo Americans, Mexican Americans, Native Americans, Asian Americans, African Americans, and numerous other groups have been living in the American Southwest without its having become a "freak" region, much less an alien nation within the nation. As

"We Are America": Pro-immigration march in Washington, DC, April 10, 2006, to protest the Sensenbrenner Bill. Courtesy of Rick Reinhard.

newcomer immigrants and their U.S.-born children across the nation continually remind us: "We are America."

When immigrants, legal or illegal, proclaim "We are America," they are demonstrating what every immigrant group has believed throughout American history: they are Americans because they believe in the promise of America, believed it before they left their countries of origin to journey to America. It's that belief, or faith, that unites them with all Americans who believe it's a privilege to live and labor in a country that values hard work and individual initiative, and that guarantees certain unalienable rights and freedoms denied many of them in their home countries. Like millions of immigrants before them, they came mainly to find jobs, to reinvent themselves, and to raise their children in a land of opportunity. That much has not changed for the majority of immigrants. But for over 11 million undocumented immigrants, living in the shadows of America can be a frightening experience. They never know the day or the hour when Immigration and Customs Enforcement (ICE) will appear at their homes or workplace with orders to deport them—from the America they consider home—to their countries of origin.

Like former presidents Ronald Reagan and George W. Bush, President Barack Obama has supported a conditional path to citizenship for eligible undocumented immigrants with no criminal records. Nonetheless, the Obama administration deported a record 1.5 million people in its first term, the majority of them Mexicans, even as those crossing the U.S.-Mexico border illegally dropped to a forty-year low. Spouses have been separated from each other, parents from their children, and brothers and sisters from one another. Before 9/11 undocumented immigrants were often allowed to stay temporarily if married to a citizen or if they were the parents of children born in the United States, but as the War on Terror converged with "border security" and "national security" after 9/11, tens of thousands of families of mixed immigration status were routinely torn apart as their undocumented members were deported. In 2012 the Obama administration deported a record-setting 400,000 undocumented immigrants, including 90,000 undocumented parents of American-born children, leaving 5,000 children in foster care. "We are the one country," said Representative Luis Gutiérrez (D) of Illinois, a leading proponent of immigration reform for over a decade, "that orphans children who have parents." The Mexican Foreign Ministry reported that 13,452 Mexican minors under the age of eighteen were deported from the United States in 2012, after spending between a few days to more than a year in adult detention centers. "We must also realize that among these hundreds of thousands of deportations are parents and breadwinners and heads of American families that are assets to American communities and have committed no crimes," said Gutiérrez.[3]

The threat of deportation has been most frightening for foreign-born children ("alien minors") who, through no fault of their own, were brought to this country illegally by their undocumented immigrant parents and have been living in fear of being deported to countries they have not lived in since they were infants. Currently there are almost 2 million undocumented children under eighteen years of age, about one-sixth of the total undocumented population. An estimated 65,000 undocumented students graduate from the nation's high schools each year, about two-thirds of whom are Latinos. According to one study, two out of three were younger than ten when they came, and three out of four were born in Mexico.[4] Many learned that they were not U.S. citizens only when they were older and could not provide social security numbers for job applications or driver's licenses, or take advantage of scholarship offers to college. As one undocumented Latina explained: "I was my class Valedictorian. I had perfect grades. I was all set to get a full scholarship to any school of my choice. It was then that they said there was a problem with my social security number.

I went home and my mother said she made it up. I didn't have one."[5] Many of these young undocumented immigrants call themselves DREAMers (from the backronym for the Development, Relief, and Education for Alien Minors Act) and have been organizing and lobbying Congress since 2001 to pass the bipartisan DREAM Act that would make undocumented youth eligible for a path to "earned citizenship" or permanent residency, provided they complete a college degree or two years of military service, and meet other eligibility requirements.

For over a decade DREAMers have been "coming out" publicly, consciously borrowing the language of the Lesbian, gay, bisexual, and transgender (LGBT) movement, to openly challenge the politics of living in fear. On January 1, 2010, four Miami-Dade County college students—Felipe Matos, Carlos Roa, Juan Rodríguez, and Gaby Pacheco—began a 1,500-mile "Trail of Dreams" walk from the Freedom Tower in Miami to Washington, DC, to urge President Obama to suspend the deportation of undocumented immigrants, and to promote awareness for just and humane immigration reform. One of the "dream walkers," Carlos Roa, a college student brought to the country when he was two years old, explained his motivation for making the trek: "We have been demonized as 'undocumented immigrants' when in reality all we want to do is contribute to this nation.... All I know is this country, and yet ... I can't legally work, I can't legally drive, I can't join the military.... It's really difficult to live your life ... [when] your dreams are shattered."[6] The dream walkers also condemned Arizona's SB 1070 initiative to require all noncitizens to carry proof of their legal status, or risk deportation: "In every community that we have walked through we met children left orphaned due to their parents' deportation.... Even more alarming, communities live in terror and distrust of the local law enforcement agency.... Our current immigration system pushes an entire population of more than eleven million human beings into a constant state of sheer paranoia.... Once our families looked to the US as a place where justice and liberty could be found.... Is the promise real when a whole state [Arizona] in this beautiful nation becomes a hub for racial injustice?"[7]

The Obama administration took a small step in 2012 to provide relief to DREAMers by implementing the Deferred Action for Childhood Arrivals Program (DACA), which enabled DREAMers to apply for a two-year deferral of deportation and made them eligible for federal work permits and driver's licenses. To qualify, DREAMers have to be under the age of thirty-one as of June 15, 2012, have come to the United States before age sixteen, be in school or have graduated from high school, have not been convicted of a felony, and "not otherwise pose a threat to national security or public safety."[8] In announcing the program, President Obama said: "These are young people who study in our schools . . . [and] pledge allegiance to our flag. They are Americans in their heart, in their minds, in every single way but one: on paper." The Department of Homeland Security, he continued, "is taking steps to lift the shadow of deportation from these young people . . . who, for all intents and purposes, are Americans."[9]

No longer in the shadows, DREAMers and their supporters are organizing, marching, and engaging in acts of civil disobedience across the country to promote the passage of the DREAM Act and challenge the politics of fear and family separation. On July 22, 2013, nine undocumented Mexican nationals, all but one raised in the United States and dubbed by the media the "Dream 9," self-deported to Mexico and then presented themselves to immigration authorities at the border in Nogales, Arizona, to seek political asylum. They all wore graduation caps and gowns to illustrate their plight as college-educated Americans without a future. Immigration officials promptly detained them and sent them to Eloy Detention Center (privately owned and operated by the Corrections Corporation of America) in south-central Arizona where they were released after seventeen days pending the outcome of their asylum petitions, which could take years. Thirty-four members of Congress wrote to President Obama on July 29, 2013, urging him to allow the Dream 9 and all DREAMers who were deported or self-deported "to come home" to the country they grew up in.[10]

Although Congress has continually failed to pass some form of comprehensive immigration reform since 1986, the DREAMers movement continues to gain support nationwide among the public as well as among members of Congress. A survey conducted by the Public Religion Research Institute reported in 2013 that 63 percent of Americans favor a way for undocumented immigrants to become citizens or legal residents, especially undocumented youth, provided they meet certain requirements. Congressional Democrats have begun to take a more proactive stance against the Obama administration's hyperactive deportation regime. On December 5, 2013, twenty-nine members of Congress, all Democrats, wrote a letter to President Obama urging him to suspend deportations and expand the deferred-action program to all undocumented immigrants who would be potential citizens under immigration reform: "Every deportation of a father, a sister, or a neighbor tears at our social consciousness," they wrote, and "every unnecessary raid and detention seriously threatens the fabric of civil liberties we swore to uphold. . . . Criminalizing American families or giving local law enforcement the responsibility to choose who stays and who goes, is not the right option."[11] Janet Murgia, president of the National Council of La Raza, a prominent Latino advocacy group, dubbed President Obama "the Deporter in Chief" for having deported almost 2 million individuals, "more than any other president in the history of the U.S."[12]

Throughout the history of civil and human rights struggles in the United States, churches and other faith-based communities have provided support and safe spaces for those escaping violence and oppression. During the Sanctuary Movement of the 1980s, for example, Catholics, Protestants, and Jews created an underground railroad of churches, synagogues, and homes for thousands of Central American refugees fleeing civil wars, fueled in part by U.S. arms support for anticommunist militias ("contras") and right-wing death squads. The movement began in Tucson, Arizona, where the Reverend John Fife opened his Southside Presbyterian Church as a "sanctuary" for undocumented refugees fleeing El Salvador in 1981, launching an international movement that included over five-hundred churches and synagogues in the United States and Canada. Over forty years later, Reverend Fife continues his faith-based advocacy, now called "No More Deaths," as a form of resistance to a border security policy that uses "death in the desert" as a deterrent to people trying to cross the border.[13]

For decades millions of church-going Latino immigrants and their families have put a human face on the "undocumented" in churches that minister to them. As one writer put it: "When members of congregations or communities are deported, detained, or torn from their families, faith leaders and their organizations are often the ones left with the painful task of helping those left behind pick up the pieces."[14] As a result, growing numbers of religious organizations, including the National Association of Evangelicals, Southern Baptist Convention, U.S. Conference of Catholic Bishops, the United Methodists' Council of Bishops, and others, are making a compelling moral case against an immigration policy that leaves many of their congregants in fear of deportation. Catholic nuns embarked on a nine-state bus tour called "Nuns on the Bus" in 2012 to protest budget cuts to programs aiding the poor, and in 2013 launched another nationwide "Nuns on the Border" tour to promote immigration reform that includes "a roadmap to citizenship for aspiring Americans, protects immigrant workers and ensures family unity."[15] United Methodist bishop Minerva Carcaño, the child of an undocumented immigrant and the first female Hispanic bishop elected in the nation's second-largest Protestant denomination, has been making the case in pulpits and podiums around the country for Christians "to stand with the sojourner," and quotes a passage from Scripture where God tells the Israelites that "the foreigner residing among you must be treated as your native-born." Her father was once that "foreigner," a Mexican who came to the United States in the 1940s under the Bracero Program, but afterward crossed the border illegally because of financial hardship. At an assembly of religious leaders in front of the U.S. Capitol in the fall 2013, Bishop Carcaño recalled the experience of millions of families forced to live in the shadows and reminded the faithful that "our immigrant brothers and sisters . . . keep working for the benefit of us all . . . picking our crops, putting food on our table, building our roads and our homes, tending to the needs of our children and our elderly parents . . . and inspiring our congregations."[16]

Rabbi Jason Kimelman-Block, deputy director of Bend the Arc: A Jewish Partnership for Justice, and dozens of other faith leaders were arrested by Capitol police, along with eight members of the House of Representatives, in an act of civil disobedience (blocking traffic) as part of the "Camino Americano: March for Immigrant Dignity and Respect." This was a day of action that gathered thousands of immigrant rights supporters in Washington, DC, on October 8, 2013, to show support for undocumented immigrants and their families. As Rabbi Kimelman-Block sat in his crowded jail cell, one of his fellow cellmates asked him, "Why do you care about this? What's your connection to this fight?" The rabbi laughed good-naturedly and said, "It's funny: if you're in the Jewish community, the answer to that question is totally obvious."[17]

White evangelical Protestants, the majority of whom (70 percent in 2011) identify as Republicans and often believe that undocumented immigrants should be punished, not rewarded, for entering the country illegally, can no longer ignore the growing numbers of Hispanics in their congregations.[18] One of the largest public opinion surveys on immigration conducted by the Public Religion Research Institute in 2013 showed that 60 percent of white evangelical Protestants support a path to citizenship provided that the immigrants meet certain requirements, like paying back taxes, learning English, and passing a background check. In 2012 a group of evangelical faith leaders founded the Evangelical Immigration Table (EIT), a coalition of diverse evangelical groups and prominent pastors whose goal is to lobby Congress for bipartisan immigration reform. EIT launched the "I Was a Stranger" campaign in 2013, calling on the more than 100,000 evangelical churches nationwide to read one scripture on immigration per day during the forty-day Christian celebration of Lent. Evangelical pastors have also been active members of the "Bibles, Badges, and Businesses for Immigration Reform," a coalition that seeks to unify the efforts of religious leaders, police and law enforcement officials, and business owners who support immigration reform. "The whole Bible is a story about people in exile," said Jenny Yang, a spokesperson for the National Association of Evangelicals.

"Almost every biblical character was a migrant at some point in their lives, including Jesus himself."[19]

PICO, a faith-based network of religious and community organizations founded in 1972 by a Jesuit priest, and representing more than one million families and one thousand congregations from forty different denominations and faiths, recently launched a national "Campaign for Citizenship" whose congregation-based organizing network includes thousands of local religious leaders and organizers spread across eleven targeted states. These religious leaders meet with elected officials in forty targeted congressional districts to persuade representatives who tend to be unsympathetic to the plight of undocumented immigrants and to the moral imperative to preserve families. These religious movements for immigration reform may have begun to influence some conservative representatives sensitive to moral and religious arguments. Representative Spencer Bachus (R) of Alabama, a conservative Christian who represents a district that in 2012 was the most Republican in the nation, in a state with the strictest anti-undocumented immigration law, made a faith-based and compassionate argument for reform of our "badly broken" immigration system. When pressed by his constituents to explain himself, Bachus, a Southern Baptist, explained, "Y'all may think I'm copping out, but with my Christian faith, it's hard for me to say that I'm gonna divide [immigrant] families up."[20]

Whether or not Congress passes legislation granting over 11 million undocumented immigrants and their families a path to earned legal status or citizenship, Latino immigrants and their children are here to stay and will continue to have a profound impact on the future of the nation. According to 2012 census projections, the non-Hispanic white population is projected to peak in 2024, at 199.6 million, up from 197.8 million in 2012. Unlike other race or ethnic groups, however, its population is projected to slowly decrease from 2024 to 2060. The Hispanic population, on the other hand, will more than double, from 53.3 million in 2012 to 128.8 million in 2060. Nearly one in three U.S. residents will be Hispanic by midcentury, if not sooner, up from about one in six today. Consequently, the census predicts, the United States will become a majority-minority nation for the first time in 2043. As one author put it, "It's not that the immigrants are 'outbreeding' the natives—it's that the natives would be depopulating themselves into oblivion without the help of immigrants."[21]

What's important about these projections is not simply the fact that the Latino population is increasing dramatically while non-Hispanic whites are decreasing, but rather that U.S. population is growing older as the outsized baby boomer generation—defined as those born between 1946 and

MEXICANS IN THE MAKING OF AMERICA

1964—approaches traditional retirement age: the population of age sixty-five and older is expected to more than double between 2012 and 2060, representing one in five U.S. residents, up from one in seven today. In 2056, for the first time, this population is projected to outnumber those 18 and under.[22] The "graying" of America threatens to leave the country with a shortage of workers to support the growing number of elderly dependents. Over two-thirds (67.2 percent) of job openings between 2012 and 2022, for example, will come from the need to replace workers who retire or permanently leave an occupation. These data suggest that Latino immigrants and their children will play an important role in replenishing the aging white workforce and retiring baby boomers. They will be the taxpayers who fund Social Security and Medicare upon which elderly white Americans depend. The Bureau of Labor Statistics (BLS) reports that Latinos already will account for three-quarters of the growth in the nation's labor force from 2010 to 2020. During the same period, Hispanics are expected to add 7.7 million workers to the labor force while the number of non-Hispanic whites in the labor force is projected to decrease by 1.6 million. Given current demographic trends, Latinos will be tomorrow's health care and medical technicians, occupations that BLS predicts will increase by 34.5 percent from 2010 to 2020.[23] The immigration problem, it turns out, may be a potential solution to the challenges created by aging baby boomers. Immigrants are younger, almost all are working age, and almost all—whether legal or not—pay taxes.[24]

Nativist pundits and politicians for decades, however, have decried the supposed practice of Mexican women crossing the border illegally to "drop anchor babies," so-called because as U.S. citizens, at age twenty-one, they can sponsor their families and relatives to legally immigrate under the "family reunification" provision of current immigration law. These family members, according to the nativist script, would take advantage of social services and create a financial burden on states already in fiscal crisis. But the data tell a different story. The total fertility rate of the United States—the total number of births per 1,000 women aged 14 to 44—remains at 1.9 births per woman, slightly below the replacement level of 2.1, and down from a high of 3.8 in 1957. The U.S. birthrate dipped in 2011 to the lowest ever recorded, according to the Pew Research Center, "led by a plunge in births to immigrant women." Contrary to the nativist nightmare of Mexican women crossing the border to give birth, the fertility rate for Mexican women in Mexico, which was 2.2 in 2012, is *lower* than that of Hispanic women in the United States, which was 2.4. Demographers attribute Mexico's declining birthrate to the rapid growth of the Mexican economy (fourteenth-largest gross domestic product in the world), urbanization, widespread availability of contraception, and growing numbers of women in the workforce. Nonetheless, births to Hispanic women in the United States would account for the continued growth of the Latino population—and the total population of the country—even if immigration were not a factor.[25]

It has often been said that "as California goes, so goes the country." Many of the demographic forces that are sweeping the nation today had their beginning in California in the 1970s, a decade or two before massive immigration from Mexico and other countries spread to other parts of the country. The backlash against Mexican immigrants in California in the 1990s is well documented, but the fears that drove the campaign for Proposition 187 to deny undocumented immigrants social, educational, and medical services never came to pass. They did not migrate to take advantage of social services and otherwise burden the state economically. The majority of Mexican immigrants to California and other states were not fleeing abject poverty so much as seeking greater economic opportunity and social mobility. With the immigrant boom long over, many California immigrant Latinos today are more settled and have relatively high rates of home ownership and rising incomes. "We're running 15 to 20 years ahead of the nation," said a demographer at the University of Southern California. "California has a large population of second-generation children who are now coming of age. The rest of the country doesn't have that."[26] A study in 2013 by the California Hispanic Chambers of Commerce and the Haas Business School at the University of California, Berkeley, reported that Latinos and Latinas created or owned some 700,000 businesses, accounting for nearly 17 percent of all businesses and contributing 650,000 jobs to the California economy. Hispanic-owned businesses make up the fastest-growing segment of the small business sector, launching at a rate nearly twice the national average. And Hispanic women, the study notes, not men, are driving the rapid rise in entrepreneurship, starting businesses six times the national average.[27]

With comprehensive immigration reform stalled in Congress for over a decade, California governor Jerry Brown has taken the lead in signing a series of immigration reform bills in fall 2013 to integrate the undocumented population of his state into American life. "While Washington waffles on immigration, California's forging ahead," Brown said. "I'm not waiting."[28] Brown bucked the trend of many states by signing into law a bill allowing undocumented immigrants to obtain driver's licenses. "This bill will enable millions of people to get to work safely and legally," Brown said in a statement issued by his office; "Hopefully, it will send a message to

Washington that immigration reform is long past due." In perhaps the most wide-reaching state law affecting the undocumented population, the Trust Act bans local and state police from holding undocumented immigrants in jail cells to facilitate their deportation for such offenses as traffic violations or selling tamales without a permit. "We're not using our jails as a holding vat for the immigration service," Brown said.[29] California also made it a crime for an employer to "induce fear" by threatening to report workers to immigration officials for work-related complaints; and the California Supreme Court ruled that qualified undocumented lawyers can be admitted to the state bar and receive licenses to practice law. These and other state-level immigration laws will affect 2.6 million people in California who are undocumented, about 7 percent of the state's population.[30] "The President should take a cue from the state of California and other locales that have rejected his deportation quota program," Executive Director Pablo Alvarado of the National Day Laborer Organizing Network said, "and reverse course on his Administration's policies of Arizonification."[31]

The fear that Latinos, now the largest single ethnic group in California (they surpassed the population of non-Hispanic whites in 2013), would transform California into "two peoples, two cultures, and two languages," in the words of Harvard political scientist Samuel Huntington, has also not come to pass. It wasn't even an accurate description of California when he wrote those words in 2004, for the Golden State had *dozens* of cultures and scores of languages long before the turn of the twenty-first century. In a state whose economy and climate are a magnet for immigrants, virtually all U.S.-born children learn English, the single most important prerequisite for assimilation into American society. Like other immigrant groups, Latinos often retain their culture and language for generations, especially in areas with high concentrations of Latinos, although most lose fluency in Spanish by the third generation. And California, with its rich medley of languages from around the world, leads the nation in raising English-dominant children. Almost 80 percent of immigrant children and the children of immigrants in California—the state with nearly 10 million foreign-born residents, the largest in the nation—have oral English proficiency. Pew Research Center surveys show that 88 percent of Hispanic adults born in the United States of immigrant parents are fluent in English, and 94 percent among third and later generations. More than two-thirds (68 percent) of adult children of Hispanic immigrants are bilingual, but by the third generation only one in four Latinos speaks "some Spanish" at home. The view that the United States will become linguistically balkanized like Belgium or Canada is simply not supported by the evidence. As one scholar of immigration noted, "The switch to English is taking place more rapidly than it has ever in American history."[32]

Another index of acculturation is intermarriage. Latinos and Asians are among the most exogamous or "out marrying" groups, driving the record high of interracial marriages, 15 percent in 2010, up from less than 1 percent in 1960. Among all newlyweds in 2010, according to the Pew Research Center, 9 percent of whites, 17 percent of blacks, 26 percent of Hispanics, and 28 percent of Asians married out. The highest percentage of interracial marriages took place in the American West, followed by the South, Northeast, and Midwest. Of the 275,500 new interracial or interethnic marriages in 2010, 43 percent were white/Latino couples, the most common type of intermarriage couple. The report also found that native-born Latino newlyweds were more than twice as likely as foreign-born Latino newlyweds to marry out—36 percent versus 14 percent. While intermarriage is not the only index of assimilation—a group can become assimilated without a high rate of intermarriage—intermarriage is more likely to occur in urban settings among the U.S.-born whose higher education, English dominance, and middle income and professional occupations facilitate "out-group" intermarriage. Pew attributes the growing trend in interracial marriages in part to changing attitudes, with more than four in ten Americans saying that "more people of different races marrying each other has been a change for the better in our society," while only about one-in-ten think it is a change for the worse. Nonetheless, while current patterns of immigration and ethnic mixing are contributing to a softening of some racial and ethnic boundaries, particularly among generations of the native-born, both race and ethnicity are likely to remain salient throughout the twenty-first century.[33]

Union membership has also been a hallmark of assimilation into American life, and Latinos have been active in unions since before the turn of the twentieth century. Today they are revitalizing labor unions, whose membership nationally in 2012 was at a historic low of 11 percent (versus 20 percent in 1983), losing a record-breaking 547,000 white members. But unions gained 150,000 new Latino and Latina members, according to the BLS, 82,000 new African Americans, and 45,000 new Asian members. "A decade ago, unions wanted to keep immigrant workers out on the theory that it would undercut wages and benefits here. But if you can't beat 'em, you join 'em," said William Gould IV, former chairman of the National Labor Relations Board under President Bill Clinton. "Now the unions' goal is to join immigrants and align with their aspirations." Latinos are more open to union membership than whites, according to Gould, because they "are often involved in institutions with a collective mentality, such as religious institutions." While the nation shed hundreds of thousands of union members in 2012, California led the nation in signing up new union members, about 110,000. Unionized Latino/a janitors, security guards, car wash workers, hotel workers, and nursing home and other caregivers have begun to enjoy some of the benefits of membership, including access to health insurance, retirement savings plans, vacations, and sick leave. Equally important, labor union participation contributes to the political incorporation of Latino immigrants and helps them overcome barriers to civic participation more generally. As one union immigrant put it: "Here at the union they teach you how to speak up, talk about what you don't like . . . and that helps you share your point of view when you go to meetings at the school [that your children attend]."[34]

Latino workers have been "speaking up" for most of the twentieth century, a process that has facilitated their gradual transition to electoral politics. Today, by the sheer force of their numbers, they play a major role in shaping the politics and cultures of cities like Miami, New York, and Chicago—and virtually every major metropolitan area in the Southwest from Los Angeles to Houston. In California, Latinos occupy 27 of 120 seats in the state legislature, up from 7 in 1984. Getting elected to city councils has proved more challenging because of the prevalence of "at large" city elections, which dilute voting power for minority candidates. Latinos and other minorities have threatened lawsuits under California's 2001 Voting Rights Act, for example, to have city council members elected by geographic district ("single-member") to ensure minority representation. The problem, explained former Republican state assemblyman Rod Pacheco, is that "years of racism, manifested in part by polarized voting, have undercut minorities' opportunities to be elected." California's counties and most of its cities, including Los Angeles and San Diego, now elect council members by geographic district, and smaller cities—Anaheim, Compton, Escondido, Whittier, Palmdale, and others—are under pressure from lawsuits to do so. Latino efforts to change election laws in cities will accelerate the decline of white-dominated local government in majority-minority areas with far-reaching consequences. The "browning" of local and state government will make it harder for nativist whites to pass laws or initiatives that target undocumented Mexican immigrants, Latino studies programs, and bilingual education.[35]

Proposition 187, for example, the 1994 California initiative to exclude undocumented immigrants from receiving state social and medical services, touched off nearly two decades of copycat laws in other states. But 187 was also a "pivot point" in changing California from an overwhelmingly Republican state to a Democratic stronghold—a "party fortress in Congress and

Courtesy of Lalo Alcaraz.

the Legislature," according to the *Los Angeles Times,* "and a dead zone for any Republican with statewide ambitions." The California electorate, observed former GOP strategist Dan Schnur, "is much less white, less religious, much less straight and much less old" than it was in the 1990s, trends that are not unique to California. In 1994 when 187 was passed, Latinos made up 10 percent of the electorate. In November 2012, they made up 20 percent, and by 2040 Latinos are projected to make up just under a third of the California electorate.[36] It's a near certainty that any party that adopts anti-immigrant or anti-Latino rhetoric will not likely win national elections in the foreseeable future. As the political commentator Dick Morris warned almost a decade before the 2012 election, "Any major politician is facing dodo bird extinction if he or she fails to reach out to Hispanics."[37] Two weeks before his election victory in 2012 against Mitt Romney, President Obama told the editors of the *Des Moines Register,* "I will just be very blunt. Should I win a second term, a big reason . . . is because the Republican nominee and the Republican Party have so alienated the fastest-growing demographic group in the country, the Latino community."[38]

How the growing population of Latinos will affect mainstream culture of America in the twenty-first century, besides local and national elections, remains an open question. Certainly the border states of California, Arizona,

New Mexico, and Texas—ground zero of the Mexican diaspora in the United States—are the leading edge bridging America with the Americas, particularly in strengthening economic and cultural ties between Mexico and the United States. The recent appearance of so many Latinos in other parts of the country, particularly the states of the Deep South, has rendered the "black and white landscape of gothic memory . . . unrecognizable," according to essayist Richard Rodriguez: "It may not look like what Faulkner described, but I bet it looks a lot more like what de Tocqueville saw. Brown illegal immigrants with Indian faces may usher the Georgian and the Virginian to a recognition that they now live within the New World—an illegal idea—and not in some distant colony of England."[39]

Indeed America is changing more rapidly in this century than many realize: it is "graying" and at the same time becoming more culturally diverse than at any time in its history, with a growing number of young, global citizens revitalizing the communities where they settle and raise families. We cannot know the answer to the question *Time* magazine posed almost twenty-five years ago: "What will the U.S. be like when whites are no longer a majority?" for certain, but if the past is any indication, America will continue to be a vibrantly pluralistic and dynamic culture. But for today's aging white population most troubled by America's changing colors, the judgment *Time* magazine rendered in 1990 is even more manifestly clear today: "For older Americans, raised in a world where the numbers of whites were greater and the visibility of nonwhites was carefully constrained, the new world will seem ever stranger. But the new world is here. It is now . . . and it is irreversibly the America to come."[40] In the America to come we will no longer have to celebrate diversity—it will have become a fundamental fact, with Asians, Africans, and Latinos from every part of the world calling the United States their home, proudly declaring, "We are America."

ABBREVIATIONS

AEMEUA	Archivo de la Embajada de México en los Estados Unidos de América, in Archivo Histórico de Secretario de Relaciones Exteriores, Mexico City
AGN	Archivo General de la Nación, Mexico City
AHSRE	Archivo Histórico de la Secretaría de Relaciones Exteriores, Mexico City
Alemán Papers	Miguel Alemán Valdés Papers, 1946–1952, Ramo de Presidentes, Archivo General de la Nación, Mexico City
Andrade Files/MX	Serie III, Legajo 2335, Expediente 2, Archivo Histórico de la Secretaría de Relaciones Exteriores, Mexico City
Andrade Files/U.S.	Naturalization Records, U.S. District Court, Western District of New York, National Archives and Records Administration, Northeast Region, New York, New York
Ávila Camacho Papers	Manuel Ávila Camacho Papers, 1940–1946, Ramo de Presidentes, Archivo General de la Nación, Mexico City
Cárdenas Papers	Lázaro Cárdenas Papers, Ramo de Presidentes, Archivo Nacional de Nación, Mexico City
Department of State	Record Group 59, Records of the Department of State, National Archives and Records Administration, Washington, DC.

Depto de Trabajo Papers	Secretario de Industria, Comercio y Trabajo, Departamento de Trabajo, Achivo General de la Nación, Mexico City
FEPC	Fair Employment Practices Committee, Record Group 228, National Archives and Records Administration, Washington, DC.
García Papers	Dr. Hector Perez García Papers, 1914–1996, Special Collections and Archives, Texas A&M University–Corpus Christi, Bell Library
GNC	Good Neighbor Commission, Texas State Library and Archives, Austin, Texas
Jester Papers	Governor Beauford H. Jester Papers, Texas State Library and Archives, Austin, Texas
MALDEF	Mexican American Legal Defense and Educational Fund Records, 1967–1984, Department of Special Collections, Stanford University Libraries, Stanford, California
NARA	National Archives and Records Administration, College Park, Maryland
OCIAA	Office of the Coordinator for Inter-American Affairs, Record Group 229, National Archives and Records Administration
Ruiz Cortines Papers	Adolfo Ruiz Cortines Papers, 1952–1958, Ramo de Presidentes, Archivo General de la Nación, Mexico City
Sánchez Papers	George I. Sánchez Papers, Benson Latin American Collection, University of Texas, Austin, Texas
Shivers Papers	Governor Allan Shivers Papers, Texas State Library and Archives, Austin, Texas
Stevenson Papers	Governor Coke Stevenson Papers, Texas State Library and Archives, Austin, Texas
Truman Papers	Subject File, Mexican Labor, Harry S. Truman Library, Independence, Missouri

NOTES

Prologue

1. I use the term "Mexican" to describe people of Mexican descent regardless of whether they are U.S.-born or citizens of Mexico, since historically little distinction was made between Mexican Americans and Mexican immigrants in the Southwest. When it is important to distinguish between U.S.-born and Mexico-born, I use the terms "Mexican American" and "Mexican immigrant" or "Mexican resident national."

2. George Lopez, "America's Mexican," www.youtube.com/watch?v=obl_tZezHPA; Ruben Navarette, Jr., "Making No Apologies for Success," www.utsandiego.com/uniontrib/20070218/news_lz1e18navar.html.

3. See Colin M. MacLachlan and William H. Beezley, *El Gran Pueblo: A History of Greater Mexico* (Upper Saddle River, NJ: Prentice Hall, 2004). On the exploration and settlement of Spanish North America, see David J. Weber, *The Spanish Frontier in North America* (New Haven, CT: Yale University Press, 1992); Herbert Eugene Bolton, *The Spanish Borderlands: A Chronicle of Old Florida and the Southwest* (1921; reprint, Albuquerque: University of New Mexico Press, 1996); John Francis Bannon, *The Spanish Borderlands Frontier, 1513–1821* (New York: Holt, Rinehart and Winston, 1970).

4. Tony Horwitz, "Immigration—and the Curse of the Black Legend," *New York Times,* July 9, 2006.

5. Ed Pooley to Neville Penrose, January 13, 1950, Box 1989/59–16, folder "Discrimination, General File, 1946–1956," Good Neighbor Commission, Texas State Library and Archives, Austin, Texas (hereafter cited as GNC). For the classic expression of shared hemispheric history, see Herbert E. Bolton, "The Epic of Greater America," *American Historical Review* 38 (April 1933): 448–474. See also Jeremy Adelman and Stephen Aron, "From Borderlands to

Borders: Empires, Nation-States, and the Peoples in Between in North American History," *American Historical Review* 104 (June 1999): 814–841.

6. Richard Rodriguez, *Brown: The Last Discovery of America* (New York: Viking, 2002), 109. I use the terms "Latino" and "Hispanic" interchangeably to refer to individuals who trace their origin or ancestry to the Spanish-speaking countries of Latin America or the Caribbean.

7. "Mexico Raises Minimum Wage by 3.9% for 2013," *Market Watch*, December 18, 2012, www.marketwatch.com/story/mexico-raises-minimum-wage-by-39-for-2013-2012-12-18-184851559.

8. "Statistical Update on Employment in the Informal Economy, June 2012," *LABORSTA*, n.d., laborsta.ilo.org/informal_economy_E.html.

9. *New York Times*, November 24, 1919. See also "Thousands of Mexicans Are Pouring into Texas," *Los Angeles Times*, June 4, 1916; and "Many Mexicans Are Coming In; Laborers Are Being Sent All Over the Country," *Los Angeles Times*, December 17, 1916.

10. Samuel P. Huntington, "The Hispanic Challenge," *Foreign Policy* (March–April 2004): 30–45.

11. Francisco E. Balderama and Raymond Rodríguez, *Decade of Betrayal: Mexican Repatriation in the 1930s* (Albuquerque: University of New Mexico Press, 1995).

12. "U.S. Spreads Net for 'Wetbacks,'" *New York Times*, June 13, 1954. See also Juan Ramón García, *Operation Wetback: The Mass Deportation of Mexican Undocumented Workers in 1954* (Westport, CT: Greenwood Press, 1980).

13. "About Us," www.ice.gov.

14. For a recent history of the western segment of the U.S.-Mexico border from 1848 to the 1930s, see Rachel St. John, *Line in the Sand: A History of the Western U.S.-Mexico Border* (Princeton, NJ: Princeton University Press, 2011).

15. Huntington, "Hispanic Challenge," 30–45.

16. Quoted in Horwitz, "Immigration."

17. Benjamin Franklin, *Observations concerning the Increase of Mankind, Peopling of Countries, & etc.* (1755; reprint, Tarrytown, NY: W. Abbatt, 1918), 224.

18. "Percent Hispanic of the U.S. Population: 1970 to 2050," *U.S. Census Bureau*, n.d., www.census.gov/newsroom/cspan/hispanic/2012.06.22_cspan_hispanics.pdf. See also Daniel Dockterman, "Statistical Portrait of Hispanics in the United States, 2009," *Pew Research Center*, February 17, 2011, table 1, http://www.pewhispanic.org/files/2013/09/2009-Statistical-Profile-Hispanics.pdf; Gretchen Livingston and D'vera Cohn, "The New Demography of Motherhood," *Pew Research Center*, May 6, 2010, pewresearch.org/pubs/1586/changing-demographic-characteristics-american-mothers.

19. Mark Hugo Lopez, Ana Gonzalez-Barrera, and Danielle Cuddington, "Diverse Origins: The Nation's 14 Largest Hispanic-Origin Groups," *Pew Research Center*, June 19, 2013, www.pewhispanic.org/2013/06/19/diverse-origins-the-nations-14-largest-hispanic-origin-groups/.

20. Norma Klahn, "Writing the Border: The Languages and Limits of Representation," in *Common Border, Uncommon Paths: Race, Culture, and National Identity in U.S.-Mexican Relations,* ed. Jaime E. Rodríguez O. and Kathryn Vincent (Wilmington, DE: Scholarly Resources, 1997), 134.

21. William A. Henry, III, "Beyond the Melting Pot," *Time,* April 9, 1990, no. 15: 28.

22. Arthur A. Ohnimus, Chief Clerk of the California Assembly, to Lic. don Miguel Alemán, President of Mexico, July 18, 1947, exp. 135.21/38, caja 166, Miguel Alemán Valdés Papers, Archivo General de la Nación (AGN), Mexico City (hereafter cited as Alemán Papers); Dan E. Garvey, Governor of Arizona, to Miguel Alemán, September 24, 1948, ibid.; José Gorostiza to Sub-secretario de la Presidencia de la República, September 7, 1955, exp. 135.21/241, caja 199, Adolfo Ruiz Cortines Papers, AGN (hereafter cited as Ruiz Cortines Papers).

23. See, for example, Alejandro Portes and Min Zhou, "The New Second Generation: Segmented Assimilation and Its Variants among Post-1965 Immigrant Youth," *Annals of the American Academy of Political and Social Science* 530 (November 1993): 74–96.

24. factfinder.census.gov/, and quoted by Roberto Suro, "Known Knowns and Unknown Knowns," in *The Hispanic Challenge: What We Know about Latino Immigration,* ed. Philippa Strum and Andrew Selee (Washington, DC: Migration Policy Institute, Woodrow Wilson International Center for Scholars, 2004), 5.

25. The term "Hispanic" was first introduced in the census in 1980, but the media began using it interchangeably with "Latins" before then. In 1970, for example, President Nixon declared the week beginning September 13 "National Hispanic Heritage Week in recognition of the gifts of people of Hispanic origin." "Hispanic Week Proclaimed," *New York Times,* August 25, 1970.

26. The Frito-Lay Company finally abandoned the "Frito Bandito" ad campaign in 1970 in response to pressure from Mexican-American civil rights activists. John R. McCarty, Vice President of Frito-Lay, Inc., to Dr. Hector P. Garcia, June 3, 1970, box 81, folder 52, Hector P. García Papers, Texas A&M University, Corpus Christi, Texas (hereafter cited as García Papers).

27. "Cultural Relations between the United States and Mexico," in *Common Borders, Uncommon Paths: Race, Culture, and National Identity in U.S.-Mexican Relations,* ed. Jaime E. Rodríguez (Wilmington, DE: Scholarly Resources, 1997), 119.

28. See Gerardo Rénique, "Race, Region, and Nation: Sonora's Anti-Chinese Racism and Mexico's Postrevolutionary Nationalism, 1920–1930s," in *Race and Nation in Modern Latin America,* ed. Nancy P. Applebaum, Anne S. Macpherson, Karin Alejandra Rosenblatt, and Peter Wade (Chapel Hill: University of North Carolina Press, 2003), 219; and Alexandra Minna Stern,

"Mestizophilia to Biotypology: Racialization and Science in Mexico, 1920–1960," ibid., 196–210.

29. The phrase is from Richard Rodríguez, *Brown: The Last Discovery of America* (New York: Viking, 2002), 112.

30. See, for example, Shannon K. O'Neil, *Two Nations Indivisible: Mexico, the United States, and the Road Ahead* (New York: Oxford University Press, 2013); and Peter H. Smith and Andrew Selee, eds., *Mexico and the United States: The Politics of Partnership* (Boulder, CO: Lynne Rienner, 2013).

1. The Genesis of Mexican America

1. See Tony Horwitz, "Immigration—and the Curse of the Black Legend," *New York Times,* July 9, 2006; and idem, *A Voyage Long and Strange: Rediscovering the New World* (New York: Henry Holt, 2008).

2. Alfred W. Crosby, *The Columbian Exchange: Biological and Cultural Consequences of 1492* (Westport, CT: Greenwood Press, 1972), 165–207; D. W. Meinig, *The Shaping of America,* vol. 1, *Atlantic America, 1492–1800* (New Haven, CT: Yale University Press, 1986); and John R. Chávez, *Beyond Nations: Evolving Homelands in the North Atlantic World, 1400–2000* (New York: Cambridge University Press, 2009).

3. Meinig, *Shaping of America,* 11.

4. *The Buried Mirror: Reflections on Spain and the New World* (Boston: Houghton Mifflin, 1992), 326. The standard work on the Spanish exploration and settlement in the New World is David J. Weber, *The Spanish Frontier in North America* (New Haven, CT: Yale University Press, 1992).

5. On the origins of race-mixing among Mexicans, see Martha Menchaca, *Recovering History, Constructing Race: The Indian, Black, and White Roots of Mexican Americans* (Austin: University of Texas Press, 2001). On recent fears that Mexicans are reconquering America, see Patrick J. Buchanan, *State of Emergency: The Third World Invasion and Conquest of America* (New York: Thomas Dunne Books/St. Martin's Press, 2006), 105–114.

6. On the subjugation and racialization of Indians and other inhabitants of western North America, see Richard Slotkin, *Regeneration through Violence; The Mythology of the American Frontier, 1600–1860* (Middletown, CT: Wesleyan University Press, 1973); Richard Drinnon, *Facing West: The Metaphysics of Indian-Hating and Empire-Building* (Norman: University of Oklahoma Press, 1997); Henry Nash Smith, *Virgin Land: The American West as Symbol and Myth* (Cambridge, MA: Harvard University Press, 1971).

7. Bernal Díaz del Castillo, *The True History of the Conquest of Mexico,* quoted in Weber, *Spanish Frontier,* 23; and Michael C. Meyer and William H. Beezley, eds., *The Oxford History of Mexico* (Oxford: Oxford University Press, 2000).

8. On Malintzin, see Camilla Townsend, *Malintzin's Choices: An Indian Woman in the Conquest of Mexico* (Albuquerque: University of New Mexico Press, 2006); Luis Rutiaga, *Los Grandes Mexicanos: Malintzin* (Mexico City: Grupo Editorial Tomo, 2004), 43–44; and Adelaida R. del Castillo, "Malintzin Tenepal: A Preliminary Look into a New Perspective," in *Essays on la Mujer,* ed. Rosaura Sánchez (Los Angeles: Chicano Studies Center, University of California, 1977).

9. In addition to Díaz del Castillo, *True History of the Conquest,* see Miguel León-Portilla, ed., *The Broken Spears: The Aztec Account of the Conquest of Mexico* (Boston: Beacon Press, 1969); Hugh Thomas, *Conquest: Montezuma, Cortés, and the Fall of Old Mexico* (New York: Simon and Schuster, 1993); and Charles Gibson, *Spain in America* (New York: Harper and Row, 1966), 24–47.

10. Díaz del Castillo, *The True History of the Conquest,* 117–127; John R. Chávez, *The Lost Land: The Chicano Image of the Southwest* (Albuquerque: University of New Mexico Press, 1984).

11. Díaz del Castillo, *True History of the Conquest,* 130.

12. León-Portilla, *Broken Spears,* xix; Gregory Rodriguez, *Mongrels, Bastards, Orphans, and Vagabonds: Mexican Immigration and the Future of Race in America* (New York: Pantheon Books, 2007), 14.

13. Díaz del Castillo, *True History of the Conquest,* 133–137.

14. Crosby, *Columbian Exchange,* 35–63; Weber, *Spanish Frontier,* 11, 28; and Suzanne Austin Alchon, *A Pest in the Land: New World Epidemics in a Global Perspective* (Albuquerque: University of New Mexico Press, 2003); Nigel Worden, *Slavery in Dutch South Africa: Captive Labor on the Dutch Frontier* (Cambridge: Cambridge University Press, 1985), 6–40.

15. Hernando Cortés, "Instrucciones dadas . . . a Francisco Cortés . . . ," in *Colección de documentos inéditos . . . de Indias,* quoted in Chávez, *Lost Land,* 11.

16. George P. Hammond and Agapito Rey, eds. and trans., *Narratives of the Coronado Expedition, 1540–1542* (Albuquerque: University of New Mexico Press, 1940). For a complete account of Spanish explorers, see Weber, *Spanish Frontier,* 30–59.

17. Weber, *Spanish Frontier,* 49.

18. Ibid.

19. P. J. Bakewell, *Silver Mining and Society in Colonial Mexico: Zacatecas, 1546–1700* (Cambridge: Cambridge University Press, 1971). On the creation of the viceroyalty and administration of the Spanish colonies, see Mark A. Burkhofer and Lyman L. Johnson, eds., *Colonial Latin America,* 8th ed. (New York: Oxford University Press, 2012), 91–104.

20. The formal municipality, Villa Real de Santa Fe, was founded a few years later, in 1610, by Oñate's successor, Pedro de Peralta, governor of New Mexico. Weber, *Spanish Frontier,* 90. See also George P. Hammond and Agapito

Rey, eds. and trans., *Don Juan de Oñate: Colonizer of New Mexico, 1595–1628*, 2 vols. (Albuquerque: University of New Mexico Press, 1953); Herbert E. Bolton, ed., *Spanish Exploration in the Southwest: 1542–1706* (1908; reprint, New York: Barnes and Noble, 1969), 199–200; Chávez, *Lost Land*, 16–19. On the settlement of El Paso, see Oakah L. Jones, Jr., *Los Paisanos: Spanish Settlers on the Northern Frontier of New Spain* (Norman: University of Oklahoma Press, 1979), 111–12.

21. Weber, *Spanish Frontier*, 23, 135.

22. Ramón Gutiérrez, *When Jesus Came, the Corn Mothers Went Away* (Stanford, CA: Stanford University Press, 1991), 95–140; Andrew L. Knaut, *The Pueblo Revolt of 1680: Conquest and Resistance in the Seventeenth-Century New Mexico* (Norman: University of Oklahoma Press, 1995); Weber, *Spanish Frontier*, 133–139.

23. Weber, *Spanish Frontier*, 81.

24. Knaut, *Pueblo Revolt*, 141–42.

25. Quoted in ibid., 142.

26. Gonzalo Aguirre Beltrán, *La poblacíon negra de México: estudio etnohistórico* (México: Fondo de Cultural Económico, 1972); Colin A. Palmer, *Slaves of the White God: Blacks in Mexico, 1570–1650* (Cambridge, MA: Harvard University Press, 1976); Theodore G. Vincent, *The Legacy of Vicente Guerrero: Mexico's First Black Indian President* (Gainesville: University Press of Florida, 2001).

27. "Why Mexico Is Backwards," *Atlantic*, July 1938, p. 9, in exp. 432.2/253–258, caja 438, Lázaro Cárdenas Papers, AGN (hereafter cited as Cárdenas Papers). For one of the earlier treatises on "whitening" and the caste system in Mexico, see Alexander Von Humboldt, *Political Essay on the Kingdom of New Spain*, vol. 1 (New York: I. Riley, 1811), 153–198. A table of mixed-race categories from mestizo to "coyote" can be found in John M. Nieto-Phillips, *The Language of Blood: The Making of Spanish-American Identity in New Mexico, 1880s–1930s* (Albuquerque: University of New Mexico Press, 2008), 27. See also Magnus Mörner, *Race Mixture in the History of Latin America* (Boston: Little, Brown, 1967).

28. Douglas R. Cope, *The Limits of Racial Domination: Plebian Society in Colonial Mexico City, 1660–1720* (Madison: University of Wisconsin Press, 1994).

29. Von Humboldt, *Political Essay*, 185–186 (italics in the original). On the granting of edicts of legitimation and the purchase of white racial status in New Spain, see Ann Twinam, "Pedro de Ayarza: The Purchase of Whiteness," in *The Human Tradition in Colonial Latin America*, 2nd ed., ed. Kenneth J. Andrien (Wilmington, DE: Scholarly Resources, 2013), 221–237.

30. Martha Menchaca, *Recovering History, Constructing Race: The Indian, Black, and White Roots of Mexican Americans* (Austin: University of Texas Press, 2001), 154–157.

31. Gutiérrez, *When Jesus Came,* 149.

32. Chávez, *Lost Land,* 21; David J. Weber, *The Mexican Frontier, 1821–1846: The American Southwest under Mexico* (Albuquerque: University of New Mexico Press, 1982).

33. Thomas E. Chávez, *Spain and the Independence of the United States: An Intrinsic Gift* (Albuquerque: University of New Mexico Press, 2002).

34. Quoted in W. J. Eccles, "The French Alliance and the American Victory," in *The World Turned Upside Down: The American Victory in the War of Independence,* ed. John Ferling (Westport, CT, Praeger, 1988), 162.

35. Quoted in Dan E. Clark, "Manifest Destiny and the Pacific," *Pacific Historical Review* 1 (March 1932), 5.

36. Weber, *Spanish Frontier,* 292; and Josefina Z. Vásquez and Lorenzo Meyer, *The United States and Mexico* (Chicago: University of Chicago Press, 1985).

37. Quoted in Charles C. Cumberland, *Mexico: The Struggle for Modernity* (New York: Oxford University Press, 1968), 134.

38. Cumberland, *Mexico,* 155.

39. Historian Richard White estimates that around 40 percent of Anglo Americans in Texas were "illegal aliens" who had crossed the border in violation of Mexican immigration laws. See Richard White, *"It's Your Misfortune and None of My Own": A History of the American West* (Norman: University of Oklahoma Press, 1991), 65.

40. John Adams, *The Works of John Adams, Second President of the United States,* vol. 10 (Boston: Little, Brown, 1850–1856), 144–145.

41. Quotation from Genesis 1:26, *American Standard Version Bible* (1901).

42. White, *"It's Your Misfortune"*; Patricia Nelson Limerick, *The Legacy of Conquest: The Unbroken Past of the American West* (New York: W. W. Norton, 1987); and Weber, *Spanish Frontier.*

43. J. C. Clopper, quoted in Arnoldo De León, *They Called Them Greasers: Anglo Attitudes toward Mexicans in Texas, 1821–1900* (Austin: University of Texas Press, 1983), 10.

44. Quotations from De León, *They Called Them Greasers,* 7–9. For the racial ideology of the Anglo Americans during this period, see Reginald Horsman, *Race and Manifest Destiny: The Origins of American Racial Anglo-Saxonism* (Cambridge, MA: Harvard University Press, 1981); and David J. Weber, " 'Scarce More Than Apes': Historical Roots of Anglo-American Stereotypes of Mexicans," in *New Spain's Far Northern Frontier: Essays on Spain in the American West,* ed. David J. Weber (Albuquerque: University of New Mexico Press, 1979).

45. Quoted in De León, *They Called Them Greasers,* 3 (italics in the original). See also Gregg Cantrell, *Stephen F. Austin: Empresario of Texas* (New Haven, CT: Yale University Press, 2001).

46. Stephen F. Austin to L. F. Linn, New York, May 4, 1835, quoted in David J. Weber, "Refighting the Alamo," in Weber, *Myth and the History of the*

Hispanic Southwest: Essays by David J. Weber (Albuquerque: University of New Mexico Press, 1988), 139.

47. Quoted in De León, *They Called Them Greasers,* 2–3. Emphasis in the original.

48. Ibid., 3–4.

49. On the history of slavery in Texas from the Spanish colonial period to the Civil War, see Randolph Campbell, *An Empire for Slavery: The Peculiar Institution in Texas, 1821–1865* (Baton Rouge: Louisiana State University Press, 1989).

50. *New York Morning News,* December 27, 1945, quoted in Frederick Merk, *Manifest Destiny and Mission in American History* (Cambridge, MA: Harvard University Press, 1963), 31–32. See also "Annexation," *United States Magazine and Democratic Review* 17 (July 1845): 5–10; and White, *"It's Your Misfortune,"* 73–75.

51. The attribution of the phrase to O'Sullivan has been disputed, but for a clear statement of his expansionist views and America's providential destiny to become a great nation, see his essay, "The Great Nation of Futurity," *United States Democratic Review* 6 (November 1839): 426–430, www.mtholyoke.edu /acad/intrel/osulliva.htm. See also Julius W. Pratt, "The Origin of 'Manifest Destiny,'" *American Historical Review* 32 (July 1927): 795–798.

52. Quoted in Clark, "Manifest Destiny," 1.

53. Ibid., 5.

54. William Seward, who negotiated the purchase of Alaska in 1867, observed the Russian settlements in the far Northwest on "the verge of the continent" and mused: "Go on and build up your outposts all along the coast, up even to the Arctic Ocean—they will yet become the outposts of my own country—monuments of the civilization of the United States in the northwest." Clark, "Manifest Destiny," 10.

55. See Timothy J. Henderson, *Mexico and Its War with the United States* (New York: Hill and Wang, 2007); John S. D. Eisenhower, *So Far From God: The U.S. War with Mexico, 1846–1848* (New York: Random House, 1989); Richard V. Francaviglia and Douglas W. Richmond, eds., *Dueling Eagles: Reinterpreting the U.S.-Mexican War, 1846–1848* (Fort Worth: Texas Christian University Press, 2000).

56. Josefina Zoraida Vázquez, "War and Peace with the United States," in *The Oxford History of Mexico,* ed. Michael C. Meyer and William H. Beezley (Oxford: Oxford University Press, 2000), 361–363.

57. Quoted in Zoraida Vázquez, "War and Peace," 368–369.

58. Michael C. Meyer and William H. Beezley, eds., *The Oxford History of Mexico* (Oxford: Oxford University Press, 2000), 3.

59. See Eisenhower, *So Far from God.*

60. See Leonard Pitt, *The Decline of the Californios: A Social History of the Spanish-Speaking Californians, 1846–1890* (Berkeley: University of California

Press, 1971); David Montejano, *Anglos and Mexicans in the Making of Texas, 1836–1986* (Austin: University of Texas Press, 1987); Chávez, *Lost Land*.

61. For a contemporary account of the dispossession and impoverishment of the Californios as a result of the Land Act, see Maria Amparo Ruiz de Burton, *The Squatter and the Don: A Novel Descriptive of Contemporary Occurrences in California* (San Francisco: S. Carson, 1885).

62. Howard Roberts Lamar, *The Far Southwest, 1846–1912: A Territorial History* (New York: W. W. Norton, 1970), 149; María E. Montoya, *Translating Property: The Maxwell Land Grant and the Conflict over Land in the American West, 1840 to 1900* (Berkeley: University of California Press, 2002); and Victor Westphall, *Mercedes Reales: Hispanic Land Grants of the Upper Río Grande Region* (Albuquerque: University of New Mexico Press, 1983).

63. T. R. Fehrenbach, *Lone Star: A History of Texas and the Texans* (New York: Macmillan, 1968), 510.

64. Paul R. Spickard, *Almost All Aliens: Immigration, Race, and Colonialism in American History and Identity* (New York: Routledge, 2007), 156–157.

65. Fernando Purcell, "Hanging Bodies, Slashed Ears and Bottled Heads: Lynching, Punishment and Race in the California Gold Rush, 1848–1853," *Hagar: Studies in Culture, Polity, Identities* 6 (Fall 2006): 85–97.

66. Pitt, *Decline of the Californios*.

67. Bruce S. Thornton, *Searching for Joaquín: Myth, Murieta and History in California* (San Francisco: Encounter Books, 2003); Charles William Goldsmith and J. T. Canales, *Juan N. Cortina: Two Interpretations* (New York: Arno Press, 1974); Pitt, *Decline of the Californios*, 215–216; Carey McWilliams, *North from Mexico: The Spanish-Speaking People of the United States* (1949; reprint, New York: Greenwood Press, 1968), 130.

68. Américo Paredes, *With His Pistol in His Hand* (Austin: University of Texas Press, 1958).

69. See, for example, Helen Hunt Jackson, *Ramona* (New York: Grosset and Dunlap, 1912); and Charles Fletcher Lummis, *Land of Poco Tiempo* (New York: Charles Scribner's Sons, 1893).

70. Quoted in Weber, *Spanish Frontier*, 341. See also, Pitt, *Decline of the Californios*, 286–290. On the origins of the black legend, see Philip Wayne Powell, *The Tree of Hate: Propaganda and Prejudices Affecting United States Relations with the Hispanic World* (New York: Basic Books, 1971).

71. Weber, *Spanish Frontier*, 336.

72. McWilliams, *North from Mexico*, 35.

73. Ibid., 34. McWilliams was not just a prolific author and editor of progressive magazines. His books on Mexican Americans represent the first serious attempt to integrate the history of Mexicans into the broader history of the United States.

74. Lummis, *Land of Poco Tiempo*, 4–5.

75. Charles F. Lummis, *The Spanish Pioneers*, 8th ed. (Chicago: A. C. Motley, 1920), 18, quoted in John Nieto-Phillips, "'When Tourists Came, the Mestizos Went Away': Hispanophilia and the Racial Whitening of New Mexico, 1880s–1940s," in *Interpreting Spanish Colonialism: Empires, Nations, and Legends*, ed. Christopher Schmidt-Nowara and John Nieto-Phillips (Albuquerque: University of New Mexico Press, 2005), 199. See also Charles Montgomery, *The Spanish Redemption: Heritage, Power, and Loss on New Mexico's Upper Rio Grande* (Berkeley: University of California Press, 2002), 20–88.

76. Laura E. Gómez, "Off-White in an Age of White Supremacy: Mexican Elites and the Rights of Indians and Blacks in Nineteenth-Century New Mexico," *Chicano-Latino Law Review* 25 (Spring 2005), 18, 21; idem, *Manifest Destinies: The Making of the Mexican American Race* (New York: New York University Press, 2007), especially ch. 3.

77. Quoted in Chávez, *Lost Land*, 92.

78. Pablo Mitchell, *Coyote Nation: Sexuality, Race, and Conquest in Modernizing New Mexico, 1880–1920* (Chicago: University of Chicago Press, 2005), 101–121; Gómez, *Manifest Destinies*, 81–116; Nieto-Phillips, *Language of Blood*.

79. McWilliams, *North from Mexico*, 36.

80. Ibid., 39.

81. On the influence of "hispanismo" in the twentieth-century Southwest, see Fredrick B. Pike, *Hispanismo, 1898–1936: Spanish Conservatives and Liberals and Their Relations with Spanish America* (Notre Dame, IN: University of Notre Dame Press, 1971), 146–165; and Ramón Gutiérrez, "Nationalism and Literary Production: The Hispanic and Chicano Experiences," in *Recovering the U.S. Hispanic Literary Heritage*, ed. Ramón Gutiérrez and Genaro Padilla (Houston, TX: Arte Público Press, 1993), 241–250.

82. McWilliams, *North from Mexico*, 37.

83. For the emergence of class and racial hierarchies in California, see Tomás Almaguer, *Racial Fault Lines: The Historical Origins of White Supremacy in California* (Berkeley: University of California Press, 1994). For Texas, see Neil Foley, *The White Scourge: Mexicans, Blacks, and Poor Whites in Texas Cotton Culture* (Berkeley: University of California Press, 1997); and Montejano, *Anglos and Mexicans*.

2. No Estás en Tu Casa

1. Rachel St. John, *Line in the Sand: A History of the Western U.S.-Mexico Border* (Princeton, NJ: Princeton University Press, 2011), 23–38; Paula Rebert, *Le Gran Línea: Mapping the United States-Mexico Boundary, 1849–1857* (Austin: University of Texas Press, 2001).

2. Erika Lee, *At America's Gates: Chinese Immigration during the Exclusion Era, 1882–1943* (Chapel Hill: University of North Carolina Press, 2003),

151–188; Grace Peña Delgado, *Making the Chinese Mexican: Global Migration, Localism, and Exclusion in the U.S.-Mexico Borderlands* (Stanford, CA: Stanford University Press, 2012), 63–72.

3. For histories of labor conflicts that developed in the Sonora-Arizona border region, see Esteban B. Calderón, *Juicio sobre la guerra del Yaqui y génesis de la huelga de Cananea* (México: Centro de Estudios Históricos del Movimiento Obrero Mexicano, 1975); and Katherine Benton-Cohen, *Borderline Americans: Racial Division and Labor War in the Arizona Borderlands* (Cambridge, MA: Harvard University Press, 2009).

4. Manuel García y Griego, "The Importation of Mexican Contract Laborers to the United States, 1942–1964: Antecedents, Operation, and Legacy," in *The Border That Joins: Mexican Migrants and U.S. Responsibility,* ed. Peter G. Brown and Henry Shue (Totowa, NJ: Rowman and Littlefield, 1983), 55; Arthur F. Corwin, "Early Mexican Labor Migration: A Frontier Sketch, 1848–1900," in *Immigrants—and Immigrants: Perspectives on Mexican Labor Migration to the United States,* ed. Arthur F. Corwin (Westport, CT: Greenwood Press, 1978), 25–37.

5. On Mexicans in the production of cotton in Texas, see Neil Foley, *The White Scourge: Mexicans, Blacks, and Poor Whites in Texas Cotton Culture* (Berkeley: University of California Press, 1997); and David Montejano, *Anglos and Mexicans in the Making of Texas, 1836–1896* (Austin: University of Texas Press, 1987). For California, see Paul S. Taylor, *Mexican Labor in the United States,* vol. 1, *Imperial Valley, California* (1930; reprint, New York: Arno Press, 1970), 1–94.

6. Quoted in Mark Reisler, *By the Sweat of Their Brow* (Westport, CT: Greenwood Press, 1976), 7–8 (quote), 19. On Mexican labor in the citrus industry in southern California, see Matt García, *A World of Its Own: Race, Labor, and Citrus in the Making of Greater Los Angeles, 1900–1970* (Chapel Hill: University of North Carolina, 2001). On Mexican railroad workers, see Samuel Bryan, "Mexican Immigrants in the United States," *Survey,* September 7, 1912, 727–728.

7. Quoted in Taylor, *Mexican Labor in the United States,* 155.

8. *Los grandes problemas nacionales* (Mexico, 1909), quoted in Arthur F. Corwin and Lawrence A. Cardoso, "Vamos al Norte: Causes of Mass Mexican Migration to the United States," in *Immigrants—and Immigrants,* 39; Trinidad Beltrán Bernal, *Problemas de tenencia de la tierra durante el Porfiriato y la Revolución (1876–1915): dos zonas zapatistas del Estado de México* (Zinacantepec: Colegio Mexiquense, 2010); and George McCutchen McBride, *The Land Systems of Mexico* (New York: American Geographical Society, 1923).

9. Quoted in Reisler, *By the Sweat of Their Brow,* 27–28. For the U.S. Department of Labor circular detailing the requirements and responsibilities of the temporary worker and the employer under the Temporary Admission program, see "Departmental Order No. 54261/202," in letter from El Embajador

de México (signature illegible) to Alberto J. Pani, Secretario de Industria, Comercio y Trabajo, June 12, 1918, exp. 15, caja 137, Departamento de Trabajo, AGN (hereafter cited as Depto de Trabajo Papers).

10. "Solution of the Labor Problem," *Star* (February 1918), in letter from Cónsul General (signature illegible), San Francisco, to Alberto J. Pani, Secretario de Industria, Comercio y Trabajo, February 1, 1918, exp. 4, caja 137, Depto de Trabajo Papers.

11. "American Labor First," *Arizona Labor Journal,* March 22, 1918, clipping attached to letter from Viceconsul de México (signature illegible), Globe, Ariz., to Secretario de Industria, Comercio y Trabajo, March 25, 1918, exp. 6, caja 137, ibid.

12. See, for example, Cónsul General (signature illegible), San Francisco, to Alberto J. Pani, Secretario de Industria, Comercio y Trabajo, February 11, 1918, exp. 29, caja 137, ibid.

13. "El Emigración de Braceros Mexicanos a Los Estados Unidos del Norte" and "México, El País de Suelo Más Rico del Mundo, con Sus Hijos Desnudos y Hambrientos," Informe del Cónsul de México, L. G. Villalpando, Kansas City, sobre las causas e la emigración de trabajadores mexicanos a los Estados Unidos, April 12, 1922, exp. 16, caja 496, ibid.

14. José Colado, Cónsul de México (Newport News, VA), "Informe Sobre Demanda de Trabajadores en Esa Región," April 3, 1918, exp. 24 and April 31, 1919, exp. 25, caja 137, ibid.; "Mexican Labor May Aid Sugar Planters Here," *Times-Picayune* (New Orleans), July 5, 1918, in letter from Jefe del Departamento (signature illegible) to Secretaría de Industria, Comercio y Trabajo, July 23, 1918, exp. 23, caja 137, ibid.

15. José Colado, Cónsul de México, "Informe de Trabajo," September 30, 1918, exp. 27, caja 137, ibid.; and Manuel S. Cárdenas to Presidente C. A. Obregón, April 21, 1921, exp. 27, caja 333, ibid.

16. The Mexican embassy instructed consuls to help workers fill out contracts with employers. "Proyecto de las Bases Que Deben Sujetarse los Contratos para la Emigración de Braceros Mexicanos con Destino a Estados Unidos," attached to Circular No. 25 from Y. Bonillas, Embajador de México, to Cónsules del Gobierno Mexicano en los Estados Unidos, June 7, 1918, exp. 16, caja 137, ibid. See also Reisler, *By the Sweat of Their Brow,* 38.

17. For letters from Americans seeking work in Mexico, see C. C. MacDonil (Charleston, WV) to Secretaría de Industria, Comercio y Trabajo, May 18, 1921, exp. 21, caja 333, Depto de Trabajo Papers; J. E. Flesher to President Obregon, February 26, 1921, exp. 20, caja 333, ibid.; Jack Russell Waltus (mechanic, WV) to President Obregon, July 21, 1921, exp. 22, caja 333, ibid.; George O. Strand (Los Angeles) to Labor Commissioner of Mexico, April 15, 1922, exp. 12, caja 508, ibid.; William L. Brown (Aransas Pass, TX) to Mexican Consul, November 12, 1922, exp. 14, caja 508, ibid. More letters from Americans can be found in exp. 6–18, caja 703, ibid.

18. See "Informe de Cónsul de México," Oklahoma City, May 6, 1922, exp. 1, caja 497, ibid.; "Informe de Cónsul de México," Dallas, July 2, 1922, exp. 2, caja 497, ibid.; "Informe de Cónsul de México," Del Río, Texas, November (no day) 1922; "Informe de Cónsul de México," Seattle, August 4, 1922, exp. 5, caja 497, ibid.; "Informe Sobre Situación del Trabajo," January 22, 1922, Cónsul de Baltimore (signature illegible), in letter from J. Poulat to Jefe del Departamento de Trabajo, Secretaría de Industria, Comercio y Trabajo, March 13, 1922, exp. 10, caja 496, ibid.

19. W. H. Grant to Department of Industry and Commerce, October 20, 1921, exp. 18, caja 333, ibid. See numerous letters from German Americans and German citizens, exp. 1–27, caja 704, ibid.

20. Oficial Mayor (signature illegible), Secretaría de Relaciones Exteriores, to Secretario de Industria, Comercio y Trabajo, November 12, 1920, exp. 24, caja 228, ibid. But the Mexican secretary of labor pointed out that U.S. Oil Companies employed far more Mexicans than Americans, and that the Americans hired were "skilled workers and supervisors who obviously required higher salaries than 'los peones.'" Secretario de Depto de Trabajo to Secretario de Gobernación, May 13, 1921, exp. 23, caja 334, ibid.

21. Enrique Conlunga, Jefe del Departamento Consultivo, to Subsecretario, Secretaría de Gobernación, March 18, 1921, exp. 23, caja 334, ibid.

22. Memorandum from J. Poulat to Ministro, Secretaría de Industria, Comercio y Trabajo, March 28, 1921, exp. 23, caja 334, ibid.

23. "Acuerdo Presidencial," February 6, 1921, in letter from Subsecretario de Secretaría de Gobernación to Secretario de Industria, Comercio y Trabajo, March 22, 1921, exp. 23, caja 334, ibid.

24. Memorandum from Jefe de la Sección (signature illegible) to Jefe del Departamento, Secretaría de Industria, Comercio y Trabajo, July 12, 1923, exp. 26, caja 704, ibid.

25. I. M. Vásquez, Cónsul de México (Laredo) to Secretario de Relaciones Exteriores, February 21, 1923, reproduced in letter from Oficial Mayor (signature illegible), Secretaría de Gobernación, to Secretario de Industria, Comercio y Trabajo, June 5, 1923, exp. 26, caja 704, ibid.

26. Memorandum from Jefe de la Sección (signature illegible) to Jefe del Departamento, Secretaría de Industria, Comercio y Trabajo, July 12, 1923; Gobernador de Jalisco (signature illegible) to Secretario de Industria, Comercio y Trabajo, June 18, 1923; Gobernador de San Luis Potosí to Jefe del Departamento, Secretaría de Industria, Comercio y Trabajo, June 13 and 25, 1923; Gobernador de Michoacán (signature illegible) to Jefe del Departamento, Secretaría de Industria, Comercio y Trabajo, July 3, 1923, exp. 26, caja 704, ibid.

27. Reisler, *By the Sweat of Their Brow*, 38.

28. Jean Meyer, *The Cristero Rebellion: The Mexican People between Church and State, 1926–1929* (New York: Cambridge University Press, 1976); Mathew

Butler, *Popular Piety and Political Identity in Mexico's Cristero Rebellion: Michoacán, 1927–1929* (New York: Oxford University Press, 2004).

29. Carey McWilliams, *North from Mexico: The Spanish-Speaking People of the United States* (1949; reprint, New York: Greenwood Press, 1968), 206.

30. "Texan Defends Mexican Labor," *Los Angeles Times,* February 24, 1928, p. 7.

31. Ibid. On the threat to public health see Natalia Molina, *Fit to Be Citizens? Public Health and Race in Los Angeles, 1879–1939* (Berkeley: University of California Press, 2006).

32. U.S. Congress, House Committee on Immigration and Naturalization, *Immigration from Countries of the Western Hemisphere,* 70th Cong., 2d sess., 1930, 619.

33. John Higham, *Strangers in the Land: Patterns of American Nativism, 1860–1925* (1955: reprint, New Brunswick, NJ: Rutgers University Press, 2002), 264–299.

34. Mathew Frye Jacobs, *Whiteness of a Different Color: European Immigrants and the Alchemy of Race* (Cambridge, MA: Harvard University Press, 1998); Mae M. Ngai, *Impossible Subjects: Illegal Aliens and the Making of Modern America* (Princeton, NJ: Princeton University Press, 2004).

35. The congressional hearings on restriction of Mexican immigration are extensive, but see U.S. Congress, House Committee on Immigration and Naturalization, *Immigration from Countries of the Western Hemisphere,* 70th Cong., 2d sess., 1930; *Immigration from Mexico,* 71st Cong., 2d sess., 1930; *Western Hemisphere Immigration,* ibid. See also David Gutierrez, *Walls and Mirrors: Mexican Americans, Mexican Immigrants, and the Politics of Ethnicity* (Berkeley: University of California, 1995); and Ngai, *Impossible Subjects.*

36. Quoted in Gary A. Greenfield and Don B. Kates, Jr., "Mexican Americans, Racial Discrimination, and the Civil Rights Act of 1866," *California Law Review* 63 (January 1975), 700. See also T. J. Woofter, Jr., *Races and Ethnic Groups in American Life* (New York: McGraw-Hill, 1933), 57.

37. Neil Foley, "Partly Colored or Other White: Mexican Americans and Their Problem with the Color Line," in *Beyond Black and White: Race, Ethnicity, and Gender in the U.S. South and Southwest,* ed. Stephanie Cole and Alison M. Parker (College Station: Texas A&M Press, 2004), 341–355; and Mario García, "Mexican Americans and the Politics of Citizenship: The Case of El Paso, 1936," *New Mexico Historical Review* 59 (April 1984): 187–204.

38. Max Sylvius Handman, "Economic Reasons for the Coming of the Mexican Immigrant," *American Journal of Sociology* 35 (January 1930): 609–610.

39. Max Sylvius Handman, "The Mexican Immigrant in Texas," *Southwestern Political and Social Science Quarterly* 7 (June 1926): 27.

40. Ibid., 40. See also Foley, "Partly Colored," 127–128.

41. See *Takao Ozawa v. United States,* 260 U.S. 178 (1922) and Ian F. Haney López, *White by Law: The Legal Construction of Race* (New York: New York University Press, 1996), ch. 4.

42. Declaration of Intention, Timoteo Andrade, no. 48281 (1929) and U.S. Department of Labor, Certificate of Arrival No. 54, both in Naturalization Records, U.S. District Court, Western District of New York, National Archives and Records Administration, Northeast Region, New York, NY (hereafter cited as Andrade Files/U.S.). See also Patrick D. Lukens, *A Quiet Victory for Latino Rights: FDR and the Controversy over "Whiteness"* (Tucson: University of Arizona Press, 2012); and Natalia Molina, "In a Race All Their Own": The Quest to Make Mexicans Ineligible for U.S. Citizenship," *Pacific Historical Review* 79 (May 2010): 167–201.

43. On the distinction between "color" and "race" in the Italian community of Chicago, see Thomas A. Guglielmo, *White on Arrival: Italians, Race, Color, and Power in Chicago, 1890–1945* (New York: Oxford University Press, 2004).

44. Petition for Citizenship, Timoteo Andrade, no. 24049 (1935), Andrade Files/U.S.

45. Although four other Mexicans had applied for naturalization, Karmuth chose Andrade's petition as a test case. Rafael de la Colina to Secretario de Relaciones Exteriores, February 17, 1936, (hereafter cited as III-2335-2), Archivo Histórico de la Secretaría de Relaciones Exteriores (AHSRE), Mexico City (hereafter cited as Andrade Files/MX). All translations are by the author.

46. Francisco Castillo Nájera to Secretario de Relaciones Exteriores, December 18, 1935, Andrade Files/MX; Luis Quintanilla to Eduardo Hay, June 17, 1936, ibid.; Espinosa, "Mexico, Mexican Americans," 124–124.

47. "Opinion of District Judge Knight, December 11, 1935, Petition No. 2272-P-24049, in the matter of Timoteo Andrade to be admitted a Citizen of the United States of America," United States District Court, Western District of New York, Andrade Files/U.S.; and *Morrison v. California,* 29 U.S 82 (1934).

48. *In re Camille,* 6 F. 256–259 (District Court, Oregon 1880); Martha Menchaca, "Chicano Indianism: A Historical Account of Racial Repression in the United States," *American Ethnologist* 20 (August 1993): 583–603.

49. Walter E. Barry to Col. C. Julian Verlarde, February 5, 1936, Andrade Files/MX; Col. C. Julian Velarde to don Eduardo Hay, February 7, 1936, ibid.

50. Mexican immigrants were entitled to vote after filing their intention to become naturalized citizens. Arnoldo De León, *In Re Rodríguez: An Attempt at Chicano Disfranchisement in San Antonio, 1896–1897* (San Antonio, TX: Caravel Press, 1979), 1–2.

51. Other cases included *In re Ah Yup,* 1 F. Cas. 223 (1878), *In re Kanaka Nian* 21 Pac. 993 (1889), *In re Saito,* 62 F. 126 (1894), *In re Camille,* 6 F. 256–259 (1880). See Ernest Evans Kilker, "Black and White in America: The Culture and Politics of Racial Classification," *International Journal of Politics, Culture, and Society* 7 (Winter 1993): 229–258; Haney-Lopez, *White by Law,* ch. 3; and

Martha Menchaca, *Recovering History, Constructing Race: The Indian, Black, and White Roots of Mexican Americans* (Austin: University of Texas Press, 2002), 282–285.

52. *In re: Rodríguez*, 81 F. 345 (W.D. Tex. 1897); Martha Menchaca, *Naturalizing Mexican Immigrants: A Texas History* (Austin: University of Texas Press, 2011), 122–125.

53. Paul S. Taylor, *Mexican Labor in the United States: Migration Statistics*. University of California Publications in Economics, vol. 6 (Berkeley: University of California Press, 1929): 242–245; Neil Foley, "Straddling the Color Line: The Legal Construction of Hispanic Identity in Texas," in *Not Just Black and White: Historical and Contemporary Perspectives on Immigration, Race, and Ethnicity in the United States*, ed. Nancy Foner and George Frederickson (New York: Russell Sage Foundation, 2004), 344.

54. *In re Rodríguez*, 81 F. 346.

55. *Elk v. Wilkins*, 112 U.S. 94 (1884). In 1924 Congress passed the Indian Citizenship Act conferring citizenship on all Native Americans in the U.S. Act of June 2, 1924, 43 U.S. Stats. At Large, Ch. 233, p. 253.

56. *In re Rodríguez*, 81 F. 349, 354–355.

57. Ibid.

58. Ariela J. Gross, "'The Caucasian Cloak': Mexican Americans and the Politics of Whiteness in the Twentieth-Century Southwest," *Georgetown Law Journal* 95 (January 2007): 337–392.

59. Recent books that view Mexican immigration as an "invasion" include Patrick Buchanan, *State of Emergency: Third World Invasion and Conquest of America* (New York: St. Martin's Press, 2006); Samuel P. Huntington, *Who Are We: The Challenge to America's National Identity* (New York: Simon and Schuster, 2005); and Peter Brimelow, *Alien Nation: Common Sense about America's Immigration Disaster* (New York: Random House, 1995).

60. Gregg Cantrell, "'Our Very Pronounced Theory of Equal Rights to All': Race, Citizenship, and Populism in the South Texas Borderlands," *Journal of American History* 100 (December 2013): 663–690; and Teresa Palomo Acosta, "In re Ricardo Rodriguez," *Handbook of Texas Online*, www.tshaonline.org /handbook/online/articles/pqitw.

61. See Edward O. Guerrant, *Roosevelt's Good Neighbor Policy* (Albuquerque: University of New Mexico Press, 1950); Bryce Wood, *The Making of the Good Neighbor Policy* (New York: Columbia University Press, 1962); Luis G. Zorrilla, *Historia de las Relaciones entre Mexico y los Estados Unidos de America, 1800–1958* (Mexico, 1977); Cesar Sepúlveda, *Las Relaciones Diplomáticos entre México y los Estados Unidos en el Siglo XX* (Monterrey, 1953).

62. See, for example, U.S. Congress, House Committee on Immigration and Naturalization, *Immigration from Countries of the Western Hemisphere*, 70th Cong., 2d sess., 1928; idem, *Immigration from Mexico*, 71st Cong., 2d sess., 1930.

63. On repatriation of Mexicans during the Depression, see Camille Guerin-Gonzales, *Mexican Workers and American Dreams: Immigration, Repatriation, and California Farm Labor, 1900–1939* (New Brunswick, NJ: Rutgers University Press, 1994); and Francisco E. Balderrama, *Decade of Betrayal: Mexican Repatriation in the 1930s* (rev. ed., Albuquerque: University of New Mexico Press, 2006).

64. "Indian Blood Bars Mexicans as Citizens," *New York Times,* December 12, 1935, clipping in Andrade Files/MX; *Buffalo Courier-Express,* December 12, 1935, clipping attached to letter from Enrique L. Elizondo to Secretario de Relaciones Exteriores, December 12, 1935, ibid.

65. Enrique L. Elizondo to Embajador de México, December 13, 1935; and Enrique L. Elizondo to Secretario de Relaciones Exteriores, January 2, 1936, ibid.

66. Enrique L. Elizondo to Secretario de Relaciones Exteriores, December 12, 1935, ibid.

67. Francisco Castillo Nájera, notes on a telephone conversation, December 13, 1935, ibid.; Telegram from Ambassador Castillo Nájera to Minister of Foreign Affairs, December 13, 1935, ibid.

68. Francisco Castillo Castillo Nájera to Secretario de Relaciones Exteriores, December 18, 1935, ibid.; Enrique L. Elizondo to Secretario de Relaciones Exteriores, January 3, 1935, ibid.; Manuel J. Sierra to Enrique L. Elizondo, January 14, 1936, ibid.

69. Francisco Castillo Nájera to Secretario de Relaciones Exteriores, December 18, 1935, ibid.

70. Testimony introduced by the Attorney for the Petitioner on March 11, 1936 and April 13, 1936, In the Matter of the Petition for Citizenship of Timoteo Andrade, Petition No. 24049, Andrade Files/U.S. All testimony is from this document.

71. Ibid.

72. On race mixing in Mexico and Latin America, see José Vasconcelos, *The Cosmic Race/La Raza Cósmica* (Baltimore, MD: Johns Hopkins University Press, 1997); Marilyn Grace Miller, *The Rise and Fall of the Cosmic Race: The Cult of Mestizaje in Latin America* (Austin: University of Texas Press, 2004); Alfonso Caso, *Indigenismo* (México: Instituto Nacional Indigenista, 1958); Richard Graham, ed., *The Idea of Race in Latin American: 1870–1940* (Austin: University of Texas Press, 1990).

73. Testimony introduced by the Attorney for the Petitioner on March 11, 1936, and April 13, 1936, In the Matter of the Petition for Citizenship of Timoteo Andrade, Petition No. 24049, Andrade Files/U.S.; Opinion, District Judge Knight, in the matter of the Petition of Timoteo Andrade, No. 2272-P-24049, June 1, 1936, ibid.

74. Francisco Castillo Nájera to Secretario de Relaciones Exteriores, December 18, 1935, Andrade Files/MX.

75. Memorandum from Castillo Nájera to Secretario de Relaciones Exteriores, December 23, 1935, ibid.; Francisco Castillo Nájera to Secretario de Relaciones Exteriores, December 24, 1935, ibid.

76. Opinion, District Judge Knight, in the matter of the Petition of Timoteo Andrade, No. 2272-P-24049, June 1, 1936, Andrade Files/U.S.

77. Luis Quintanilla to Eduardo Hay, June 17, 1936, Andrade Files/MX.

78. Francisco Castillo Nájera to Secretario de Relaciones Exteriores, December 24, 1935, ibid.

79. Luis Quintanilla to Eduardo Hay, June 17, 1936, ibid.

80. Ibid.

81. Glenn E. Hoover, "Our Mexican Immigrants," *Foreign Affairs* 8 (October 1929–July 1930), 104.

82. Stefan Kühl, *The Nazi Connection: Eugenics, American Racism, and German National Socialism* (Princeton, NJ: Princeton University Press, 2002).

83. "Mexicans Barred?" *Dallas Journal,* n.d., clipping in Andrade Files/MX. He also suggested that Andrade could have claimed that being half Spanish was the same as being half African, since "the Moorish infiltration onto Spain would reasonably be represented by this time in the blood of practically all the families of Spain."

84. See Jack D. Forbes, *Aztecas del Norte: The Chicanos of Aztlán* (Greenwich, CT: Fawcett Publications, 1973), 13.

85. Sammy Howe to Department of State, March 9, 1940, Decimal File 811.4016/267, Record Group 59, Records of the Department of State, National Archives and Records Administration (NARA), College Park, MD (hereafter cited as Department of State).

86. *Takao Ozawa v. United States,* 260 U.S. 178 (1922); Haney López, *White by Law,* ch. 4; Neil Foley, "Mexican Americans and the Faustian Pact with Whiteness," in *Reflexiones 1997: New Directions in Mexican American Studies,* ed. Neil Foley (Austin: University of Texas Press, 1998), 59–60.

87. *United States v. Bhagat Singh Thind,* 261 U.S. 204 (1923); and Haney López, *White by Law,* 89.

88. George I. Sánchez to Nelson A. Rockefeller, December 31, 1941, box 31, folder 9, George I. Sánchez Papers, Benson Latin American Collection, University of Texas, Austin, TX (hereafter cited as Sánchez Papers).

3. Becoming Good Neighbors

1. On the international consequences of racial injustice in the United States during World War II, see Justin Hart, "Making Democracy Safe for the World: Race, Propaganda, and the Transformation of U.S. Foreign Policy during World War II," *Pacific Historical Review* 73 (February 2004), 49–84; and R. A. Humphreys, *Latin America and the Second World War,* vol. 1 (London: Institute of Latin American Studies, University of London, 1981), 1–14.

2. "Spanish-Americans in the Southwest and the War Effort," Report No. 24, Office of War Information, August 18, 1942, Decimal File, 811.4016/444, box 3804, Department of State.

3. Carey McWilliams to Nelson Rockefeller, October 15, 1942, box 1717, folder "Carey McWilliams Plan," Office of the Coordinator for Inter-American Affairs, RG 229, NARA (hereafter cited as OCIAA).

4. George I. Sanchez to Nelson A. Rockefeller, December 31, 1941, box 31, folder 9, Sánchez Papers; idem, *Forgotten People: A Study of New Mexicans* (Albuquerque: University of New Mexico Press, 1940).

5. Quoted in Edward O. Guerrant, *Roosevelt's Good Neighbor Policy* (Albuquerque: University of New Mexico Press, 1950), 1. See also Bryce Wood, *The Making of the Good Neighbor Policy* (New York: Columbia University Press, 1961); and Fredrick B. Pike, *FDR's Good Neighbor Policy: Sixty Years of Generally Gentle Chaos* (Austin: University of Texas Press, 1995).

6. Quoted in Irwin F. Gellman, *Good Neighbor Diplomacy: United States Policies in Latin America, 1933–1945* (Baltimore: Johns Hopkins University Press, 1979), 24.

7. Gellman, *Good Neighbor Diplomacy*, 25. On the multiple meanings of "intervention" in the context of international jurisprudence, including "diplomatic intervention," see Charles G. Fenwick, "Intervention: Individual and Collective," *American Journal of International Law* 39 (October 1945): 645–663.

8. Dicurso por Lic. Ramón Beteta, Subsecretario de Relaciones Exteriores de México, en la Conferencia Inter-Americana para la Consolidación de la Paz, December 19, 1936, attached to letter from Lic. Ramón Beteta to Sr. General Lázaro Cárdenas, February 12, 1937, Cárdenas Papers. Translations of documents are by the author.

9. On Mexico's nationalization of the foreign-owned petroleum industry, see Lorenzo Meyer, *México y los Estados Unidos en el Conflicto Petrolero, 1917–1942* (Mexico City: Colegio de México, 1968); Jonathan C. Brown and Alan Knight, eds., *The Mexican Petroleum Industry in the Twentieth Century* (Austin: University of Texas Press, 1992).

10. Francisco Castillo Nájera, *Relaciones Futuras Entre México y Los Estados Unidos* (Washington, DC, 1942), 20, exp. 577.1/25, caja 977, Manuel Ávila Camacho Papers, AGN (hereafter cited as Ávila Camacho Papers).

11. Castillo Nájera, *Relaciones Futuras,* ibid. See also María Emilia Paz, *Strategy, Security, and Spies: Mexico and the U.S. as Allies in World War II* (University Park: Pennsylvania State University Press, 1997), 108.

12. Quoted in Carey McWilliams, *North from Mexico: The Spanish-Speaking People of the United States* (1948; reprint, New York: Greenwood Press, 1968), 256–257.

13. On the politics of wartime cooperation between Mexico and the United States, see Luis G. Zorilla, *Historia de las relaciones entre México y los Estados*

Unidos de América, vol. 2 (Mexico City: Editorial Porrúa, 1977), 483–509; and Stephen R. Niblo, *War, Diplomacy, and Development: The United States and Mexico, 1938-1954* (Wilmington, DE: Scholarly Resources, 1995), 89–122.

14. Max Paul Friedman, *Nazis and Good Neighbors: The United States Campaign against the Germans of Latin America in World War II* (Cambridge: Cambridge University Press, 2003), 2.

15. Report, "The Military Importance of Northeastern Brazil," August 24, 1942, box 610, folder "Military Importance of N.E. Brazil, 5th Column Activities, Germans in Brazil, the Japanese and Italians in Brazil, Prominent Brazilians in the 5th Column," OCIAA. See also Stanley E. Hilton, *Hitler's Secret War in South America 1939-1945: German Military Espionage and Allied Counterespionage in Brazil* (Baton Rouge: Louisiana State University, 1981).

16. Hitler's African colonies "would provide the strategic position ... from which to launch an air attack for the invasion and conquest of Latin America." See *La "Quinta Columna" en las dos Américas: La Conquista de la América Latina es el Objetivo Final de Hitler,* 20-page pamphlet, n.d., p. 19, exp. 550/9, caja 824, Ávila Camacho Papers.

17. Report, "The Military Importance of Northeastern Brazil," OCIAA.

18. Friedman, *Nazis and Good Neighbors,* 2.

19. "He [Ávila Camacho] Fooled Hitler," *Chicago Daily News,* January 24, 1942, clipping attached to letter from Ricardo G. Hill, Cónsul General de México, to Manuel Ávila Camacho, exp. 704/52, caja 1137, Ávila Camacho Papers.

20. "La Quinta Columna Vuelve la Cara hacia el Norte," typescript, n.d., by Hal Burton, in exp. 704.1/124–1, caja 1302, Cárdenas Papers; Niblo, *War, Diplomacy, and Development,* 65; Paz, *Strategy, Security, and Spies,* 146–208.

21. *Excelsior,* November 20, 1942; Alberto Alegria Arteaga to Manuel Ávila Camacho, November 23, 1943, exp. 550/44–56, caja 845, Ávila Camacho Papers; Niblo, *War, Diplomacy, and Development,* 77. The Mexican Secret Service reported that the Japanese were preparing an invasion of Panama and Tehuantepec, Oaxaca, in an attempt to blockade U.S. shipping. Servicios Secretos, Memorandum estrictamente confidencial exclusivo para ... Manuel Ávila Camacho, March 9, 1942, exp. 606.3/17, caja 993, Ávila Camacho Papers.

22. Castillo Nájera, *Relaciones Futuras,* ibid. On the use of Mexican airfields, see Stetson Conn and Byron Fairchild, *The United States Army in World War II,* vol. 1, *The Western Hemisphere* (Washington, DC: Government Printing Office, 1989), 331–363. I am indebted to military historian Roger Spiller for suggesting this source.

23. Bulletin, "Mexico Demands Change," July 2, 1946, box 4–14/178, folder "Mexican Politics," Governor Coke Stevenson Papers, Texas State Library and Archives, Austin, Texas (hereafter cited as Stevenson Papers). "Mexico 'Fixed Star' in United Nations' Galaxy," *Christina Science Monitor,* July 1, 1942, clip-

ping attached to letter from L. Couttolenc to Lic. Jesús González Gallo, July 6, 1942, exp. 550/44–32, caja 844, Ávila Camacho Papers.

24. For Texas, see Thomas A. Guglielmo, "Fighting for Caucasian Rights: Mexicans, Mexican Americans, and the Transnational Struggle for Civil Rights in World War II Texas," *Journal of American History* 92 (March 2006): 1212–1237; and Emilio Zamora, *Claiming Rights and Righting Wrongs in Texas: Mexican Workers and Job Politics during World War II* (College Station: Texas A&M Press, 2009).

25. Those regarded as potential fifth columnists in Mexico included *trotskistas, falangistas, sinarquistas,* and *nazi-fascistas.* Manuel J. Bezares and Francisco Gallegos to Manuel Ávila Camacho, April 2, 1943, exp. 541.1/56, caja 681; Servicios Secretos, Memorandum estrictamente confidencial exclusivo para . . . Manuel Ávila Camacho, June 4, 1942, exp. 606.3/17, caja 993, Ávila Camacho Papers.

26. David Paull Nickles, *Under the Wire: How the Telegraph Changed Diplomacy* (Cambridge, MA: Harvard University Press, 2003), 137–160; World War I Documents Archive, "Zimmerman Note," wwi.lib.byu.edu.

27. "Risible Embuste Del Senador Lee," *Excelsior,* May 9, 1940, clipping with memorandum from Pierre de L. Boal to Secretary of State, May 9, 1940, Decimal File 812.00B/515, Microfilm LM 130, reel 16, Department of State. Texas congressman and chair of the committee, Martin Dies, wanted Leon Trotsky and Mexican muralist Diego Rivera to testify before his committee. August Raymond Ogden, *The Dies Committee: A Study of the Special House Committee for the Investigation of Un-American Activities, 1938–1944* (Washington, DC: Catholic University Press, 1945), 172.

28. Elis M. Tipton to Walter H. C. Laves, October 9, 1942, and Elis M. Tipton to Vice-President (Henry A. Wallace), October 10, 1942, box 1717, folder "Paul Horgan," OCIAA.

29. "En Mexico No Existe Una Quinta Columna," *El Universal,* n.d., clipping sent by Pierre de L. Boal to Secretary of State, June 4, 1940, Decimal File 812.00N/160, reel 18, Department of State. Of the seven major newspapers in Mexico City in 1941 *(El Universal, Excelsior, La Prensa, Novedades, El Nacional, Universal Gráfico, Últimas Noticias),* only one, *La Prensa,* was consistently anti-U.S. before the U.S. entry into the war. J. F. McGurk to Secretary of State, September 30, October 3, and October 15, 1941, Decimal File 812.911/331, reel 64, Department of State.

30. Quoted in Lars Schoultz, *Beneath the United States: A History of U.S. Policy toward Latin America* (Cambridge, MA: Harvard University Press, 1998), 309. See also David Kahn, *Hitler's Spies: German Military Intelligence in World War II* (New York: Macmillan, 1978).

31. Quoted in Schoultz, *Beneath the United States,* 309; Friedman, *Nazis and Good Neighbors,* 8.

32. "Nazi Activities in Mexico," FBI Memo, sent by J. Edgar Hoover to Adolf A. Berle, April 8, 1940, Decimal File 812.00N/112, reel 18, Department of State. See petitions of Mercedes Córdova Vda. De Kruse to Manuel Ávila Camacho, August 15, 1942; Juan Hintze to Manuel Ávila Camacho, June 17, 1943; and María Culebro Escandón de Schulte to Manuel Ávila Camacho, May 12, 1944; all in exp. 550/35–6, caja 826, Ávila Camacho Papers.

33. "Informe Confidencial A-3, sobre las Actividades Alemanes en México," typescript, October 13, 1939, in letter from Eduardo Villaseñor to Lázaro Cárdenas, October 22, 1939; and "El Nazismo en Mexico," typescript, May 23, 1940, exp. 704.1/124–1, caja 1302, Cárdenas Papers.

34. *La Quinta Columna en las dos Américas,* Ávila Camacho Papers. German nationals in Mexico opposed to Hitler formed La Liga Antinazi de Habla Alemana and the Movimiento Antinazi de Alemania Libre en México. See "Diez Años de Barbarie Nazi," February 17, 1943, exp. 710.1/101–91, caja 1191, Ávila Camacho Papers.

35. John Bright and Josephine Fierro de Bright, "Mexican Americans of the Southwest," p. 5, report attached to letter from John Bright to Walter H. C. Laves, November 10, 1942, box 1717, folder "Spanish-Speaking Project," OCIAA. For examples of German propaganda in Mexico, see *Der Deutsche Volkswirt* ("Die Wirtschaft im Neuen Deutschland" and "Das Neue Reich und das Ausland"), No. 12/13, January 1941, exp. 707/174, caja 1142, Ávila Camacho Papers; and *Informe Político Aleman,* exp. 606.3/17, caja 993, ibid.

36. Senador Joaquín Martínez Chavarría to Manuel Ávila Camacho, August 19, 1941, exp. 550/9, caja 824, ibid.; Alfonso Guerra to Lic. J. Jesús González Gallo, September 12, 1941, exp. 550/33, caja 825, ibid.

37. John C. Dreier to Sumner Welles et al., December 15, 1942, Decimal File 811.4016/508, box 3805, Department of State. On "Sinarquista cells" in California and Texas, see "Report of the Spanish-Speaking Peoples in the Southwest," Field Report, March 14 to April 7, 1942, reel 70, Fair Employment Practices Committee (FEPC), RG 228, NARA (hereafter cited as FEPC).

38. Confidential Memorandum from J. Edgar Hoover to Adolf A Berle, Jr., July 26, 1940, Decimal File 812.00N/316–1/2, reel 18, Department of State. Hoover cites the same states, in the same order, as the Zimmerman Note, and both missives inexplicably omit California.

39. Marcelo Mejia Baeza to Manuel Ávila Camacho, December 30, 1941, exp. 550/44–5, caja 830, Ávila Camacho Papers; Memorandum estrictamente confidencial . . . para Manuel Ávila Camacho, attached to letter from Carmen Aguilar and Francisco Venegas, February 22, 1943, exp. 606.3/17, caja 993, ibid.; Luis Audirac to Manuel Ávila Camacho, December 23, 1941, exp. 545.3/75, caja 788, ibid.

40. Francisco Domínguez Novoa to Manuel Ávila Camacho, March 12, 1941, exp. 133.2/12, caja 140, ibid. The Mexico City Newspaper, *El Hombre Libre,* published numerous articles attacking Jews for being "tricky" and "deceitful."

Josephus Daniels to Secretary of State, November 26, 1940, Decimal File 812.4016/110, reel 3, Department of State; and J. F. McGurk to Secretary of State, September 30, 1941, Decimal File 812.911/331, reel 64, ibid.

41. "Patriotas de México y de toda la América Latina. Alerta!" Handbill of PNSM, enclosure sent by Pierre de L. Boal to Secretary of State, June 9, 1940, Decimal File 812.00N/225, reel 18, ibid.

42. J. Salvador S. Sánchez to Lic. Jesús González Gallo, May 30, 1942, exp. 702.11/201, caja 1032, Ávila Camacho Papers.

43. "Ezequiel Padilla and Family," typescript, n.d., n.a. in exp. 709/56, caja 1186, ibid. Author's translation.

44. A "state of war" indicated that Mexico would defend itself against attack, but its military lacked the training and resources to join allied armies on the battle fronts. Manuel Ávila Camacho, "México en Estado de Guerra, Mensaje al H. Congreso de la Unión de los Estados Unidos Mexicanos," May 1942, exp. 550/44-2, caja 828, ibid.; *El Mundo,* May 29, 1942, in letter from J. Rubén Romero to Manuel Ávila Camacho, June 10, 1942, exp. 550/44-32, caja 844, ibid.; and Harold D. Finley to Secretary of State, May 25, 1942, Decimal File 812.911/26, reel 65, Department of State.

45. "Mexico Es un Gran Aliado," *El Continental,* June 7, 1942, in letter from Raúl Michel, Cónsul General de México, to Manuel Ávila Camacho, June 11, 1942, exp. 550/44-32, caja 844, Ávila Camacho Papers.

46. Embajador Castillo Nájera to Manuel Ávila Camacho, March 27, 1942, exp. 705.1/53, caja 1159, ibid.; Loyal L. Greeley to Manuel Ávila Camacho, April 29, 1943, exp. 705.1/53, caja 1159, ibid. On the Lend-Lease agreement with Mexico, see Conn and Fairchild, *United States Army,* 354–355.

47. "Cifras que demuestran la cooperación de México en minerales y materias primas al esfuerzo bélico de los Estados Unidos," report attached to letter from Ezequiel Padilla to C. Lic. J. Jesús González Gallo, July 28, 1943; and "Reglas Para Una Cooperación Económica entre Nuestro País y Los Estados Unidos," *El Nacional,* July 18, 1943, clipping in exp. 577.1/36, caja 977, Ávila Camacho Papers.

48. Donald W. Rowland, *History of the Office of the Coordinator of Inter-American Affairs* (Washington: Government Printing Office, 1947), 3–10; Claude Curtis Erb, "Nelson Rockefeller and United States—Latin American Relations, 1940–1945 (PhD diss., Clark University, 1980), ch. 1.

49. Memorandum from David J. Saposs to Walter H. C. Laves, May 11, 1942, box 1717, folder "Spanish-Speaking People's Congress," OCIAA.

50. Nelson Rockefeller to Manuel Ávila Camacho, May 31, 1943; Manuel Ávila Camacho to Sr. Nelson A. Rockefeller, June 1, 1943, exp. 577.1/36, caja 977, Ávila Camacho Papers.

51. The Spanish Americans of the Southwest and the War Effort, p. 2, report attached to letter from R. Keith Kane to Dr. David J. Saposs, July 4, 1942, box 1717, folder "OWI—Miscellaneous," OCIAA.

52. David J. Saposs, Report on Rapid Survey of Resident Latin American Problems and Recommended Program, April 3, 1942, box 339, Legal Division, Hearings, 1944–1946, folder "Hearing, Background Material," FEPC; copy of report also in folder "Program for Cooperation of Spanish-Speaking Minorities in the United States," box 1717, OCIAA.

53. Dennis Chavez to Mr. Waterbury, April 30, 1942, Decimal File, 811.4016/358, box 3804, Department of State; Robert Meza, LULAC Council #1, to Congressman Richard M. Kleberg, July 27, 1942, reel 66, FEPC.

54. Harry Frantz to Hart Stilwell, January 23, 1943, Central Files, box 57, folder "Spanish and Portuguese-Speaking Minorities in the U.S," OCIAA. Mexican Ambassador Castillo Nájera told Ávila Camacho that the OCIAA "tiene a su cargo la directa aplicación de la política del buen vecino del Gobierno Federal."Memorandum para el C. Presidente de la República del C. Embajador Francisco Castillo Nájera, September 21, 1942, exp. 577.1/36, caja 977, Ávila Camacho Papers.

55. Joseph E. Weckler to Stanley A. Harris, April 17, 1943, Central Files, box 57, folder "Spanish and Portuguese-Speaking Minorities in the U.S," OCIAA.

56. Victor Borella to Thomas Kilpatrick, November 24, 1943, Central Files, box 57, folder "Spanish and Portuguese-Speaking Minorities in the U.S," OCIAA.

57. Dale Adams, "Saludos Amigos: Hollywood and FDR's Good Neighbor Policy," *Quarterly Review of Film and Video* 24 (May 2007): 289–295. The OCIAA also collaborated with the Mexican movie industry to produce a film in Michoacán to portray native Mexican life with accuracy and sensitivity. Memorandum para el C. Presidente de la República, Ávila Camacho Papers.

58. Memorandum for Files, Second Inter-Agency Meeting on Problems of the Spanish Speaking . . . , December 11, 1942, box 1717, folder "Reports: Inter-Agency Meetings," OCIAA.

59. L. A. Wicks to Gov. Stevenson, box 4–14/156, folder "Interracial Discrimination," Stevenson Papers.

60. Case Study, Division of American Republics, September 12, 1941, Decimal File, 811.4016, box 3804, Department of State.

61. Sumner Welles to William P. Blocker, November 25, 1941, Decimal File, 811.4016/323A, box 3804, ibid.

62. William P. Blocker to Secretary of State, January 8, 1942, Decimal File 811.4016/319, box 3804, ibid.

63. Joseph C. Crew to Coke Stevenson, February 17, 1945, Decimal File 811.4016/2–1745, ibid.; Chargé d'Affaires of the Embassy of Mexico to Acting Secretary of State, May 23, 1945, Decimal File 811.4016/5–1045, ibid.; John Willard Carrigan to Major William L Breese, May 15, 1945, Decimal File 811.4016/5–1045, ibid.; Luis L. Duplan to Gov. Stevenson, September 30, 1943, box 4–14/156, folder "Interracial Discrimination," Stevenson Papers.

64. *El Tornillo,* n.d., clipping attached to letter from E. W. Eaton to Secretary of State, July 29, 1927, Decimal File 811.4016/7–2947, Department of State.

65. Fidencio Soria B. to Gov. Coke Stevenson, February 21, 1945, box 1989/59–18, folder "Mexicans Burned to Death in Fisher County," GNC. See also Joseph C. Crew to Coke Stevenson, February 17, 1945, Decimal File 811.4016/2–1745, Department of State; Chargé d'Affaires of the Embassy of Mexico to Acting Secretary of State, May 23, 1945, Decimal File 811.4016/5–1045, ibid.; John Willard Carrigan to Major William L Breese, May 15, 1945, Decimal File 811.4016/5–1045, ibid.; Case Study, Division of American Republics, ibid.

66. Guy W. Ray to Secretary of State, October 6, 1943, and attached editorial from *Mañana,* Decimal File 811.4016/713, box 3806, ibid.

67. See, for example, Luis L. Duplan, Consul of Mexico (Austin) to George I. Sánchez, April 23, 1943, box 25, folder 8, Sánchez Papers. Numerous letters of complaint from Mexican consuls in Austin, Dallas, and other cities can be found in box 4-14/155, folder "Good Neighbor Commission," Stevenson Papers.

68. "Bad Neighbors," *Time,* February 7, 1944, www.time.com/time/magazine.

69. Joseph F. McGurk (Chargé d'Affaires ad Interim, U.S. Embassy) to Secretary of State, February 4, 1942, box 1717, folder "Program for Cooperation of Spanish-Speaking Minorities in the United States," OCIAA.

70. William P. Blocker to Cordell Hull, "Results of a Confidential Survey of the Problem of Racial Discrimination Against Mexican and Latin American Citizens in Texas and New Mexico," February 27, 1942, p. 13, Decimal File 811.4016/337, box 3804, Department of State.

71. Luis L. Duplan to George I. Sanchez, April 23, 1943, printed in *Laredo Times,* editorial, July 11, 1943, clipping attached to William P. Blocker to Lawrence Duggan, June 29, 1943, Decimal File 811.4016/611, box 3805, ibid.

72. Case Study, Division of American Republics, ibid. The Mexican consul in Austin compiled a list of signs proscribing the rights of Mexicans. See Luis L. Duplan to George I. Sánchez, April 23, 1943, reel 66, FEPC.

73. *Hernandez v. Texas,* 251 S.W. 2d 531, rev'd, 347 U.S. 475 (1954). Also see Michael A. Olivas, ed., *"Colored Men" and "Hombres Aquí": Hernandez v. Texas and the Emergence of Mexican-American Lawyering* (Houston, TX: Arte Público Press, 2006); and idem, "The 'Trial of the Century' That Never Was: Staff Sgt. Macario García, the Congressional Medal of Honor, and the Oasis Café," *Indiana Law Journal* 83 (2008): 1391–1403.

74. William P. Blocker to Secretary of State, September 2, 1943, Decimal File 811.4016/687, box 3806, Department of State; Laurence Duggan to Edward Stettinius, February 17, 1944, Decimal File 811.4016/803, box 3806, ibid.; PFC. George M. Villarreal to Gov. Stevenson, November 19, 1943, box 4-14/156, folder "Interracial Discrimination," Stevenson Papers.

75. Case Study, Division of American Republics, Department of State; Raúl Michel to Sr. Lic. Jesús González Gallo, September 11, 1942, exp. 573.12/15, caja 972, Ávila Camacho Papers.

76. Carlos A. Calderón, Consul General of Mexico, "Address Delivered to Good Neighbor Commission of Texas," August 18, 1944, III-813-1(I), Archivo Histórico de la Secretaría de Relaciones Exteriores, Mexico City (hereafter cited as AHSRE); "Minutes of the Fifth Meeting of the Good Neighbor Commission," August 18, 1944, box 4–14/169, folder "Good Neighbor Commission 1944," Stevenson Papers; "Consul General Sees Era of Mexico-U.S. Friendship," *Fort Worth Press,* May 6, 1944, clipping attached to letter from Carlos A. Calderón to Lic. J. Jesús González Gallo, June 29, 1944, exp. 573.12/25, caja 972, Ávila Camacho Papers.

77. Quoted in Otey M. Scruggs, "Texas and the Bracero Program, 1942–1947," *Pacific Historical Review* 32 (February 1963), 254.

78. Manuel García y Griego, "The Importation of Mexican Contract Laborers to the United States, 1942–1964: Antecedents, Operation, and Legacy," in *The Border That Joins: Mexican Migrants and U.S. Responsibility,* ed. Peter G. Brown and Henry Shue (Totowa, NJ: Rowman and Littlefield, 1983), 59–60.

79. One Mexican man, Alberto Ochoa, explained to the president that when he married an *"americana,"* her brothers threatened to kill him. Alberto Ochoa to Manuel Ávila Camacho, May 14, 1942, exp. 575.1/33, caja 974, Ávila Camacho Papers. See letters to Manuel Ávila Camacho from Erasmo P. Guzmán (Raymond, MN), August 12, 1941, extracto 47553; Faustino Gutiérrez (Synder, TX), December 5, 1942, extracto 42768; Pedro Nuñez (Hamlin, TX), September 21, 1942, extracto 35174; Salvador Puga (Stockton, CA), February 23, 1943, extracto 7499; Pedro López (Slayton, TX), January 5, 1943, extracto 941; all in exp. 575.1/17, caja 974, ibid.

80. Jesús Prado y demás firmantes to Ávila Camacho, December 3, 1941, exp. 575.1/22, caja 974, ibid.; "Bofetón a La Política del Buen Vecino," *Excelsior,* November 26, 1941, and "Delicados," *Novedades,* November 28, 1941, clippings attached to letter from Harold D. Finley to Secretary of State, November 29, 1941, Decimal File 811.4016/315, Department of State (translated by the author).

81. See, for example, letters and telegrams to Manuel Ávila Camacho from C. Guadarrama and Dámaso E. Sosa, February 14, 1942; José Sánchez Gutiérrez and José Dávalos Alvarez, July 8, 1943; José Hexiquio Ortega, May 12, 1943; Salvador Pérez, Presidente de la Cámera de Comercio de la Piedad de Cabadas, Michoacán, January 18, 1944; Luis Novoa Moreno, January 18, 1944, exp. 546.6/120–7, caja 794, Ávila Camacho Papers.

82. Ignacio García Téllez to Secretario de Relaciones Exteriores, May 2, 1942, exp. 546.6/120–4, caja 974, ibid.

83. Juan J. Herrera to Manuel Ávila Camacho, May 22, 1942, exp. 546.6/120–4, caja 974, ibid. See also letters from José Alamo, president of the Comisión Honorífica Mexicana, in Mesa, Arizona, to Manuel Ávila Camacho, May 4, 1942; and Lic. Agustín Rodríguez Ochoa, Confederación de Trabajadores Mexicanos en Norte América, to Secretario del Trabajo y Previsión Social, April 29, 1942; both in exp. 546.6/120–4, caja 794, ibid.

84. Ezequiel Padilla responded that "no negotiation exists with the U.S. government to allow 50,000 Mexican workers to provide labor in Texas." Telegram from Cámara de Trabajores Mexicanos Afiliados a la CTM to Manuel Ávila Camacho, March 30, 1943; Ezequiel Padilla to Lic. J. Jesús González Gallo, April 6, 1943, exp. 546.6/120–4, caja 794; telegram from Confederación de Trabajadores Mexicanos de Norteamérica, Local 8, to Manuel Ávila Camacho, April 3, 1943; Manuel Tello a Secretario Particular del Presidente de la República, April 12, 1943, exp. 546.6/120–4, caja 794, ibid.

85. Theodore G. Miles to Manuel Ávila Camacho, February 14, 1944, exp. 575.1/17, caja 974, ibid.

86. Adolfo de la Huerta to Lic. Ezequiel Padilla, Informe Número 103 sobre mi última jira por la region Sur de los Estados Unidos, April 25, 1943, exp. 546.6/120–7, caja 794, ibid.; Adolfo de la Huerta to Lic. J. Jesús González Gallo, April 28, 1943, exp. 546.6/120–7, caja 794, ibid.

87. Jack Danciger to Earl Warren, August 25, 1943, Decimal File 811.4016/696, box 3806, Department of State.

88. Despite the ban many continued to petition the Mexican government for bracero contracts to Texas. See, for example, letters to Manuel Ávila Camacho from Nestor Roldán y Angel Galicia P., August 2, 1943, extracto 24388; Juan M. García, May 24, 1943, extracto 16838; and Marcelino Ortiz, January 15, 1945; all in exp. 546.6/120–5, caja 794, Ávila Camacho Papers.

89. On nationalization of the oil industry, see Lorenzo Meyer, *Mexico and the United States in the Oil Controversy, 1917–1942* (Austin: University of Texas Press, 1972).

90. "Mexico's All-American Diplomat," *New York Herald Tribune,* February 14, 1943, clipping attached to letter from Cónsul General Ricardo G. Hill to Lic. Ezequiel Padilla, February 15, 1943, exp. 131/8, caja 117, Ávila Camacho Papers.

91. Quoted in Neil Foley, *The White Scourge: Mexicans, Blacks, and Poor Whites in Texas Cotton Culture* (Berkeley: University of California Press, 1997), 206. See also Guglielmo, "Fighting for Caucasian Rights."

92. Pauline R. Kibbe to the members of the Good Neighbor Commission, December 29, 1944, box 4–14/169, folder "Good Neighbor Commission 1944," Stevenson Papers.

93. H.B. 909, copy in enclosure no. 3, attached to Blocker to Hull, "Results of a Confidential Survey," Department of State; "'Mexican' Bill Introduced,"

April 15, 1941, newspaper clipping, n.a., enclosure no. 2, attached to Blocker to Hull, "Results of a Confidential Survey," ibid.

94. Radio Program, "What Does It Take to Get the American People Together," March 3, 1941, enclosure no. 2, attached to Blocker to Hull, "Results of a Confidential Survey," ibid.; Samuel Walker, *Hate Speech: The History of an American Controversy* (Lincoln: University of Nebraska Press, 1994), 55.

95. *State v. Klapprott*, 22 A. 2d 877 (1941). See also David Little, "Tolerance, Equal Freedom, and Peace: A Human Rights Approach," in *Religion and Human Rights: Toward an Understanding of Tolerance and Reconciliation*, ed. David Little and David Chidester (Atlanta, GA: Academic Exchange, Emory University, 2001), 3-30.

96. "'Mexican' Bill Introduced," April 15, 1941, newspaper clipping, no name, enclosure no. 2, attached to William P. Blocker to Cordell Hull, "Results of a Confidential Survey of the Problem of Racial Discrimination against Mexican and Latin American Citizens in Texas and New Mexico," Feb. 27, 1942, p. 17, Decimal File 811.4016/337, Box 3804, Department of State.

97. "Racial Prejudices Must Be Eradicated," *El Universal*, April 23, 1941 (translation), enclosure no. 2, attached to Blocker to Hull, "Results of a Confidential Survey," ibid.

98. Inter-office memo from Mr. Dawson to Mr. Bursley, May 16, 1941, Decimal File 811.4016/288, ibid. An amendment to include Indians was added to the Spears Bill in 1945.

99. Editorial, *El Nacional,* April 24, 1941, enclosure no. 2, attached to Blocker to Hull, "Results of a Confidential Survey," ibid.

100. *El Paso Herald-Post,* April 15, 1943, clipping attached to memo from William P. Blocker to Secretary of State, April 16, 1943, Decimal File 811.4016 /530, box 3805, ibid.

101. Stephen E. Aguirre to Secretary of State, July 23, 1943, Decimal File 811.4016/633, box 3805, ibid.; Luis L. Duplan to Richard M. Kleberg, July 16, 1943, Decimal File 811.4016/634, box 3805, ibid.

102. Francisco Castillo Nájera to Cordell Hull, July 23, 1943, attached to Memorandum of Conversation, July 24, 1943, Decimal File 811.4016/637, box 3805, ibid.

103. Herbert S. Bursley to Secretary of State, September 19, 1943 and attached inter-office memo, Division of the American Republics, September 30, 1943, Decimal File 811.4016/703; Guy W. Ray to Secretary of State, April 3, 1946, Decimal File 811.4016/4-346, ibid.

104. Enrique González Martínez, Presidente, Comité Mexicano Contra El Racismo, to Manuel Ávila Camacho, August 2, 1944, exp. 546.1/1, caja 789, Ávila Camacho Papers; "El Papel de Texas en las Relaciones Interamericanas," *Fraternidad,* August 1, 1944, exp. 546.1/1, caja 789, ibid.; J. F. McGurk to Philip Bonsal and Laurence Duggan, March 25, 1944, Decimal File 811.4016/810, box

3806, Department of State; *El Nacional,* March 27, 1945, clipping attached to letter from David Thomasson to Secretary of State, March 27, 1945, Decimal File 811.4016/3–2745, ibid.; *El Nacional,* September 23, 1945, clipping in letter from Robert F. Hale to Secretary of State, September 24, 1945, Decimal File 811.4016/9–2445, ibid.

105. Chris P. Fox to Gov. Stevenson, February 23, 1943, with enclosed newspaper clipping and letter to *Time* magazine, box 4–14/169, folder "Good Neighbor Commission 1944," Stevenson Papers.

106. W. S. Gandy to Gov. Stevenson, n.d., box 4–14/156, folder "Interracial Discrimination," ibid.

107. *Houston Post,* February 19, 1944, attached to letter from William P. Blocker to Secretary of State, February 28, 1944, Decimal File 811.4016/787, box 3806, Department of State. On numbers of Mexican Americans graduating from the University of Texas in the 1940s, see Ruth Ann Douglass Fogartie, *Texas-Born Spanish-Name Students in Texas Colleges and Universities,* Inter-American Education Occasional Papers No. 3 (Austin: University of Texas Press, 1948), 14–15.

108. George Messersmith, Memorandum, July 22, 1943, attached to letter from George Messersmith to Joseph F. McGurk, July 23, 1943, Decimal File 811.4016/680, box 3806, Department of State.

109. Messersmith to McGurk, July 23, 1943.

110. *Dallas Times Herald,* February 10, 1944, clipping, box 3, folder "Clippings and Releases," War Manpower Commission, RG 211, Region X, NARA.

111. Jack Danciger to Gov. Stevenson, December 15, 1943, box 4–14/156, folder "Interracial Discrimination," Stevenson Papers. Danciger was an honorary Mexican consul in Fort Worth.

112. *Terrell Wells Swimming Pool v. Rodriguez,* 182 S.W.2d 824 (Tex. Civ. App. 1944); *El Paso Herald-Post,* February 3, 1944, clipping in letter from William P. Blocker to Secretary of State, February 4, 1943, Decimal File 811.4016/778, box 3806, Department of State; Albert Treviño to Gov. Stevenson, November 10, 1944, box 4–14/169, folder "Interracial Discrimination 1944," Stevenson Papers.

113. *Lopez v. Seccombe* 71 F. Supp. 769 (S.D. Cal. 1944). See also George A. Martinez, "Legal Indeterminacy, Judicial Discretion and the Mexican-American Litigation Experience: 1930–1980," *U.C. Davis Law Review* 27 (1994): 565–566.

114. *El Paso Herald-Post,* January 10, 1945, clipping in letter from William P. Blocker to Secretary of State, January 11, 1945, Decimal File 811.4016/1–1145, Department of State; William P. Blocker to Secretary of State, August 9, 1945, Decimal File 811.4016/8–1445, ibid.

115. William P. Blocker to Secretary of State, March 6, 1945, Decimal File 811.4016/3–545, ibid.

116. William Prescott Allen to Manuel Ávila Camacho, March 20, 1944, exp. 546.6/120–7, caja 794, Ávila Camacho Papers.

117. Memorandum from Sen. Lic. Antonio Villalobos to Manuel Ávila Camacho, February 26, 1945, exp. 575.1/17, caja 974, ibid. See also Lic. Sen. Antonio Villalobos to Manuel Ávila Camacho, February 21, 1945; and Lic. J. Jesús González Gallo to Lic. Antonio Villalobos, February 28, 1945; both in exp. 575.1/17, caja 974, ibid.

118. George Messersmith to William P. Blocker, February 2, 1945, Decimal File 811.4016/2–245, Department of State.

119. Transcript of radio comments of Stuart Long, September 17, 1945, attached to letter from William P. Blocker to Secretary of State, October 8, 1945, Decimal File 811.4016/10–845, ibid.

120. Maury Maverick to Lawrence W. Cramer, June 10, 1942, Legal Division, Hearings, 1944–1946, box 339, folder "Hearing, Background Material," FEPC.

121. Philip W. Bonsal to Sumner Welles, May 13, 1943, Decimal File, 811.4016/547 1/2, box 3805, Department of State; Minutes of the Conference on Inter-American Relations in Texas, December 17–18, 1943, box 4–14/169, folder "Good Neighbor Commission 1944," Stevenson Papers.

122. *Fraternidad,* July 1, 1945, box 1989/59–16, folder "Discrimination, General File, 1946–1956," GNC; Enrique González Martínez, Presidente, Comité Mexicano Contra El Racismo, to Manuel Ávila Camacho, August 2, 1944, exp. 546.1/1, caja 789, Ávila Camacho Papers.

123. Jacob I. Rodriguez to Editor, *San Antonio Express,* August 25, 1953, folder "Comal County," box 1989/59–17, GNC.

124. *El Nacional,* November 10, 1945, clipping in letter from David Thomasson to Secretary of State, November 13, 1945, Decimal File 811.4016/11–1345, Department of State.

125. *Excelsior,* June 11, 1945, in a letter from George Messersmith to Secretary of State, June 11, 1945, Decimal File 812.4016/6–1145, ibid.; *Los Angeles Times,* June 12, clipping in Memorandum from Asa E. Phillips, Jr., to Mr. Carrigan, June 18, 1945, Decimal File 812.4016/6–1345, ibid.; Office Memorandum from Mr. Carrigan to Dr. Munro, June 21, 1945, Decimal File 811.4016/6–2145; George Messersmith to Secretary of State, June 12, 1945, Decimal File 812.4016/6–1245, reel 1, ibid.

126. *Fraternidad,* July 1, 1945, clipping attached to letter from William P. Blocker to Secretary of State, Decimal File 811.4016/7–2545, ibid.

127. The population of foreign-born Mexicans in Texas in 1940 was 159,266, compared to 134,312 in California. See *Sixteenth Census of the United States: 1940,* vol. 2: *Characteristics of the Population,* pt. VI: Pennsylvania—Texas, table 15: "Texas Foreign-Born White, 1910 to 1940, and Total Foreign Born, 1850 to 1900, by Country of Birth, for the State," 781; ibid., pt. I: United States Summary and Alabama—District of Columbia, table 15: "California, Foreign-Born White, 1910 to 1940, and Total Foreign Born, 1850 to 1900, By Country of

Birth, For the State," 533. On the origins of exclusion of California's nonwhite populations, see Tomás Almaguer, *Racial Fault Lines: The Historical Origins of White Supremacy in California* (Berkeley: University of California Press, 1994).

128. Dreier to Sumner Welles et al., December 15, 1942, Decimal File 811.4016/508, box 3805, RG 59, Department of State.

129. On the Sleepy Lagoon trial, see Eduardo Obregón Pagán, *Murder at the Sleepy Lagoon: Zoot Suits, Race, and Riot in Wartime L.A.* (Chapel Hill: University of North Carolina Press, 2003); Carey McWilliams, *North from Mexico,* 228–233; and David G. Gutiérrez, *Walls and Mirrors: Mexican Americans, Mexican Immigrants, and the Politics of Ethnicity* (Berkeley: University of California Press, 1995), 126–130.

130. Quoted in Edward J. Escobar, *Race, Police, and the Making of a Political Identity: Mexican Americans and the Los Angeles Police Department, 1900–1945* (Berkeley: University of California Press, 1999), 212–213.

131. Elis M. Tipton to Walter H. C. Laves, October 9, 1942, box 1717, folder "Paul Horgan," OCIAA.

132. Bright and Fierro de Bright, "Mexican Americans of the Southwest," 6, report attached to letter from John Bright to Walter H. C. Laves, Nov. 10, 1942, box 1717, folder "Spanish-Speaking Project," ibid.

133. Information Directives, attached to memorandum from Harry W. Frantz to Wallace K. Harrison, August 5, 1943, box 1459, folder "Content: Directives, Long-range," OCIAA.

134. Activities in Los Angeles, report from Alan Cranston to Elmer Davis, November 28, 1942, p. 3, box 1717, folder "Spanish-speaking Minorities," ibid.

135. William G. MacLean, Meeting ... on Spanish Speaking Minority Problem on the Pacific Coast, November 5, 1942, Decimal File 811.4016/468, box 3805, Department of State; Memorandum for the files, n.a., November 3, 1942, box 1717, folder "OWI—Miscellaneous," OCIAA.

136. Activities in Los Angeles, report from Alan Cranston to Elmer Davis, November 28, 1942, pp. 2–3, box 1717, folder "Spanish-speaking Minorities," ibid.; Summary of the Conference of Agencies of the Government ... on the Los Angeles Situation, attached to memorandum from Louis T. Olom to Walter H. C. Laves, November 18, 1942, box 1717, folder "Reports: Inter-Agency Meetings," ibid.

137. John Edgar Hoover to Adolf A. Berle, Jr., January 6, 1945, Decimal File 811.4016/1–645, Department of State.

138. Peter Richardson, "Carey McWilliams: The California Years" (2005), p. 5, http://repositories.cdlib.org/escholarship/.

139. Harry F. Henderson to Nelson Rockefeller, November 12, 1942, box 1717, folder "Spanish-speaking Minorities," OCIAA; Nelson Rockefeller to Harry F. Henderson, n.d., ibid.

140. Memorandum from Joseph E. Weckler to Victor Borella, January 29, 1943, box 1717, folder "Spanish-speaking Minorities," ibid.

141. On the emergence of the pachuca persona and a new Mexican-American female identity, see Elizabeth R. Escobedo, "The Pachuca Panic: Sexual and Cultural Battlegrounds in World War II Los Angeles," *Western Historical Quarterly* 38 (Summer 2007): 133–156. See also Luis Alvarez, *The Power of the Zoot: Youth Culture and Resistance during World War II* (Berkeley: University of California Press, 2008); Pagán, *Murder at the Sleepy Lagoon.*

142. Adolfo de La Huerta to Lic. Ezequiel Padilla, Informe No. 109, May 8, 1943, exp. 546.6/120–7, caja 794, Ávila Camacho Papers.

143. Fletcher Bowron to Philip W. Bonsal, Chief, Division of American Republics, Department of State, August 3, 1943, Decimal File 811.4016/695, box 3806, Department of State.

144. Henry S. Waterman to Secretary of State, September 24, 1943, Decimal File 811.4016/705, box 3806, ibid. (Cano quote); Maria Lorosco to Manuel Ávila Camacho, June 18, 1943, exp. 575.1/46, caja 974, Ávila Camacho Papers.

145. Octavio Paz, *Labyrinth of Solitude, the Other Mexico, and Other Essays* (New York: Grove Press, 1985), 13–14.

146. *Time,* June 21, 1943, clipping attached to letter from G. S. Messersmith to Secretary of State, June 19, 1943, Decimal File 811.4016/570, box 3805, Department of State.

147. G. S. Messersmith to Secretary of State, June 19, 1943, Decimal File 811.4016/570, box 3805, ibid.

148. The Mexican Visitor General of Consulates in Los Angeles, Adolfo de la Huerta, reported Downey's comment to the Mexican president. Telegram from Adolfo de la Huerta to Lic. J. Jesús González Gallo, June 10, 1943, exp. 575.1/46, caja 974, Ávila Camacho Papers.

149. G. S. Messersmith to Secretary of State, June 25, 1943, Decimal File 811.4016/572, box 3805, Department of State.

150. Memorandum of Conversation between George S. Messersmith and Laurence Duggan, June 21, 1943, Decimal File 812.021/156, reel 22, ibid.

151. Guy W. Ray, second secretary of the U.S. embassy in Mexico, to the Secretary of State, June 22, 1943, Decimal File 811.4016/577, box 3805, ibid.

152. Guy W. Ray to Secretary of State, June 17, 1943, Decimal File 811.4016 /568, box 3805, ibid.

153. Guy D. Ray to Secretary of State, June 26, Decimal File 811.4016/619, box 3805, ibid. (quote); Ray to Secretary of State, June 17, 1943, ibid.; Herbert. S. Bursley to Secretary of State, June 26, 1943, Decimal File 811.4016/590, box 3805, ibid.

154. William P. Blocker to Secretary of State, August 3, 1943, Decimal File 811.4016/651, box 3806, ibid.; William P. Blocker to Secretary of State, August 20, 1943, Decimal File 811.4016/664, box 3806, ibid.

155. McWilliams, *North from Mexico,* 257.

4. Defending the Hemisphere

1. On FDR's Good Neighbor Policy, see Bryce Wood, *The Making of the Good Neighbor Policy* (New York: Columbia University Press, 1961); Edward O. Guerrant, *Roosevelt's Good Neighbor Policy* (Albuquerque: University of New Mexico Press, 1950), and Frederick B. Pike, *FDR's Good Neighbor Policy: Sixty Years of Generally Gentle Chaos* (Austin: University of Texas Press, 1995).

2. Department of Defense, Office of the Deputy Assistant Secretary of Defense for Military Manpower and Personnel Policy, *Hispanics in America's Defense* (Washington, DC: Government Printing Office, 1990); "Voces Oral History Project," http://www.lib.utexas.edu/voces/; Maggie Rivas-Rodriguez et al., eds., *Legacy Greater than Words: Stories of U.S. Latinos and Latinas of the WWII Generation* (Austin: University of Texas Press, 2006).

3. A complete listing can be found in a thick binder accompanying the "Informe Final del Trabajo sobre el Servicio Militar," 1946, III-805-1, AHSRE. For notices of deaths of Mexican nationals in the U.S. Army, see Francisco Castillo Nájera to Secretario de Relaciones Exteriores, January 29 and February 10, 1945, and other casualty lists, III-795-1 (II), AHSRE.

4. U.S. citizens evading induction in Mexico included mainly men with non-Hispanic surnames, such as Lawrence Anderson, Peter Wood, Charles Butler, Thomas White, John Wilson, and William Brandon. Lic. Guillermo Ostos, Jefe del Departamento, to Director General de Población, November 16, 1943; and U.S. Ambassador to Secretario de Relaciones Exteriores, March 7 and May 11, 1944; both in III-2470-13, AHSRE.

5. *Sixteenth Census of the United States: 1940, Population,* vol. 2: *Characteristics of the Population,* pt. VI: Pennsylvania—Texas, table 15: "Texas Foreign-Born White, 1910 to 1940, and Total Foreign Born, 1850 to 1900, by Country of Birth, for the State," 781; ibid., pt. I: United States Summary and Alabama—District of Columbia, table 15: "California, Foreign-Born White, 1910 to 1940, and Total Foreign Born, 1850 to 1900, by Country of Birth, for the State," 533.

6. "Signicativo Agasajo al Cónsul General de Mexico," *La Prensa,* May 20, 1944, and "C. C. Honors Mexican Consul," *San Antonio Light,* May 19, 1944, clippings attached to letter from Carlos A. Calderón to Lic. J. Jesús González Gallo, June 29, 1944, exp. 573.12/25, caja 972, Ávila Camacho Papers. I use "Mexicans" to refer to Mexican Americans as well as Mexican nationals.

7. See, for example, Adolfo de La Huerta (Los Angeles) to Lic. J. Jesús González Gallo, May 8, 1943, exp. 546.6/120–7, caja 794, ibid.

8. "El Gobierno de México, desde tiempo inmemorial, incansablemente ha estado haciendo todo lo posible por lograr el retorno a la Patria de los mexicanos que radican en los Estados Unidos" ("Informe Final del Trabajo sobre el Servicio Militar," p. 3).

9. See, for example, Ernesto Galarza, *Merchants of Labor: The Mexican Bracero Story, an Account of the Managed Migration of Mexican Farm Workers in California, 1942–1960* (Charlotte, CA: McNally and Loftin, 1964); and Deborah Cohen, *Braceros: Migrant Citizens and Transnational Subjects in the Postwar United States and Mexico* (Chapel Hill: University of North Carolina Press, 2011).

10. "Lasting Neighborly Ties," *Fort-Worth Star-Telegram,* clipping attached to letter from Carlos A. Calderón, Cónsul de México (San Antonio) to Lic. J. Jesús González Gallo, June 29, 1944, exp. 573.12/25, caja 972, Ávila Camacho Papers.

11. Tomás Oropeza Ramirez to Manuel Ávila Camacho, July 31, 1943, extracto 2397, exp. 575.1/4, caja 974, ibid. See also letters to Foreign Minister Ezequiel Padilla, July 17, 1942, caso de Raymundo Hernández, III-630-7, AHSRE; Adolfo Ruíz, caso de Ramón Novarro Samaniegos, August 14, 1942, III-630-22, ibid.

12. Petition of Marcos Gomez et al. to Congreso de La Unión Mexicana, May 12, 1942, III-630-7, ibid.

13. Lieutenant R. L. Vasquez, CSM, to Manuel Ávila Camacho, March 28, 1943, exp. 575.1/4, caja 974, Ávila Camacho Papers.

14. Memorandum to Walter H. C. Laves from Dora Thea Hettwer, November 11, 1942, box 1717, folder "OWI—Miscellaneous," OCIAA.

15. Felipe Carvajal to Franklin Delano Roosevelt, October 21, 1942, exp. 575.1/4, caja 974, Ávila Camacho Papers.

16. "Informe Final del Trabajo sobre el Servicio Militar," p. 22; "Otros dos Mexicanos Mueren en la Guerra," *El Universal,* May 24, 1944, in letter from José Gorostiza to Cónsul de México (Douglas, Arizona), December 2, 1944, III-800-1 (III), AHSRE.

17. "Un Mexicano Cocina Para Eisenhower," *El Continental,* July 20, 1944, III-800-1 (II), ibid.

18. "Family Gives Seven of Eleven Sons to U.S. Service," *Fresno Bee,* November 26, 1942; and "Five Sons in Service," *El Paso Herald Post,* November 26, 1944, III-800-1 (II), ibid.

19. Memorandum from Q. C. Taylor, State Headquarters for Selective Service, Austin, Texas, in letter from Santiago A. Campbell to Secretario de Relaciones Exteriores, October 7, 1942, III-803-1 (I), ibid.

20. C. Palacios Roji to Capt. Robert W. Platte, October 10, 1942; "U.S. Now Can Induct Mexican Nationals into Service Here," *El Paso Times,* May 29, 1942, in letter from Raúl Michel to Embajador de México, May 29, 1942, III-802-1 (II), ibid.

21. Manuel Aguilar, Consul of Mexico, Los Angeles to Local Board No. 199, September 26, 1942; and letters to Local Boards No. 223, 174, 199, and 217; both in III-808-2 (II), ibid.

22. Memorandum from Q. C. Taylor, Austin, Texas, in letter from Santiago A. Campbell to Secretario de Relaciones Exteriores, October 7, 1942, III-803-1 (I), ibid.

23. Anexo 10, "Mexicanos Incorporados en el Ejército de los Estados Unidos Hasta el 31 de Octubre de 1943," in letter from Ezequiel Padilla to Secretario de la Defensa Nacional, January 26, 1944, III-785-1, ibid. I was unable to find a single case of a resident U.S. citizen being drafted into the Mexican armed forces.

24. Ricardo C. Hill, Consul General of Mexico, Chicago, to Col. Paul H. Armstrong, Director, Illinois State Selective Service System, July 27, 1942, III-803-1 (I), ibid.; José M. Gutiérrez to Local Board No. 1, Tuma, Arizona, October 3, 1942, III-775-1, ibid.; and Oscar F. González to Local Board 120, Los Angeles, September 1, 1943, III-2005-34, ibid.

25. See letters to Manuel Ávila Camacho from Cresencio Mayo de González (Taft, TX), October 1, 1942; José Alamo (Mesa, AZ), August 26, 1942; Juan Márquez (Watsonville, CA), November 9, 1942; and Atilano Venegas (Chicago, IL), March 30, 1943; all in exp. 575.1/4, caja 974, Ávila Camacho Papers.

26. Rafael de la Colina, Consul General of Mexico, New York, to United States Selective Service, August 20, 1942, III-808-2(2), AHSRE; José M. Gutiérrez to Selective Service, Local Board No. 1, Tuma, Arizona, October 3, 1942, III-775-1, ibid.

27. See George J. Sanchez, *Becoming Mexican American: Ethnicity, Culture, and Identity in Chicano Los Angeles, 1900–1945* (New York: Oxford University Press, 1993); and David G. Gutiérrez, ed., *Between Two Worlds: Mexican Immigrants in the United States* (Wilmington, DE: Scholarly Resources, 1996).

28. See, for example, Zamarripa to Secretario de Relaciones Exteriores, February 4, 1942; Rafael Osuna B. to Secretario de Relaciones Exteriores, November 29, 1941; and Ernesto Hidalgo to Rafael Osuna B, December 30, 1941; all in III-801-1 (II), AHSRE.

29. "Bajo ningún argumento legal podía México reclamar como nacionales suyos a los hijos de mexicanos nacidos en aquélla Nación [U.S.]. La doble nacionalidad, [en] circunstancias . . . que producen un estado de guerra, ha creado situaciones difíciles de resolver, y durante el último conflicto los casos de este tipo fueron más graves" ("Informe Final del Trabajo sobre el Servicio Militar," p. 10).

30. "Que los Mexicanos Aquí Deben Engrosar Las Filas," *Las Noticias* (Del Rio, TX), October 22, 1942, in letter from M. Tomás Morlet to Cónsul General de México, October 24, 1942; and *Los Mexicanos en los Estados Unidos y la Guerra* (México, 1942); both in III-803-1(I), AHSRE; Manuel Tello to C. Waldo Romo Castro, April 22, 1943, exp. 575.1/4, caja 974, Ávila Camacho Papers.

31. Pearl M. Baker, Local Board No. 203–91 (Alhambra, CA) to Victor Alvidrez, April 2, 1943; and Vicente Peralta Coronel, Cónsul General de México to Secretario de Relaciones Exteriores, August 24, 1943; both in III-809-1 (II), AHSRE.

32. Convenio Militar, Artículo IV: "Los nacionales de cada País que . . . son 'residentes técnicos' del último País, conocidos como 'residentes fronterizos'

[border residents] deberán ser considerados como residentes del País en el que de hecho viven, para los fines del servicio militar" ("Informe Final del Trabajo sobre el Servicio Militar," pp. 6–7).

33. José M. Gutiérrez, Consul of Mexico, to Selective Service Local Board No. 159 (El Centro, CA), April 7 and May 18, 1943; José M. Gutiérrez to Director, Selective Service Headquarters (Sacramento, CA), May 27, 1943, III-808-1; and Alfredo Elías Calles to Cónsul de México (Calexico, CA) December 21, 1943; all in III-811-1 (II), AHSRE.

34. Fernando Rueda, Vicecónsul Encargado, to Cónsul General de México (Los Angeles), October 2, 1943, III-812-3, ibid.

35. In one case, the Department of State informed the Mexican ambassador that the local draft board would take the "necessary steps to enforce these obligations" on Ignacio Terán, a resident Mexican national who left the United States after May 16, should he attempt to reenter the United States. G. Howland Shaw, for the Secretary of State, to Francisco Castillo Nájera, Ambassador of Mexico, November 24, 1943, III-811-1 (II), ibid.

36. Department of State to the Mexican Ambassador, November 22, 1943, III-811-1 (II), ibid.

37. Ezequiel Padilla to Herbert S. Bursley, January 22, 1943; and Herbert S. Bursley to Manuel Ávila Camacho, January 22, 1943; both in exp. 545.22/153, caja 774, Ávila Camacho Papers; "Informe Final del Trabajo sobre el Servicio Militar," pp. 6–7.

38. Arthur A. Holmes, Selective Service Appeal Section, to Adolfo G. Dominguez, Consul of Mexico in Detroit, July 31, 1942, III-800-1 (I), AHSRE; "Informe Final del Trabajo sobre el Servicio Militar," pp. 24–25, 30.

39. Col. Vicente Peralta C., Consul General of Mexico, San Francisco, to Local Board No. 19, October 15, 1942, III-808-2 (II), AHSRE; "Informe Final del Trabajo sobre el Servicio Militar," p. 22.

40. Secretary of War to Secretary of State, August 15, 1944; Lic. Alfonso García Robles to Embajador de México, February 26, 1944, III-772-2 (I), AHSRE.

41. Rubén E. González to Embajada de México, January 5, 1944; Secretary of State to Chargé d'Affaires ad interim of Mexico, May 22, 1944, III-772-2(I), ibid.

42. Omar Josefé to Secretario de Relaciones Exteriores, August 27, 1940, III-802-1 (II), ibid.; "Draft Call Proves Big Success," *Los Angeles Daily News*, November 6, 1943, in letter from Vicente Peralta C. to Secretario de Relaciones Exteriores, November 9, 1943, III-780-3, ibid.

43. Eugenio Aza, Cónsul de México (Fresno, CA) to Pvt. Leandro Palomo, March 8, 1943, III-772-2 (I), ibid.; Eugenio Aza, Consul of Mexico, to Commanding Officer (Camp Roberts, CA), February 16, 1943; and Col. J. M. Moore to Señor Don Eugenio Aza, February 24, 1943; both in III-772-2 (II), ibid.

44. Eugenio Aza, Cónsul of México, to Commanding Officer (Camp Roberts, CA), June 28, 1943, III-772-2 (II), ibid.

45. See, for example, the case of forty-three-year-old Benito Chávez Rivera, non-English-speaking and *físicamente agotado* (worn-out) from years of strenuous physical labor, who asked a Mexican consul to request his release from the army. Arturo M. Elías, Cónsul de México (Douglas, AZ) to Secretario de Relaciones Exteriores, June 25, 1943, III0–806–2, ibid.

46. Adolfo de La Huerta to Lic. Ezequiel Padilla, June 17, 1942, exp. 575.1/4, caja 974, Ávila Camacho Papers.

47. See letter from Squadron 201 pilot to his mother five months before he died: Crisóforo Salido Grijalva to Rosario G. Magallanes, August 5, 1944; and "Orgullosos de que su Hijo Murió como un Héroe," *El Universal,* June 15, 1945, III-795-1 (I), AHSRE. On the deaths of Mexican pilots in the Mexican expeditionary force, see telegrams from Embajador Castillo Nájera to Secretario de Relaciones Exteriores, July 30 and August 6, 1945, ibid.

48. Luis I. Duplan, Cónsul of México (Austin), to Cónsul General de México (San Antonio), March 8, 1944, III-803-1 (III), ibid.

49. Luis L. Duplan, Cónsul of México (Austin), to Cónsul General de México (San Antonio), March 19, 1944, ibid.

50. Carlos Palacios Roji, Cónsul Encargado, to Secretario de Relaciones Exteriores, March 28, 1944, III-803-1 (III), ibid.

51. Mexican Ambassador to Cordell Hull, Secretary of State, June 1, 1943, III-772-2(I), ibid.; Alfredo Elías Calles, Cónsul de México (Los Angeles) to Embajador de México, April 17, 1943, III-772-2(I), ibid.

52. Sumner Welles, for the Secretary of State, to Francisco Castillo Nájera, Ambassador of Mexico, June 12, 1943, III-772-2(I), ibid.; Vicente Peralta Coronel, Cónsul General de México (Los Angeles) to Andrew García Esparza, August 2, 1943, ibid. (emphasis added)

53. G. Howland Shaw for the Secretary of State to Francisco Castillo Nájera, Ambassador of Mexico, April 7, 1943, III-772-2(I), ibid.

54. J. A. Ulio, Adjutant General, to Mr. Constantino Marino, May 28, 1943, III-772-2 (I), ibid.

55. Jaime Torres Bodet, Subsecretario de Relaciones Exteriores, to Francisco Castillo Nájera, Ambassador of Mexico, June 10, 1943, III-772-2 (I), ibid.; Salvador Duhart M., Primer Secretario to Cónsul de México en Salt Lake City, December 12, 1942, III-772-2 (II), ibid. (emphasis added)

56. Francisco Castillo Nájera to Cónsules Generales de México en Nueva York, Chicago, San Francisco, El Paso, and San Antonio, November 25, 1942, III-772-2 (I), ibid.

57. In addition to seeking reclassification from "1-A" to "3-A," many Mexicans sought to be discharged from the army to return to Mexico to take care of their families. See, for example, Manuel Aquilar to Local Board, No. 219 (Los Angeles), December 14, 1943, III-806-1, ibid.

58. Ricardo G. Hill to Local Board No. 107, Chicago, IL, October 31, 1942; C. Palacios Roji to Capt. Robert W. Platte, October 10, 1942, III-775-1, ibid.; "Informe Final del Trabajo sobre el Servicio Militar," p. 15.

59. Transcript of letter from Col. R. Esmay in letter from Federico Gutiérrez Pastor to Secretario de Relaciones Exteriores, March 9, 1944, III-775-1, AHSRE.

60. Jóse Gorotiza, Director General, to Jesús José H. Rentaría, November 17, 1944, III-772-2 (I), ibid. Consuls handled thousands of cases involving Mexican servicemen trying to obtain the family allowance. "Informe Final del Trabajo sobre el Servicio Militar," p. 29.

61. Cor. Vicente Paralta (Los Angeles) to Sr. Benigno Corona y Téllez, October 8, 1943, III-775-2, AHSRE.

62. Jack Leighter to Francis Alstock, October 31, 1942, box 1717, folder "Spanish-speaking Minorities," OCIAA.

63. Raúl Michel, Mexican Consul of El Paso, to Cónsul de México, Denver, CO, October 30, 1942, III-775-2, AHSRE; Adolfo de la Huerta to Lic. Ezequiel Padilla, Informe Número 103 sobre mi Última Gira por la Region Sur de los Estados Unidos, April 25, 1943, exp. 546.6/120–7, caja 794, Ávila Camacho Papers.

64. G. C. Wilmoth, El Paso District Director, Immigration and Naturalization Service, to Raúl Michel, Consul General of Mexico, July 14, 1942, III-802-1 (II), AHSRE.

65. On the denial of the board to allow one Mexican draftee permission to visit dying relatives in Mexico, see Fernando Rueda to Cónsul de México, May 25, 1944, III-772-2 (I), ibid.

66. "Brief taken from the report of investigation made by Mr. Emiliano de la Garza, District Attorney at Nuevo Laredo, Tamaulipas, in regard to the death of Miguel Meza," attached to letter from Raúl Michel, Consul General of Mexico (El Paso), to Mr. Chas. A. Ruiz, April 4, 1945, III-806-1, ibid.

67. Ezequiel Padilla to Cónsul de México, Calexico, CA, October 30, 1942; and Telegram from Cónsul Gutiérrez, Calexico, CA, to Secretaría de Relaciones Exteriores, October 15, 1942; both in III-803-1 (I), ibid.

68. Serapio Martínez Pérez to Lic. Ezequiel Padilla, October 19, 1942, exp. 575.1/4, caja 974, Ávila Camacho Papers.

69. Jack Leighter to Francis Alstock, October 31, 1942, box 1717, folder "Spanish-speaking Minorities," OCIAA.

70. Pedro Mena to Manuel Ávila Camacho, December 26, 1942, extracto 44091, exp. 575.1/4, caja 974, Ávila Camacho Papers.

71. "Creo firmemente . . . que ha de venir una metamorfosis completa en el ambiente internacional y, como consecuencia directa, ha de modificarse la situación social de nuestros compatriotas en este país, principalmente en el Estado de Texas, en el que tantos incidentes penosos se registran, no solo motiva-

dos por la discriminación de los mexicanos en los lugares públicos, sino por los atropellos y atentados que estos sufren, registrándose, en estos casos, actos de verdadera denegación de justicia de parte de las autoridades inferiores" (De la Huerta to Padilla, Informe Número 103).

72. Lic. Alfonso García Robles to Embajador de México, July 1, 1944, III-772-2 (I), AHSRE.

73. José Infante (Minatare, NE) to Ezequiel Padilla, March 21, 1941, III-801-1 (II), ibid.; Comisión Honorífica Mexicana to Manuel Ávila Camacho, November 30, 1942, extracto 42954, exp. 575.1/4, caja 974, Ávila Camacho Papers.

74. Marciano M. Zamarripa to Presidente Ávila Camacho, March 10, 1941, III-801-1 (II), AHSRE; "Spanish-Americans in the Southwest and the War Effort," Report No. 24, Office of War Information, August 18, 1942, Decimal File, 811.4016/444, box 3804, Department of State.

75. José Tarquino Dávila Loubet to Manuel Ávila Camacho, February 23, 1943, exp. 575.1/4, caja 974, Ávila Camacho Papers.

76. Amada Valles Macias (Stockton, CA) to President Ávila Camacho, February 16, 1943, exp. 575.1/4, caja 974, ibid.

77. Ernésto Hidalgo to Sra. Refugio M. de Romero, January 3, 1942, exp. 575.1/4, caja 974; *El Continental* [El Paso], n.d., clipping attached to letter from Raúl Michel to Lic. Jesús González Gallo, exp. 550/44–9–32, caja 833, ibid.

78. Raúl Michel, Cónsul General, El Paso to Embajador de México, March 22, 1945, III-772-2(I), AHSRE.

79. Jesús José Holguin Rentería, transcribed in letter from José Gorostiza, Director General, to Cónsul General de México, El Paso, November 18, 1944, III-772-2 (I), ibid.

80. Carlos Palacios Rojí to Cónsul de México, March 30, 1944; Secretary of State to the Chargé d'Affaires ad interim, May 23, 1944, III-772-2 (I), ibid.

81. Ibid. That Garibaldi was "mistaken" as an Indian soldier may well have been a greater insult to Garibaldi and his mother than having been refused service as a Mexican, given the long history of discrimination against Indians in both Mexico and the United States.

82. "Mexican-Indian Battle Flares," *San Diego Union*, October 17, 1940, III-800-1 (III), ibid.

83. Manuel Aguilar, Consul of Mexico, to Chairman, Selective Service System, November 16, 1942, III-808-2 (II), ibid.

84. See, for example, Selective Service Form 351: "Permit of Local Board for Registrant to Depart from the United States," III-811-1 (II), ibid.

85. "Mexican-Indian Battle Flares," *San Diego Union*, October 17, 1940, III-800-1 (III), ibid.

86. Memorandum from Brigadier General J. Watt Page, Texas State Director of Selective Service, to All Local Boards, May 27, 1943, III-772-2(II), ibid.

87. "Wounded Again—At Home . . . ," newspaper clipping, n.d., box 1989/59–18, folder "Discrimination Correspondence, 1949–1950," GNC.

88. Rear Admiral H. H. Good, USN, War Department, to Queens Machine Company, September 24, 1943, III-772-2 (I), AHSRE.

89. Nathalie E. Panek, War Production Board, to Lawrence W. Cramer, FEPC Secretary, August 12, 1942; Frieda S. Miller, State Council of Defense, to Governor Herbert H. Lehman (New York), March 3, 1942; Sidney Hillman, Council of National Defense, to Secretary of War, November 12, 1942; and Abner Green, American Committee for Protection of the Foreign Born, to Lawrence Cramer, September 25, 1942; all in reel 66, FEPC.

90. Atilano Venegas to Manuel Ávila Camacho, March 30, 1943, exp. 575.1/4, caja 974, Ávila Camacho Papers. Most complaints came from California: Francisco Castillo Nájera, Embajador de México, to Cordell Hull, Secretary of State, June 24, 1942; and Francisco Castillo Nájera to Adolfo de la Huerta, Visitador General de Consulados (Los Angeles), June 20, 1942, legajo 1457–9, Archivo de la Embajada de México en los Estados Unidos de América, in AHSRE (hereafter cited as AEMEUA). See also Will W. Alexander, "Aliens in War Industries," *Annals of the American Academy of Political and Social Science* 223 (September 1942): 138–143.

91. Felipe Carvajal to Franklin Delano Roosevelt, October 21, 1942, exp. 575.1/4, caja 974, Ávila Camacho Papers; "Los Mexicanos en Texas," *Fraternidad*, June 1944, 7–8, exp. 546.1/1, caja 789, ibid.

92. Memorandum and copy of Section 11, Employment of Aliens, Public Act No. 671, 76th Congress, attached to letter from Francisco Castillo Nájera, Embajador de México, to Cordell Hull, Secretary of State, June 24, 1942; Memorandum Confidencial from Francisco Castillo Nájera to Sección Norteamericana, Comisión México-Norteamericana de Defensa Conjunta, June 27, 1942; Francisco Castillo Nájera to Will W. Alexander, War Manpower Commission, January 5, 2943; and Cónsul Vicente Peralta (San Francisco) to Embajador de México, December 9, 1942; all in legajo 1457–9, AEMEUA.

93. "Joint Statement by the Secretary of War, the Attorney General, the Secretary of the Navy and the Chairman of the Maritime Commission on the Employment of Aliens," June 7, 1943; and "State Legislation Restricting the Participation by Aliens in Certain Occupations and Professions," typescript, Research Unit, Immigration and Naturalization Service, n.d.; both in reel 71, FEPC.

94. "Judge Naturalizes Fighters for American Democracy," *San Diego Union*, June 12, 1942, clipping in III-630-7, AHSRE.

95. "Esto fue sin duda alguna, un incentivo poderoso para que regular número de mexicanos optaran por naturalizarse como nacionales de los Estados Unidos y gozar de tal prerrogativa, máxime que de esa suerte, prácticamente aseguraban su futuro" ("Informe Final del Trabajo sobre el Servicio Militar," p. 24). The phrase "una necesidad moral" appears on p. 21. See also Efraín G.

Domínguez, Cónsul de Fort Worth, to Secretario de Relaciones Exteriores, January 22, 1946; and José Gorostiza to Cónsul de México en Fort Worth, February 11, 1946, III-745-3, AHSRE.

96. See Circular No. 2, transcribed in letter from Vicente Sanchez Gavito to Consuls in New York, Texas, California, and Illinois, attached to letter from Jack Dancinger, Honorary Consul, to Secretaría de Relaciones Exteriores, February 2, 1945, III-808-1, ibid.

97. The *Washington Post,* for example, reported that Mexicans were "doing their fair share of the fighting—250,000 of them, out of a total population of two million." It also noted that San Antonio, with a population of 300,000, "one-third of them Mexicans, has furnished some 51,000 troops." Of the 1,400 San Antonians killed, nearly half were of "Spanish-American or Mexican stock." "Mexicans in the War," *Washington Post,* May 4, 1944, and numerous other clippings from U.S. and Mexican newspapers of Mexican nationals and Mexican Americans wounded, killed, and decorated for bravery, in III-800-1 (II) AHSRE.

98. *Congressional Record,* April 24, 1945, quoted in Carey McWilliams, *North from Mexico: The Spanish-Speaking People of the United States* (1948; reprint, New York: Greenwood Press, 1968), 260.

99. Not all decorated Mexican Americans received the attention of Medal of Honor recipients. Pedro Cano, winner of the Distinguished Service Cross for heroism, received his medal in the mail. Indignant citizens of his hometown, Edinburg, Texas, demanded that the U.S. Army make a formal presentation of the award. An army general from Washington, DC, came to Edinburg to award Cano the medal at a banquet paid for by the citizens of Edinburg. *The Austin American Statesman,* March 20, 1947, folder "Discrimination, Correspondence 1950–51—General Files, 1944," box 1989/59–18, GNC.

100. Discurso pronunciado por el señor Cónsul General Gustavo Ortiz Hernán, en ocasión de los festejos ofrecidos con motivo de la ciudad de San Antonio, Texas, October 23, 1945, III-802-1 (I), AHSRE. One of the Medal of Honor recipients, Macario García, was a Mexican national who was refused service in a Texas café and subsequently charged with "aggravated assault." See Michael Olivas, "The 'Trial of the Century' That Never Was: Staff Sgt. Macario Garcia, the Congressional Medal of Honor, and the Oasis Café," *Indiana Law Journal* 83 (2008): 1390–1403.

101. For a complete list of Mexican nationals who received medals in the U.S. Army, see "Nómina de los mexicanos alistados en el ejército de los Estados Unidos de América," Lista IV—Condecorados, III-818-1 (V), AHSRE.

102. Darlis A. Miller, "Hispanos and the Civil War in New Mexico: A Reconsideration," *New Mexico Historical Review* 54 (April 1979): 105–123; Jerry Don Thompson, *Mexican Texans in the Union Army* (El Paso: Texas Western Press, 1986); "Mexican Texans in the Civil War," *Handbook of Texas,* www.tshaonline.org/handbook; Department of Defense, *Hispanics in America's*

Defense; and Col. Gilberto Villahermosa, "America's Hispanics in America's Wars," *Army Magazine* (September 2002), www.ausa.org/webpub/DeptArmy-Magazine.nsf.

103. David López, "Saving Private Aztlan: Preserving the History of Latino Service in Wartime," *Diálogo,* condor.depaul.edu/~dialogo; Villahermosa, "America's Hispanics in America's Wars"; and Phillip Gonzales and Ann Massmann, "Loyalty Questioned: Nuevomexicanos in the Great War," *Pacific Historical Review* 75, no. 4 (2006): 629–666.

104. José de la Luz Sáenz, *Los Mexico-Americanos en la Gran Guerra: y su contingente en pró de la democracia, la humanidad y la justicia* (San Antonio, TX: Artes Gráficas, 1933).

105. See especially Julio Moreno, *Yankee Don't Go Home: Mexican Nationalism, American Business Culture, and the Shaping of Modern Mexico, 1920–1950* (Chapel Hill: University of North Carolina Press, 2003); and Stephen R. Niblo, *War, Diplomacy, and Development: The United States and Mexico* (Wilmington, DE: Scholarly Resources, 1995), 89–119.

106. Sir Ernest Mason Satow, *Satow's Diplomatic Practice,* 6th ed. (New York: Oxford University Press, 2009), 567–568. On the influence of the Act on the United Nations Charter, particularly with respect to Articles 51–54 on collective self-defense, see Robert C. Hilderbrand, *Dumbarton Oaks: The Origins of the United Nations and the Search for Postwar Security* (Chapel Hill: University of North Carolina Press, 1990), 163–169.

107. Thomas Rath, "Que el cielo un soldado en cada hijo te dio . . .': Conscription, Recalcitrance and Resistance in Mexico in the 1940s," *Journal of Latin American Studies* 37 (2005), 511; and "Reglas Para Una Cooperación Económica entre Nuestro País y Los Estados Unidos," *El Nacional,* July 18, 1943, clipping in exp. 577.1/36, caja 977, Ávila Camacho Papers.

108. Martin Binkin, *Blacks and the Military* (Washington, DC: Brookings Institute, 1982). On biased treatment of Mexican nationals by draft boards, see Jack Leighter to Francis Alstock, October 31, 1942, box 1717, folder "Spanish-speaking Minorities," OCIAA; Raúl Michel, Mexican Consul of El Paso, to Cónsul de México, Denver, Col., October 30, 1942, III-775-2, AHSRE; G. C. Wilmoth, El Paso District Director, Immigration and Naturalization Service, to Raúl Michel, Consul General of Mexico, July 14, 1942, III-802-1 (II), ibid.; de la Huerta to Padilla, Informe Número 103. On the refusal of immigration officials on the border to allow Mexican nationals to return to Mexico, see "Informe Final del Trabajo sobre el Servicio Militar," p. 13.

109. Bernardo Blanco, Consul of Mexico, Sacramento, to Mayer E. F. Leiten, Head of Selective Service, July 31, 1942, III-800-1 (1), AHSRE.

110. Manuel García y Griego, "The Importation of Mexican Contract Laborers to the United States, 1942–1964: Antecedents, Operation, and Legacy," in *The Border That Joins: Mexican Migrants and U.S. Responsibility,* ed. Peter G. Brown and Henry Shue (Totowa, NJ: Rowman and Littlefield, 1983).

5. Braceros and the "Wetback" Invasion

1. "Mexicans Convert Border into Sieve," *New York Times*, March 27, 1950, legajo 1453-1; "Protección a Nuestros 'Espaldas Mojadas,'" *Excelsior*, October 16, 1951; "Los 'Espadas Mojadas' Invaden Varias Industrias de Edos. Unidos," *Excelsior*, November 19, 1951, legajo 1454-3, AEMEUA.

2. "Mexican Border-Jumpers Set Two-a-Minute Mark in April," *New York Times*, May 10, 1953, in letter from Rafael Nieto, Mexican Embassy, to Luis Padilla Nervo, Secretario de Relaciones Exteriores, May 11, 1953, legajo 1454-3, AEMEUA. On the Bracero Program, see Ernesto Galarza, *Merchants of Labor: The Mexican Bracero Story, an Account of the Managed Migration of Mexican Farm Workers in California, 1942–1960* (Charlotte, CA: McNally and Loftin, 1964); and Kitty Calavita, *Inside the State: The Bracero Program, Immigration, and the I.N.S.* (New York: Routledge, 1992).

3. "Mexicans Convert Border into Sieve."

4. "Thousands of Mexicans Illegally Cross U.S. Border Each Month," *Los Angeles Times*, May 2, 1950; Mae M. Ngai, *Impossible Subjects: Illegal Aliens and the Making of Modern America* (Princeton, NJ: Princeton University Press, 2005), 147–152.

5. "Mexican Border-Jumpers."

6. Quoted in letter from Gus Garcia to George I. Sanchez, July 21, 1949, box 16, folder 19, Sánchez Papers.

7. "Southern Border," *Washington Post*, July 23, 1953, clipping attached to letter from José T. Delgado, Cónsul de México (Washington, DC), to Secretario de Relaciones Exteriores, July 27, 1953, legajo 1454-3, AEMEUA.

8. "The 'Wetback' Influx," *New York Times*, April 17, 1953; "Brownell Tours 'Wetback' Border," *New York Times*, April 16, 1953; "Government Maps War on Wetbacks," *Los Angeles Times*, June 10, 1954.

9. Manuel García y Griego, "The Importation of Mexican Contract Laborers to the United States, 1942–1964: Antecedents, Operation, and Legacy," in *The Border That Joins: Mexican Migrants and U.S. Responsibility*, ed. Peter G. Brown and Henry Shue (Totowa, NJ: Rowman and Littlefield, 1983), 55.

10. Mark Reisler, *By the Sweat of Their Brow: Mexican Immigrant Labor in the United States, 1900–1940* (Westport, CT: Greenwood Press, 1976), 24.

11. "Arrangement for migration to the United States of Mexican farm labor," *Department of State Bulletin* 8 (August 8, 1942), 689–690, in legajo 1451-22, AEMEUA.

12. Regional Office Newsletter No. 18, June 1951, Bishop's Committee for the Spanish Speaking, box 142, folder 2, García Papers. On the first seven years of the bracero program, see Wilbert E. Moore, "America's Migration Treaties during World War II," *Annals of the American Academy of Political and Social Science* 262 (March 1949), 31–38.

13. Press Release, Embajada de Mexico, "Sindicato Americano Nacional de Trabajadores Agrícolas [SANTA, as the NFLU was called in Spanish]," September 9, 1948, legajo 1452-7, AEMEUA; U.S. Scuttles Plan to Import Mexican Nationals," *Fresno Citizen,* September 17, 1948, legajo 1452-7, ibid. See also "California Jobs Going to Mexicans in Areas Having Huge Idle Rolls," *New York Times,* March 28, 1950, legajo 1453-1, ibid.

14. "Mexican 'Wetbacks' a Complex Problem," *New York Times,* January 18, 1953.

15. Leocadio and Ismael Ochoa to Manuel Ávila Camacho, August 9, 1942, and scores of other letters and telegrams to President Ávila Camacho in exp. 546.6/120, caja 793, Ávila Camacho Papers.

16. Telegram from Felix Cabañas to Manuel Ávila Camacho, September 23, 1945, exp. 546.6/120-1, caja 793, ibid.; John Mraz and Jaime Vélez Storey, *Trasterrados: braceros vistos por los hermanos Mayo* (Mexico City: Secretaría de Gobernación, AGN: Universidad Autónoma Metropolitana, 2005).

17. "Braceros Mexicanos Víctimas en EE. UU.," *Acción,* October 11, 1943 in letter from Owen W. Gaines to Secretary of State, October 19, 1943, Decimal File 811.4016/720, box 3806, Department of State; see also inter-office memorandum, Division of the American Republics, September 24, 1943, Decimal File 811.4016/722, box 3806, ibid.

18. George Messersmith to Philip W. Bonsal, November 26, 1943, Decimal File 811.4016/749, ibid.

19. George I. Sánchez to Rev. Robert E. Lucey, July 24, 1950, box 124, folder 2, García Papers; Isaac S. Valdéz, Angel Acero y demás firmantes to Manuel Ávila Camacho, August 13, 1942, exp. 546.6/120, caja 793, Ávila Camacho Papers.

20. Acuerdo al Secretario de la Defensa Nacional, Manuel Ávila Camacho, February 2, 1945, exp. 546.6/120, caja 793, ibid.; Memorandum, Department of State to Ambassador of Mexico, January 14, 1946; Memorandum, Embajador de México to Secretary of State, January 3, 1946, legajo 1452-3, AEMEUA.

21. "Manpower Problems in Texas, 1943–1944," *Texas Almanac* (1945–1946), in letter from Luis L. Duplan, Cónsul de México (Austin) to Secretario de Relaciones Exteriores, October 27, 1945, legajo 1451-22, ibid.

22. "Like the Other One," *Valley Evening Monitor* (McAllen, TX), April 25, 1948, in letter from Lauro Izaguirre, Cónsul of México (McAllen, TX), to Secretario de Relaciones Exteriores, April 28, 1948, legajo 1452-7, ibid.

23. "'No es Alarde,' Informa el Estado Que México Niego la Petición de Mandar Trabajadores," typescript in letter from Efraín G. Domínguez, Cónsul de México (Austin) to Secretario de Relaciones Exteriores, legajo 1452-7, ibid.; "Jester Apologizes to Aleman," *Amarillo Daily News,* April 25, 1949, in letter from Alfonso Guerra, Oficial Mayor, to Secretario de Relaciones Exteriores, May 12, 1949, exp. 130/280, caja 117, Alemán Papers.

24. Martin F. Carpenter, U.S. Employment Service, to Rafael Aveleyra, Consul General of Mexico (Mexican Embassy), May 2, 1949, legajo 1454–1, AEMEUA.

25. Ben Laney to Miguel Alemán, July 10, 1947, exp. 546.6/1–32, caja 594, Alemán Papers.

26. "Memorandum . . . desde Pine Bluff, Arkansas . . . a la Secretaría de Relaciones Exteriores," October 21, 1948; Angel Cano del Castiollo, Consul of Mexico, to E. T. Miller, U.S. Employment Service, October 23, 1948; Notarized Affidavit of A. A. Hughes, October 11, 1948; Robert E. Wilson, Department of State Division of Mexican Affairs, to Rafael de la Colina, November 5, 1948; and U.S. Department of Justice, "Minimum Requirements for Housing and Hygienic Living Conditions for Mexican Agricultural Laborers," September 27, 1948; all in legajo 1453–3, AEMEUA.

27. Yellen was found innocent of the charge. Ben Yellen to President Adolfo Ruiz Cortines, July 9, 1958; "Yellen and Ruiz Innocent," *Brawley News,* July 19, 1958, clipping attached to Ben Yellen to President Adolfo Ruiz Cortines, July 21, 1958; Ben Yellen to Commissioner of Insurance, July 21, 1958, exp. 548.1/706, caja 899, Ruiz Cortines Papers.

28. For examples of braceros who suffered serious illnesses, injuries, and accidents, as well as widows and other family members who sought compensation for braceros who died in accidents, see letters to President Manuel Ávila Camacho from Balbina Mejía Vda. De la O. (San Francisco), April 16, 1945, exp. 571.1/68, caja 975; Altagracia Estrada Flores Vda. De Pérez (Santa Barbara), June 19, 1944, exp. 575.1/67; José A. Domínguez (AZ), July 27, 1944, exp. 575.1/66; Macario Urbieta Sánchez y demás firmantes (Sheridan, WY), July 16, 1944, exp. 575.1/72; Susana Meza Vda. De Serrano Mireles Francisco Espejal (WA), September 7, 1944, exp. 575.1/78; Leopoldo Aviña (MI), December 27, 1944, exp. 575.1/93; all in Ávila Camacho Papers.

29. For a list of the complaints of Mexican railway workers in the first months of the Railroad Bracero Program, see letter from Alfredo Elias Calles, Mexican Consul (Los Angeles), to E. C. Rinehard, War Manpower Commission, July 13, 1943, reel 66, FEPC.

30. F. J. Holliday to Manuel Ávila Camacho, December 19, 1944, exp. 546.6 /120–5, caja 794, Ávila Camacho Papers. See also Secretary of State to the Ambassador of Mexico, January 7, 1946, legajo 1452–1, AEMEUA. On the bilateral negotiations inaugurating the Railroad Bracero Program in 1943, see Barbara A. Driscoll, *The Tracks North: The Railroad Bracero Program of World War II* (Austin: University of Texas Press, 1999), 67–74.

31. Rita Halle Kleeman, "Hi, Amigos!" *New York Herald Tribune,* October 21, 1945, in letter from Ernesto Galarza, Pan-American Union, to Embajador Rafael de la Colina, legajo 1451–22, ibid.

32. Lazar A. Bautista to Superintendent of Southern Pacific Company, September 17, 1944; and "Memorandum para el Sr. Presidente de la República:

Datos Sobre los Braceros Mexicanos," November 2, 1944, exp. 546.6/120–7, caja 794, Ávila Camacho Papers.

33. Guadalupe S. Miranda, Pascual Hernández, and Juan Cervantes to A. T. Mercier, president of Southern Pacific, quoted in letter from J. A. Small, president of Ferrocarril Sud-Pacífico de México, to Lic. J. Jesús González Gallo, May 2, 1944, ibid.

34. "Mexico Asks Fair Play for Its Workers in U.S.A.," *PM Examiner,* September 23, 1945, in legajo 1452–1, AEMEUA.

35. Memorandum para Acuerdo Presidencial, "Regreso de Trabajadores Mexicanos," November 21, 1945; Memorandum from Mexican Ambassador, Antonio Espinosa de los Monteros to Manuel Ávila Camacho, November 14, 1945; and Acuerdo Presidencial, "Planes de Repatriación . . . ," in letter from Manuel R. Palacios to Manuel Ávila Camacho, December 13, 1945; all in exp. 546.6/120–1, caja 793, Ávila Camacho Papers.

36. "Temporary Admission of Nationals of Mexico . . . to Engage in Agricultural Employment under the Agreement of February 21, 1948 Governing the Migration of Mexican Workers," jointly issued by the Commissioner of Immigration and Naturalization and the Director of the United States Employment Services, April 8, 1948, legajo 1452–6, AEMEUA; and Luis G. Salinas to Miguel Alemán, October 19, 1947, exp. 546.6/1–32, caja 594, Alemán Papers.

37. Agreement signed by Maurice L. Stafford, First Secretary of the Embassy of the United States, and Alfonso Guerra, Oficial Mayor, Ministry of Foreign Relations, and diplomatic notes from Raymond H. Geist, Chargé d'Affaires ad interim (U.S.), to Rafael de la Colina, Chargé d'Affaires ad interim (Mexico), February 20, 1948, legajo 1452–8, AEMEUA.

38. "Instructivo Para Los Trabajadores Agrícolas Mexicanos (Braceros) que Vayan A Prestar Sus Servicios, Transitoriamente a Los Estados Unidos," Comisión Intersecretarial al Encargada de Los Asuntos de Los Trabajadores Emigrantes, March 27, 1948, legajo 1452–6, ibid.

39. "Instructivo Para Los Trabajadores." On the efforts of the Mexican government to inform braceros of their rights and responsibilities, see also "Consejos a los Trabajadores Mexicanos que pasan a los Estados Unidos, contradados por la 'War Food Administration'" (Administración de Alimentos en Tiempo de Guerra, 1944, Secretaría de Relaciones Exteriores, Departamento de Información para el Extranjero, exp. 546.6/120–30, caja 796, Ávila Camacho Papers); "Los Braceros," 1946, Secretaría del Trabajo y Previsión Social, 1946, exp. 546.6/120–30, caja 796, ibid.

40. "Agreement Not to Employ Illegal Workers," Anexo "B," and "Occupational Diseases and Accidents," Anexo "C," Centro de Contratación de Trabajadores Ilegales en Harlingen, Texas, n.d., legajo 1453–5, AEMEUA.

41. "Boletín Informativo Publicado por el Comisionado de Inmigración y Naturalización y Director Federal del Servicios de Empleos," n.d., attached to

letter from Gustavo Padrés, Jr., Cónsul Comisionado de San Antonio, to Secretario de Relaciones Exteriores, April 5, 1951, legajo 1452–6, ibid.

42. "Thousands of Mexicans."

43. Paul J. Reveley, Department of State, to Rafael de la Colina, Charge d'Affaires ad interim of Mexico, September 3, 1948; Rafael Nieto, Consejero, to Secretario de Relaciones Exteriores, September 4, 1948, legajo 1452–8, AEMEUA.

44. "Informe Concentrado de los Sucesos Registrados en Esta Frontera, Relacionado con Nuestros Braceros," Raúl Mitchel, Cónsul General de México (El Paso), October 19, 1948; Jay C. Stilley, "Special Bulletin," October 26, 1948, legajo 1453–1, ibid.

45. "Flagrante Contradicción del Convenio Entre México y E.U.," *Excelsior,* October 17, 1948; "Es una Esclavitud Voluntaria Para los Mexicanos, *Excelsior,* October 19, 1948; clipping, "Fué un Acto Desesperado de EE. UU. la Admisión de Braceros," n.p., October 21, 1948; "U.S. Abandons Move to Keep Mexicans Out," *New York Times,* October 17, 1948; and "México Rompió Ayer el Pacto con E.U. Relativo a los Braceros," *Excelsior,* October 19, 1948; all in legajo 1453–1, AEMEUA.

46. "Immigration Head Denies 'Pressure,'" *El Paso Times,* October 21, 1948, legajo 1453–1, ibid.

47. Raúl Michel, Consul General of Mexico, to George C. Wilmoth, U.S. Immigration Service, October 16, 1948, legajo 1453–1, ibid.

48. Alfonso Anaya, Presidente, Asociación Mexicana de Periodistas, October 20, 1948, exp. 546.6/1–32, caja 594, Alemán Papers.

49. Rafael de la Colina, Encargado de Negocios ad interim, to Secretario de Relaciones Exteriores, October 18, 1948; and State Department Note no. 4946, October 18, 1948, attached to letter from Rafael de la Colina; both in legajo 1452–8, AEMEUA; and LULAC Resolution No. 2, June 12, 1949, attached to letter from Jacob I. Rodriguez to President Miguel Aleman, June 29, 1949, exp. 546.6/1–32, caja 594, Alemán Papers.

50. Paul Daniels, Department of State, to Rafael de la Colina, Chargé d'Affaires ad interim, October 22, 1948, attached to letter from Rafael de Colina to Secretario de Relaciones Exteriores, October 22, 1948, legajo 1452–8, AEMEUA.

51. Raúl Michel, Cónsul de México (El Paso) to Embajador de México, December 18, 1948, legajo 1453–1, ibid.

52. "U.S. Moves to Strengthen Guard against 'Wetbacks,'" *San Antonio Express,* December 8, 1948, legajo 1453–1, ibid.

53. "Border Patrol Increased to Halt Illegal Entries," *Corpus Christi Caller,* July 25, 1949, clipping attached to letter from Augusto Mehene, Cónsul de México (Corpus Christi, TX) to Cónsul General de México (San Antonio), July 26, 1949, legajo 1452–8, ibid.

54. Carmen Gallegos González to Manuel Ávila Camacho, April 17, 1946, exp. 546.6/120, caja 793, Ávila Camacho Papers.

55. José Hernández Serrano to Manuel Ávila Camacho, July 2, 1945, exp. 546.6/120, caja 793, ibid.

56. Radio Address, B. Tarkington Dowlen, "Should the U.S. Import 100,000 Mexican Farm Laborers?" typescript in letter from Alfredo Elías Calles, Cónsul de México (Los Angeles), to Embajador de México, April 1, 1943, legajo 1457–13, AEMEUA.

57. F. B. Hair to President Miguel Aleman, June 19, 1952, exp. 671/12179, caja 1039, Alemán Papers.

58. "An Obligation on Our Soil," *Brownsville Herald,* May 6, 1943, in letter from Enrique R. Ballesteros to Secretario de Relaciones Exteriores, May 7, 1943, legajo 1457–13, AEMEUA.

59. Louis Levand to President Miguel Alemán, March 10, 1947; "Two Are Killed in Crowd Trying to See President," *Wichita Beacon,* March 4, 1947, in letter from Josephus Daniels to Miguel Alemán, March 5, 1947, exp. 571.1/9, caja 698, Alemán Papers.

60. Typescript of speech by Miguel Alemán, March 3, 1947, on the occasion of President Truman's visit to Mexico City, exp. 571.1/9, caja 698, ibid.; Secretary of State George Marshall to President Miguel Aleman, May 22, 1947, exp. 135.2/37, caja 155, ibid.

61. Hubert H. Humphrey to President Miguel Alemán, September 22, 1949, exp. 136.1/35, caja 168, ibid.

62. State of the Union Address, January 7, 1948, in letter from Julián Sáenz, Embajada de México, to Lic. Rogerio de la Selva, Secretario de la Presidencia de la República, January 8, 1948, exp. 606.3/126, caja 718, ibid. See also *To Secure These Rights: Report of the President's Committee on Civil Rights* (Washington: Government Printing Office, 1947).

63. "Los Estados Unidos Contribuyen a Que los Trabajadores Mexicanos Entren Ilegalmente al País," translation into Spanish of article in the *Washington Star,* April 8, 1951, exp. 671/14501, caja 1062, Alemán Papers.

64. President Harry S. Truman to President Miguel Alemán, July 14, 1951, David Stowe Papers, Subject File, Mexican Labor, 1951, box 7, Harry S. Truman Library, Independence, MO (hereafter cited as Truman Papers); Miguel Alemán to President Harry S. Truman, July 27, 1951, exp. 671/14501, caja 1062, Alemán Papers. See also "Text of Truman Message on 'Wetbacks,'" *New York Times,* July 14, 1951.

65. Adela S. de Vento to Presidente Adolfo Ruiz Cortines, June 8, 1953, exp. 548.1/122, legajo 1, caja 893, Ruiz Cortines Papers.

66. "Wetback Inquiry Gets Instructions," *New York Times,* April 12, 1951; Respuesta de Carl W. Strom, Cónsul General de los Estados Unidos, al Discurso Inaugural del Dr. Guerra en la Conferencia sobre Trabajadores Migratorios, July 16, 1951, exp. 671/14501, caja 1062, Alemán Papers.

67. See García y Griego. "Importation of Mexican Contract Laborers," 63.

68. Ernesto Galarza, *Merchants of Labor: The Mexican Bracero Story* (Charlotte, CA: McNally and Loftin, 1964), 61, quoted in García y Griego, "Importation of Mexican Contract Laborers," 65.

69. Quoted in Juan García Ramon, *Operation Wetback: The Mass Deportation of Mexican Undocumented Workers in 1954* (Westport, CT: Greenwood Press, 1980), 111.

70. "Mexico—Silver Treasures for a Song," American Airlines advertisement, attached to letter from Geroge C. Van Nostrand, American Airlines of Mexico, S.A., to Rogerio de la Selva, Secretaría de la Presidencia, April 22, 1952, exp. 293/2462, caja 908, Alemán Papers.

71. The President of Sociedades Unidas de Hispano Americanos de Los Angeles urged President Ruiz Cortines to negotiate more favorable contracts for Mexican workers. Dr. Sandoval to Presidente Adolfo Ruiz Cortines, December 12, 1953, exp. 548.1/122, legajo 1, caja 893, Ruiz Cortines Papers.

72. The Mexican government had no juridical basis for preventing its citizens from emigrating. "Mexican Farm Workers Flooding into U.S.," *Journal and Press Dispatch* (CA), January 29, 1954, in exp. 548.1/122, legajo 10, caja 893, ibid.; Circular Num. 3/54, from Lic. Agustín Yañez, Gobernador de Jalisco, to Presidente Municipal, January 19, 1954, exp. 548.1/122, legajo 8, caja 893, ibid.

73. The American Farm Bureau Federation and the National Council of Farmer Cooperatives also testified in favor of renewing the Bracero Program. "Crop Loss Feared in 'Wetback' Jam," *New York Times*, February 6, 1954, clipping in exp. 548.1/122, legajo 10, caja 893, ibid.

74. President Ruiz Cortines received hundreds of telegrams and letters from labor leaders, journalists, students, and ordinary citizens congratulating him for his "patriotic and revolutionary" stand defending the rights of braceros in the U.S. See telegrams and letters in exp. 548.1/122, legajos 1 to 9, caja 893, ibid.

75. The Association of Mexican Farm Workers in El Paso, representing "Mexico de Afuera," wrote to President Ruiz Cortines that the association "no tolera que individuos sin escrúpulos sigan cometiendo inhumanas arbitrariedades con nuestra clase campesina, no solamente en los Estados Unidos, sino también en la República Mexicana." J. Jesús Ávila to Presidente Adolfo Ruiz Cortines, January 22, 1954, exp. 548.1/122, legajo 7, caja 893, ibid.

76. "U.S., Mexico Agree Again on Laborers," *West Memphis News,* April 1, 1954, in letter from Luis García Larrañaga to Secretario de Gobernación, May 12, 1954, exp. 548.1/122, legajo 11, caja 893, ibid.

77. Ernesto Galarza to Embajador Rafael de la Colina, August 6, 1949 legajo 1454–1; Rafael de la Colina to Subsecretario de Relaciones Exteriores, August 15, 1949, legajo 1454–1, AEMEUA; and "U.S. Plans to Curb Alien Farm Labor, *New York Times,* April 14, 1950, legajo 1453–6, ibid.

78. Regional Office Newsletter No. 18, García Papers.

79. García y Griego, "Importation of Mexican Contract Laborers," 64–65. See also Juan Ramón García, *Operation Wetback: The Mass Deportation of Mexican Undocumented Workers* (Westport, CT: Greenwood Press, 1980); Eleanor M. Hadley, "A Critical Analysis of the Wetback Problem," *Law and Contemporary Problems* 21 (Spring 1956): 334–357; Kelly Lytle Hernández, "The Crimes and Consequences of Illegal Immigration: A Cross-Border Examination of Operation Wetback, 1943 to 1954," *Western Historical Quarterly* (Winter 2006): 421–444.

80. See letters to President Manuel Ávila Camacho from José I. López, August 6, 1944; Melchor Casas, August 2, 1944; Ignacio Puente, July 28, 1944; both in exp. 546.6/120–3, caja 974; Dr. Manuel Morreno Barrera to Manuel Ávila Camacho, February 13, 1945; Francisca Estrada y demás firmantes, February 26, 1945; both in exp. 546.6/120–4, caja 974; María Efraina Rocha, May 24, 1944, exp. 546.6/120–7, caja 974; all in Ávila Camacho Papers.

81. "Wetback Bill Pledged," *New York Times,* March 30, 1954, clipping attached to letter from Luis García Larrañaga to Secretario de Relaciones Exteriores, April 30, 1954, exp. 548.1/122, legajo 11, caja 893, Ruiz Cortines Papers.

82. "Mexican Horde Repulsed by Border Patrol," *Chicago Tribune,* February 2, 1954; "The Wetback Problem Is Serious" and "Thousands Hunt U.S. Farm Jobs in Border Towns," *Los Angeles Times,* January 28, 1954, clippings in exp. 548.1/122, legajo 10, caja 893, ibid.

83. "U.S. Spreads Net for 'Wetbacks,'" *New York Times,* June 13, 1954; "Wetback War," *Missourian,* July 17, 1954, clipping in exp. 162/11, caja 281, ibid.

84. "Operation Wetback," *Handbook of Texas,* www.tshaonline.org/handbook.

85. For examples of United Press articles published in Mexico, see "Será Detenido el Exodo Ilegal de Braceros en E.U., *El Nacional,* June 11, 1954; "11,000 'Espaldas Mojadas' han sido Detenidos en la Operación," *El Universal,* July 19, 1954. Historian Manuel García y Griego notes that Mexican newspapers and "the annual report of DATAM played down the campaign, with only a single sentence in reference to the event." See García y Griego, "Importation of Mexican Contract Laborers," 91, n. 79.

86. "Nosotros los mexicanos de Chicago, opinamos que estas deportaciones . . . garantizan que los métodos usados por las autoridades de inmigración en los estados unidos, constituyen una completa desviación de los deberes de los mas altos representantes del Gobierno de México." Hilario Aleman, United Packinghouse Workers of America, to President Adolfo Ruiz Cortines, September 27, 1954, exp. 546.6/55, caja 883, Ruiz Cortines Papers.

87. On support for deportation generally, see, for example, *Daily Review,* July 14, 1954, in box 1977/081–483, folder "Wetbacks," Governor Allan Shivers Papers, Texas State Library and Archives, Austin, TX (hereafter cited as Shivers

Papers); and Harry Kane to Presidente Adolfo Ruiz Cortines, January 28, 1954, exp. 548.1/122, legajo 8, caja 893, Ruiz Cortines Papers.

88. "Wetback Trek May Become Death March," *Laredo Times,* June 5, 1953, exp. 546.6/55, caja 883, ibid.

89. David H. Moore (Yuma, AZ) to President Adolfo Ruiz Cortines, June 26, 1954, exp. 548.1/122, legajo 11, caja 893, ibid. A Spanish-speaking Anglo who worked for years in the bracero contract office in Hidalgo, Texas, felt pity for "estas probecitas [*sic*] criaturas que abandonan su Patria y su familia para venir a buscarse el pan de cada día en este País del Tío Sam." Fred. L. Johnston to Presidente Adolfo Ruiz Cortines, February 21, 1957, exp. 546.137, caja 884, ibid.

90. "Government Maps War."

91. "Sneaking into the United States," *Newark News,* February 25, 1954; "Keeping the Communists Out," *Time,* March 15, 1954; and "The Americas," *Newsweek,* March 22, 1954, clippings in exp. 162/11, caja 281, Ruiz Cortines Papers.

92. "McCarran and the Alien," *New York Times,* August 23, 1951.

93. "Keeping the Communists Out"; and "The Americas."

94. Quoted in García y Griego, "Importation of Mexican Contract Laborers," 66. See also "Drive on Wetbacks Termed a Success," *New York Times,* March 10, 1955.

95. Mexico's population increased by 39.4 percent (over nine million) between 1950 and 1960, among the highest growth rates in the world. See Paul Cross Morrison, "Population Changes in Mexico, 1950–1960," *Revista Geográfica* 32, no. 59 (2nd Semester, 1963): 79–92.

96. "Proyecto Para la Creación de la Comisión Nacional de Colonización y de Relaciones con los Mexicanos de Exterior," in letter from Mario Lasso to Presidente Adolfo Ruiz Cortines, April 1, 1954; "El Gobierno Mexicano Invita a La Repatriación," May 14, 1954, *Noticias* (Chicago), in letter from Mario Lasso to Enrique Rodríguez Cano, Secretaría de la Presidencia de la República, May 16, 1954, exp. 111/1438, caja 27, Ruiz Cortines Papers.

97. García y Griego, "Importation of Mexican Contract Laborers," 66.

98. "Data Sought on Mexican Maids Here," *Washington Post,* May 12, 1956, in letter from Manuel Tello, Embajador, to C. José Gorostiza, Secretaría de Relaciones Exteriores, May 12, 1956, legajo 1450–18, AEMEUA. The Mexican ambassador reported to the Foreign Minister that numerous young women were employed as domestic servants, "sin ninguna libertad, casi en calidad de esclava, con un sueldo a juicio del patrón, y, si la muchacha protesta, es encarcelada." Oscar Rabasa, P.O. del Secretario de Relaciones Exteriores, to Embajador de México, October 5, 1956; Oscar Rabasa to Cónsul General de México (San Antonio), October 22, 1956; and Manuel Tello, Embajador de México, to Secretario de Relaciones Exteriores, October 23, 1956; all in ibid.

99. Varden Fuller, "No Work Today! Plight of America's Migrants," Public Affairs Pamphlet No. 190 (1953), in letter from Lura Street Jackson to Secretaría

de la Presidencia, January 26, 1953, exp. 704/48, caja 1274, Ruiz Cortines Papers.

100. "Hands across the Border," report of the Inter-American Council of the Barberton Chamber of Commerce, 1945, in letter from Ruby M. Platt to Manuel Ávila Camacho, March 21, 1946, exp. 546.6/120–6, caja 794, Ávila Camacho Papers.

101. A. T. Mercier (Southern Pacific Company) and D. J. Russell (Northwestern Pacific Railroad Company and San Diego & Arizona Eastern Railway Company) to Nuestros Amigos Mexicanos, September 16, 1945, exp. 546.6/120, caja 793, ibid.

102. Sidney P. Osborn to President Elect Miguel Aleman, November 15, 1946, exp. 544.1/33–4, caja 553, Alemán Papers. See also Earl Warren, Governor of California, to Lic. don Miguel Alemán, December 2,1947, exp. 135.2/296, caja 159, ibid.; Fletcher Bowron, Mayor of Los Angeles, to Miguel Aleman, January 13, 1947, exp. 544.1/33–4, caja 553, ibid.

103. S. H. Strathman, executive secretary of Associated Farmers of California, Inc., to Manuel Ávila Camacho, January 14, 1944, and attached Resolution No. 5, exp. 546.6/120–7, caja 794, Ávila Camacho Papers.

104. "Thousands of Mexicans."

105. George I. Sánchez to Rev. Robert E. Lucey, July 24, 1950, box 124, folder 2, García Papers.

106. Quoted in "Mexico, the Latin North American Nation: A Conversation with David Thelen," *Journal of American History* 86 (September 1999): 467–480.

107. "Short on Labor, Farmers in the U.S. Shift to Mexico," *New York Times,* September 5, 2007.

108. Quoted in "Mexican Immigration no Threat to U.S.," *Los Angeles Times,* April 24, 1977.

109. McWilliams, *North from Mexico: The Spanish-Speaking People of the United States* (1948; reprint, New York: Greenwood Press, 1968), 304.

110. Geri Smith and Keith Epstein, "On the Border: The 'Virtual Fence' Isn't Working," *BusinessWeek,* February 7, 2008, www.businessweek.com/stories /2008-02-06/on-the-border-the-virtual-fence-isnt-working.

111. "U.S. Border Patrol Sector Profile—Fiscal Year 2012," http://www.cbp .gov/sites/default/files/documents/usbp_sector_profile_3.pdf.

6. The Chicano Movement

1. See, for example, *Houston Chronicle,* July 27, 1949, in letter from J. A. Kiesling to Gov. Allan Shivers, July 28, 1949, folder "Good Neighbor Commission," box 1997/081–357, Shivers Papers.

2. Quoted in Thomas S. Sutherland, "Texas Tackles the Race Problem," *Saturday Evening Post,* January 12, 1952, p. 22.

3. In Texas, the League of United Latin American Citizens (LULAC, founded in 1929) and the American G.I. Forum (1948); and in California, the Mexican-American Political Association (MAPA, 1959) and the highly successful Community Service Organization (CSO, 1947). Zaragosa Vargas, "In the Years of Darkness and Torment: The Early Mexican American Struggle for Civil Rights, 1945–1963," *New Mexico Historical Review* 76, no. 4 (Summer 2001): 382–413; and idem, *Labor Rights Are Civil Rights: Mexican American Workers in Twentieth-Century America* (Princeton, NJ: Princeton University Press, 2005), chs. 4–6.

4. For the standard work on the Mexican-American generation, see Mario T. García, *Mexican Americans: Leadership, Ideology, and Identity, 1930–1960* (New Haven, CT: Yale University Press, 1989). For an overview of the Chicano Movement, see Carlos Muñoz, *Youth, Identity, Power: The Chicano Generation* (New York: Verso, 1989).

5. Carl Allsup, *The American G.I. Forum: Origins and Evolution* (Austin: University of Texas Press, 1982), 30–33; Ignacio M. García, *Hector P. García: In Relentless Pursuit of Justice* (Houston, TX: Arte Público Press, 2003), 1–75.

6. William Blocker, American consul general in Ciudad Juárez, offered Texas governor Coke Stevenson his confidential opinion that "the principal source of racial discrimination reports is emanating from a very small group of Mexican-Americans whose motives are, obviously, not to the best interest of our state and country." William P. Blocker to Gov. Stevenson, October 2, 1943, box 4–14/155, folder "Good Neighbor Commission," Stevenson Papers.

7. Vaughn M. Bryant, memo to Neville G. Penrose, March 25, 1953, box 1989/59–16, folder "Discrimination, General Correspondence," GNC.

8. Jose Maldonado, sworn deposition, June 30, 1949, box 1989/59–16, folder "Discrimination, General File, 1946–1956," ibid.

9. Thomas S. Sutherland to Dr. Hector P. García, May 27, 1949, box 1989/59–16, folder "Discrimination, General File, 1946–1956," ibid.; Norman Rozeff, "García, Hector Pérez," *Handbook of Texas Online,* www.tshaonline .org/handbook/online/articles/fga52.

10. The United States also returned to the Mexican government the remains of hundreds of Mexican nationals who served in the U.S. Army and died overseas during the war. See the numerous files in III-1608-1 to III-1609-1, 1946–1950, AHSRE.

11. Dr. Hector P. García to Gov. Beauford Jester, January 11, 1949, box 4–14/82, folder "Three Rivers Case," Governor Beauford H. Jester Papers, Texas State Library and Archives, Austin, TX (hereafter cited as Jester Papers).

12. "GI of Mexican Origin Denied Rites in Texas to Be Buried in Arlington," *New York Times,* January 13, 1949; Lupe Longoria, Statement made to the Three Rivers Chamber of Commerce, January (n.d.), 1949, box 130, folder 34, García Papers. See also Patrick J. Carroll, *Felix Longoria's Wake: Bereavement,*

Racism, and the Rise of Mexican American Activism (Austin: University of Texas Press, 2003).

13. T/Sgt. Gale Harris to Gov. Beauford Jester, January 14, 1949, box 4–14/82, folder "Three Rivers Case," Jester Papers.

14. James J. Green to Gov. Beauford Jester, January 27, 1949, box 4–14/82, folder "Three Rivers Case," ibid.

15. Many governors, including Earl Warren of California, and mayors of major cities attended Miguel Alemán's inauguration, as did Nelson Rockefeller and many other officials of the U.S. government. Nelson A. Rockefeller to Miguel Alemán, December 10, 1946; Earl Warren to Miguel Alemán, December 14, 1946, exp. 544.1/33–4, caja 553, Alemán Papers.

16. Parents' Petition to Gov. Beauford Jester, January 15, 1949; James J. Green to Gov. Beauford Jester, January 27, 1949; and William McGill to Mr. Hart, February 13, 1949, box 4–14/82, folder "Three Rivers Case," Jester Papers.

17. "Jester Apologizes to Aleman," *Amarillo Daily News,* April 25, 1949, attached to letter from Alfonso Guerra, Oficial Mayor, to Secretario de Relaciones Exteriores, May 12, 1949; and "Jester Plans Mexican Tour," *Amarillo Globe,* April 25, 1949; both in exp. 130/280, caja 117, Alemán Papers.

18. "Descansa y en el Cementerio de Arlington un Héroe Mexicano," *El Universal,* February 17, 1949; "Funeraria Niego sus Servicios a un Soldado México-Americano," *La Prensa* (San Antonio), January 12, 1949; and Efraín G. Dominguez, Cónsul de México (Austin), to Secretario de Relaciones Exteriores, January 24, 1949; all in III-1608-1 (II), AHSRE.

19. U. W. Walker to President of Mexico, October 4, 1949, exp., 546.6/1–32, caja, 594, Alemán Papers.

20. J. F. Gray to Lloyd Bentsen May 5, 1949; Lloyd Bentsen to J. F. Gray, May 10, 1949, box 4–14/82, folder "Three Rivers Case," Jester Papers.

21. L. M. Granados to Gov. Beauford Jester, January 15, 1949, box 4–14/82, folder "Three Rivers Case," ibid.

22. George I. Sánchez to Roger Baldwin, January 4, 1942 and September 21, 1942, box 2, folder 17, Sánchez Papers. See also Rubén Donato and Jarrod S. Hanson, "Legally White, Socially 'Mexican': The Politics of De Jure and De Facto School Segregation in the American Southwest," *Harvard Educational Review* 89 (Summer 2012): 202–225.

23. Jorge C. Rangel and Carlos M. Alcala, "Project Report: De Jure Segregation of Chicanos in Texas Schools," *Harvard Civil Rights-Civil Liberties Law Review* 7 (March 1972), 314.

24. Transcript of radio comments of Stuart Long, September 17, 1945, attached to letter from William P. Blocker, American consul (Ciudad Juárez) to Secretary of State, October 8, 1945, Decimal File 811.4016/10–845, Department of State.

25. See George A. Martinez, "Legal Indeterminacy, Judicial Discretion and the Mexican-American Litigation Experience: 1930–1980," *U.C. Davis Law Review* 27 (1994), 555, 576.

26. *Independent School District v. Salvatierra,* 33 S.W. 2d 790 (Tex. Civ. App. 1930). For an excellent summary of the desegregation cases from these three states, see James A. Ferg-Cadima, "Black, White and Brown: Latino School Desegregation Efforts in the Pre- and Post- *Brown v. Board of Education* Era," *MALDEF* (May 2004): 1–47. See also Guadalupe San Miguel, Jr., *"Let All of Them Take Heed": Mexican Americans and the Campaign for Educational Equality in Texas, 1910–1981* (Austin: University of Texas Press, 1987).

27. *Independent School District v. Salvatierra.*

28. Ibid. See also San Miguel, *"Let All of Them Take Heed,"* 78–80; and Carl Allsup, "Education Is Our Freedom: The American GI Forum and the Mexican American School Segregation in Texas, 1948–1957," *Aztlan* 8 (1979): 27–50.

29. *Alvarez v. Owen,* No. 66625 (San Diego County Super. Ct. filed April 17, 1931); Robert R. Alvarez, Jr. "The Lemon Grove Incident: The Nation's First Successful Desegregation Court Case," *Journal of San Diego History* 32 (Spring 1986): 116–135; Richard R. Valencia, *Chicano Students and the Courts: The Mexican American Legal Struggle for Educational Equality* (New York: New York University Press, 2008), 19–21.

30. *Mendez v. Westminster School District,* 64 F. Supp. 544, 549 (D. Cal. 1946), aff'd, 161 F.2d 774 (9th Cir. 1947). See also Christopher Arriola, "Knocking on the Schoolhouse Door: *Mendez v. Westminster,* Equal Protection, Public Education, and Mexican Americans in the 1940's," *La Raza Law Journal* 8 (Fall 1995): 166–207; and Philippa Strum, *Mendez v. Westminster: School Segregation and Mexican-American Rights* (Lawrence: University of Kansas Press, 2010).

31. *Plessy v. Fergusson,* 163 U.S. 537 (1896).

32. *Brown v. Board of Education of Topeka,* 347 U.S. 483 (1954). See also Charles Wollenberg, *All Deliberate Speed; Segregation and Exclusion in California Schools, 1855–1975* (Berkeley: University of California Press, 1976), 132.

33. Quoted in Richard R. Valencia, "The Mexican Struggle for Equal Educational Opportunity in *Mendez v. Westminster:* Helping to Pave the Way for *Brown v. Board of Education,*" *Teachers College Record* 107 (March 2005), 408.

34. LULAC and American G.I. Forum members also described discrimination against Mexican Americans as "Nazi" racism. See, for example, Joe Zapata to Gov. Allan Shivers, n.d., telegram attached to letter, William L. McGill to Tom S. Sutherland, April 14, 1950, box 1989/59–18, folder "Discrimination Correspondence, 1949–1950," GNC.

35. Complaint to Enjoin Violation of Federal Civil Rights and for Damages, in the United States District Court for the Western District of Texas, box 79, folder 4, Sánchez Papers; *Delgado v. Bastrop Independent School District,* Civil No. 388 (W.D. Tex., June 15, 1948).

36. Final Judgment, Minerva Delgado et al., vs. Bastrop Independent School District et al., June 15, 1948, box 79, folder 5, Sánchez Papers. See also San Miguel, *"Let All of Them Take Heed,"* 123–126.

37. For recent research on this case, see Michael A. Olivas, ed., *"Colored Men" and "Hombres Aquí": Hernández v. Texas and the Emergence of Mexican American Lawyering* (Houston, TX: Arte Public Press, 2006); and Ignacio M. García, *White but Not Equal: Mexican Americans, Jury Discrimination and the Supreme Court* (Tucson: University of Arizona Press, 2009).

38. *Pete Hernández v. State of Texas,* Texas Court of Criminal Appeals, No. 25,816 (1952), Opinion by Judge Davidson at 6.

39. *Sanchez v. State,* 243 S. W. 2d 700 (1951).

40. Appellant's Brief, *Pete Hernández v. State of Texas,* Court of Criminal Appeals, No. 25,816, 16–17; *Hernández v. Texas,* 251 S.W. 2d 531.

41. *Hernández v. Texas,* 347 U.S. 475 (1954). Justice Warren also cited an earlier case, *Hirabayashi v. United States,* 320 U.S. 81 (1943), in which a Japanese American was indicted for failing to comply with curfew laws imposed on citizens of Japanese ancestry: "Distinctions between citizens solely because of their ancestry are by their very nature odious to a free people whose institutions are founded upon the doctrine of equality."

42. *Hernández v. Texas,* 347 U.S. 475 (1954).

43. Editorial, *Fort Worth Star-Telegram,* March 4, 1952, box 1989/59–16, folder "Discrimination, general correspondence [1950–1957]," GNC.

44. Unsigned letter to "Dear Sir" [Gov. Shivers], November 13, 1950, box 1989/59–18, folder "Mexicans Burned to Death in Fisher County," ibid.

45. Casualty figures taken from press reports in 1951, reproduced and cited in Mario T. García, *Mexican Americans: Leadership, Ideology, and Identity* (New Haven, CT: Yale University Press, 1989), 210.

46. John P. Schmal, "Hispanic Contributions to America's Defense," *Puerto Rico Herald,* November 11, 1999, www.puertorico-herald.org/issues/vol3n46/HispanicContributions-en.html.

47. Quoted in Ruth D. Tuck, *Not with the Fist: Mexican Americans in a Southwest City* (New York: Harcourt, Brace, 1946), 221.

48. Quoted in Jacques Levy, *Cesar Chavez: Autobiography of La Causa* (New York: W. W. Norton, 1975), 8; John R. Chávez, *The Lost Land: The Chicano Image of the Southwest* (Albuquerque: University of New Mexico Press, 1984), 134–135.

49. The union underwent a series of name changes and affiliations after 1962 (when it was called an association or committee) before receiving its own charter in 1972 as the United Farm Workers Union of the AFL-CIO, the largest federation of labor unions in the United States. For simplicity, I refer to the union in its various iterations as the United Farm Workers Union (UFW).

50. The literature on the Cesar Chavez and the UFW is vast, but see Matt García, *From the Jaws of Victory: The Triumph and the Tragedy of Cesar Chavez*

and the Farm Worker Movement (Berkeley: University of California Press, 2012); Miriam Pawel, *The Union of Their Dreams: Power, Hope, and Struggle in Cesar Chavez's Farm Worker Movement* (New York: Bloomsbury Press, 2009); Jacques Levy, *Cesar Chavez: Autobiography of La Causa* (New York: W. W. Norton, 1975); and "The Fight in the Fields: Cesar Chavez and the Farmworkers' Struggle," *PBS,* www.pbs.org/itvs/fightfields/cesarchavez.html.

51. "El Plan de Delano," chavez.cde.ca.gov/ModelCurriculum/Teachers /Lessons/Resources/Documents/El_Plan_De_Delano.pdf.

52. "Robert F. Kennedy Statement on Cesar Chavez, March 10, 1968, re-search.archives.gov/description/194027; Steven W. Bender, *One Night in America: Robert Kennedy, Cesar Chavez, and the Dream of Dignity* (Boulder, CO: Paradigm Publishers, 2008), 29–32.

53. Mark Day, *Forty Acres: Cesar Chavez and the Farm Workers* (New York: Praeger, 1971), 76.

54. Susan Ferriss and Ricardo Sandoval, *The Fight in the Fields: Cesar Chavez and the Farmworkers Movement* (New York: Harcourt Brace, 1997), 86–123; García, *From the Jaws of Victory,* 40–43; Jan Young, *The Migrant Workers and Cesar Chavez* (New York: Julian Messner, 1974), 160.

55. John Kenneth Galbraith, *The Affluent Society* (Boston: Houghton Mifflin, 1958), 1.

56. Michael Harrington, *The Other America: Poverty in the United States* (Baltimore, MD: Penquin, 1962), 3–4, 12.

57. "Letter from Birmingham Jail," April 16, 1963, mlk-kpp01.stanford .edu/index.php/resources/article/annotated_letter_from_birmingham/.

58. Julie Leininger Pycior, *LBJ and Mexican Americans: The Paradox of Power* (Austin: University of Texas Press, 1997), 7–22 (quote on 18); William M. Epstein, *Democracy without Decency: Good Citizenship and the War on Poverty* (University Park: Pennsylvania State University Press, 2010); and Edward R. Schmitt, *President of the Other America: Robert Kennedy and the Politics of Poverty* (Amherst: University of Massachusetts Press, 2010).

59. See, for example, *Revolutionary Activities within the United States— The American Indian Movement,* Ninety-fourth Congress, 2nd session (Washington, DC: Government Printing Office, 1976); Paul Chaat Smith and Robert Allen Warrior, *Like a Hurricane: The Indian Movement from Alcatraz to Wounded Knee* (New York: New Press, 1996).

60. Reies Tijerina, *They Called Me "King Tiger": My Struggle for the Land and Our Rights* (Houston, TX: Arte Público Press, 2000), 63 (first quote), 11 (second quote). On conflicts over land grants in New Mexico, see David Correia, *Properties of Violence: Law and Land Grant Struggle in Northern New Mexico* (Athens: University of Georgia Press, 2013); and María E. Montoya, *Translating Property: The Maxwell Land Grant and the Conflict over Land in the American West, 1840–1900* (Berkeley: University of California Press, 2002).

61. Quoted in Richard Gardner, *Grito! Reies Tijerina and the Land Grant War of 1967* (New York: Bobbs-Merrill, 1970), 120; and Lorena Oropeza, "The Heart of Chicano History: Reies López Tijerina as a Memory Entrepreneur," *The Sixties: A Journal of History, Politics and Culture* 1, no. 1 (June 2008): 49–67.

62. Michael Jenkinson, *Tijerina: Land Grant Conflict in New* Mexico (Albuquerque, NM: Paisano Press, 1968), 58–59; Peter Nabokov, *Tijerina and the Courthouse Raid* (Albuquerque: University of New Mexico Press, 1969), 216; Chávez, *Lost Land,* 138–141.

63. Jenkinson, *Tijerina,* 61–62.

64. Gardner, *Grito!,* 117–132; Chávez, *Lost Land,* 139–140; Jenkinson, *Tijerina,* 61–70; Nabokov, *Tijerina and the Courthouse Raid,* 51.

65. Poverty figures in Patricia Bell Blawis, *Tijerina and the Land Grants: Mexican Americans in Struggle for Their Heritage* (New York: International Publishers, 1971), 108.

66. Gardner, *Grito!,* 114.

67. Nabokov, *Tijerina and the Courhouse Raid,* 85–156. The raid was also covered by the Paris edition of the *New York Times,* which, Nabokov notes, "gloated over having its stereotype of Wild West primitivism borne out" (ibid., 157).

68. Nabokov, *Tijerina and the Courhouse Raid,* 253; Blawis, *Tijerina and the Land Grants,* 100–101.

69. Quoted in Blawis, *Tijerina and the Land Grants,* 97.

70. Santa Fe *New Mexican,* June 5, 1968, quoted in Blawis, *Tijerina and the Land Grants,* 129.

71. Quoted in Gardner, *Grito!,* 121.

72. Quoted in Blawis, *Tijerina and the Land Grants,* 130.

73. Quoted in ibid., 139; Chávez, *Lost Land,* 141.

74. Blawis, *Tijerina and the Land Grants,* 98. On Tijerina's participation in the march and black-brown coalition politics in the 1960s and 1970s, see Gordon K. Mantler, *Power to the Poor: Black-Brown Coalition and the Fight for Economic Justice, 1960–1974* (Chapel Hill: University of North Carolina Press, 2013), 71–73, 145–149, 156–158.

75. Quoted in Blawis, *Tijerina and the Land Grants,* 99.

76. Ernesto B. Vigil, *The Crusade for Justice: Chicano Militancy and the Government's War on Dissent* (Madison: University of Wisconsin Press, 1999).

77. Rodolfo Gonzales and Alberto Urista [Alurista, pseud.], "El Plan Espiritual de Aztlán," *El Grito del Norte* (Albuquerque, NM), 2, no. 9 (July 6, 1969): 5; and "El Plan de Aztlán," www.colorado.edu/StudentGroups/MEChA/MEXA plana.html.

78. David G. Gutiérrez, *Walls and Mirrors: Mexican Americans, Mexican Immigrants, and the Politics of Identity* (Berkeley: University of California Press, 1995), 185.

79. Chávez, *Lost Land,* 142–144. See also Forbes, *Aztecas del Norte,* ch. 1.

80. Chávez, *Lost Land,* 145.

81. Ignacio M. García, *United We Win: The Rise and Fall of La Raza Unida Party* (Tucson: University of Arizona, Mexican American Studies Research Center, 1989); Muñoz, *Youth, Identity, Power,* 99–126; and Teresa Palomo Acosta, "Raza Unida Party," *Handbook of Texas Online,* www.tshaonline.org/hand book/online/articles/war01.

82. Quoted in Rodolfo Acuña, *Occupied America: A History of Chicanos,* 3rd ed. (New York: Harper-Collins, 1988), 339.

83. For a listing of all the candidates affiliated with LRUP in over one hundred elections from 1970 to 1978, see "The Candidates Who Ran During the Years of La Raza Unida in Texas," *La Raza Unida Party Reunion,* n.d., www.larazaunidapartyreunion.org/Candidates.html.

84. In Texas alone, a change of only 50,000 votes would have put Nixon in the White House. Henry A. J. Ramos, *The American GI Forum: In Pursuit of the Dream, 1948–1983* (Houston, TX: Arte Público Press, 1998), 88.

85. Ignacio M. García, *Viva Kennedy: Mexican Americans in Search of Camelot* (College Station: Texas A&M University Press, 2000); Manuel G. Gonzales, *Mexicanos: A History of Mexicans in the United States* (Bloomington: University of Indiana Press, 1999), 207.

86. Muñoz, *Youth, Identity, Power,* 134–149; David Montejano, *Quixote's Soldiers: A Local History of the Chicano Movement, 1966–1981* (Austin: University of Texas Press, 2010), 89; Carey McWilliams, *North from Mexico: The Spanish-Speaking People of the United States* (1948; reprint, New York: Praeger, 1990), 289.

87. Quoted in Montejano, *Quixote's Soldiers,* 87 (first quote), 95 (second quote). For the full text of the Plan de Santa Barbara, see www.nationalmecha .org/documents/EPSB.pdf.

88. Mario T. García and Sal Castro, *Blowout!: Sal Castro and the Chicano Struggle for Educational Justice* (Chapel Hill: University of North Carolina Press, 2011); Armando Navarro, *Mexican American Youth Organization: Avant-Garde of the Chicano Movement in Texas* (Austin: University of Texas Press, 1995), 99; Muñoz, *Youth, Identity, Power,* 64–73; Montejano, *Quixote's Soldiers,* 61; Gonzales, *Mexicanos,* 208–211; McWilliams, *North from Mexico,* 287–290.

89. George Mariscal, ed., *Aztlán and Viet Nam: Chicano and Chicana Experiences of the War* (Berkeley: University of California Press, 1999), 27.

90. Quoted in Lorena Oropeza, *!Raza Si! !Guerra No!: Chicano Protest and Patriotism during the Vietnam War Era* (Berkeley: University of California Press, 2005), 27.

91. Ibid., 61–65 (quote on 64).

92. Ibid., (quote on 65).

93. Ibid., (quote on 61).

94. Quoted in Julian E. Zelizer, *Arsenal of Democracy: The Politics of National Security in America from World War II to the War on Terrorism* (New York: Basic Books, 2010), 206 (first quote); Stewart Burns, *To the Mountaintop: Martin Luther King Jr.'s Sacred Mission to Save America, 1955–1968* (New York: Harper, 2004), 320 (second quote); see also F. Michael Higginbotham, *Ghosts of Jim Crow: Ending Racism in Post-Racial America* (New York: New York University Press, 2013), 3.

95. Quoted in Oropeza, *!Raza Si!,* 89.

96. Martin Luther King, Jr., *A Testament of Hope; The Essential Writings and Speeches of Martin Luther King, Jr.,* ed. James Melvin Washington (San Francisco: Harper & Row, 1986), 233.

97. Quoted in Dwight N. Hopkins, "Keeping the Dream Alive," in James Echols, ed., *I Have a Dream: Martin Luther King Jr. and the Future of Multicultural America* (Minneapolis, MN: Fortress Press, 2004), 64.

98. Navarro, *Mexican American Youth Organization,* 183; Oropeza, *!Raza Si!,* 76–79.

99. Ralph Guzman, "Mexican American Casualties in Vietnam," *La Raza* 1, no. 1 (1970): 12–15; Acuña, *Occupied America,* 346; Gonzales, *Mexicanos,* 212; Oropeza, *!Raza Si!,* 67.

100. World War II veteran and Bexar county commissioner (San Antonio) Albert Peña, Jr., quoted in Oropeza, *!Raza Si!,* 159.

101. Quoted in ibid., 127.

102. David Shaw and Richard Vasquez, "Contradictory Reports Given in Slaying of Columnist Salazar," *Los Angeles Times,* August 30, 1970; Henrique Hank Lopez, "Ruben Salazar Death Silences a Leading Voice of Reason," *Los Angeles Times,* September 6, 1970. See also Acuña, *Occupied America,* 346–350; Gonzales, *Mexicanos,* 212–213.

103. Helen Rowan, "A Minority Nobody Knows," *Atlantic* (June 1967): 47–52.

7. Brave New Mundo

1. According to one journalist, the phrase was first used in 1978 to refer to Hispanic appointees in the Carter administration: "The blacks had the decade of the '60s; women had the '70s. The '80s will be the decade for Hispanics." Frank del Olmo, "Latino 'Decade' Moves into the '90s," *Los Angeles Times,* December 4, 1989.

2. Arthur S. Fleming et al., to the President [Nixon] et al., "Letter of Transmittal," April 1974, U.S. Commission on Civil Rights, *Counting the Forgotten: The 1970 Census Count of Persons of Spanish Speaking Background in the United States* (Washington, DC: Government Printing Office, 1974), especially 34–55; and Committee on Post Office and Civil Service, Subcommittee on Census and Statistics, *Effect of Census Statistics on Federal Aid Programs and*

Federal Reporting Requirements, 93rd Congress, 2nd sess. (Washington, DC: Government Printing Office, 1974): 1–78.

3. Office of Management and Budget, "Directive No. 15, Race and Ethnic Standards for Federal Statistics and Administrative Reporting," 1977, wonder .cdc.gov/wonder/help/populations/bridged-race/directive15.html; Benjamin Francis-Fallon, *Minority Reports: The Emergence of Pan-Hispanic Politics, 1945–1980* (forthcoming, Harvard University Press), 341–345. On the development of a "panethnic consciousness" among Mexicans and Puerto Ricans in Chicago in response to unfair labor practices, see Felix Padilla, *Latino Ethnic Consciousness: The Case of Mexican Americans and Puerto Ricans in Chicago* (South Bend, IN: Notre Dame University Press, 1985).

4. On the efforts of the Census Bureau and Latino leaders to agree on how the 1980 census should count "Spanish-origin" people, see Griselda Cristina Mora, "De Muchos, Uno: The Institutionalization of Latino Panethnicity, 1960–1990" (PhD diss., Princeton University, 2009), 127–221; and "Approaching the 1980 Census: Changes Should be Implemented to Reduce an Undercount of the Hispanic Population," Testimony of the Mexican American Legal Defense and Educational Fund (MALDEF) to the U.S. Senate Committee on Governmental Affairs," April 9, 1979, box 37, folder 47, Mexican American Legal Defense and Educational Fund Records, Department of Special Collections, Stanford University Libraries, Stanford, CA (hereafter cited as MALDEF).

5. On the role of Hispanic leaders in persuading the census to adopt the "Hispanic" category in the 1980 census and census administrators willingness to accommodate them, see Harvey M. Choldin, "Statistics and Politics: The 'Hispanic Issue' in the 1980 Census," *Demography* 23 (August 1986): 403–418; and "Hispanics and the 1980 Census," Testimony of the Mexican American Legal Defense and Educational Fund to the Subcommittee of Census and Population, Committee on Post Office and Civil Service, April 17, 1979, box 37, folder 46, MALDEF.

6. On the complications and controversies surrounding census terminology and the different meanings ascribed to Latino and Hispanic as ethnic labels, see David E. Hayes-Bautista and Jorge Chapa, "Latino Terminology: Conceptual Basis for Standardized Terminology," *American Journal of Public Health* 77 (1987): 61–68; and Suzanne Oboler, *Ethnic Labels, Latino Lives: Identity and the Politics of (Re)Presentation in the United States* (Minneapolis: University of Minnesota Press, 1995), 3–6.

7. Richard Rodríguez, "The Salsa Zone: Mexico's New President Speaks English in Public while U.S. Candidates Speak Spanish. Fade-out for Nativism," *Los Angeles Times,* July 9, 2000.

8. Elizabeth S. Rolph, *Immigration Policies: Legacy from the 1980s and Issues for the 1990s* (Santa Monica, CA: Rand, 1992), 6; Roger Daniels, *Guarding the Golden Door: American Immigration Policy and Immigrants since 1882*

(New York: Hill and Wang, 2004), 129–144; idem, *Coming to America,* 2nd ed. (New York: HarperCollins, 2002), 338–344.

9. Mercedes Olivera, "Immigration Rocketing, Former INS Chief Says," *Dallas Morning News,* February 28, 1980.

10. John D. Skrentny, *The Minority Rights Revolution* (Cambridge, MA: Harvard University Press, 2002), 144 (quote) and ch. 7; and Dean Kotlowski, *Nixon's Civil Rights: Politics, Principle and Policy* (Cambridge, MA: Harvard University Press, 2002), 138, 264.

11. Barry Goldwater to Bryce Harlow, January 6, 1969, quoted in Nancy MacLean, *Freedom Is Not Enough: The Opening of the American Workplace* (Cambridge, MA: Harvard University Press, 2006), 180.

12. The phrase was used in the title of a report issued in 1966 by the National Education Association: *The Invisible Minority: Report of the NEA-Tuscon Survey on the Teaching of Spanish to the Spanish-Speaking,* www.nea.org/assets /img/content/The_Invisible_Minority.pdf. See also Helen Rowan, "A Minority Nobody Knows," *Atlantic* (June 1967): 47–52. On the evolution of NCLR from a Chicano organization to a panethnic "Hispanic" one, see Mora, "De Muchos, Uno," 31–126.

13. "Latin Tempo-A Single Voice," quoted in Mora, "De Muchos, Uno," 115–116.

14. Mora, "De Muchos, Uno," 116; "About Us," *NCLR,* www.nclr.org/index .php/about_us/.

15. "The Translation of Our Name," *NEA,* www.nea.org/assets/img/content /The_Invisible_Minority.pdf; Mora, "De Muchos, Uno," 37.

16. Pamela G. Hollie, "Courting the Hispanic Market," *New York Times,* December 26, 1983"; Frank del Olmo, "Latino 'Decade' Moves into '90s," *Los Angeles Times,* December 14, 1989. See also Melissa Renee Mendoza, "The Latino Giant: A Growing Population and Its Impact on U.S. Advertising" (MA thesis, University of Texas, 2008), ch. 1: "A Market Is Born"; and Arlene M. Dávila, *Latinos Inc.: The Marketing and Making of a People* (Berkeley: University of California Press, 2001).

17. "Frito Bandito Ad Attacked as Racist," *Washington Post,* December 11, 1969; Norman Smith, "The Spoils of Victory: The Conquest of the Frito Bandito," *Revista Chicano-Riqueña,* no. 3 (Verano, 1975): 35–45.

18. Philip H. Dougherty, "Madison Avenue Takes a Trip to the Moon," *New York Times,* June 29, 1969.

19. Thomas Martinez, "How Advertisers Promote Racism," *Civil Rights Digest* 2 (Fall 1969), 20; Smith, "Spoils of Victory," 42; Chon A. Noriega, *Shot in America: Television, the State, and the Rise of Chicano Cinema* (Minneapolis: University of Minnesota Press, 2000), 35–50, passim; and Michael White, *A Short Course in International Marketing Blunders: Mistakes Made by Companies That Should Have Known Better* (Novato, CA: World Trade Press, 2002), 139–140.

20. Earl Golz, "Latins Plan Protest of 'Frito Bandito,'" *Dallas Morning News,* April 3, 1971.

21. "Advertising: Ban the Bandito," *Newsweek,* December 22, 1969, 82, quoted in Smith, "Spoils of Victory," 42.

22. John R. McCarty to Vicente T. Ximenes, February 25, 1970, doc. 132.24, García Papers; Smith, "Spoils of Victory," 38; and White, *Short Course in International Marketing Blunders,* 140.

23. "How about Frito Amigo?" *Washington Post,* June 2, 1971, doc. 132.21, García Papers.

24. Vicki Stone, "Attack Frito Bandito," *Hutchison News* (Kansas), February 14, 1971, doc. 132.26, ibid.

25. *La Raza* 1, no. 4 (June 1971), 26, quoted in Noriega, *Shot in America,* 46.

26. Quoted in White, *Short Course in International Marketing Blunders,* 146.

27. "How about Frito Amigo?"; and "La Campaña del Frito 'Bandito,' un Insulto a Mexicanos," *El Sol de Texas* (Dallas), January 15, 1971, doc. 132.25, García Papers.

28. Henry Allen, "Bandito Business," *Washington Post,* April 29, 1971.

29. Henry A. J. Ramos, *The American GI Forum: In Pursuit of the Dream, 1948–1983* (Houston, TX: Arte Público Press, 1998), 111–116; MacLean, *Freedom Is Not Enough,* 177–180.

30. "Why Boycott Coors," n.d., García Papers.

31. EEOC v. Adolph Coors Co. et al., U.S. District Court . . . of Colorado (1975), doc. 124.51, ibid.; "'Coors Boycott' in Texas—No Tóme Cerveza Coors," November 11, 1975, doc. 124.51, ibid; Ramos, *American GI Forum,* 112.

32. Steve Emmons, "Teamsters, Women Unite," *Los Angeles Times,* August 10, 1976.

33. "10-Year Coors Boycott Ends as Unions Win Concessions," *Los Angeles Times,* August 19, 1987; Ramos, *American GI Forum,* 114.

34. Letter from Joseph Coors to Fellow American, n.d. [1976], doc. 79.23, García Papers.

35. Don Williamson, "Calls for Coors Boycott Echo again after Speech to Blacks Brews a Storm," *San Diego Union,* March 12, 1984; idem, "Coors, L.A.'s NAACP Reach Agreement over Buying," *San Diego Union,* April 7, 1984.

36. "Beer Company Signs Pact with Rights Group," *New York Times,* April 10, 1984.

37. Janet Simons, "Coors Turns Boycotters into Buyers," *Advertising Age,* February 27, 1986.

38. "Latino Groups Protest Agreement with Coors," *Los Angeles Times,* November 13, 1984; "The Beer and the Boycott," *New York Times Magazine,* January 31, 1988.

39. Ivan Vasquez, "Historical Synopsis of the American G.I. Forum Affirmative Action Team," 15–18, doc. 213.1, García Papers; American G.I. Forum

Affirmative Action Team, "Good Faith Efforts: Chronology of Negotiations," doc. 213.1, ibid.; Simons, "Coors Turns Boycotters into Buyers."

40. Simons, "Coors Turns Boycotters into Buyers."

41. Laurie Becklund, "Latino Groups Protest Agreement with Coors," *Los Angeles Times,* November 13, 1984. The AFL-CIO ended its boycott in 1987. Oswald Johnston, "AFL-CIO Ends 10-Year Boycott of Coors Beer," *Los Angeles Times,* August 20, 1987.

42. Jonathan Tasini, "The Beer and the Boycott," *New York Times,* January 31, 1988.

43. Ibid.; Steven Greenhouse, "The Coors Boys Stick to Business," *New York Times,* November 30, 1986."

44. Lee May, "Latinos Aim for Progress via Politics," *Los Angeles Times,* July 27, 1987; Zaragosa Vargas, *Crucible of Struggle: A History of Mexican Americans from Colonial Times to the Present Era* (New York: Oxford University Press, 2011), 350–351.

45. Geoffrey Godsell, "Hispanics in the U.S.: Ethnic 'Sleeping Giant' Awakens," *Christian Science Monitor,* April 28, 1980 (quote); Andy Rose, "Group Regards Latino Vote as Sleeping Giant to be Awakened," *Los Angeles Times,* November 17, 1986.

46. Robert Lindsey, "Brown Power: Growing Hispanic Populace Alters Mainstream," *Dallas Morning News,* February 19, 1979; Rose, "Group Regards Latino Vote as Sleeping Giant."

47. Campbell J. Gibson and Emily Lennon, *Historical Census Statistics on the Foreign-born Population of the United States: 1850–1990* (Washington, DC: U.S. Bureau of the Census, 1999), www.census.gov/population/www/documentation/twps0029/twps0029.html.

48. Alejandro Portes and Rubén Rumbaut, *Immigrant America: A Portrait,* 3rd ed. (Berkeley: University of California Press, 2006), 367.

49. "Carter Ends Mexican Summit without Arranging Oil Purchase," *Crimson,* February 17, 1979.

50. Jimmy Carter, "Communication to Congress," quoted in David Gutiérrez, *Walls and Mirrors: Mexican Americans, Mexican Immigrants, and the Politics of Ethnicity* (Berkeley: University of California Press, 1995), 200.

51. Fuchs quote in Richard L. Strout, "Punish the Alien's Boss," *Christian Science Monitor,* November 7, 1980.

52. Quoted in Daniel J. Tichenor, *Dividing Lines: The Politics of Immigration Control in America* (Princeton, NJ: Princeton University Press, 2002), 250.

53. Tichenor, *Dividing Lines,* 250.

54. "Notre Dame's President Offers Solutions on Aliens," *New York Times,* August 24, 1981.

55. Howard Swindle, "Los Angeles Swells with Aliens," *Dallas Morning News,* May 31, 1980. On the history of the Border Patrol, see Kelly Lytle Hernández,

Migra!: A History of the Border Patrol (Berkeley: University of California Press, 2010).

56. Peter H. Schuck, *Citizens, Strangers, and In-Betweens: Essays on Immigration and Citizenship* (Boulder, CO: Westview Press, 1998), 12; William A. V. Clark, "Residential Patterns: Avoidance, Assimilation, and Succession," in *Ethnic Los Angeles,* ed. Roger Waldinger and Mehdi Bozorgmehr (New York: Russell Sage, 1996), 115; Lindsey, "Brown Power."

57. Donnel Nunes, "U.S. Puts Number of Illegal Aliens under 5 Million," *Washington Post,* January 31, 1980.

58. "Testimony of William French Smith, Attorney General, before the Senate Subcommittee on Immigration and Refugee Policy . . . ," July 30, 1981, in Nicholas Laham, *Ronald Reagan and the Politics of Immigration Reform* (Westport, CT: Prager, 2000), 48; Nunes, "U.S. Puts Number of Illegal Aliens under 5 Million."

59. Lawrence H. Fuchs, "Select Commission on Immigration and Refugee Policy: Development of a Fundamental Legislative Policy," *Willamette Law Review* 17 (1980): 141–150 (quote 144).

60. James Nelson Goodsell, "Mexico Is Expected to Squelch Any Reagan Hopes of More Oil," *Christian Science Monitor,* December 26, 1980; Alan Riding, "Mexico Brings Trump Card, Oil, to Talks with U.S.," *New York Times,* January 5, 1981; Brad Knickerbocker, "Reagan Eyes Proposals for Guest Workers," *Christian Science Monitor,* May 22, 1981.

61. On the conflict within the Reagan White House over the recommendations of the task force, including how to deal with "illegal aliens," see Thomas R. Maddux, "Ronald Reagan and the Task Force on Immigration, 1981," *Pacific Historical Review* 74 (May 2005): 195–236. For a comprehensive overview of the four-year legislative history of the Immigration Reform and Control Act, see Nancy Humel Montwieler, *The Immigration Reform Law of 1986* (Washington, DC: Bureau of National Affairs, 1987).

62. "Immigration Hikes Urged: Doubled Canadian, Mexican Quotas Proposed," *Dallas Morning News,* January 26, 1982; Jack M. Kneece, "Hispanic Group Calls Reagan Plan 'Most Repressive,'" *Dallas Morning News,* July 31, 1981 (quote). On the politics of immigration reform in the 1980s, see Daniel J. Tichenor, *Dividing Lines: The Politics of Immigration Control in America* (Princeton, NJ: Princeton University Press, 2002), 242–288.

63. Quotes in Laham, *Ronald Reagan,* 47–48.

64. "Text of the Second Reagan-Mondale Debate," *Washington Post,* October 22, 1984.

65. Marlene Cimons, "Senate Votes Amnesty for Aliens, Sets Ceiling on Annual Immigration," *Los Angeles Times,* August 18, 1982.

66. Juan F. Perea, ed., *Immigrants Out!: Nativism and the Anti-Immigrant Impulse in the United States* (New York: New York University Press, 1997), 2; Laham, *Ronald Reagan,* 166–170.

67. John M. Crewdson, "Critics Attack Reagan on Immigration Reform," *New York Times,* August 1, 1981.

68. Quoted in Laham, *Ronald Reagan,* 57.

69. Cimons, "Senate Votes Amnesty for Aliens." MALDEF president Vilma Martinez took issue with the amnesty provision because it "takes all undocumented, regardless of their equities, and requires them to serve in a 10-year temporary status without full protection of their labor and civil rights." Kneece, "Hispanic Group Calls Reagan Plan 'Most Repressive.'"

70. Tichenor, *Dividing Lines,* 263.

71. Task Force on Undocumented Workers. Quote in Laham, *Ronald Reagan,* 64.

72. Jack Boettnet, "President's Immigration, Refugee Plans Criticized," *Los Angeles Times,* September 26, 1981. Others argued that "there is no such thing as a temporary worker program." See Douglas S. Massey and Zai Liang, "The Long-Term Consequences of a Temporary Worker Program: The U.S. Bracero Experience," *Population Research and Policy Review* 8 (September 1989): 199–226.

73. Boettnet, "President's Immigration, Refugee Plans Criticized."

74. James Fallows, "Immigration Bill Stirs Up Melting Pot of Controversy," *Los Angeles Times,* February 5, 1984; Robert Pear, "Immigration Bill Is Hardly Home Free," *New York Times,* April 8, 1984; Robert Pear, "The Immigration Bill's Melting Pot," *New York Times,* July 2, 1984 (Kemp and Hance quotes).

75. Schuck, *Citizens, Strangers, and In-Betweens,* 94. For a chronology of legislation from 1972 to the passage of IRCA, see Robert Pear, "The Immigration Bill: Step by Step," *New York Times,* October 21, 1986.

76. The "Texas Proviso" of the McCarran-Walter Act (1952) stipulated that employers committed no crime in hiring unauthorized immigrants so long as they did not smuggle, transport, or "harbor" them. Kitty Calavita, *Inside the State: The Bracero Program, Immigration, and the I.N.S* (1992; reprint, New Orleans, LA: Quid Pro Quo Books, 2010), 71–75; Luis Plascencia, *Disenchanting Citizenship: Mexican Migrants and the Boundaries of Belonging* (New Brunswick, NJ: Rutgers University Press, 2012), 10; Michael C. LeMay, *Anatomy of a Public Policy: The Reform of Contemporary American Immigration Law* (Westport, CT: Praeger, 1994), 10.

77. See, for example, Jay Matthews, "Upsurge in Illegal Aliens Is Reported: Word Gets Home That Work Is Easy to Find despite New Law," *Washington Post,* July 9, 1987; Patrick McDonnell, "Border Arrests of Illegal Aliens up 2 Months in Row," *Los Angeles Times,* March 2, 1988; "Illegal Aliens: Still Coming," *Economist,* no. 7799 (February 1993), 26.

78. United States Government Accounting Office, *Immigration Reform: Employer Sanctions and the Question of Discrimination: Report to the Congress* (Washington, DC: Government Printing Office, 1990), 3–4; "IRCA-related

Discrimination: Actions Have Been Taken to Address IRCA-related Discrimination, But More is Needed," Statement of Lowell Dodge, Director, Administration of Justice Issues, before the Subcommittee on Immigration and Refugee Affairs, Committee on the Judiciary, U.S. Senate (Washington, DC: Government Printing Office, 1992): 1–8.

79. Muzaffar Chishti, "Immigrant Sanctions against Immigrant Workers," *WorkingUSA* (March/April 2000): 71–76; Michael J. Wishnie, "Prohibiting the Employment of Unauthorized Immigrants: The Experiment Fails," *University of Chicago Legal Forum* (January 2007): 193–640.

80. Fay S. Joyce, "Jesse Jackson Crosses into Mexico to Denounce an Immigration Bill," *New York Times,* May 15, 1984.

81. Peter Schuck, "The Politics of Rapid Legal Change: Immigration Policy in the 1980s," in Marck Landy and Martin Levin, eds., *The New Politics of Public Policy* (Baltimore, MD: Johns Hopkins University Press, 1995), 49–50, quoted in Tichenor, *Dividing Lines,* 262.

82. Douglas S. Massey, Jorge Durand, and Nolan J. Malone, *Beyond Smoke and Mirrors: Mexican Immigration in an Era of Economic Integration* (New York: Russell Sage, 2002), 91–93.

83. Tichenor, *Dividing Lines,* 267–274 (quotes on 274); Timothy J. Henderson, *Beyond Borders: A History of Mexican Migration to the United States* (Malden, MA: Wiley-Blackwell, 2011), 115–117.

84. Massey et al., *Beyond Smoke and Mirrors,* 84.

85. "Ilegal Border Traffic Rising Again; Population Pressures in Mexico Are Forcing More Young Workers North to Find Employment," *Christian Science Monitor,* October 16, 1991; David Johnston, "Border Crossings Near Old Record," *New York Times,* February 9, 1992; Jorge G. Castañeda, "Again, People Are Mexico's No. 1 Export," *Los Angeles Times,* March 24, 1992.

86. John Dillin, "U.S. Beefs Up Border Patrol after Protests from States about Costs of Immigration," *Christian Science Monitor,* February 7, 1994.

87. David Clark Scott, "Mexico Unhappy with U.S. Border Policy," *Christian Science Monitor,* March 15, 1994.

8. Fortress America

1. Hans P. Johnson, *Undocumented Immigration to California: 1980–1993* (San Francisco: Public Policy Institute of California, 1996): 1–132; Rebecca Trounson, "California's Population Growth to Slow in Coming Decades," *Los Angeles Times,* April 25, 2012.

2. Frank del Olmo, "Se Habla Inglés: Prop. 63, a Cruel Joke, Could Cost Us Dearly," *Los Angeles Times,* August 28, 1986.

3. Geoffrey Pullum, *The Great Eskimo Vocabulary Hoax and Other Irreverent Essays on the Study of Language* (Chicago: University of Chicago Press, 1991), 118.

4. "California Makes English Official Language of State," *Toronto Star,* November 5, 1986; Marcia Chambers, "California Braces for Change with English as Official Language," *New York Times,* November 26, 1986.

5. Six other states declared English their official language: Georgia, Illinois, Indiana, Kentucky, Nebraska, and Virginia. John R. Emshwiller, "California Voters Expected to Make English the State's Official Language," *Wall Street Journal,* October 31, 1986. One of the earliest signs of language nativism occurred in south Florida when Dade County voters rescinded a resolution that declared the county to be officially bilingual. Olmo, "Se Habla Inglés."

6. Geoffrey Nunberg, "An 'Official Language' for California?" *New York Times,* October 2, 1986; "Putting English First," *Washington Post,* November 12, 1988; "No Official Language: A Federal Judge Knocks Down Arizona's English-only Law," *Time,* February 19, 1990, 82.

7. Russell Baker, "Dealing with California," *New York Times,* December 7, 1986.

8. For a full text of the memo, see " 'Witan Memo' III," *Southern Poverty Law Center,* October 10, 1986, www.splcenter.org/get-informed/intelligence -report/browse-all-issues/2002/summer/the-puppeteer/witan-memo-iii.

9. Zita Arocha, "Chavez Quits U.S. English Organization: Ex-Reagan Aide Objected to Memo," *Washington Post,* October 20, 1988; Justin Akers Chacón and Mike Davis, *No One Is Illegal: Fighting Racism and State Violence on the U.S.-Mexico Border* (Chicago, IL: Haymarket Books, 2006), 245–246.

10. Quoted in Jeff Biggers, *State Out of the Union: Arizona and the Final Showdown over the American Dream* (New York: Nation Books, 2012), 70–71; Tony Castro, "Hispanics in California Now Match White Population," *VOXXI,* July 3, 2013. Whites were already less than 50 percent of the population in California by 2000. See Todd S. Purdum, "Non-Hispanic Whites a Minority, California Census Figures Show," *New York Times,* March 30, 2001.

11. Robin Dale Jacobson, *The New Nativism: Proposition 187 and the Debate over Immigration* (Minneapolis: University of Minnesota Press, 2008); and Jeffrey R. Margolis, "Closing the Doors to the Land of Opportunity: The Constitutional Controversy Surrounding Proposition 187," *University of Miami Inter-American Law Review* 26 (Winter 1994): 363–401.

12. Peter Schrag, *Not Fit for Our Society: Immigration and Nativism in America* (Berkeley: University of California Press, 2010), 170–171.

13. Joseph Nevins, *Operation Gatekeeper: the Rise of the 'Illegal Alien' and the Making of the U.S.-Mexico Boundary* (New York: Routledge, 2002), 87.

14. Joan Beck, "Proposition 187: Hidden Backlash," *Times-Picayune,* November 5, 1994.

15. Quotes from Jacobson, *New Nativism,* 31, 34, 43.

16. "Why Proposition 187 Won't Work," *New York Times,* November 20, 1994; Patrick J. McDonnell, "Proposition 187 Measure Passes despite California Diversity," *Los Angeles Times,* November 13, 1984.

17. Ron Unz, "Proposition 187 Brings Us to a Moral Precipice," *Orange County Register,* October 30, 1994.

18. James E. Garcia, "Kemp, Bennett Unlikely Allies with Proposition 187 Opponents," *Austin American-Statesman,* November 20, 1994.

19. Philip Martin, "Proposition 187 in California," *International Migration Review* 29 (Spring 1995): 255–263 (Clinton quote, 258); Roberto Suro and Dan Balz, "Proposition 187 Dominates, Divides California Races," *Austin-American Statesman,* November 3, 1994; "Nueva Marcha de Estudiantes en Los Angeles, Contra la 187," *La Jornada,* November 3, 1994; Roberto Suro, "Latino Marches Add Unpredictable Element as Proposition 187 Vote Nears," *Washington Post,* November 5, 1994; "Judge Blocks Most of California's Prop. 187," *Salt Lake Tribune,* December 15, 1994.

20. Jorge Durand, Douglas S. Massey, and Emilio A. Parrado, "The New Era of Mexican Migration to the United States," *Journal of American History* 86 (September 1999), 532; Norman Caufield, *NAFTA and Labor in North America* (Urbana: University of Illinois Press, 2010), 103–104.

21. Schrag, *Not Fit for Our Society,* 171.

22. "Latin American Leaders Attack California's New Proposition 187," *Star Tribune,* December 10, 1994.

23. Ugo Pipitone, "187: la Limpieza Étnica del Vecino," November 1, 1994, *Diario de Juárez,* December 2, 1994; Juan José Hinojosa, "187: La Raíz del Problema," *Proceso,* November 14, 1994; Emilio Pradilla Cobos, "Neoliberalismo, TLC [NAFTA], y Xenofobia en EU," November 3, 1994, November 5, 1994; and Elena Gallegos y Emilio Lomas, "Reitera México su Rechazo a la Propuesta 187," *La Jornada,* November 10, 1994.

24. Alicia Di Raddo, "The Times Poll: Fear of Crime Is the Unifying Factor in O.C.," *Los Angeles Times,* October 25, 1993.

25. For an insightful analysis of Latino stereotypes in film, see Charles Ramirez-Berg, *Latino Images in Film: Stereotypes, Subversion, and Resistance* (Austin: University of Texas Press, 2002), esp. 66–86.

26. For a history of policing the U.S.-Mexico border, see Kelly Lytle Hernández, *Migra!: A History of the Border Patrol* (Berkeley: University of California Press, 2010); and Peter Andreas, *Border Games: Policing the U.S.-Mexico Divide* (Ithaca, NY: Cornell University Press, 2000).

27. On Clinton's immigration policy, see Office the President, *Accepting the Immigration Challenge: The President's Report on Immigration* (Washington, DC: Government Printing Office, 1994): 1–66.

28. Nevins, *Operation Gatekeeper,* 61–94; Bill Ong Hing, *Defining America through Immigration Policy* (Philadelphia, PA: Temple University Press, 2004), 184–205; "La Operación Guardían, tan Nociva como la Propuesta 187, *La Jornada,* November 6, 1994.

29. Wayne Cornelius, "Death at the Border: Efficacy and Unintended Consequences of U.S. Immigration Control Policy," *Population and Development*

Review 27, no. 4 (December 2001): 661–685; Wendy Brown, *Walled States, Waning Sovereignty* (New York: Zone Books, 2010), 110 (quote); Hing, *Defining America,* 189; B. Drummond Ayres, Jr., "Stepped-up Border Staff Cuts Illegal Crossings," *Austin American-Statesman,* December 13, 1994; Elise Ackerman, "Finally, an Effective Fence," *U.S. News and World Report,* October 19, 1998. For a narrative account of fourteen Mexicans, the "Yuma 14," abandoned by their "coyote" and left to die in the Arizona desert, see Luis Alberto Urrea, *The Devil's Highway: A True Story* (Boston, MA: Little, Brown, 2004).

30. Karl Eschbach, Jacqueline Hagan et al., "Death at the Border," *International Migration Review* 33, no. 2 (Summer 1999): 430–454: and Cornelius, "Death at the Border," 29.

31. Richard Rodriguez, "The 'Great Wall of America' and the Threat from Within," *Los Angeles Times,* September 5, 2010.

32. Susan Ferriss, "Mexican Farmers Charge NAFTA Wrecking Corn Trade: Free Trade Erodes Traditional Base of Rural Economy," *Edmonton Journal,* September 7, 2003.

33. Demetrios G. Papademetriou, John J. Audley, Sandra Polaski, and Scott Vaughan, *NAFTA's Promise and Reality: Lessons from Mexico for the Hemisphere* (Washington, DC: Carnegie Endowment for International Peace, 2004), 6, 48; Caufield, *NAFTA and Labor in North America,* 103–106; Belinda Coote, *NAFTA: Poverty and Free Trade in Mexico* (Oxford: Oxfam Publications, 1995), 21–22; Mike Davis, "The Great Wall of Capital," in *Against the Wall: Israel's Barrier to Peace,* ed. Michael Sorkin (New York: New Press, 2005), 90–97.

34. Elisabeth Malkin, "Nafta's Promise, Unfulfilled," *New York Times,* March 23, 2009.

35. Lawrence Downes, "Immigration Standoff in Phoenix," *New York Times,* December 10, 2007.

36. U.S. Congress, *Illegal Immigration Reform and Immigrant Responsibility Act of 1996, Conference Report,* 104th Cong., 2nd sess. (Washington, DC: Government Printing Office, 1996); Austin T. Fragomen, Jr., "The Illegal Immigration Reform and Immigrant Responsibility Act of 1996: An Overview," *International Migration Review* 31 (Summer 1997): 438–460.

37. Carolyn Wong, *Lobbying for Inclusion: Rights Politics and the Making of Immigration Policy* (Stanford, CA: Stanford University Press, 2006), ch. 6; Nina Newton, *Illegal, Alien, or Immigrant: The Politics of Immigration Reform* (New York: New York University Press, 2008), ch. 4; Durand et al., "The New Era of Mexican Migration to the United States"; "INS Reverses Earlier Decision to Release Criminal Immigrants," *Boca Raton News,* February 18, 1999.

38. Timothy A. Hacsi, *Children as Pawns: The Politics of Educational Reform* (Cambridge, MA: Harvard University Press, 2001), 91–94; Deidre Martinez, *Who Speaks for Hispanics? Hispanic Interest Groups in Washington* (Albany, NY: SUNY Press, 2009), 100–101.

39. For an analysis of Bush's proposed reform of the agricultural worker program, see Camille J. Bosworth, "Guest Worker Policy: A Critical Analysis of President Bush's Proposed Reform," *Hastings Law Review* 56 (May 2005): 1095–1120; Dan Eggen and Helen Dewar, "Bush Weighing Plan for Mexican Guest Workers," *Washington Post,* July 25, 2001.

40. Quoted in Brown, *Walled States, Waning Sovereignty,* 116–117.

41. Brian T. Connor, "A New Pearl Harbor? Analogies, Narratives, and Meanings of 9/11 in Civil Society," *Cultural Sociology* 6, no. 1 (March 2012): 3–25. On the military perspective of the comparison, see Fred L. Borch, "Comparing Pearl Harbor and '9/11,': Intelligence Failure? American Unpreparedness? Military Responsibility?" *Journal of Military History* 67, no. 3 (July 2002): 845–860.

42. Elizabeth C. Borja, *Brief Documentary History of the Department of Homeland Security, 2001–2008* (Washington, DC: Government Printing Office, 2008), 2–32; Stephen Dinan, "New Mexico Leader Hits Lax Border Security," *Washington Times,* August 22, 2005.

43. "Homeland Chief Vows Border Crackdown," *New York Daily News,* August 24, 2005.

44. The priority mission of CBP can be found on their website: www.cbp .gov/xp/cgov/about/.

45. Duncan Hunter, "Terrorists Work to Infiltrate Southern U.S. Border," *Washington Times,* June 12, 2008.

46. George Cahlink, "New Homeland Security Chairman Sees Larger Role for UAVs in Border Security," *Defense Daily,* October 14, 2005.

47. Davis, "The Great Wall of Capital," 93.

48. George W. Bush, "Renewing America's Purpose," *On the Issues,* February 9, 2000, www.ontheissues.org/Archive/Purpose_George_W__Bush.htm.

49. Robert Pear and Carl Hulse, "Immigration Bill Fails to Survive Senate Vote," *New York Times,* June 28, 2007.

50. Rachel L. Swarns, "Tough Border Security Bill Nears Passage in the House," *New York Times,* December 14, 2005. For an overview of the bill and the protest marches that followed its passage in the House, see Leo R. Chavez, *The Latino Threat: Constructing Immigrants, Citizens, and the Nation* (Stanford, CA: Stanford University Press, 2008), 152–176.

51. Table 8.1: "Selected Immigrant Rights Marches, Spring 2006," 36, in Xóchitl Bada, Jonathan Fox, and Andrew Selee, *Invisible No More: Mexican Migrant Civil Participation in the United States* (Washington, DC: Woodrow Wilson International Center for Scholars, 2006); "Churches Take Immigration Reform Fight into the Streets," *National Catholic Reporter,* March 31, 2006; Adrian D. Pantoja and Cecilia Menjívar, "The Spring Marches of 2006: Latinos, Immigration, and Political Mobilization in the 21st Century," *American Behavioral Scientist* 52, no. 4 (December 2008): 499–506.

52. Roberto Suro, "Out of the Shadows, into the Light," in *Rallying for Immigrant Rights: The Fight for Inclusion in 21st Century America,* ed. Kim Voss and Irene Bloemraad (Berkeley: University of California Press, 2011), 251.

53. Richard Rodriguez, "Mexicans in America," *Cato Unbound,* August 14, 2006 (quote), www.cato-unbound.org/. For an analysis of the bills main provisions, see Allen Thomas O'Rourke, "Good Samaritans Beware: The Sensenbrenner-King Bill and Assistance to Undocumented Immigrants," *Harvard Latino Law Review* 9 (Spring 2006): 195–208.

54. "Senator Kennedy Rallies for Immigration Reform," April 10, 2006, www.tedkennedy.org/ownwords/event/immigration_rally.

55. Quoted in Suro, "Out of the Shadows," 255.

56. Michael A. Fletcher and Jonathan Weisman, "Bush Signs Bill Authorizing 700-Mile Fence for Border," *Washington Post,* October 27, 2006.

57. On the DREAMer immigrant youth movement, see Walter J. Nicholls, *The DREAMers: How the Undocumented Youth Movement Transformed the Immigrant Rights Debate* (Stanford, CA: Stanford University, 2013).

58. Herbert A. Sample, "Governor Talks of Closing Mexico Border," *Sacramento Bee,* April 20, 2005, quoted in Chavez, *Latino Threat,* 142–143; David Von Drehle, "The Great Wall of America," *Time,* June 19, 2008; Carolina Gomez y Laura Poy, "Una Nueva Barda Provocará que haya más Pérdida de Vidas," *La Jornada,* October 1, 2006 (quote); "Califican de 'Inhumano' del Muro en la Frontera," *El Universal,* October 1, 2006; and "Gobiernos de América Latina Rechazan el Muro: 'Erróneo y Lamentable', Dicen," *La Jornada,* October 5, 2006.

59. Peter Andreas, *Border Games: Policing the U.S.-Mexico Divide* (Ithaca, NY: Cornell University Press, 2000), 51–84.

60. Richard Rodriguez, "The 'Great Wall of America' and the Threat from Within," *Los Angeles Times,* September 5, 2010.

61. See website for Minuteman Project, minutemanproject.com/jim-gilchrist.

62. Harel Shapira, *Waiting for José: The Minutemen's Pursuit of America* (Princeton, NJ: Princeton University Press, 2013), 2.

63. Quoted in Roxanne Lynn Doty, *The Law into Their Own Hands: Immigration and the Politics of Exceptionalism* (Tucson: University of Arizona Press, 2009), 59–60.

64. Quoted in Peter Monaghan, "Minding America," *Chronicle of Higher Education,* April 22, 2013.

65. Shapira, *Waiting for José,* 22.

66. Ibid., 121.

67. Quoted in David Holthouse, "Minutemen, Other Anti-Immigrant Militia Groups Stake Out Arizona Border," *Intelligence Report,* no. 118 (Summer 2005), Southern Poverty Law Center, www.splcenter.org.

68. A photograph of the Arizona Minuteman wearing the T-shirt can be found in Chavez, *Latino Threat,* 141.

69. "Bush Decries Border Project," *Washington Times,* March 25, 2005.

70. For a summary of the bill's main provisions, see Mara Knaub, "SB 1070: What It Says," *Tribune Business News,* May 30, 2010. For a complete text of the bill, see www.azleg.gov/legtext/49leg/2r/bills/sb1070s.pdf. On nativist and antifederal government politics leading to the passage of SB 1070, see Biggers, *State out of the Union.*

71. Lisa Magaña, "Arizona's Immigration Policies and SB 1070," in *Latino Politics and Arizona's Immigration Law, SB 1070,"* ed. Lisa Magaña and Erik Lee (New York: Springer, 2013), 20.

72. Tom Barry, "Securing Arizona: What Americans Can Learn from Their Rogue State," *Boston Review* (March/April 2011): 30–39; Tim Alberta, "Rubio Stares Down the Right over 'Undocumented Democrats,'" *National Journal,* January 18, 2003.

73. Quoted in Randal C. Archibold, "Arizona Enacts Stringent Law on Immigration," *New York Times,* April 23, 2010.

74. Tellingly, the bill did not ban courses on Native Americans, African Americans, or Asian Americans. For the text of the bill, see http://www.tuc sonsentinel.com/local/report/042910_1070_text/text-sb-1070-arizona-illegal -immigration-law/.

75. Biggers, *State out of the Union,* 179; James E. Garcia, "Banning Ethnic Studies Won't End Idea," *Arizona Republic,* February 4, 2014. See also Cindy Carcamo, "Ethnic Studies Ban Is Upheld: A Judge Finds Most of an Arizona Law to be Constitutional," *Los Angeles Times,* March 13, 2013; and Lourdes Medrano, "Tucson District in Turmoil over State Ban on Ethnic Studies," *Christian Science Monitor,* May 4, 2011.

76. National Council of State Legislatures, *Immigrant Policy Project,* September 6, 2013, www.ncsl.org/issues-research/immig/immgration-report-august -2013.aspx; "Anti-Illegal Immigration Laws in States," *New York Times,* April 22, 2012.

77. Paul Taylor, Ana Gonzalez-Barrera, Jeffrey S. Passel, and Mark Hugo Lopez, "An Awakened Giant: The Hispanic Electorate Is Likely to Double by 2030," *Pew Research Center,* November 14, 2012, www.pewhispanic.org/2012/11 /14/an-awakened-giant-the-hispanic-electorate-is-likely-to-double-by-2030/.

Epilogue

1. "Beyond the Melting Pot," *Time,* April 9, 1990; Jeffrey S. Passel, D'vera Cohn, and Ana Gonzalez-Barrera, "Net Migration from Mexico Falls to Zero— and Perhaps Less," *Pew Research Center,* April 23, 2012, www.pewhispanic .org/2012/04/23/net-migration-from-mexico-falls-to-zero-and-perhaps-less/.

2. Peter Brimelow, *Alien Nation: Common Sense about America's Immigration Disaster* (New York: Harper Perennial, 1996), xix.

3. Julia Preston, "Record Number of Foreigners Were Deported in 2011," *New York Times,* September 7, 2012; David Grant, "Deportations of Illegal Immigrants in 2012 Reach New US Record," *Christian Science Monitor,* December 24, 2012; Esther Yu-Hsi Lee, "United States Deported over 13,000 Unaccompanied Mexican Minors Last Year," *ThinkProgress,* July 25, 2013, thinkprogress.org/immigration/2013/07/25/2350861/13000-unaccompanied-mexican-minors-deported-from-us/; Mark Hugo Lopez and Anna Gonzalez-Barrera, "High Rate of Deportations Continue under Obama despite Latino Disapproval," *Pew Research Center,* September 19, 2013, www.pewresearch.org/fact-tank/2013.

4. William Perez and Daniel G. Solorzano, *We Are Americans: Undocumented Students Pursing the American Dream* (Sterling, VA: Stylus, 2009), xxv.

5. Quoted in Walter J. Nicholls, *The DREAMers: How the Undocumented Youth Movement Transformed the Immigrant Rights Debate* (Stanford, CA: Stanford University Press, 2013), 6; Michael Matza, "Study Details Demographics of 'Dreamer' Immigrants," *Philadelphia Inquirer,* August 14, 2013.

6. Quoted in Marie Friedman Marquardt et al., *Living 'Illegal': The Human Face of Unauthorized Immigration* (New York: New Press, 2013), 250.

7. "Trail of DREAMs Official Statement on SB 1070," *Trail of Dreams,* April 24, 2010, www.trail2010.org/blog/2010/apr/24/official-statement-sb1070-arizona/.

8. "Consideration of Deferred Action for Childhood Arrivals Process," *U.S. Citizenship and Immigration Services,* n.d., www.uscis.gov/humanitarian/consideration-deferred-action-childhood-arrivals-process.

9. "Remarks by the President on Immigration," *The White House,* June 15, 2012, www.whitehouse.gov/the-press-office/2012/06/15/remarks-president-immigration.

10. Gene Demby, "The Dream 9 Pushes the Envelope (and Their Allies' Buttons)," *NPR News,* August 20, 2013, www.npr.org/blogs/codeswitch/2013/08/20/; Cindy Carcamo, "'Dream 9' Released from Immigration Detention," *Los Angeles Times,* August 7, 2013. For the letter to President Obama, see www.scribd.com/doc/156837022/Letter-to-President-Obama-Re-DREAM-9#download; Lizbeth Mateo, twitter.com/LizbethMateo.

11. Robert P. Jones et al., *What Americans (Still) Want from Immigration Reform: American Public Opinion March–November 2013* (Washington, DC: Public Religion Research Institute, 2013), publicreligion.org/site/wp-content/uploads/2013/11/2013.Immigration_Phase2.WEB-copy.pdf. Text of letter: i2.cdn.turner.com/cnn/2013/images/12/05/gutierrez.remarks.and.letter.to.obama.pdf

12. "Is Obama Still Deporter in Chief?" *National Public Radio,* March 17, 2014, http://www.npr.org/2014/03/17/290860495/is-obama-still-deporter-in-chief.

13. "Rev. John Fife Continues Immigrant Humanitarian Work 25+ Years after Launching Sanctuary Movement," *Democracy Now!,* April 23, 2007, www.democracynow.org/2007/4/23/rev_john_fife_continues_immigrant_humanitarian#.

14. Jack Jenkins, "Welcoming the Newcomer: How Faith Groups Are Rallying the Religious behind Immigration Reform," *National Hispanic Christian Leadership Conference,* March 25, 2013, www.americanprogress.org/issues/religion/news/2013/03/25/57840/welcoming-the-newcomer-how-faith-groups-are-rallying-the-religious-behind-immigration-reform/>.

15. Sandy Strauss, "Nuns on the Border," *Pennsylvania Council of Churches, Ministry of Public Advocacy,* May 23, 2013, pachurchesadvocacy.org/weblog/?p=14995.

16. Lilly Fowler, "Methodist Bishop Minerva Carcaño on the Front Lines of Immigration Battle," *Religious News Service,* March 8, 2013, www.religionnews.com/2013/03/08/methodist-bishop-minerva-carcano-on-front-lines-of-immigration-battle/; Jack Jenkins, "Why Faith Groups Are Rallying behind Immigration Reform," *Religion and Politics,* November 13, 2013, religionandpolitics.org/2013/11/13/why-faith-groups-are-rallying-behind-immigration-reform/; idem, "Welcoming the Newcomer."

17. Quoted in Jenkins, "Why Faith Groups Are Rallying behind Immigration Reform"; "Rabbi to Risk Arrest as Thousands Rally on National Mall for Immigration Reform," *ImmigrationProf Blog,* October 5, 2013, lawprofessors.typepad.com/immigration/2013/10/national-mall-rally-on-october-8.html.

18. "Trends in Party Identification of Religious Groups," *Pew Research Center,* February 2, 2012, www.pewforum.org/2012/02/02/trends-in-party-identification-of-religious-groups/.

19. Public Religion Research Institute, "Republicans and Evangelicals Support a Path to Citizenship with Basic Requirements for Immigrants Living in the Country Illegally," *Public Religion Research Institute,* April 16, 2013, publicreligion.org/research/2013/04/april-2013-religion-politics-tracking-survey/; Jenkins, "Welcoming the Newcomer."

20. Quoted in Jenkins, "Why Faith Groups Are Rallying Behind Immigration Reform"; "Campaign for Citizenship," *PICO National Network,* www.piconetwork.org/issues/immigration; Greg Sargent, "A Conservative Christian in a Deep Red District Makes Case for Immigration Reform," *Washington Post,* August 23, 2013; Rep. Spencer Bachus, "Immigration," *Congressman Spencer Bachus,* March 13, 2013, bachus.house.gov/immigration/; Richard Fausset, "Alabama Enacts Anti-Illegal-Immigration Law Described as Nation's Strictest," *Los Angeles Times,* June 10, 2011.

21. "U.S. Census Bureau Projections Show a Slower Growing, Older, More Diverse Nation a Half Century from Now," *U.S. Census Bureau,* December 12, 2012, www.census.gov/newsroom/releases/archives/population/cb12-243.html;

Jonathan V. Last, *What to Expect When No One's Expecting: America's Coming Demographic Disaster* (New York: Encounter Books, 2013), 115.

22. Ibid.

23. "U.S. Census Bureau Projections"; "Employment Projections: 2012–2022 Summary," *Bureau of Labor Statistics,* December 19, 2013, www.bls .gov/news.release/ecopro.nr0.htm; Rakesh Kochhar, "Labor Force Growth Slows, Hispanic Share Grows," *Pew Research Center,* February 13, 2012, www .pewsocialtrends.org/2012/02/13/labor-force-growth-slows-hispanic-share -grows-2/; "Overview of the 2010–20 Projections," *Bureau of Labor Statistics,* March 29, 2012, www.bls.gov/ooh/about/projections-overview.htm.

24. See Dowell Myers, *Immigrants and Boomers: Forging a New Social Contract for the Future of America* (New York: Russell Sage Foundation, 2007).

25. Laird W. Bergad, *Hispanics in the United States: A Demographic, Social, and Economic History* (Cambridge: Cambridge University Press, 2010), 99–113; Gretchen Livingston and D'Vera Cohn, *U.S. Birth Rate Falls to a Record Low: Decline Is Greatest among Immigrants* (Washington, DC: Pew Research Center, 2012); Rodolfo Tuiran, Virgilio Partida, Octavio Mojarro, and Elena Zúñiga, "Fertility in Mexico: Trends and Forecast," 483–506, www.un.org/esa/popula tion/publications/completingfertility/RevisedTUIRAN-PARTIDApaper .PDF; Sabrina Tavernise, "Fertility Rate Stabilizes as the Economy Grows," *New York Times,* September 6, 2013.

26. Gosia Wozniacka, Elliot Spagat, and Amy Taxin, "California Latinos Show Deep Roots in US," *ABC News,* December 21, 2013, abcnews.go.com/ US/wireStory/california-latinos-show-deep-roots-us-21298668.

27. Alexandra Bjerg, "Hispanic-Owned Businesses Fueling the Economic Recovery in California," *California Economic Summit,* October 17, 2013, www .caeconomy.org/reporting/entry/hispanic-owned-businesses-fueling-the-eco nomic-recovery-in-california; StacyT, "Hispanic-Owned Businesses," *Hispanic Post,* October 18, 2013, www.hispanicpost.com/2013/10/hispanic-owned-busi nesses-fueling-the-economic-recovery-in-california/.

28. Patrick McGreevy, "Brown Signs California Immigration Bills, Wins Activists' Kudos in Pressing for Reform," *Washington Post*, October 6, 2013, www.washingtonpost.com/politics/brown-signs-california-immigration-bills -wins-activists-kudos-in-pressing-for-reform/2013/10/06/71b1dac8-2ecb-11e3 -9ccc-2252bdb14df5_story.html.

29. Timm Herdt, "Immigration Reform, Slowed in D.C., Moves Ahead in California," *San Francisco Examiner,* September 19, 2013, http://www.sfexam iner.com/sanfrancisco/immigration-reform-slowed-in-dc-moves-ahead-in -california/Content?oid=2582042; "California Gov. Jerry Brown Signs Slew Of Immigration Laws, Challenges Congress To Follow His Lead," *Fox News Latino,* October 7, 2013, www.latino.foxnews.com/latino/politics/2013/10/07/california -gov-jerry-brown-signs-laws-protecting-undocumented-immigrants-and/ (Brown quote).

30. Sharon Bernstein, "California Governor Urges Faster Immigration Reform," *Reuters,* May 14, 2013, www.reuters.com/article/2013/05/15/us-usa -immigration-california-idUSBRE94E02820130515.

31. "California Gov. Jerry Brown Signs Slew Of Immigration Laws, Challenges Congress To Follow His Lead," *Fox News Latino,* October 7, 2013, www .latino.foxnews.com/latino/politics/2013/10/07/california-gov-jerry-brown -signs-laws-protecting-undocumented-immigrants-and/.

32. Samuel P. Huntington, "The Hispanic Challenge," *Foreign Policy* (March/ April 2004): 30–45; Shirin Hakimzadeh and D'Vera Cohn, *English Usage among Hispanics in the United States* (Washington, DC: Pew Hispanic Center, 2007), i–iii; Anna Gorman, "Immigrants' Children Grow Fluent in English," *Los Angeles Times,* November 30, 2007; "MPI Date Hub, California," *Migration Policy Institute,* n.d., www.migrationinformation.org/datahub/state2.cfm?ID=CA.

33. Wendy Wang, "The Rise of Intermarriage," *Pew Research Center,* February 16, 2012, www.pewsocialtrends.org/2012/02/16/the-rise-of-intermarriage/; Simon Marcson, "A Theory of Intermarriage and Assimilation," *Social Forces* 29, no. 1 (1950): 75–78.

34. Kathleen Miles, "Unions Gain Latino Members, Could Be Unions' Saving Grace," *Huffington Post,* January 25, 2013, www.huffingtonpost.com/2013/01/25 /unions-latino-members-saving-grace_n_2543486.html; Chris Haller, "Labor Union Participation Helps Latino Immigrants Overcome Barriers to Civic Engagement," *EngagingCities,* December 21, 2011, engagingcities.com/article/labor -union-participation-helps-latino-immigrants-overcome-barriers-civic-engagement.

35. Jean Merl, "State Voting Law Spurs Change," *Los Angeles Times,* September 15, 2013; Elliot Spagat, "Latinos Still Face Electoral Hurdles in California," *Daily Democrat,* December 28, 2013.

36. Mark Z. Barabak, "Prop. 187 as a Pivot Point," *Los Angeles Times,* October 14, 2013; and Cathleen Decker, "Poll Shows Republicans Losing Ethnicity, Age Battle in California," *Los Angeles Times,* November 11, 2013.

37. Quoted in Lowell Ponte, "Mexamerica," *Front Page Magazine,* January 2, 2004, archive.frontpagemag.com/readArticle.aspx?ARTID=14775.

38. Mike Allen, "Lessons Learned from 2012," *Politico,* www.politico.com /news/stories/1112/83273_Page2.html.

39. "Mexicans in America," *Cato Unbound,* August 4, 2006, www.cato-un bound.org/2006/08/14/richard-rodriguez/mexicans-america.

40. "Beyond the Melting Pot," *Time,* April 9, 1990.

ACKNOWLEDGMENTS

Like most histories, *Mexicans in the Making of America* builds on the works of many scholars. I would like to acknowledge some of them: Teresa Palomo Acosta, Rodolfo Acuña, Tomás Almaquer, Luis Alvarez, Gabriela Arredondo, Alicia Schmidt Camacho, Albert Camarillo, Ernesto Chávez, John Chávez, Miroslava Chávez-García, Arnoldo De León, Ignacio García, Mario T. García, Matt García, Manuel García y Griego, Juan Gomez-Quiñones, Gibert G. González, Richard Griswold del Castillo, David Gutiérrez, Ramón Gutiérrez, Kelley Lytle Hernández, Carey Mc-Williams, Pablo Mitchell, Natalia Molina, Armando Navarro, Douglas Monroy, David Montejano, Maria Montoya, Anthony Mora, Michael Olivas, Lorena Oropeza, Monica Perales, Stephen Pitti, Raúl Ramos, Andrés Resendez, Vicki Ruiz, Guadalupe San Miguel Jr, George Sánchez, Zaragosa Vargas, and Emilio Zamora. I am especially thankful to those who have taken time to read all or parts of the manuscript, including Patrick Foley, John Chávez, David Gutiérrez, Tom Holt, Vicki Ruiz, Kenneth Andrien, Zaragosa Vargas, and Richard White. I would also like to thank the anonymous readers for Harvard University Press, and Joyce Seltzer, senior executive editor at Harvard University Press, whose high standards and wise counsel have made it a joy and privilege to work with her.

I have been fortunate to receive a number of research fellowships over the years that have provided time off from my teaching duties to conduct research in archives in the United States and Mexico. I would like to thank the John Simon Guggenheim Foundation, the National Endowment for the Humanities, the Woodrow Wilson International Center for Scholars, the Fulbright Senior Research Fellowship at the Centro de Investigación y Docencia Económicas in Mexico, the American Philosophical Society, the American Council of Learned Societies, and the Institute for Historical Studies at the University of Texas.

My colleagues in the Clements Department of History at Southern Methodist University and the Clements Center for Southwest Studies have been a source of encouragement and support, and have extended a warm welcome to me as a new member of the faculty. Thanks especially to Ken Andrien, John Chávez, Ed Countryman, Crista Deluzio, Jeffrey Engel, Andrew Graybill, Kenneth Hamilton, Tom Knock, Alexis McCrossen, John Mears, Dan Orlovsky, Sherry Smith, and Kathleen Wellman for their support of the graduate program in Borderlands/Southwest studies.

My sister Teresa and brother Patrick continue to support my need to study our past and share stories about growing up absurd as Hibernian Mexican Americans. Patrick has read every word of the book with a critical eye from his perch in southern California. His insights have been invaluable in helping me understand the changing culture and politics of his adopted state. Sister Teresa has kept me grounded with her traditional Mexican cooking and devotional practices, including getting me started on creating a home altar to remember who I am and where I come from.

My own family has been the bedrock of my life. The love and support of Angela and our three daughters—Sabina, Bianca, and Sophia—have sustained me over the years in more ways than I can adequately express, and for that I am deeply grateful. I am blessed beyond words for them.

INDEX

American Indian Movement (AIM), 163, 165–166, 176
American Jewish Congress (AJC), 156
American Me (film), 208
American Revolution, expansionism in wake of, 23–24
amnesty policies: backlash against, 200–201; border control issues and, 214–215; DREAM Act provisions for, 217, 224; immigration reform and proposals for, 179–180, 193–197; political discourse concerning, 5
Anaya, Toney, 189
"anchor babies" issue, 199, 204, 233–234
Anderson, Martin, 194
Andrade, Timoteo, 52–63, 66, 84, 257n45
Anglo Americans: American identity linked to, 6, 8; antiwar movement and, 175–178; Chicano movement and, 149; colonial history and privileging of, 13–27; fear of Mexican immigrants among, 6–8, 48–49, 219–220; Hispanophilia of, 34–36; history of Mexican immigration and, 2–3; land expropriation and westward expansion by, 31–33; Minutemen network and, 219–220; population comparison with Latinos, 4; post-independence Mexico and, 24–25; preservation of dominance through anti-immigration policies for, 48–50; projected minority status for, 203–204, 212–213, 219–239; racial stereotyping of Mexicans by, 33–34, 37–38, 48–51, 75–87; second-generation Mexican Americans and, 153; Spanish colonization and, 23–24; Texas Americanization and, 24–27; wartime security concerns over Mexicans by, 70
Anheuser-Busch brewing company, 188
Anti-Defamation League of B'nai B'rith, 187
antidiscrimination legislation: immigration reform and, 194–195; U.S.-Mexican relations and, 82–84
anti-immigration policies: cultural limits of, 11–12; early history of, 15–16; emergence in 1980s of,

179–182; European and Asian immigration restrictions and, 49; Good Neighbor policy as response to, 56–57; historical evolution of, 40; racial stereotyping in, 48–49; state-based initiatives, emergence of, 206–224
anti-Semitism, U.S. history of, 8
antiwar movement, 163; Chicano movement and, 174–178
"apochamiento," Mexican immigrants and process of, 10–11
Argentina, German ties with, 71
Arias Sierras, Daniel (Mrs.), 100
Arismendi, Ezequiel, 130
Arizona: Anglo American minority status in, 222–224; anti-immigrant vigilante groups in, 221; border crossings in, 3; English-only legislation in, 201–202, 212; illegal immigration legislation in, 200–224; Mexican border with, 3, 40; Spanish colonization in, 19; transborder migration in, 42
Arkansas, bracero workers in, 130
Armijo, Manuel, 29
Army McCarthy hearings, 143, 159
Arteaga Santoya, Armando, 107
Asian immigrants: citizenship restrictions and, 51, 62–63; discrimination against, 51, 62–63, 90, 155–156, 195; entry restrictions on, 49, 182; intermarriage by, 236–239; population growth of, 190
Asian Indians, racial classification of, 62–63
assimilation: immigrant patterns of, 9–10; intermarriage by immigrants and, 236–239; by Mexican Americans, 10–12; by Spanish colonials, 20–27
Associated Farmers of California, 145
Association of Mexican Farm Workers, 291n75
Austin, Stephen, 27
Ávila Camacho, Manuel: discrimination against Mexicans and, 64–66, 68, 71–73, 80–82, 85, 88–89, 93; Global Settlement program and, 121–122; illegal immigration and, 129, 145; Mexican military service in World War II and, 99, 101, 112, 120

California: Alien Land Laws in, 53–54; anti-immigration legislation in, 200–224, 234–239; Arizona border enforcement with, 222–224; bracero workers in, 130; defense industries in, Mexican workers at, 116; demographic projections for, 233–239; discrimination against Mexicans in, 88, 90–95; garment industry labor issues in, 191; illegal immigrant labor in, 146–147; internment of Japanese immigrants in, 90; Latino/a elected officials in, 189–190, 222–224, 237–239; mestizos in, 22–23; Mexican border with, 3; Mexican immigrant workers in, 43, 81–82, 84; Mexican military service in World War II and, 98–100, 104, 113–114; Mexican property rights in, 53–54; as Mexican territory, 26–27; school segregation in, 154–156; Spanish colonial heritage in, 36–37; statehood for, 32–33; U.S. acquisition of, 27–31; World War II security concerns in, 71

Camarota, Steven, 213

"Camino Americano: March for Immigrant Dignity and Respect.," 231

"Campaign for Citizenship," 232

Canada: bilingualism in, 201; colonization of, 13; Mexican military service in, 99–100; U.S. immigration quotas with, 193–194

Cananea Consolidate Copper Company, 42

Cano, Pedro, 283n99

Cano del Castillo, A., 93

Carcaño, Minerva, 230–231

Caribbean: colonization history in, 13; immigrant migration patterns from, 8; U.S. intervention in, 65

Carmichael Stokely, 165

Carranza, Venustiano, 46

Carrasco, Ernesto, 110

Carter, Jimmy, 190–191

Carvajal, Felipe, 99

Castañeda, Carlos, 89

Castillo, Leon, 182

Castillo Nájera, Francisco, 57–60, 66, 72, 84–85, 108

Castro, Sal, 173

Catholic Church: Mexican anticlerical policies and, 48; Mexicans' conversion to, 23–27; Mexican traditional practices and, 35–36; pro-immigrant movements and, 230–231; segregation of Mexican members in, 78, 85

Celler, Emanuel, 138

Cempoalan people, 17

Center for Immigration Studies, 202, 213

Center for North American Border Studies, 197

Central American immigrants: faith-based support for, 230; migration patterns of, 8; population growth of, 191–192

Chapel of San Miguel, 20

Chavez, Cesar, 147; economic empowerment and, 164–165; political activities of, 171–178; Tijerina and, 168; United Farm Workers Union and, 148, 160–164, *161, 163*

Chavez, Dennis, 73

Chávez, Eddie, 168

Chávez Rivera, Benito, 106, 279n45

Chertoff, Michael, 213

Chicano Associated Student Organization, 178

Chicano movement, 148–178; Alianza Federal de Mercedes and, 168–169; Crusade for Justice and, 169–170; decline of, 176–178; National Council of La Raza and, 183–184; political careers within, 170–178; student organizations in, 172; Vietnam War military service and, 173–174

children of immigrants: Americanization of, 9–10, 153–155, 212; deportation of, 227–239

Chinese Exclusion Act (1882), 49

Chinese immigrants: citizenship restrictions on, 51, 59, 62–63; entry restrictions on, 49, 60; as laborers, 44; in Mexico, 46; racist policies concerning, 16

Christian Science Monitor, on U.S.-Mexican relations, 68

Churchill, Winston, 82

Cinco de Mayo celebrations, 8–9

Cisneros, Henry G., 189

citizenship. *See also* "path to citizenship"
policies: defense industry requirements for, 115–116; for illegal
immigrants, 227–239; Mexican
immigrants' push for, 206; military
service in World War II linked to,
96–104, 108–111; for resident Mexican
nationals, postwar policies concerning, 116–117; restrictions on, for
immigrant populations, 39, 51–63, 147
citrus industry, Mexican labor in, 43
Civil Homeland Defense group, 219–221
Civil Rights Act of 1964, 164, 183
civil rights movement: bracero workers
and, 139–140; California discrimination against Mexicans and, 91;
Chicano movement and, 160–164,
177–178; immigration policies and,
181–182, 194–195; Latinos and, 183;
Mexican immigrants and Mexican
Americans and, 63, 69–70, 148;
pro-immigration activism and,
229–239; school segregation and,
155–158; Texas discrimination against
Mexicans and, 87–89
Civil War, Mexican military service in,
118–119
Clements, William, 192
Clinton, Bill, 198–199, 201, 204, 208, 210
Coca-Cola, Hispanic marketing by, 184
Cold War era, Mexican immigrants as, 5
colonization of America: by Europeans,
15–27; history of, 13–27
Colorado, English-only legislation in,
201–202
Colorado Civil Rights Commission,
186–187
Colors (film), 208
Columbus Day, Hispanic perspective on,
184
Comisión Nacional de Colonización, 144
Comité Contra la Penetración Nazi- Fas-
cista (Committee against Nazi- Fascist
Penetration), 71
Comité de Habla Hispana of the United
Packinghouse Workers of America,
142
Comité de Vecinos de Lemon Grove
(The Lemon Grove Neighbors
Committee), 154

Comité Mexicano Contra el Racismo
(Mexican Committee against Racism),
85, 89
Comité pro México de Afuera (Commit-
tee for the Protection of Mexicans
Living Abroad), 85, 291n75
Committee for the Survival of a Free
Congress (CSFC), 187–188
Committee on Inter-American Rela-
tions, 87
Communism: civil rights movement
and, 159; decline of anticommunist
movement and, 168–169; FBI
investigations of, 92; Operation
Wetback and fear of, 142–143
Community Service Organization
(CSO), 160
Confederación de Trabajadores
Mexicanos en Norte América, 99, 126
Congreso Nacional de Pueblos de Habla
Española (National Spanish- Speaking
People's Congress), 99
Congressional Medal of Honor: for
Latino veterans, 159; for Mexican
veterans, 117–119, *118,* 283n99
Congress of Industrial Organizations
(CIO), 139. *See also* American
Federation of Labor and Congress of
Industrial Organizations (AFL-CIO)
Connor, Roger, 197–198
contract labor clause, Mexican laborers
and, 44
Convención Nacional Democrática
(National Democratic Convention),
207
Coors, Joseph, 187
Coors, Peter, 189
Coors, William, 187–188
Coors Brewing Company, national
boycott of, 184, 186–189
Corona, Bert, 168
Coronado, Francisco Vásquez de, 15,
19–20
Corpus Christi Caller newspaper, 87
corridos (ballads), 33
Cortés, Hernán, 16–18, 20
Cortés Moctezuma, Isabel Tolosa, 20–21
Cortez, Gregorio, 33
Cortez, Romaldo, 33
Cortina, Juan, 33

Cortines, Ruiz, 142, 144, 291n75
coyotes, illegal immigration and use of, 209
Cranston, Alan, 91
criminal activities by immigrants, stereotypes concerning, 34, 91, 149, 207
criminal penalties: in antidiscrimination laws, 83, 113; criminalization of illegal immigration and, 5, 211–224, 234–239
Criollo Spaniards, ethnic identity of, 22
"Cristero Rebellion," 48
Cronkite, Walter, 192
cross-border workers. *See also* guest worker proposals: draft policies in World War II concerning, 102; legalization for, 192–193
Crusade for Justice, 169–170
Cuauhtémoc, 18
Cuba, U.S. relations with, 65
Cuban immigrants: in Florida, 202; "marielitios" immigration and, 190; population growth of, 191–192
cultural discourse: anti-immigrant themes in, 207–208; Arizona SB 1070 proposals for, 223–224; elevation of European culture and, 37; English language ascendancy and, 201; Hispanophilia and, 34–35; illegal immigration legislation and, 202–204; Latino impact on, 238–239; Mexican immigrants in, 6, 10–12, 48–49
Cuoto, Bernardo, 29
Cushing, Caleb, 28

Daniels, Paul, 135
A Day without a Mexican (film), 146–147
DeAnda, James, 157
debt peonage, in Mexico, 43–44
"Decade of the Hispanic," 178–179, 189, 200, 225
Deck, Allan, 195
defense industries in World War II, Mexican workers in, 115–116
Deferred Action for Childhood Arrivals (DACA) Program, 228–229
De la Colina, Rafael, 135
De la Cruz, Sara, 52
De la Huerta, Adolfo, 81–82, 93, 105
de la Luz Sáenz, José, 119
Delano Grape Strike, 161–164

De Las Casas, Bartolomé, 34
de Léon, Ponce, 15
De Léon Carpio, Ramiro, 207
Delgado, Minerva, 156
Delgado v. Bastrop Independent School District, 157
Del Rio Manifesto, 172
de-Mexicanization, Mexican concern over, 45–46
Democratic Party: Hispanic relations with, 177–178; immigration politics and, 56; Mexican American political activism and, 171–178
De Neve, Felipe, 36
Denver Crusade for Justice, 186–187
Department of Homeland Security, 5, 147, 213–214; children of immigrants and, 229; Secure Border Initiative, 221
deportation of Mexicans: Arizona SB 1070 proposals for, 223–224; discrimination against Mexican veterans and, 117; farm labor shortage and, 124–125; during Great Depression, 40; illegal immigration and, 129–147; under Obama, 227–230; under Operation Wetback, 141–147; post-9/11 increase in, 216–217; Proposition 187 proposals for, 205–206; streamlined process for, 197–198
De Soto, Hernando, 15, 20
Development, Relief and Education for Alien Minors (DREAM) Act, 217; children of immigrants and, 228–239
Devlin, Frederick T., 58–59
Diaz, José, murder of, 91
Díaz, Porfirio, 31, 43
Díaz del Castillo, Bernal, 17–18
Díaz Ordaz, Gustavo, 166
Dickson, Fagan, 83
Dillingham Commission. *See* United States Immigration Commission
discrimination. *See also* segregation: against African Americans, 12, 51–53, 61–63, 121–122; against Asian Americans, 51, 62–63, 90, 155; against immigrant workers, 196–197; against Mexicans, 39–40, 48, 64–65, 69–70, 75–95; against Mexican veterans, 97–98, 103–104, 112–122; against resident Mexican nationals, 75–81, *77,*

resident nationals, 46, 68, 70–71; pro-Nazi German-Americans and, 83

Germany, Mexican relations with, 65–72

Ghandi, Mahatma, 162

G.I. Bill of Rights, 159; resident Mexican nationals participation in, 116–117

Gilchrist, Jim, 219–220

gobalism, American multiculturalism and, 1–12

Goldwater, Barry, 183

Gómez, Marcos, 99

Gonzales, Henry B., 160, 171, 172, 175

Gonzales, Manuel C., 83, 88, 104, 107

Gonzales, Rodolfo "Corky," 168, 169–170

González, Rubén E., 104

Good Neighbor policy, 56–57, 60, 63–66, 69; California discrimination against Mexicans and, 90–95; illegal immigration and, 137; Mexicans in U.S. army and, 96–97; Texas discrimination against Mexicans and, 75–76, 88

Gould, William IV, 236–237

Government Accounting Office (GAO), discrimination against immigrant workers, data from, 196–197

Granados, L. M., 152

grape boycott, 161–164

The Grapes of Wrath (Steinbeck), 160

Great Britain, Mexican military service in, 99–100

Great Depression: Mexican immigration during, 5, 40; Mexican repatriation during, 57

Greater Mexico concept, transnational migration and, 2

Green, James, 151

Green, Jerome T., 154

"Guardia Blanca" (oil industry security force), 46

guest worker proposals, immigration reform and, 192–197, 212–215, 217

Gutiérrez, José Angel, 171

Gutiérrez, Luis, 227

Haiti, U.S. relations with, 65

Hance, Kent, 196

Handman, Max, 50–51

Hanjoor, Hanji, 221

Harper's Weekly, on Spanish Americans, 36

Harrington, Michael, 164

Harris, Gale, 151

Harte, Bret, 34

Hay, Eduardo, 57

Hayakawa, S. I., 201, 212

head tax on immigrants, 44, 126

Henderson, Harry F., 92

Herald (Los Angeles newspaper), 92

Heritage Foundation, 187

Hernandes v. Driscoll CISD, 157

Hernandez, Antonia, 195

Hernández, Guadalupe, *111*

Hernández, Jorge, 218

Hernández, Pete, 157

Hernández, Ramón, *111*

Hernandez, Richard, 185

Hernandez v. Texas, 78

Herrera, John J., 76, 81, 157

Herrera, Silvestre, 173–174

Herrera Horta, Ginés de, 21

Herrerias, Ignacio, 94

Hesburgh, Theodore, 191

Hispanic Medal of Honor, 119

Hispanic population. *See also* Latino population; Mexican immigrants: business marketing to, 184; business ownership in, 234–239; Coors brewery boycott and, 186–189; electoral politics and, 189–190; emerging identity of, 178–184; growth of, 190–192; U.S. Census classification of, 179–181, 303n5

Hispanophilia, emergence of, 34–35

Hispanophobia, in Southwestern U.S., 34

Hitler, Adolf, 61, 64, 262n16

Holguin Rentería, Jesús José, 113

Hoover, Glenn, 60

Hoover, J. Edgar, 70–71, 92

Horne, Tom, 223

Horn, James, 201

House Bill 909 (Racial Equality/Equal Accommodations Bill) (Texas), 83–84

House Concurrent Resolution 105 (Caucasian Race Resolution) (Texas), 82–84, 87–88

House Un-American Activities Committee, 70

housing discrimination against Mexicans, Texas laws involving, 80–81

Houston, Sam, 26

Martinez, Vilma, 195
Martínez Pérez, Serapio, 110–111
Matos, Felipe, 228
Mauermann, Gus B., 107
Maverick, Maury, 89
Maxey, Thomas S., 55
Maya peoples, 16
Mazzoli, Romano L., 193
McBride, Robert H., 193–194
McCain, John, 214–215
McCarran, Pat, 143
McCarty, John R., 184
McDonald's, 184, 207
McGown, Floyd, 54–55
McMinn, T. J., 56
McVeigh, Timothy, 213
McWilliams, Carey, 34–35, 37, 48, 65, 92, 147, 251n73
medical services for braceros, 130–131, 132–134
medical services illegal immigrants, anti-immigration policies restricting, 203–205
Melville, Herman, xiii
Mendez v. Westminster, 155–156, 173
Mercier, A. T., 131
Messersmith, George, 87–89
mestizo population: Anglo American suspicion of, 25–27; in California, 36–37; citizenship rights for, 54–63; in colonial America, 2; history of, 13–15; power structure among, 22–23; racial hierarchy among, 21–23, 36–38; Spanish colonial intermixing with, 20–21
Mexican American Legal Defense and Educational Fund (MALDEF), 178; bilingual legislation and, 202; Coors brewery boycott and, 186–187; illegal immigration debate and, 192, 194–195
Mexican American Political Association (MAPA), 168
Mexican Americans: Chicano movement and, 148–178; citizenship rights demanded by, 147; Coors hiring discrimination against, 186–189; demonstrations against anti-immigrant legislation by, 215–224; economic power for, 164–165; educational achievement of, 172–178;

electoral politics and, 189–190; growing power in Southwest of, 180; illegal aliens linked to, 194–195; political involvement of, 170–178; second generation, social and political status of, 51–52 (*See also* Mexican immigrants; resident Mexican nationals); terminology involving, 243n1; Vietnam War military service of, 173–178; World War II military service, 97, 101–122
Mexican American Youth Organization (MAYO), 171, 172
Mexican Army: border control by, 135; Mexican military service in World War II and, 97, 102–103
Mexican Farm Labor Program Agreement (1942): amendments to, 132–134; expiration in 1953 of, 139; Mexican cancellation of, 135; postwar extension of, 97, 121–122, 124, 126; renewal in 1954 of, 139–147; termination in 1964 of, 144–145; U.S. discrimination of Mexicans and, 48, 79–81; Wilmoth open border violation of, 134–135
Mexican immigrants. *See also* Latino population; resident Mexican nationals; second-generation Mexican-Americans: American multiculturalism and influence of, 1–12; backlash against, 206–224; birthrates in U.S. of, 7; in California garment industry, 191; citizenship restrictions on, 39, 51–63; cultural marginalization of, 37–38; debate over restrictions on, 40; demonstrations against anti-immigrant legislation by, 215–224; discrimination against, 39–40, 64–65, 69–70, 75–81, 77, 79; economic power for, 164–165; English-only legislation and, 201–202; fear of, 4–5; gang activity in California by, 90–91, 207–208; growth in 1980s of, 190–192; guest worker proposals and, 192–193; history of, 2–3; immigration policies and restrictions on, 49–50, 181–183, 193–194; indigenous origins of, 15–27; labor as motivation for, 3–4, 39–40; mestizo heritage of, 20–22, 50–51;

Mexican immigrants. *(continued)*
military service in World War II by,
64–65, 96–122; passing as "Spanish"
by, 35–37, 58; public opinion concerning, 207–224; racial classifications for,
50–51; recent decline in, 225;
repatriation to Mexico of, 57;
self-repatriation back to Mexico
during World War II, 110–111, *111*;
stereotyping of, 33–34, 37–38, 48–49,
74, 136, 207–208; terminology
involving, 243n1; transborder
migration patterns of, 7–8, 39–41;
unsafe working conditions for, 74,
81–82, 84, 131–132, 197, 287n28
Mexican Revolution (1910–1920), 43, 64,
149
Mexico: agribusiness operations in,
146–147; American immigration into,
45–47, 97–98; Americanization in,
10–11; annexation of territory from,
15–16, 28–31, 39; ban on Texas
participation in Bracero Program by,
75–85, 87–88; border control problems
in, 40, 124–125, 134–136, 199;
boundary with U.S., 3, *14,* 40, 68;
braceros agreements and, 126–136;
defense industry citizenship requirements and, 116; draft policies in,
120–122; drug cartels in, 208, 218–219;
exodus of workers from, 45–47,
134–136, 144–147; fence construction
opposed by, 218; foreign investment in,
210; honoring of Mexican war veterans
in, 117; immigrants' return to, 47–48;
inadequate repatriation services for
braceros in, 132; independence from
Spain and, 24; *maquiladoras* (factories) and, 166; Mexican military
service in World War II and, 96–122;
military ties with U.S. and, 96–122; oil
reserves in, 192; Operation Wetback
supported by, 142–147; recolonization
proposal in, 144; U.S. anti-
immigration policies opposed by, 207;
U.S. relations with, 23–27, 56–95,
136–147, 213–215; World War II and,
64–65, 92–95, 99–122
Mexico-North American Commission
for Economic Cooperation, 72

Meza, Miguel, 110
Michel, Raúl, 135
Mid-Atlantic States: bracero working
conditions in, 131–132; immigration
patterns in, 10; Mexican immigrant
workers in, 191
Mid Continent Casualty Insurance
Company, 130–131
Midwestern United States: braceros
working conditions in, 131; Mexican
immigrant workers in, 4, 10, 45, 191;
state anti-immigration legislation in,
223–224
migrant workers. *See also* farm workers:
guest worker proposals, 192–193;
illegal immigration of, 135–147;
Mexican immigrants as, 41–47;
postwar surge in, 123–126; rate of
return to Mexico by, 47–48; school
segregation for children of, 152–153
Miles, Theodore G., 81
Military Agreement (Convenio Militar),
102–104, 108
military service of Mexicans: all-
Mexican military units and, 105–106;
discrimination of Mexicans in, 97–98,
103–104, 112–122; DREAM act
provisions and, 217–224; heroism of
Mexican Americans in, 117, 283n97,
283n99; language issues for Mexicans
in, 104–105; Mexican immigrants and
resident nationals in, 96–122, 283n97;
segregation of African Americans in,
97; in Vietnam, 173–178
Miller brewing company, 188
minimum wage laws, illegal immigration and, 197
mining: early Mexican laborers in,
32–33, *42,* 42–43; in Mexico, labor
conditions in, 46; in post-
independence Mexico, 24; in Spanish
colonies, 16, 19–20
Minuteman Project, 219–221
"Minutemen" network, 219–221
mission enterprises, Spanish colonization of Mexico and, 23
Mississippi, bracero workers in, 130
Mitchell, H. L., 126
Mittelstaedt, R. E., 113–114
Mi Vida Loca (film), 208

mixed-race populations: citizenship restrictions for, 52–63; eugenics movement and, 60; school segregation policies and, 154–156; Spanish colonization and, 21–22

Moctezuma, 16–17

Molina, Gloria, 189

Molina Enrique, Andrés, 43

Mondale, Walter, 162, 194

Monroe Doctrine, 120

Monsiváis, Carlos, 10

Montalban, Ricard, 185

Montoya, Joseph, 168

Moore, David, 142–143

Morales, Ysaias, 150

Morris, Dick, 238

Morrison v. California, 53

Movimiento Estudiantil Chicano de Aztlán (MEChA), 172, 176; Coors brewery boycott and, 186–187

multiculturalism in America: Chicano movement and, 149; overview of, 1–12

multilingualism in America, overview of, 1–12, 201–202

Muñiz, Ramsey, 171

Murguía, Janet, 216–217, 229–230

Murieta, Joaquín, 33

Murphy, John, 186

NAACP Legal Defense Fund, 158–159, 177

Napolitano, Janet, 147

Narvaez Spíndola, Manuel, 103–104

National Association for the Advancement of Colored People (NAACP), 61; Coors brewery boycott and, 187–188; National Council of La Raza and, 183; school segregation and, 156

National Association of Evangelicals, 230–232

National Association of Latino Elected and Appointed Officials (NALEO), 160

National Bilingual Education Act, 160

National Chicano Moratorium Committee, 176–178

National Conference of Catholic Bishops, 190, 195, 230

National Council of La Raza (NCLR), 178, 183–184, 194–195, 216–217, 229–230

National Council of State Legislatures, 223–224

National Defense Act of 1916, 109

National Farm Labor Union (NFLU), 126

National Farm Workers Association (NFWA), 160–161

National Guard, border control assistance from, 198–199

national identity card proposals, illegal immigration and, 197

nationalism, of Mexican immigrants, 98–99

National Lawyers Guild, 92, 156

National Mexican-American Anti-Defamation Committee (NMAADC), 185

National Organization of Women (NOW), 187

National Origins Quota Act (1924), 181

national security issues, U.S.-Mexican relations and, 64–95

National Socialist Party, 61, 71; pro-Nazi German-Americans and, 83; Texas discrimination against Mexicans compared with, 76, 85–86

National Student Association, 186–187

National University of Mexico, 95

National Youth Administration, 61

Native Americans. *See also* American Indian Movement (AIM); indigenous peoples: Chicano movement and, 160, 168–178; citizenship restrictions for, 51–63; cultural marginalization of, 37–38; decimation by contagious disease of, 18; Indohispano movement in New Mexico and, 165–169; mestizo and blurred identity of, 59–63; in Mexico, 16–17; objections to classification of Mexicans as Indians by, 113–114; origins of Mexicans and, 15–27; pre-colonial history of, 13–15; racist policies concerning, 16, 26–27; school segregation of, 155–156

nativist ideology: anchor baby myth, 233–239; English-only legislation and, 201–203; Minutemen networks and, 219–224

Naturalization Act (1790), 49, 51–54, 60–61

Railroad Bracero Program, 131, 145
Railroad Retirement Fund, bracero
  involuntary contributions to, 132
Raissi, Lotfi, 221
Ramírez, Felipe, 112
Rand Corporation, English proficiency
  of Latinos, survey of, 201–202
Raspberry, William, 186
Ray, Guy, 76
Raynosa, Creuz, 191
Reagan, Ronald, 163, 187, 192–197
Reno, Janet, 208, 213
Republican Party: Hispanic relations
  with, 177–178; immigration politics
  and, 56; Latino demographics and,
  237–238
Reserve Officers' Training Corps
  (ROTC), citizenship restrictions on
  scholarships in, 109
residentes fronterizos (border residents),
  draft policies concerning, 102
resident Mexican nationals: citizenship
  rights for, 48–63; discrimination
  against, 75–81, *77, 79,* 84; military
  service in World War II by, 64–65,
  96–122; naturalization applications in
  1990s by, 206–207; postwar citizenship policies for, 116–117; protest of
  Operation Wetback by, 142; security
  concerns during World War II about,
  70; terminology involving, 243n1
Reuther, Walter, 139
Reza, Salvador, 210
Rice, Ben H., 156–157
Richardson, Bill, 213
Rico Ferrat, Carlos, 146
Rio Grande (Rio Bravo), as natural
  boundary, 40–41
Roa, Carlos, 228
Rockefeller, Nelson, 65 73, 91–92
Rodríguez, Cleto, 117, *118*
Rodríguez, Jacob I., 88–89
Rodríguez, Juan, 228
Rodríguez, Ricardo, 53–63
Rodríguez, Richard, 180, 216, 239
Romney, Mitt, 238
Roosevelt, Eleanor, 76
Roosevelt, Franklin D.: Columbus Day
  declaration by, 8; Executive Order
  9066 and, 90; Global Settlement

program and, 121–122; Good
  Neighbor policy of, 56–57, 60, 63–66,
  69, 75–76; immigrant citizenship
  rights and, 58; Latin American policy
  under, 64–95; Mexican military
  service in World War II and, 99, 112;
  Padilla and, 82; Sleepy Lagoon murder
  case and, 92
Roosevelt, Theodore, 119
Ross, Fred, 160
"Rough Riders," Mexican enlistment in,
  119
Roybal, Edward, 160, 170–171
Ruiz, Elvira, 130–131

Salazar, Rubén, 176
Salinas de Gortari, Carlos, 207, 210
Saludos Amigos (film), 75
Salvadorans, migration patterns of, 8
Samora, Julian, 177, 183
Sánchez, Alfonso, 167–168
Sanchez, David, 174–176
Sánchez, George I., 63, 87, 89, 146
Sánchez, Robert, 87
Sanctuary Movement, 230
San Diego and Arizona Eastern Railway
  Company, 145
Saposs, David, 73
SB 1070 (Arizona), 200–201, 221–224;
  student protests against, 228
Scaroni, Steve, 146
Schnur, Dan, 238
school segregation of Mexican children,
  153–158; Chicano movement protests
  against, 173–178
Scott, Winfield, 29
second-generation Mexican-Americans:
  Anglo-Americans and, 152–153;
  Chicano movement and, 148–178;
  social and economic status of, 51–52;
  World War II military service by, 97,
  101
Secure Fence Act (2006), 2, 147, 217
segregation: in California, 90–91;
  Chicano movement and, 149–178; of
  immigrants and African Americans,
  51, 113; impact of World War II on,
  63–65, 152–153; of Mexican immigrants and residential nationals,
  75–82, 148; of Mexican military

personnel, 105, 112–122, 151–153; school segregation of Mexicans and, 153–156; of World War I military units, 119

Select Commission on Immigration and Refugee Policy (SCIRP), 190–193

Selective Service System: Mexicans drafted by, 100, 102, 104, 119–120; racial categories used by, 113–114

Selective Training and Service Act of 1940, 98, 100, 109, 121

Sensenbrenner, Jim, 214–215

September 11, 2001 terrorist attacks, immigration reform and, 212–224

Servicemen's Dependents Allowance Act, 109

Seven cities of Cíbola and Quivira, myth of, 18–19

Seward, William, 250n54

sexuality: inter-racial dating and, 80–81; of mestizo women, Anglo-American stereotypes concerning, 26–27

Silva, France, 119

Simcox, Chris, 219–220

Simpson, Alan K., 193, 210–211

Simpson-Mazolli Bill, 193–197. *See also* Immigration Reform and Control Act (IRCA)

slavery: Coors' remarks on, 188; Spanish colonialism and, 21–22; in Texas, 27–28

Sleepy Lagoon Defense Committee (SLDC), 92

Sleepy Lagoon trial (1942), 90–92

Smith, Lamar, 211

Smith, William French, 193

Solis, José Luis, 210

Soria, Fidencio, 76

source-country diversity, immigration reform and, 198

Southern Baptist Convention, 230–232

Southern Pacific Railway, 131, 145

Southern United States: Mexican immigrant workers in, 4, 7–8, 10, 45, 191; state anti-immigration legislation in, 223–224

Southwest Council La Raza, 178

Southwestern United States: border control operations in, 123–124; braceros workers in, 134; Chicano movement in, 148–149, 164–178;

cultural discourse of Latinos in, 239; demand for Mexican labor in, 39–40, 45; discrimination against Mexicans in, 39–40, 64–65, 75–81, 148–178; electoral politics of Mexican Americans in, 171–178, 237–239; Europeanization of heritage in, 34–38; Hispanophilia in, 34–35; history of Mexican presence in, 2–3, 10, 15–16, 98; Mexican American population growth in, 180; Mexican farm workers in, 39–40, 45, 75–82; Mexican landowners in, 31–32; Mexican military service in World War II and, 99; Operation Wetback in, 141–147; population demographics in, 225–226; Spanish colonization of, 13–16, 18–20; surge of Mexican immigrants to, 48–49, 98, 123–147; in U.S.-Mexican War, 28–31

Southwest Voter Registration and Education Project, 177

Spanish Americans, ethnic identity as, 34–37, 58–63

Spanish colonialism: Anglo American Hispanophilia concerning, 35–36; cultural heritage of, 35–38; history of, 13–27; impact in North America of, 2–3; map of exploration, *14*; Mexican independence and, 24; slavery and, 21–22; United States relations and, 23–24

Spanish Fantasy Heritage, in Southwestern U.S., 34–38

Spanish language, prevalence in America of, 1–12

Spears, J. Franklin, 88

Special Mexican Relations Committee, 92

Squadron 201 (all-Mexican military unit), 105

sterilization laws, immigration laws modeled on, 61

Stevenson, Coke, 75–76, 87

Stockton, Robert, 29

Stowe, David H., 137–138

student protests: California discrimination against Mexicans and, 94; Chicano movement and, 171–178; by children of immigrants, 228–239; Texas discrimination against Mexicans and, 90